Savage Kin

Native Peoples of the Americas

Laurie Weinstein, Series Editor

Savage Kin

Indigenous Informants and American Anthropologists

Margaret M. Bruchac
Foreword by Melissa Tantaquidgeon Zobel

FIRST PEOPLES
New Directions in Indigenous Studies

UNIVERSITY OF ARIZONA PRESS   TUCSON

The University of Arizona Press
www.uapress.arizona.edu

ISBN-13: 978-0-8165-3706-8 (cloth)
ISBN-13: 978-0-8165-3939-0 (paper)

Cover design by Sara Thaxton
Cover photo: Bertha Parker Pallan, Mark Raymond Harrington, and Irwin Hayden, Nevada, c. 1929.
Courtesy of the Museum of Northern Arizona, Snow Collection, MS-31542-12.

Publication of this book is made possible in part by a grant from the Andrew W. Mellon Foundation, and
by the proceeds of a permanent endowment created with the assistance of a Challenge Grant from the
National Endowment for the Humanities, a federal agency.

Library of Congress Cataloging-in-Publication Data
Names: Bruchac, Margaret M., author.
Title: Savage kin : indigenous informants and American anthropologists / Margaret M. Bruchac ; foreword
   by Melissa Tantaquidgeon Zobel.
Other titles: Native peoples of the Americas.
Description: Tucson : University of Arizona Press, 2018. | Series: Native peoples of the Americas | Includes
   bibliographical references and index.
Identifiers: LCCN 2017047717 | ISBN 9780816537068 (pbk. : alk. paper)
Subjects: LCSH: Anthropological ethics—History—20th century. | Indians of North America. | Cultural
   relations.
Classification: LCC GN33.6 .B78 2018 | DDC 174.9301—dc23 LC record available at https://lccn.loc
   .gov/2017047717

Printed in the United States of America
♾ This paper meets the requirements of ANSI/NISO Z39.48-1992 (Permanence of Paper).

Contents

Series Foreword

Native Peoples of the Americas is a multivolume series that covers North, Middle, and South America. Each volume takes unique methodological approaches—archaeological, ethnographic, ecological, and/or ethnohistorical—to culture areas and regions and to themes that link areas across time and space. This volume, written by Margaret Bruchac, looks at a major theme that links Native American and First Nations peoples across Native North America. It examines the "collecting" of Native stories and artifacts by anthropologists, many of whom were charged by their mentor and the father of the discipline, Franz Boas, to salvage these materials at the turn of the twentieth century because Native groups were believed to be quickly disappearing as a result of modernity.

Savage Kin: Indigenous Informants and American Anthropologists turns the term *savage* on its head. Whereas late nineteenth- and early twentieth-century social Darwinism linked savage to pretty much any group/person not white, Bruchac uses the term ironically to refer not to the ethnic origins but to the behaviors of white anthropologists who so voraciously appropriated Native cultures. White anthropologists such as Frederic Putnam, Franz Boas, Frank Speck, Mark Harrington, and William Fenton were doing what they were expected to do—collect information, stories, objects (even secretive, ritual objects), for showcasing, whether that showcasing was intended for sale, publication, or museum display. They enlisted Native informants such as George Hunt, Jesse Cornplanter, and Gladys Tantaquidgeon to serve as gatekeepers for their cultures and communities. Complicated individuals such as Arthur Parker tried to play both sides. It is no wonder then that Vine Deloria Jr., in his book *Custer Died for Your Sins*, wrote a chapter sarcastically titled "Anthropologists and Other Friends." "Into each life," Deloria wrote, "some rain must fall. Some people have bad horoscopes, others take tips on the stock market. . . . But Indians have been cursed above all other people in history. Indians have anthropologists" (78–79).

Bruchac's book shows the complicated and messy side of those anthropologist/ Native relationships. She describes failures and successes, marriages and divorces, Hollywood Indians, conflicts between traditional and modern Natives, and the loss of a lot of "stuff." Masks, regalia, wampum belts, and other materials considered to be sacred and ceremonial were appropriated by the collectors/anthropologists, who believed themselves much more capable of housing these materials than the tribes. Indeed, her book is really a prequel to the NAGPRA (Native American Graves Protection and Repatriation Act) of

1990 that aimed to recover materials lost to salvage anthropology. So many materials were collected, including skeletal remains, funerary objects, cultural patrimony, sacred objects, and documents, that Bruchac asks at the beginning of this book, "Where did our stuff go?"

I had my own lesson in "Where did our stuff go" when I was researching documents at the former location of the Museum of the American Indian/ Heye Foundation in New York City on West 155th Street. When I was there in the late 1980s, I came across a treasure trove of letters written by various collectors and archaeologists (such as Mark Harrington) to George Gustav Heye. I was amazed by the sheer number of materials that were shipped back to New York City. Heye directed his collectors to purchase items at trading posts, or work with local tribes to directly purchase their wares; some of his collectors even dug up grave goods. These materials were all sent back by railcar to New York, where Heye first stored things in his own apartment, before using his wealth (as an heir to the Standard Oil fortune) to move the collection to a more permanent home and exhibit space on West 155th Street. While I was at the museum to do my own project, I never forget those letters, especially the ones dealing with grave goods—they opened my eyes to the business of collecting. While Heye was well intentioned—he wanted to create a museum to showcase American Indian artifacts, and thus preserve them for the future—the other side of that coin is that Native peoples lost control over many of their materials.

Writing from the perspective of both an anthropologist and a Native person (Abenaki), Bruchac has crafted a forceful and insightful study of the relationships that anthropologists created with American Indians. She looks at the intellectual traditions that shaped anthropological inquiries and collecting, and the reasons why Native informants were willing to help these anthropologists in their endeavors. Another aspect of this book that makes the stories so compelling is that many of the Native people who were sought out by the anthropologists were women. Women were the gatekeepers of knowledge. They befriended the anthropologists (e.g., Gladys Tantaquidgeon and Frank Speck), taught them the language and the lore, and were the "passes" into tribal circles.

This book is a must-read for anyone who wishes to delve into the history behind NAGPRA, the history of anthropology, and how knowledge was acquired from Native groups all over the world. It should make us question this whole process of collecting and retelling stories that are not our stories to tell.

Laurie Weinstein, PhD
Series Editor, Native Peoples of the Americas
Danbury, Conn., June 2017

Foreword

Consider the moccasin flower (*Cypripedium acaule*)—also referred to as the lady's slipper—a plant indigenous to Algonkian territory. For the flower to grow, a *Rhizoctonia* fungus must feed the seeds. Later, that same fungus extracts nutrients from the grown plant for its own food. Young bees enter a space they can escape only through a tight spot under the stigma, leaving behind some pollen and carrying more to sister plants. Flora, fauna, and fungi work together in reciprocity. Once the plant flowers, it takes on a shape that Algonkian people recognize as the center seam Eastern Woodland Indian moccasin. Mohegan children learn from their elders that it is best not to transplant or pick this flower, not only because it is beautiful and delicate but because it grows in the territory of the Little People, known in my Mohegan language as Makiawisug. In Mohegan tradition, the Little People who wear these moccasins (and who can shapeshift into tiny whippoorwills) are known to grant wishes and lead people to healing herbs in the forest.

Storied beings like this plant offer lessons about the ways Indigenous peoples are rooted in the world. The moccasin flower teaches many things, including the fact that all beings are related; and that to survive and procreate we must live in reciprocity with our fungal, floral, and faunal kin. The lifeways of this plant connect humans with other-than-human beings, and lessons like this explain how it is possible to be linked to multiple kin communities. For myself, I am directly related to both flora and fauna, since Mohegans are the Wolf People, and I am also Ôsowunáw, the flower on the corn plant (or "the thing that changes"). In the Indigenous worldview, plants, animals, and people are routinely linked as collaborative kin. In the mainstream human world, not all relationships are quite so collaborative or sustainable.

In the annals of the early years of American anthropology, there are many examples of potentially collaborative research relationships that devolved into nonreciprocal, nonsustainable harvests of cultural knowledge and patrimony. Many non-Native male researchers share the dubious distinction of collecting sensitive materials from vulnerable Native gatekeepers (both male and female) whom they claimed as kin; this misuse and abuse of trust equates to "picking the moccasin flowers." It was also a breach of cultural protocols for male anthropologists (Native or non-Native) to represent themselves as knowledgeable about women's issues. Nonetheless, most of the extensive scholarly research they conducted in anthropology and archaeology remains uncredited to the Native men, women, and communities who preserved it (and also researched it)—one of many silences that this book hopes to set aright.

The case histories, herein, show how five early twentieth-century anthropologists developed nonreciprocal kinship relationships with Native culture experts.

1. Tlingit George Hunt married two high-ranking Native women, whose information he sold to Franz Boas, who in turn called Hunt's people barbarous and dug up their sacred sites for personal bounty.
2. Abenaki storyteller Beulah Tahamont married and worked with Arthur Parker (a Seneca descendant, lacking tribal status), who sold ethnographic and funerary objects and offered virtually no gratitude for his wife's contributions to his scholarship.
3. Parker's sister, Endeka, and Tahamont's daughter, Bertha, assisted anthropologist Mark Harrington in field analysis, making groundbreaking discoveries in archaeology. Bertha Parker also mingled ethnographic research with the protection of sacred knowledge; yet her memory was nearly erased from the scientific record, and her research notes are commingled with those of Harrington.
4. Six Nations traditionalist Jesse Cornplanter was recruited by then doctoral student William Fenton, a man who leveraged artifacts away from his subjects, interfered with tribal politics, and pirated Cornplanter's research to advance his own career.
5. Anthropologist Frank Speck brought Mohegan gatekeeper Gladys Tantaquidgeon along as a researcher when visiting Northeast tribes and incorporated her contributions into his own papers so that they, too, are scarcely recognized. Tantaquidgeon also offered insights into kinships with other-than-human beings (such as the Makiawisug), even though these beliefs were routinely ignored or denigrated by white male researchers.

For many Native people, especially Native women, these five tales will feel disturbingly autobiographical. From the time I was a child, growing up at my family's Tantaquidgeon Indian Museum, encounters with anthropologists were preceded by warnings to be vigilant and treat these interlopers with suspicion. This is particularly understandable when you consider that the Tantaquidgeon museum maintains an iconic example of contact-era Algonkian wampum (the "Uncas collar") that has remained continually in Native hands since the day it was made. While interactions with anthropologists on our home territory were generally congenial, my great aunt Gladys Tantaquidgeon made me aware that anthropologists had also appointed themselves as the gatekeepers of our histories. One word from them about anything they perceived as a lapse in the maintenance of our tribal culture could permanently call into question our own history, and potentially undermine our tribal sovereignty.

Over time, I personally witnessed the fraught nature of this connection between anthropological research and tribal sovereignty, while gaining greater awareness of the profound importance of gender relations. In 1989 the Mohegans were denied federal status on the grounds that patriarchal leadership had been fractured during the First and Second World Wars, a time when most of the men were away, fighting as soldiers. In subsequent findings, anthropological reviewers were surprised to "discover" that Mohegan women had handled tribal business during the war years—as, in fact, they had for most of the tribe's history.

Although later federal reviewers corrected their mistake, many other anthropologists have never corrected the erroneous research of their predecessors. These successors have continued to benefit from and build upon earlier mistakes, sometimes teaming up with politicians to misrepresent tribal histories and erase tribal futures. Whether declaring an archaeological site violable so the land could be used by the state, claiming an artifact was "not sacred" so a museum could keep it, concealing museum records, revealing sacred or patrimonial (or "matrimonial") knowledge, assuming the status of an expert on the tribe in academic venues, or violating tribal research protocols, outside researchers have posed a real and constant threat. If we are ever to recover from these issues, the ethics of engagement call for serious reconsideration. For that reason, I view this book not only as an excellent recounting of the ways in which museums illicitly obtained and misidentified artifacts but also as a call for truth and reconciliation. The words within these pages are a must-read/first-read for all Native experts and museum professionals entering artifact discussions.

By revealing the true, dark side of Indigenous artifact collecting in the twentieth century, Bruchac calls into question the data and assumptions generated by Speck, Harrington, Fenton, Parker, Boas, and their contemporaries. Their omissions and misrepresentations are not, as might be supposed, simple errors that could be corrected by more research. Some of their findings continue to serve as foundational knowledge on the tribal communities they studied. Some of the artifacts they collected—whose supposed "history" has been used to disprove tribal cultural practices and tribal claims—need to be reconsidered. More importantly, this book subtly points out that the individuals and tribal nations who did not actively participate in collaborations with anthropologists were, and are, often neglected and presumed bereft of culture, simply because they made the difficult (and likely informed) decision not to play their game.

And so I return to kinship. What anthropology is missing is the medicine of true kinship. Natives who read this book may burst into tears to find that the injustices they have personally experienced (and which, in many cases, have been denied) are finally seeing the light of day. Anthropologists and museum professionals who read it may suddenly understand what the Natives have been "fussing" about for so long. This book puts truth and honesty on the table as a starting point for a new day of discussion. It is also surprisingly hopeful, showing that, when at their best, the relationships between Natives and anthropologists in the early twentieth century offered glimmers of true reciprocal kinship upon which modern-day descendants can build.

Indigenous notions of open and accepting kinship have a great legacy on this continent. Tribal nations created alliances and confederacies that lasted thousands of years. Considering the attention that was afforded to the mechanics of Indigenous kinship patterns by twentieth-century anthropological scholarship, one might suppose that this notion would already be highly regarded. Yet to truly appreciate Indigenous kinship philosophy requires seeing beyond the presumed boundaries of gender, nationality, and even species. Indigenous kinship allows differing communities to cohabit a shared ecosystem for many generations, and even, in the aftermath of war, to make peace by making new relatives. Indigenous kinship allows one person to trust another person with their children, as their own. Indigenous kinship respects the embodied knowledge of elders, the wise insights of dreams, and the unquestionable importance of caring for sacred objects. If this book shows us anything, it is that our Indigenous ancestors were too quick to trust. During the era of salvage anthropology, when Natives embraced non-Natives as collaborators or kin, they lost much of their cultural wholeness (through the misuse and theft of objects and Indigenous knowledge systems, and through research that isolated individual tribal citizens) rather than salvaging it. Natives lost control over beloved stories and objects, they saw their family members disrespected, and they felt betrayed at the highest level.

Some of the most painful levels of loss were associated with artifacts that, in tribal communities, told stories about the living; in museums, they were conscripted into telling stories about the dead. The process of extracting these objects—from burials, from ceremonial use, from the hands of tribal keepers, and from their Indigenous cultural contexts—left gaping holes that have yet to be repaired. For non-Natives who remain mystified by the intensity of Native concerns over "artifacts," it is crucial to remember that these objects have agency. They are alive. They are our kin. That is why Native people struggle over flawed classifications, argue for repatriation, resist offers to loan back artifacts, and shudder to see their property displayed and reinterpreted using research that—as Bruchac has shown—can be woefully ill informed or culturally flawed.

Surely, Native traditionalists and anthropologists alike will experience discomfort with some of the tales in this book, especially the evidence of predecessors who engaged in questionable and possibly dangerous research. Bruchac shows how Boas, Harrington, Speck, Fenton, and Parker were, and continue to be, regarded as luminaries in the profession. She also shows that other-than-human beings, especially the beings embodied in the artifacts they collected, were, and still are, respected by Native communities as culture heroes of a different sort. In general, the Native gatekeepers in this book showed considerable respect to the anthropologists with whom they worked. Women like Beulah Tahamont, Bertha Parker, and Gladys Tantaquidgeon offered crucial insights and warnings regarding the delicacy of other-than-human kinships, but their white male research partners often fell short in the realm of reciprocal respect.

Our Native world is, at heart, an inherently reciprocal one, in which stories, gifts, and ideas are exchanged with open curiosity and consideration. It is also a world in which information may be denied to an outsider if they do not respect the appropriate keepers of that knowledge, and those keepers are often women. The anthropological discipline, as the study of culture, can benefit from considering some of the omissions and misnomers in scholarship delineated by Bruchac in this text. This is not merely an academic matter. Issues of representation can mean life or death for a Native community.

To move forward, we need to look back, in order to avoid repeating a broken gait down a twisted road that might trap us in a dangerous place. Native people are more than merely scouts, gatekeepers, and signposts pointing the way to knowledges that can benefit academic researchers. When anthropologists and historians are called on to testify for or against Indigenous nations—on issues like federal recognition, repatriation, land claims, cultural patrimony, resource development, site protection, and anything else associated with cultural and political sustainability—they have an ethical responsibility to question the version of Indigenous history that was created by culture heroes like Speck, Fenton, Parker, Harrington, and Boas. In some cases, these researchers preserved important knowledges that might otherwise have been lost in a kind of search and rescue mission. But that mission neglected the widely recognized ethical boundary of "First, do no harm." In the process of salvaging, many complex knowledge system protocols were ignored, enabling the theft of cultural patrimony and leading to the misconstrual of recorded information. It is therefore critical that we question their beliefs, just as they questioned ours. Anthropology can move forward by acknowledging its past failings, by redressing the wrongful placement of many sacred tribal objects in non-Native hands, and by returning objects and histories to Indigenous homelands, where they can hold a place of honor and live in reciprocity with human and other-than-human beings, like the moccasin flowers.

Melissa Tantaquidgeon Zobel

Preface and Acknowledgments

It was a snowy April day in Goose Bay, Labrador, in 2008, and I had just finished a presentation on recovering hidden histories in Algonkian territory when a dignified elderly man stood up to make a statement. Identifying himself as Innu on his mother's side, Winston White proudly stated that his father, fur dealer and Indian trader Richard White, had been instrumental to the success of anthropologist Frank Gouldsmith Speck's research in Labrador nearly a century earlier.[1] The two men had corresponded for years, but once Speck had collected the things he desired, the letters stopped. Although many decades had passed, Winston wanted someone to pick up the dropped threads: "Our work together was not done. We miss him."

In my travels across Indian Country, there have been many similar scenarios. Whenever I meet with members of those Native communities visited by early anthropologists—in an Algonquin camp, a Mohawk longhouse, a Mohegan museum, or a Penobscot canoe—there are poignant stories of encounter and exchange, embrace and abandonment. Some visitors, adopted as kin, came around again and again. Others came and went rapidly, taking tribal patrimony with them, leaving behind confusion and loss. In every locale, relationships that began a century ago are not yet finished, even though the participants are long dead. To recover a better sense of those encounters, I set forth to examine the extant correspondence, hoping to find clues to the social relations and material exchanges that shaped ethnological collections.

This research was particularly encouraged, informed, and inspired by the many Indigenous intellectuals, elders, and gatekeepers that I have been lucky to know. My encounter with Mohegan Medicine Woman Gladys Tantaquidgeon was brief but inspirational, and I am deeply grateful for the wise advice and friendship of her successor, Melissa Tantaquidgeon Zobel. Great thanks are offered to Tuscarora scholar Richard W. Hill Sr., former Coordinator of Deyohahá:ge, the Indigenous Knowledge Centre at Six Nations Polytechnic Institute at Ohsweken, who so generously shared his wampum research and cultural insights. For key insights on the importance of historical interpretation and living history performance, I am grateful to Linda Coombs (Aquinnah Wampanoag). For their ongoing work on repatriation, I am grateful to Christine Abrams (Seneca), Chair of the Haudenosaunee Standing Committee on Burial Rules and Regulations; Faithkeeper and Repatriation Officer G. Peter Jemison (Seneca); Faithkeeper and Chief Oren Lyons (Onondaga); Indian Nations attorney Shannon Keller O'Loughlin (Choctaw); and Condoled Chief Curtis Nelson (Kanesatake Mohawk), among many others.

Many librarians and curators provided absolutely invaluable assistance as I prowled through the archives of the American Philosophical Society, Canadian Museum of History (formerly the Canadian Museum of Civilization), Cornell University Library, Indian Lake Museum, National Museum of the American Indian (formerly the Museum of the American Indian/Heye Foundation), New York State Museum, Peabody Museum of Archaeology and Ethnography at Harvard, Phillips Library of the Peabody Essex Museum, Rochester Museum and Science Center, Southwest Museum of the American Indian (now part of the Autry Museum), Tantaquidgeon Indian Museum, and the University of Pennsylvania Museum of Archaeology and Anthropology (Penn Museum), among others. Their names are so numerous that, at the risk of forgetting some, I must whole-heartedly thank them all.

Financial support for this research came through awards from the Franklin Library Resident Research Fellowship and Phillips Fund for Native American Research Fellowship from the American Philosophical Society, the Ford Foundation Postdoctoral Fellowship for Excellence in College and University Teaching from the National Research Council of the National Academies, the Katrin H. Lamon Native American Scholar in Residence Fellowship from the School for Advanced Research, and the Career Enhancement Fellowship for Junior Faculty from the Andrew W. Mellon Foundation and Woodrow Wilson Foundation.

Thanks are due to many academic colleagues, starting with Kevin McBride, Françoise Dussart, and the late Joseph Comprone at the University of Connecticut, who encouraged the proposal that developed into this book. During my sabbatical year in Santa Fe, fellow resident scholars—James Brooks, Kitty Corbett, Aimee Garza, Craig Janes, Theresa McCarthy, Nicole Taylor, and Julie Weis—provided insight on the evolving manuscript. I am especially grateful to Nancy Mithlo (Apache), for her brilliant company and keen insights. During that same year, Chip Colwell introduced me to Stephen Hayden and Diane Boyer, who shared crucial materials documenting the relationship between Bertha Parker and Julian Hayden.

In 2013 Robert Preucel and Timothy Powell recruited me to join Frank Speck's anthropology department at the University of Pennsylvania. Many thanks to Anita Allen, Richard Leventhal, Susan Lindee, Adriana Petryna, Rogers Smith, Deborah Thomas, and Greg Urban, among other colleagues at Penn, for mentoring support. Field research funding was provided by the Penn Museum Director's Field Research Funds, with thanks to Julian Siggers and Steven Tinney. A grant from Penn's University Research Foundation enabled me to follow Speck's tracks even further into the field, revealing more connections and more questions.

The challenge of tracking long-past relations was, at times, more like a hunting expedition than archival research. My father, the late Adirondack taxidermist Joseph E. Bruchac, taught me that tracks on the ground (like words on the page) tell only part of the story; one must also observe more subtle clues in the broken branches and scattered signs that indicate where someone has passed by. And so, I covered a lot of territory seeking written, material, geographical, cultural, and ephemeral evidence to link places, people, narratives, and objects that have long been separated. Whenever I fell too far down a rabbit hole (literally or figuratively), I was guided back by steady hands. My late in-laws William and Nancy Kennick, my brother, Joe Bruchac, and my Indigenous academic colleagues—most notably Lisa Brooks (Abenaki), Kahente Horn-Miller (Kahnawake Mohawk), Kehaulani Kauanui (Hawaiian), Malinda Maynor Lowery (Lumbee), and Alyssa Mt. Pleasant (Tuscarora)—provided inspiration and support at critical junctures in time and space. For transcribing assistance, special thanks go to April Heaslip. For their infinite patience and fine company, I am indebted to my darling husband, Justin Kennick, and my feline writing companions, Grey and Mkazitok.

Great thanks are offered to my patient editors at the University of Arizona Press, Allyson Carter and Laurie Weinstein, and to the anonymous reviewers of both the book proposal and the final manuscript. During the final stages of editing, I benefited from the invaluable mentoring support of George Nicholas. Additional words of appreciation and thankfulness go out to my many friends across Indian Country (you know who you are), who convinced me that the stories in this book must be told, to inspire ever more interesting research.

Margaret M. Bruchac
November 2017

Savage Kin

Introduction

A Few Thoughts on Naming

> I once asked an old man: Are *all* the stones we see about us here alive? He reflected a long while, and then replied, "No! But *some* are." This qualified answer made a lasting impression on me.
>
> —Irving Hallowell, "Ojibwa Ontology, Behavior and World View"

Names matter. They signify and communicate conceptions of identity, kinship, and power. Traditionally, my Algonkian Indian kin (like many other Indigenous peoples) do not live in a conceptual world governed by humans alone; they recognize the coexistence of "other-than-human" beings (animals, shapeshifters, ancestral spirits, natural forces, etc.) living side by side with humans. For the Ojibwe (also called Ojibwa and Anishinaabe), for example, all human and other-than-human beings are construed as "persons," living causal agents with the capacity to manifest, transform, and direct power.[1] These beliefs were integrated into hunting, harvesting, and healing traditions and linked to specific locales in the physical landscape. As anthropologist Frank Gouldsmith Speck observed a century ago, Algonkian hunters employed specialized speech, decorative clothing, and even ritually marked "meat pans" to explicitly speak to and respect the animals being hunted.[2] As contemporary Abenaki historian Lisa Brooks notes, the physical necessity of sharing natural resources in a literal and conceptual "common pot" continues to influence how Indigenous people talk about and occupy shared ecosystems over time.[3] Respect and reciprocity are crucial considerations. Any person who meddles with the delicate balance between human and other-than-human worlds—by disrespecting relationships, stealing property, abusing power, or otherwise transgressing cultural norms—might be rightfully accused of behaving, in effect, like a social "savage." One must move carefully to avoid potential offense, since all persons can be unpredictable.

The machinations of Euro-American colonization forced unexpected changes on Indigenous people, not the least of which was the loss of control over the independent shaping of their own names and identities. The Indigenous were classed by colonizers as primitives, aboriginals, and savages. The thought

patterns associated with these antiquated names still linger, making it difficult to choose a generic term that will not offend. The French word *sauvage*,
for example, which roughly translates to people of the forest, did not truly
recognize Indigenous people as owners of the forests they inhabited. Nor did
the English word *savage*, which was deployed to position the Indigenous as
primitives vis-à-vis the theoretically more advanced white Euro-American settler societies.[4] *Indian*, another long-standing term with lingering popularity
in pop culture, has an equally fraught history.[5] Even though many among
the Indigenous claim that term for themselves (collectively referring to North
America as "Indian Country," for example), it is still widely used as a pejorative.
There are other possibilities, like the terms *American Indian* (commonly used
in the nineteenth and twentieth centuries) and *Native American* (which came
into use during the human rights movements of the 1970s), but these, too,
link Indigenous identity to a colonial settler state (America) that interrupted
Indigenous sovereignties.

The concept of imagining North American Indigenous people as "savages"
was central to the anthropological project because it positioned them as theoretically uncivilized and primitive and, therefore, perfect candidates for study
as "Others." As Edward Said notes, the establishment of categorical distinctions among different groups of people was instrumental to the process of colonizing. Western colonizers constructed "institutions, vocabulary, scholarship,
imagery, doctrines, even colonial bureaucracies and colonial styles" to control
not just the lives but also the images of colonized subjects.[6] Maori scholar
Linda Tuhiwai Smith similarly characterizes colonial terminology as a racial-
izing system that normalizes, empowers, and reproduces itself by positioning
people of color in permanent opposition to white Europeans.[7] As Alejandro
Haber observes, "Indians themselves had little chance to take part in defining
what was considered to be Indian."[8] Colonizing terms and approaches had
wide-ranging influence in literature, science, history, and other fields of research that, until quite recently, routinely marginalized Indigenous knowledges
and oral traditions.[9] Even in the presumably objective field of ethnohistory, Indigenous people were often positioned in opposition to the non-Indigenous as
conceptual (if not literal) "cannibals."[10] Anthropologist Audra Simpson insists
that virtually all forms of ethnographic identification, even the use of the term
Indigenous, can be problematic when they evoke an exotic "Other" without
regard for the specificities of sovereign identities.[11]

How, then, can we collectively name Native people and nations without
using colonizing terminology? I am tempted to use the Abenaki term *alnôba*,
which simply means "human being" (or, more specifically, a Native person as
distinct from a non-Native person).[12] Yet to do so would be Abenaki-centric
at the risk of ignoring hundreds of other Indigenous languages and nations

on the North American continent. So, at the risk of overgeneralizing, I will use both *Native* and *Indigenous* as all-encompassing terms for the aboriginal peoples who are commonly referred to as Native Americans or American Indians in the United States, and as Aboriginals and First Nations in Canada. The term *Indian*, when it appears, will generally reflect a direct transcription from a historical text that may or may not have pejorative meaning. The term will also be used when it represents a named group, event, or concept (e.g., the "Indian Reorganization Act," the "American Indian Movement"). In all cases, the terms *Indian, Native*, and *Indigenous* will be capitalized, since these terms are not simply adjectives but are proper nouns designating socially constructed groups. Whenever possible and appropriate, I will also use tribal names to reflect the identities that Indigenous individuals and groups claim for themselves.

These names may, I realize, generate some confusion. For example, readers will encounter Mohegan, Wampanoag, Abenaki, and other New England tribal nations who are collectively identified as Algonkian Indians (a cultural category), speaking various dialects of Algonquian (a linguistic category), and participating in a pan-Indian "Algonquin Council." Those tribal nations share some cultural similarities with, but are politically and geographically separate from, the Algonquin nation in Quebec (now identified as the Kitigan Zibi Anishinaabeg). All of these Algonkian peoples differ from another broad cultural grouping identified culturally as Iroquois or Haudenosaunee ("people of the longhouse"), speaking various dialects of Iroquoian (another linguistic category). Before the 1720s, the Haudenosaunee (Mohawk, Oneida, Onondaga, Cayuga, and Seneca) were known to colonial settlers as the Five Nations Iroquois Confederacy. Since the inclusion of the Tuscarora, they have been identified as the Six Nations Iroquois Confederacy.[13] Since both cultural and historical specificity are required, I will note, in each chapter, which names were in use for the Indigenous groups being discussed at any particular moment in time.

Not incidentally, the original working title for this project was "Consorting with Savages." The term *savage* was intended as a categorical distinction to classify white collectors who swept through Indigenous communities in search of treasures (evoking Indigenous stories of cannibal spirits in human form). Like Mik'maq author Daniel Paul, who titled his book *We Were Not the Savages*, I had hoped to simply turn the sobriquet in reverse.[14] When early readers took issue with the title, I sought alternatives. Suggestions included "Consorting with Western Barbarians," "Saving or Savaging," "Dances with Documents," "Conversational Crossings," "Resisting Capture," and "Relationship Status, Complicated."[15] One possibility was "Inside Out," evoking a more nuanced representation of the complex positionalities of these early research partners, many of whom danced across multiple cultural divides. Another option was

"Other-Than-Ourselves," a play on words that resonates with Algonkian conceptions of the categories of "humans" and "other-than-humans," while also referencing the routine anthropological practice of "othering" those who are not like "us" (whoever "us" might be). In the end, we settled on the title *Savage Kin*.

During the era of salvage anthropology, Indigenous and anthropological "selves" and "others" were, of course, complicated individuals with links to multiple kin communities. Even when they did not fit neatly into binary categories, they had to locate themselves somewhere. Were they strangers or friends, allies or enemies, informants or research partners? As my colleague Françoise Dussart noted in an early discussion about this work, we are all positioned within existing and shifting relationships, where "no one encounters anyone for the first time, no one exchanges for the first time." All human social interactions proceed on the premise that persons are "inevitably lived and perceived as versions of other persons."[16] The data in anthropological records, according to Marilyn Strathern, must therefore always be seen as reflecting "some kind of interaction or dialogue between persons, imagined or not, a crucial source of indeterminacy."[17] Thus, when we examine anthropological correspondence, it is helpful to consider just what kind of "person" each individual participant was perceived to be, which persons they were related to, and who they were seeking to engage (or avoid, or appease) during an anthropological encounter.

In many of those early encounters, multiple persons were present: in physical form as human beings, in ethereal form as other-than-human beings, in memory as ancestral cultural advisors, and in imagination as future audiences. Early anthropologists believed themselves to be almost uniquely capable of capturing authentic records and representations of the Indigenous that would remain influential and meaningful for generations. The early Indigenous informants who left written records were also talking to future beings, by agreeing to record oral traditions that might otherwise have been lost to memory. Some of those culturally coded messages, which are not always perceptible to outsiders, are still tucked away in correspondence and field notes, waiting to be read.

Anthropological archives preserved many kinds of texts: oral traditions, family anecdotes, ritual speech, object histories, field notes, scientific observations, and everyday conversation, to name just a few. Arguably, none of these texts were as straightforward as they might seem to be. Errors in translation, cultural biases, and Euro-centric theoretical models slipped in-between the lines of this cross-cultural discourse. As a result, some Indigenous oral traditions were regarded as historically "factual" and "real" experiences; others were seen as mythological (and therefore apparently "false") stories. Anthropological texts were constructed as seemingly objective observations of on-the-ground encounters, but is it possible that some of them were closer to speculative "fiction?" How can we discern and discuss the difference?

One of Frank Speck's students, A. Irving Hallowell, encountered an Ojibwe framing device that, although it might seem dated, remains relevant as a means of distinguishing between anecdote and myth. Among the Algonkian peoples of the Upper Great Lakes region, "stories" are typically classed into two distinct categories:

> 1. News or tidings (*tdbdtcamowin*), i.e., anecdotes, or stories, referring to events in the lives of human beings (*anicindbek*). In content, narratives of this class range from everyday occurrences, through more exceptional experiences, to those which verge on the legendary. . . . 2. Myths (*dtiso/kanak*), i.e., sacred stories, which are not only traditional and formalized; their narration is seasonally restricted and is somewhat ritualized.[18]

Human beings were always considered to be the authors and central characters of "news or tidings," even if they happened to be recounting personal encounters with other-than-human beings. "Myths," in contrast, were believed to have been originally scripted and inhabited by "living entities who have existed from time immemorial." Interestingly, the characters who inhabit these myths tend to "behave like people. . . . There is social interaction among them and between them and anicindbek."[19] And, of course, those mythological beings depended on human narrators to transmit their stories.

Using this framing device, we might designate anthropologists as a new class of beings ("academic beings") who, during the early twentieth century, began scripting stories related to themselves and their interactions with "Indigenous beings." Within the frame of this metaphor, anthropological "news or tidings" would include everyday encounters in the office and in the field, casual exchanges with informants, narrative reports and routine publications, and anecdotes (humorous and otherwise). The category of anthropological "myth" would include the stories that academic beings recount about those intellectual ancestors who have assumed larger-than-life form, through ritually significant encounters, with special cachet attached to transcultural acts (e.g., adoption, naming) that signify enhanced power or status. The tellings of these stories are not (like Native myths) seasonally restricted, but they are ritualized, having long been circulated within departments, institutions, and professional recitations (including conferences, publications, and websites) that keep ancestral memories alive.

The chapters of this book are filled with these kinds of stories. Some of these stories (like some of those Ojibwe stones) are more alive than others. They fill the gaps in anthropological literature and public memory by revealing the human dimensions of almost legendary encounters between memorable predecessors. Many of the early anthropologists imagined themselves to be heroes engaged in dangerous search and rescue missions, recovering cultures from extinction, seeking treasures to fill the halls of the great museums. Despite herculean efforts, some of their missions failed, and some of their collections quite literally went up in flames. To explain such troubles, their Indigenous informants spoke of uncanny influences: ancestral spirits, prophetic dreams, shape-shifters, and warnings from other-than-human beings. The more personal anecdotes illuminate complex gender relations, power dynamics, and social entanglements that propelled some individuals into the light and others into the shadows. This book shines a bit of light into those shadows, revealing some stories that have been waiting a very long time to be told.

1

Watching the Collectors

Dialogical and Material Encounters

> If you want to understand what a science is, you should look in
> the first instance not at its theories or its findings, and certainly
> not at what its apologists say about it; you should look at what the
> practitioners of it do.
>
> —Clifford Geertz, "Thick Description"

Around the turn of the twentieth century, a number of
North American museums—including the American Museum of Natural
History at Columbia University; the Robert S. Peabody Museum of Archaeology and Ethnography at Harvard University; the Museum of the American
Indian/Heye Foundation in New York City; and the University of Pennsylvania Museum of Archaeology and Anthropology in Philadelphia—launched
collecting expeditions into Native American and First Nations communities.[1]
Indigenous peoples were, at the time, presumed to be poised on the brink of
either irreversible extinction or inescapable modernity, and collectors sought to
preserve relics of the past for study and display. Many collectors (in common
with religious missionaries, social reformers, and stage agents) subscribed to
social evolutionary theories that positioned the Indigenous as culturally un-
developed when compared to white Americans and Europeans.[2] As a result,
exhibitions often emphasized the exoticism of Indigeneity, using objects to
illustrate distinctions between supposedly "primitive" (Native American) and
"advanced" (Euro-American) cultures. As Donna Haraway notes in her analysis
of ethnographic dioramas, exhibitions were also gendered and classed in ways
that reflected elite white masculine ideals and achievements.[3]

Despite class, gender, and ethnic divides, anthropology was often a collaborative endeavor. Indigenous individuals were enlisted as guides, interpreters,
artisans, procurers, and translators. These relationships began to blur the roles
of anthropologist/informant, kin/outsider, and collector/collected. Some white
anthropologists insisted on maintaining a detached and strictly objective social
and intellectual distance. Others developed such close friendships with Indigenous subjects and communities that they "went Native," being ritually adopted

Figure 1 Franz Boas (*left*) and George Hunt (*right*) posing with an unnamed Kwakwaka'wakw woman who is spinning yarn while rocking a cradle. Vancouver Island, c. 1894. Photograph by Oregon C. Hastings. Image # 11604. Courtesy of the American Museum of Natural History Library.

and transformed from outsiders to kin.[4] Looking back at these relations, David Browman and Steven Williams, authors of *Anthropology at Harvard: A Biographical History, 1790–1940*, have suggested that the "strong Indigenous-based contribution" should be recognized as a "critical thread in the origins of our field."[5] Taking that analogy a bit further, the evidence in correspondence and field notes suggests that, in some locales, Indigenous interlocutors were responsible for weaving the material that incorporated that critical thread. Yet they rarely gained credit as intellectual equals. Their efforts were largely obscured by power relations and cataloging practices that separated people from objects, objects from communities, and communities from their stories.

With this in mind, one could ask whether Franz Boas inspired George Hunt, Hunt inspired Boas, or Hunt's wives informed and inspired both of them. We could reasonably trace Irving Hallowell's interest in Algonkian Ojibwe ontology not just by looking to his mentor, Frank Speck, or to Speck's mentor, Boas, but to the crucial data provided by Speck's Indigenous informants. A reexamination of Speck's relations with his collaborator Gladys Tantaquidgeon and her mentor, Fidelia Fielding, reveals the beginnings of what would become a lasting engagement with Indigenous ontologies and Algonkian landscapes. Fenton's entire career in Haudenosaunee studies would have been impossible without the generosity of his Seneca friends. Is it not possible that early anthropological researchers were influenced and guided by their Indigenous informants, as much as (if not more than) their academic colleagues?

Putnam's Boys and Converse's Salon

The intense focus on North American Indigenous peoples in Americanist anthropology began, in a sense, with Lewis Henry Morgan's seminal text, *League of the Ho-dé-no-sau-nee or Iroquois,* and also with his *Ancient Society; or, Researches in the Lines of Human Progress from Savagery through Barbarism to Civilization.*[6] Each of these promoted the notion that Indigenous groups (even the exceptional Iroquois) were evolving toward either disappearance or civilization, depending upon the degree to which they were willing or able to acculturate to Euro-American lifeways.

A less ethnocentric and more relativistic approach to anthropology emerged under the leadership of Frederic Ward Putnam, at around the same time that he recruited Franz Boas to work on the 1893 World's Columbian Exposition on the grounds of the Chicago Field Museum of Natural History. Putnam, who directed archaeological research for the Peabody Museum of Archaeology and Ethnography at Harvard University, was determined to establish a comprehensive program in anthropology somewhere in America. In Chicago, he hoped to build on the success of the Columbian Exposition and the concurrent "World's Fair Congress of Anthropology," which brought together most of North America's anthropological scholars.[7] When financial limitations at Harvard and political differences at the Field Museum blocked opportunities in those venues, Putnam turned his attentions to the American Museum of Natural History (AMNH) and Columbia University in New York City. With Harvard's permission, in 1894 Putnam accepted a half-time appointment at AMNH's Division of Archaeology and Ethnology, which he immediately renamed "Anthropology" to accommodate and encourage the increasing linkages between archaeological excavating and ethnological work. He then hired Boas as an assistant for ethnology and physical anthropology. Boasting of his early success at Columbia, Putnam wrote, "I have the best equipment of any anthropological museum in the country and I'll show Chicago I can go them one better."[8] AMNH supported a series of wide-reaching archaeological expeditions, including Harlan Smith's midwestern mapping of mounds and earthworks in 1892 and the 1897 Jesup North Pacific Expedition with Smith and Boas.

In 1899 Boas was appointed as Columbia's first professor of anthropology; by 1905 he had left his post at AMNH to consolidate the teaching of anthropology at Columbia into a single department, which he chaired. A highly influential researcher and educator, Boas developed theories of "cultural relativism" and "historical particularism" that were progressive for the time, given the prevalence of social evolutionary thought and cultural racism.[9] Unlike many of his colleagues, he viewed Native cultures as relatively cohesive and complete, situated within their own logics of development and governed by their own laws. His attempts to discredit Darwinian social evolutionary theory and scientific racism might have laid the path for a more holistic, reflexive, and inclusive anthropology, were it not for lingering inequalities that continued to influence relations on the ground.[10] As George Stocking Jr. has observed, cultural relativism can easily morph into moral relativism and apologism if one ignores the impact of class and power inequalities on cultural continuity and survival.[11]

To chart the distribution and diffusion of Indigenous worldviews, material practices, and cultural traits, Boas collected and interpreted both archaeological and ethnographic data. Museums expected collectors to largely focus on physical material, but Boas recognized that "any array of objects is always only an exceedingly fragmentary presentation of the true life of a people," since objects derived meaning through use. He wrote,

> All of these [objects] are used in the daily life of the people, and almost all of them receive their significance only through the thoughts that cluster around them. For example, a pipe of the North American Indians is not only a curious implement out of which the Indian smokes, but it has a great number of uses and meanings, which can be understood only when viewed from the standpoint of the social and religious life of the people.[12]

Boas therefore called for studies of the "psychological as well as the historical relations of cultures" to answer the questions that specimens could not address.[13] Even so, there was an inherent lack of reflexivity. Non-Indigenous collectors assumed roles as the interpreters of Indigenous societies and religions, while overlooking the influence of their own psychologies. Where a white researcher might see that pipe as an inanimate object, practical implement, and/or ritual tool, an Indigenous user might see the same pipe as an animate conveyer of messages, an active participant in ceremony, and an agent with transformative powers that could be activated through prayer and medicine. Such Indigenous object ontologies cannot necessarily be understood by gazing into a museum case or interviewing a lone informant; they are best understood (and are often protected) within a living cultural complex.

Writing in *Invisible Genealogies: A History of Americanist Anthropology*, Regna Darnell notes that the intellectual and theoretical dimensions of anthropological research were shaped by Boas's insistence on "ethnographic salvage" to recover data from geographically distinct and presumably vanishing cultural groups.[14] Indigenous cultural material, human remains, and data were collected and sorted through various fields of study—archaeology, physical anthropology, cultural anthropology, linguistic anthropology, and psychological analysis—that generated their own conceptual, methodological, and even cultural divisions. Scientific researchers typically positioned themselves as elite intellectuals vis-à-vis their Indigenous subjects. The material they collected was organized, analyzed, cataloged, curated, and interpreted, in most cases, in the absence of consultation with Indigenous knowledge-bearers, and without consideration for Indigenous philosophies and sensitivities. Over time, institutional memories about these collections replaced Indigenous memories to such a degree that speculative theories and opinions, if voiced by a prominent enough researcher, were routinely accepted as fact. Even exhibit labels could become tools of erasure when they replaced Indigenous identifiers with scientific jargon. Yet, during the salvage era, there were some unexpected locales where Indigenous perspectives were more equitably expressed and listened to.

During the early twentieth century, anthropological theories were also being formulated outside the academy, in the salon hosted by Harriet Maxwell Converse in New York City. Converse was a wealthy poet, social activist, and honorary chief among the Six Nations Haudenosaunee (Iroquois).[15] She might be considered, in a sense, "the midwife of anthropology," since she hosted Putnam's lectures and helped to recruit Boas's students. Her close friendship with Ely Parker, the "educated Seneca Indian" who had served as Lewis Henry Morgan's primary informant, made her a relative expert on Six Nations Haudenosaunee culture.[16] Converse's guests in the salon included seasoned field archaeologists such as Harlan Ingersoll Smith and George Hubbard Pepper, journalists such as Udo Joseph Keppler, and artists such as John William Fenton and Casper Mayer. She also hosted Native guests, notably Abenaki actor/model Elijah Tahamont and other residents of the New York Indian colony. The most eager audience for these gatherings consisted of a small cohort of promising eighteen-to-nineteen-year-olds: Mark Raymond Harrington, Alanson Buck Skinner, Frank Gouldsmith Speck, William Jones, and Arthur Caswell Parker.[17] Imagine the scene: a group of eminent white scholars and brilliant young men, all desirous of studying Indians, urged on by a wealthy white female visionary and her influential friends. The voices of Native women and traditional Native leaders were conspicuously absent, which may explain some of the gender and culture biases that infused early anthropological theory and practice.

Putnam, who frequently offered lectures at Converse's, was always in search of "enthusiastic but little-schooled amateur" archaeologists who had (or desired) experiential field learning, with or without college degrees. He also sought to recruit talented Native students for academic study, and found just such a prospect in William Jones (Sauk-Fox), who was then a graduate of Hampton Institute and Phillips Andover Academy and a medical student at Harvard. Jones recalled his first meeting with Putnam in 1867:

> My meeting with Professor Putnam was the very nicest talk I believe I ever had with an elderly man, excepting perhaps one or two with Dr. Bancroft. He took me right in, and told me just exactly what I wanted to know without the least possible questioning of my part except one or two times. . . . The field he opened to me is certainly wide, with room enough for hundreds of intelligent workers.[18]

Jones abandoned his dream of being a doctor to become an anthropologist. After graduation from Harvard in 1900, he went to Columbia to study under Boas. He received the President's University Fellowship in 1900, completed his master's study, and was immediately appointed as a University Fellow and assistant in anthropology for 1901–3.[19] His doctoral study led him to work among his own people (the Sauk and Fox), and he became the first Native American student to receive a PhD in anthropology at Columbia. His 1904 dissertation, "Some Principles of Algonkin Word Formation," was immediately published in *American Anthropologist*.[20] Jones accepted a position at the Chicago Field Museum and seemed destined for a productive career, but his elite training and sense of privilege apparently led him astray. In 1909 he was murdered in the Philippines by the Ilongot people he was studying. The records reflect the cause: Jones disdained and insulted the Natives, whom he characterized as "more like beasts than human beings." During a dispute over the delivery of balsa rafts, he manhandled and threatened to detain a tribal elder. This transgressive action provoked violent retribution.[21] There were several brief obituaries, but the anthropological community reacted to Jones's death with a curious silence.[22]

The only other Native American student on Putnam's radar who showed as much promise as Jones was Arthur Parker. Perhaps, with proper training, he could be shaped into an excellent anthropologist. Research depended, after all, on interactions with Indigenous informants, so who better to gather information than one of their own? In retrospect, Jones and Parker shared a similar personal flaw: they were each willing to use their Indian identities to exert positional privilege as cultural experts, without any culturally specific training or political standing to do so in their respective tribal nations. In effect, they behaved like cultural (if not genetic) "white men." Like other researchers who had Native ancestry, and like some of the white researchers who had honorary tribal adoptions, these men were socially marked as "Indians," but they did not exert any traditional authority within their Indigenous communities. There were, of course, moments when they crossed cultural borderlines, capturing revelatory insights that accurately reflected Indigenous experience, but much of their work obscured the agency and influence of the Indigenous knowledge keepers who assisted them.

Authenticating Indians

During the salvage anthropology era, everyone was searching for authentic "Indians." Scientific collectors promoted the notion that they were rendering a great service to humanity by preserving what was about to be forever lost. To do so, they had to identify and establish fixed social, geographical, and political boundaries between tribal individuals and nations. Franz Boas, in collaboration with his student Edward Sapir, devised geocultural and linguistic groupings (including Iroquoian and Algonquian) that are still widely recognized as useful categories, and are routinely used by Native people today to identify themselves. Collectors sought to assemble distinctive collections that would effectively represent these cultural groups.

Since amateur and professional collectors were not bound by any particular code of ethics, they routinely engaged in what can be seen, in retrospect, as acts of deception (purchasing and alienating known patrimonial objects) and desecration (excavating and removing human remains and funerary objects from gravesites). These practices crossed and altered conceptions of tribal boundaries, identities, and property rights. Ethnological data, theory, and practice became inextricably linked with unequal power relations in the field. As Michael Ames astutely observes in his *Cannibal Tours and Glass Boxes: The Anthropology of Museums*, "museums are cannibalistic in appropriating other peoples' material for their own study and interpretation."[23] Once boxes had been constructed, collectors were expected to fill them, but none of these objects walked into museums under their own power. Each collection resulted from some sort of direct interaction with Indigenous makers (living or dead), Indigenous culture (recognized or not), and Indigenous assistants (willing or not). In museum settings, these objects came to symbolize not the living Indigenous cultures that created them but fragments of the presumably vanishing (or already vanished) cultures of the past.[24] Ironically, the salvage project caused some of the very losses it was predicated upon. If Native cultures were not vanishing when it began, they were in danger of vanishing when it ended.

This work was positioned against the backdrop of an intensive civilizing project in the Americas. White settler populations sought to claim and expand into Indigenous landholdings across the continent, and federal Indian policy advocated the alteration, if not elimination, of traditional Indigenous culture through forced education, assimilation, acculturation, and relocation.

In the aftermath of the western Indian wars, Native American Indian communities also faced increasing pressures to restructure tribal governance and accept American citizenship as a means to expedite their political transition to modernity. Popular discourse and stereotypes of the era suggested that American Indians were helpless to resist the loss of traditional ways and assimilation into mainstream white society.[25] This made a compelling argument for the large-scale capturing of their culture. Exhibitions at prominent institutions like Columbia, Harvard, and the Smithsonian were widely promoted as authoritative means of understanding Indians (or at least understanding white cultural beliefs about Indians).[26] As Curtis Hinsley notes, in *The Smithsonian and the American Indian: Making a Moral Anthropology in Victorian America*, the collecting of American Indian material became entangled with Victorian social mores, shaping white American conceptions of Indians as exotic alien "others."[27] The "vanishing Indian" label became a floating signifier that could be selectively applied to deny Indigenous modernity and survivance. Philip Deloria has suggested, in *Indians in Unexpected Places*, that modernized Indians were, in a sense, dislocated in time: not civilized, not white, and, therefore, not "modern."[28]

The material collected varied widely in style and quality, from unique objects to replicas produced explicitly for sale. Conceptual divisions between present and past were such that museums emphasized older materials, on the assumption that these would be more authentic. Yet there were no common protocols for dating and organizing collections; each collector and each museum applied somewhat idiosyncratic systems of their own devising. Objects were physically sorted in ways that imperfectly reflected (or overtly distorted) Indigenous origins and meanings.[29] The anthropological salvage project generated an enormous volume of records—field notes, letters, sketches, photographs, and other manuscripts—that could potentially provide context, but these papers (if they were kept at all) were often scattered into different institutions and archives. It is difficult to tell, from this distance, exactly what cultural data was recorded, how much of the original documentation was kept, and how much was accidentally or intentionally discarded. For example, George Gustav Heye, founder of the Museum of the American Indian/Heye Foundation, was passionate about acquiring thousands of Indian objects (approximately 700,000, at best count) through expeditions, purchases from dealers, and exchanges with other museums.[30] Yet he was reportedly so uninterested in cultural details that one of his collectors, Mark Harrington, wrote:

> I have something real—and unpleasant—for you. I have been writing you that I had been sending in full information with my specimens, but I was wrong. All of a sudden I remembered that George Heye did *not* want detailed information on

specimens. On ethnological specimens he wanted only the name of the thing and the tribe; on archaeological, only the name of the thing and the site; all other information he deliberately threw away. I found this on one of my early visits to the museum after a collecting trip.[31]

Luckily, many of Harrington's notes were eventually preserved in the Museum of the American Indian/Heye Foundation archives, but they were rarely well organized. Museum curators routinely sorted and stored objects by type or by collector, thereby obscuring personal names, tribal identities, and other crucial cultural data; the erasures introduced by these cataloging choices still cause confusion in Indigenous collections today.

Talking with the Collectors, Excavating the Archives

When I first sought to locate materials that might document Indigenous commentary on those early anthropological encounters, I expected to find only a few letters, but I discovered much more. A number of the Indigenous participants in the anthropological project were surprisingly eloquent and prolific letter writers. Some letters survived in small tribal and family archives, but these were often detached from the objects under discussion. An impressively large body of correspondence was preserved and housed in non-Indigenous locations (academic offices, museum records, libraries, and institutional archives). Indigenous writers were typically classified as "informants" rather than "intellectuals," and the bulk of their writings (when they were preserved) were subsumed into the archives of the scholars who studied them. This organizational scheme might create the impression that Indigenous knowledge was preserved largely as a by-product of the production of academic knowledge. Yet, as the case studies in this book demonstrate, the letters to and from collectors, dealers, museums, state agents, tribal leaders, and informants reveal intimately negotiated relationships and arguments that are only glimpsed in formal publications. This discovery makes Indigenous intellectual and social contributions to the foundational knowledges of anthropology far more visible.

Indigenous intellectuals are not particularly well represented in the early ethnographic literature, in large part because different stories were being told about them. Natives were positioned as ethnographic subjects, not as scholars; and as informants, not theorists. White scholars believed themselves to be capable of discerning precisely which Indigenous people and practices were most "authentic" (and they still do so today).[32] In seeking authenticity, anthropologists often sought out less-educated Indians, developing a special fondness for impoverished or illiterate informants who could be convincingly represented as the "last" of their tribe. Potential informants were subjected to multiple levels of validation. Did they wear traditional dress and speak their language? Were they "real Indians" or "show Indians"? Did they have access to any desirable artifacts they might be willing to sell? Native people who were too savvy or resistant to the collecting process need not apply. In other words, the process of vetting informants, like the process of selecting artifacts, was socially negotiated and racially marked from the outset. By studying the surviving evidence of dialogical as well as material encounters, we can illuminate key moments of intersection, collaboration, and contestation.

For example, buried amid routine correspondence, in multiple museums, there are scores of strikingly articulate personal letters largely written in English about specific objects in the collections. In the personal papers of prominent anthropologists, there are similar assemblages of letters that reveal details of social interactions and economic negotiations in the field, recording working relationships that, in some cases, lasted for decades. Some of these letters are chatty and warm, others are scathingly critical; all reveal complicated exertions of personal power. These letters often constitute "hidden transcripts": private, subaltern critiques of power expressed as a means of resistance.[33] The same archives also preserve speeches, petitions, and other documents intended as "public transcripts" to assert tribal presence and sovereignty in the face of American and Canadian state domination. Indigenous agents, by turns, provoked, resisted, negotiated, translated, and sometimes scripted collecting encounters. Following Pierre Bourdieu's approach, the textual evidence can be mined to determine how their discourse shaped the circulation of both symbolic and real capital, as individual and collective identities, relations, and positions shifted over time.[34] Taken as a whole, this correspondence reveals some of the messy social negotiations behind the polished constructions that appeared in anthropological publications. Perhaps not surprisingly, these letters suggest that the anthropologists were not always in control.

Here, it is important to note that, by 1900, few Indigenous communities in North America were as socially isolated or "primitive" as collectors might imagine. In some locales, Native individuals and tribal communities were fully fluent in English, French, or Spanish, after having interacted with Europeans for centuries. A surprising number of Native people volunteered to supply data and material for museum collections; some actively promoted the tribal identities that researchers most wanted to see.[35] Some of the most prolific informants were self-selected volunteers who collected (and occasionally invented) material for anthropological consumption. There were also charismatic performers and shape-shifters who danced their way into view, even while "playing Indian" to enhance their social and economic status. Some of these individuals (e.g., Elijah Tahamont a.k.a. "Dark Cloud" and Oscar de Corti a.k.a. "Iron Eyes Cody") became very successful in Hollywood films.[36] Rather than simply handing over unfiltered data, these Native people took an active role in shaping Indian imagery and feeding the American hunger for Indian culture.

A fuller understanding of these relationships can be gained through what I call "reverse ethnography," a process designed to illuminate some of the microhistories embedded within the *longue durée* of the anthropological project. These microhistories, sometimes traceable through objects, are often highly visible in correspondence, especially during an era when so much routine communication was conducted and recorded through written letters. After densely reading through four decades' worth of anthropological correspondence from about 1900 to 1940, I realized that Indigenous informants played a much larger role in ethnographic collecting than they are typically credited for. They were not just naïve victims; they were arguably co-creators of the Americanist school of anthropology. They contributed important embodied experiences and subaltern perspectives, and mediated access to tribal knowledges, while providing desired information and artifacts. For their own reasons (often put into writing), some of them persisted in supporting the anthropological project, even under criticism from their own kin and communities. As guides and translators, they offered nuanced interpretations and (when necessary) blunt critiques. The written records of this discourse—often collaborative, sometimes contentious, always complicated—reveal the degree to which anthropologists depended on, were challenged by, and sometimes chose to conceal the intelligence of their Indigenous informants.

2

Finding Our Dances

George Hunt and Franz Boas

> They say here is he who is finding out all our Dances then he goes
> and tell it to Dr Boas.
>
> —George Hunt to Franz Boas, March 4, 1898

It started with seawater. In 1883, two years after completing his PhD dissertation in physics, titled "Beiträge zur Erkenntniss der Farbe des Wassers" (Contributions to the understanding of the color of water), Franz Uri Boas (1858–1942) set forth on an expedition to Baffin Island in the Canadian north.[1] There, during a grueling winter while his ship was frozen in, he experienced his first in-depth encounters with Indigenous people. He had intended to study geography, water, and culture but soon found himself intimately dependent on Inuit technology for survival. He commissioned fur clothing from Inuit women, hired Inuit men as translators and guides, slept in their igloos, and ate their food. In his letter diary to his sweetheart Marie Krackowizer (on a page marked with a small spot of blood from the seal liver he had just tasted), he expressed an observation that was radical in its cultural relativity:

> I often ask myself what advantages our "good society" possesses over that of the "savages" and find, the more I see of their customs, that we have no right to look down upon them. Where amongst our people could you find such hospitality as here? Where are people so willing, without the least complaint, to perform *every* task asked of them? We have no right to blame them for their forms and superstitions which may seem ridiculous to us. We "highly educated people" are much worse, relatively speaking.[2]

Boas's second encounter with the Indigenous happened in a less arduous and more familiar setting closer to home, when he met members of the Nuxalk Nation (Bella Coola) performing as an exhibit at the Königliches Museum für Völkerkunde (Royal Ethnological Museum) in Berlin. After conducting linguistic interviews with these people, Boas joined an expedition to British Columbia to learn more. These experiences sparked what would become a lifelong interest in Northwest Coast cultures and a permanent relocation to the United States in 1887.[3]

In 1888 Boas embarked on his university career, starting at Clark University, where he rapidly advanced from docent to chair of a new Department of Anthropology. His interests in physical anthropology and craniometric measurements led him back to the Northwest Coast where, at Fort Rupert, British Columbia, he crossed paths with George Hunt, a man of mixed Tlingit and English ancestry. Hunt had been working as a court interpreter for Superintendent of Indian Affairs Israel Powell since 1879, and he appeared to be more fluent in English and acculturated than many of his neighbors. In a diary entry on June 13, 1888, Boas wrote that Hunt's help would be "of the greatest value," since otherwise, "the only way I can get people is to drag them in by the hair."[4] He successfully recruited Hunt as a guide for several expeditions. By 1892 Boas had resigned his position at Clark and been hired by Frederic Ward Putnam, from the Peabody Museum at Harvard, to organize the anthropological exhibitions at the Chicago World's Fair. To manage the Kwakwaka'wakw camp and performances at the fair, Boas again recruited George Hunt, sealing the foundation of a partnership that would last for more than four decades.[5]

Anthropological informants such as George Hunt—born into a high-ranking First Nations family, fluent in English, adept at navigating across cultures, with social access to tribal traditionalists—were ideal. Within their first few years of working together, Boas and Hunt co-authored three books of Kwakiutl texts (between 1902 and 1905).[6] Boas also published nine research articles and additional texts composed largely of material collected by Hunt.[7] Hunt composed thousands of handwritten manuscript pages—now distributed across the archives at the American Philosophical Society (APS), American Museum of Natural History, and Columbia University—filled with observations of traditional activities, narratives of oral traditions, descriptions of sacred practices, sketches of family crests and coppers, diagrams of houses, maps, and linguistic notes.[8] Since Boas was paying by the page, each was meticulously numbered and cataloged. These men negotiated the parameters of these projects and payments by exchanging thousands of pages of correspondence; Hunt also kept field notebooks and account books of his own. A surprisingly large quantity of this raw material (including, by my count, approximately 2,400 pages at APS alone) remains unpublished.

Hunt's correspondence with Boas reveals social undercurrents that shaped the circulation of both symbolic and real capital. Hunt idolized Boas, who, in a sense, invented "Hunt, the collector," by enticing him to locate, identify, and procure virtually all the materials on his patron's wish list, regardless of the logistical challenges. Hunt eagerly responded to any request, from stealing icons to excavating graves to dismantling buildings, often knowingly violating

Figure 2 Franz Boas relaxing in Ruth Benedict's living room, c. 1930s. Photographer unknown. Courtesy of the Library of Congress.

cultural protocols to do so. He promoted himself as the primary (if not sole) interlocutor of Northwest Coast culture, denouncing the reliability of other sources, even his own kin. He assured Boas that whatever he did not know, he could find out, given sufficient time and money and the right informants. Although their partnership has been touted as a positive example of cross-cultural collaboration, their correspondence shows that they intentionally marginalized the influence of nonliterate Indigenous female sources by privileging scientific approaches and male perspectives. The ethnographic material that entered Boas's hands was, in effect, gendered and filtered in ways that obscured the female authorities in Hunt's own household.

Origin Stories

George Hunt's Indigenous identity came from his mother, Anislaga (also called Anain, Ansnaq, and Mary Ebbetts), a Tlingit woman of the Gaanax.adi clan, Raven phratry, from Tongass, Alaska. In the 1840s she accompanied her father, a highly ranked chief, on a trip to Port Simpson, on the Nass River in Vancouver, British Columbia. There, she met Robert Hunt from Dorsetshire, England, chief factor at the Hudson's Bay Company (HBC) post. The details of their courtship are vague, but marriages between high-ranking First Nations Native women and HBC employees were encouraged as a strategy to facilitate trade and ensure peace. Anislaga (1823–1919) and Robert (1828–93) shared a life together that was explicitly bicultural. Their wedding was a traditional Tlingit ceremony with a potlatch giveaway of blankets and trade goods, and their homes were HBC houses at Port Simpson and Fort Rupert.[9]

Anislaga's Raven clan people (like other clans among the Northwest Coast First Nations) traced their origins to a nonhuman animal, bird, reptile, or other creature that, according to traditional narratives, had chosen to transform itself into human form. In her clan origin story, a raven flew into the location now known as Hardy Bay. Origin narratives such as these were ritually recounted at Winter Festivals and potlatches, reminding all "how the ancestors long ago met with tribulations and adventures; how they were harassed or rescued by spirits and monsters; how benevolent spirits appeared in visions and invested their 'protégés' with charms; and how ancient warriors conquered their enemies in warfare."[10] These narratives were also carved onto totem poles that were ceremonially (and sometimes competitively) "stood up" at significant locations.[11] Anislaga contracted master carvers to sculpt her clan origin story onto two totem poles: one was placed over her mother's burial site in Tongass and a copy was erected near her home in Fort Rupert.[12] Although she was living in a mixed English and Native household and community, Anislaga retained other Tlingit customs reserved for high-status women, including weaving Chilkat blankets and curating engraved bracelets, coppers, and other family treasures. Among the First Nations of the Northwest Coast, clan property included physical material (land, houses, canoes, clothing, masks, crests, coppers, and so on), performative activities (songs, dances, rituals), names (personal names and house names), and dreams. Traditionally, women inherited and exercised rights of control over this tangible and intangible heritage, including representations of clan ancestors.[13]

The Hunts had seven daughters and four sons. The daughters forged cross-cultural marriages with other newcomers to the territory. Annie married H. Spencer, a Canadian fur trader who set up a salmon cannery at Alert Bay. Jane married a Welshman, Henry Cadwallader, and Elizabeth married a Scottish Lowlander, Daniel Wilson.[14] Three of the sons—George, Eli, and William—married Native women. George (1854–1933) made the most strategic matches by marrying, in succession, two Kwakwaka'wakw (also called Kwakiutl) *wi'oma*, women of noble families and high rank: Lucy Homikanis (who died in 1908) and Tsukwani Francine (who outlived him). With the assistance of his mother, his missionary school education, and his wives, George Hunt developed fluency in Tlingit, English, and Kwak'wala, and a unique level of exposure to Northwest Coast First Nations traditional knowledge.

Negotiating Terms and Translating Kwakwaka'wakw Culture

Hunt's work for Boas largely focused not on his own Tlingit community but on his wives' people, the Kwakwaka'wakw. Members of this tribal group knew Hunt from childhood, and allowed him to participate in regional potlatches and ceremonies, but did not consider him a tribal member or potlatch chief in his own right.[15] Northwest Coast Indigenous societies accorded high rank and distinction to women as carriers and inheritors of tradition and discouraged men from interfering with female roles (and vice versa).[16] For example, among the Tlingit, as one man reported to Marius Barbeau, a man is only "entitled to a Tongas dance or whatever dance my wife gives me through marriage."[17] Similar restrictions were in place among the Kwakwaka'wakw, so that men could only perform the rituals that their wives' families permitted. As a result, certain categories of gender-specific knowledge were largely inaccessible to outsiders. Yet Hunt stepped in front of his wives to assume the role of cultural gatekeeper, asserting a gendered intellectual authority that was routine for Europeans but foreign to the Indigenous.

In his letters and field notes, George Hunt frequently referenced his mother, wives, and sisters as primary informants, but in his publications, they were accorded neither authority nor authorship. Boas may be responsible for these

Figure 3 The Hunt family at Tsaxis, 1894. *Second from left, back row*: George Hunt, Lucy Homikanis Hunt, and Franz Boas. *Seated, right*: Anislaga Mary Ebbets Hunt (George's mother) surrounded by her grandchildren. Photograph by Oregon C. Hastings. Courtesy of the American Philosophical Society.

erasures, given his preconceived notions about Indigenous knowledge, gender, authenticity, and cultural evolution. Like many others who denied modernity to the Indigenous, Boas believed that "authentic Indians" could only be found in isolated locales at the far reaches of civilization. He observed matrilineal descent and female status but believed the inheritance system among the Kwakwaka'wakw to be "an abnormal development," suggesting that the passing of rank from mother to son (bypassing her husband) evidenced an imperfect evolutionary stage in what was presupposed to be a natural "transition of a maternal society to a paternal society."[18] He downplayed the value of women's knowledge of food-gathering, cooking, and marriage rites. Even after he gained fluency in the Kwak'wala language, Boas appears to have made little effort to communicate directly with Native women (or with ordinary people) about everyday life. Instead, he solicited data coded by rank and gender, with men's perspectives taking prominence.[19]

When Boas had first arrived in the territory, the Kwakwaka'wakw were curious about this stranger who had so many questions. Was he a prospector? Was he a government agent? The letters suggest that, early on, Hunt realized that a collaboration with Boas could serve the interests of traditional leaders who were keen to resist strictures imposed by the Anglican Church Missionary Society and Canadian authorities. Hunt had been repeatedly warned by Reverend Hall, who informed him, in no uncertain terms, that any performances of dances, ceremonies, and potlatches would draw unwanted attention, and could land Hunt in jail. Boas, on the other hand, assured Hunt and others that these practices should continue, in part so that he could observe and accurately record them. He insisted that he would not interfere with them; in fact, he promised that he would advocate for the tribes. In a letter to Chief Hemasaka, he said: "The Kwakiutl have no better friend than I. Whenever I can, I speak for you. . . . I have told the chiefs in Ottawa and the chiefs in England many times, that the potlatch and that the dance are not bad."[20]

Despite (or, perhaps, because of) this avowed support for the preservation of tradition, Boas was well positioned to observe and collect vast quantities of Kwakwaka'wakw property. He and Hunt coordinated the physical removal (through both excavation and purchase) of human remains, ritual objects, dance regalia, and totem poles, and the recording of any related songs or oral narratives that went with them. Boas, along with fellow purchasers like George Gustave Heye, insisted that every object be old and authentic and not newly constructed.

> Besides these, we want a good and carefully selected collection of masks and
> dancing-implements, but you must not take any new and shabby mask. We want
> only good old carvings with good painting; and for every single mask we must have

the history written down carefully in Kwakiutl; and if the mask has a song, you must record the song with it, as you have been in the custom of doing.[21]

This museological collecting was so extensive that it began to fracture traditional continuity in a region that so heavily depended on material objects—masks, boxes, instruments, and so on—to both embody and enable ritual relationships. Metaphorically and literally, Boas promised to preserve these Kwakwaka'wakw treasures by capturing them in more durable boxes, along with the narratives that gave them meaning.[22] Although he likened this process to the traditional carved wooden boxes made by Northwest Coast peoples to preserve cultural treasures, there was a key difference: Boas's boxes would not keep these things alive; they would be taken away and, in effect, entombed in museums.

As Boas's man in the field, Hunt traveled widely, using small (easily concealed) notebooks to record interviews and cultural performances. He collected multiple renditions of oral tradition, writing in Kwak'wala, and edited these before translating them into English.[23] In the field and at home, he would discuss his findings with knowledge-bearers and, more importantly, with his wife Lucy, who provided additional insights that made their way into Hunt's lengthy explanatory letters to Boas. Agnes Cranmer, Hunt's granddaughter, recalled that Hunt's writing required a great deal of cogitation: "When he was writing at his table and could not think what to put down next he would get up and take a long walk fast to get it clear in his head."[24] These methods raise interesting questions: Was Hunt strictly recalling stories, or was he reconstructing (perhaps even constructing) them? Did he blend oral tradition with creative narrative invention? Boas wondered the same: "Do you get these meanings from the old people, or do you translate them from your own knowledge of the language?"[25]

Although Indigenous oral traditions typically display some degree of narrative coherence among individual tradition keepers, Hunt does not appear to have been a carrier or keeper of those traditions in any ritual sense. Hence, he admitted, he found it difficult to procure straightforward answers: "If you ask ten Indians about one History not two of them would speak it the same."[26] He patiently explained his method of devising comprehensive narratives: "That is why I go first to the story owner family then I go next to the Enemee [enemy] family, and I always find lots of Defference Between the two, and very little more talk with some of the other People then I get the whole thing Right."[27] He reiterated this concern in subsequent letters, articulating the method he developed to reconcile "rival" storytellers: "I Don't go to and take these stories from one man"; instead, he would collect two variants before going to a "third man and ask him to tell me the same story. then I get the whole story."[28] In some cases, Hunt reported, it was difficult to discern the owners of particular traditions, stories, and objects; so he often sought out knowledgeable old women, "for they seems to know more about the old times then the Men Do."[29]

The "old times," of course, were the times that Boas was most interested in. Although some Northwest Coast Indians were then actively engaged in adapting old stories to new purposes and producing new art objects for the tourist trade, Boas was quite insistent that all materials collected must be old rather than new. Collectors had inspired a minor industry in the making of reproductions, and Boas's suspicions were aroused by a carved stone head and by "reproductions of older implements that have gone out of use."[30] He told Hunt, "Your friends are making them in order to show what the Indians used to do in older times," but, he cautioned,

> Since this is the case, you had better not get any specimens of this kind. It gives me great concern to think that in continuing this work you might get specimens that are not in reality what you and I suppose them to be, and I believe it would be better if you did not try to get any more material for some time. . . . It will be all right if you continue with your manuscripts.[31]

Over the course of nearly four decades of working with Boas, Hunt became increasingly skilled in both procuring authentic objects and narratives and creating them. He was instrumental not only in collecting and composing stories but in reinventing the representations of "Kwakiutl" culture that appeared in staged performances, on film, and in the museum. Hunt convinced his family members and traditionalists to stage potlatches, Winter Dances, and Hamat'sa (a ritualistic "cannibal" dance) for Boas's benefit, despite the fact that these activities were explicitly banned by the Canadian government. Hunt and his neighbors were fully aware of the potential theatrical impact and transgressive power of these public representations. Their wild performance at the World's Columbian Exposition in Chicago, for example, became more than just a tourist attraction; it was an overt act of resistance to Canadian authorities who had banned Indigenous ceremonies.[32] Hunt even attempted to dictate the forms this resistance should take by denouncing other public representations of Northwest Coast culture. In 1907, for example, he informed Boas that Charles F. Newcombe, photographer and collector for the Chicago Field Museum, had been duped by his Native models: "How they Dressed themselves, that kind of Dressing is never seen here sence the world was made. Charles Nowel got it from the Bible for that is the way the Romens use to Dress themselves in war." Hunt circulated Newcombe's photographs to other Indians, who "only laughed and say that white men is Esely [easily] foold."[33]

Unexpected Consequences

Hunt faced many unexpected challenges: disease, legal woes, financial hardship, physical losses, and the suspicions of his neighbors. On reading through his correspondence year by year, project by project, one sees that a surprising number of accidental deaths coincided with ritual disturbances (e.g., staging of forbidden ceremonies, thefts of objects, grave robbing). Among Northwest Coast peoples, Indigenous religious beliefs conceptualized transgressive actions as evidence of witchcraft. "Witchcraft," however, is an imprecise English word for characterizing the troubles that might emerge from breaches, intended or otherwise, of carefully mediated relationships among human and other-than-human worlds. Trouble might come from ephemeral forces, ancestral spirits, or human enemies. People perceived direct causal links between ritual breaches and personal troubles (e.g., illness, loss, death), and employed charms, spoken words, and ritual activities (personal, familial, or communal) as a means to address and appease ancestral spirits and supernatural forces. Hunt made no explicit written associations between his actions and the losses that surrounded him, but his neighbors may have perceived more than mere coincidence.[34]

Hunt often took pains to conceal his collecting activities from his neighbors, by meeting in secret and by keeping small notebooks in which he could surreptitiously record his observations at ceremonial events. Even so, Indigenous gatekeepers and Canadian authorities alike were watching. During an 1898 trip, for example, Hunt reported that his secret reporting on ritual activities had been discovered.

> I made one trip to Alert Bay and as soon as the Indians found out that it was me [they] all came and some of them looked angry to me and some of them was laughing these where the Halls school Boy, and they say here is he who is finding out all our Dances then he goes and tell it to Dr Boas . . . for they say that they see on some paper where you say that the Hamats'a Do Eat mans flesh and kills men and Eat them up, now they say in the old times they Did Do this thing But now the Hamatsa is made to give Property away. and I walked away from them. . . . Now my Dear Friend you see that the Halls school Boys is kicking against us yet. But I in hopes that we will get the Best of them yet.[35]

Boas provided reassurance and encouraged Hunt to continue. Ethnographic research was profitable, and the pay received for providing a single-story manuscript could be more lucrative than an entire season of working in the canning factory.

Similar criticism surfaced after George's sisters Sarah and Jane had provided lodging and assistance for Harlan Ingersoll Smith during the American Museum of Natural History's Jesup Expedition.[36] They knew that Smith was excavating graves to collect crania for scientific study, but the sisters were, apparently, unprepared for the resulting publicity. An interview in the Victoria newspaper, accompanied by sketches of the women, portrayed Northwest Coast Indians as primitive cannibals feasting on the remains of the dead. Sarah and Jane were outraged at Mrs. Smith's part in crafting these representations. George wrote to Boas:

> She [Mrs. Smith] went to Victoria Put something against my sisters, in the news Papers. . . . Ever senc [since] they Read the Paper of what Mrs Smith say about them . . . and the names she called them, there, I am shame to talk about, so my sisters got that Wild about thing, that they went and report to the Indians. . . . Said that they will never let Mr Smith come to Fort Rupert again to still [steal] there grave again.[37]

The alarm over these representations did not end there. In Victoria, Chief Hemasaka heard about a speech in which Boas had described his tribe as cannibals, and as the most primitive people of all.

> Now here is another thing Hemasaka Went Down to Victoria, and some one told him a speach that you made about that you have Been, all Round the World, and seen Every thing changed for the Best, Except the Kwakiutl tribe, that there still Living on the Daid [dead] People, and I was called in a feast, and after he told this news, all the People told me that they Dont want you or me to see the Dance of any kind again, so you see that I know friend even Mr Spencer and [my] sisters are against me now. now you are the only one I have now. the only thing I am wishing for is my life Be speard [spared].[38]

In a response that seems almost tone-deaf, Boas insisted that Mr. and Mrs. Smith were "full of praise for your sisters and your mother," and suggested it would be unwise to "be on unfriendly terms with Spencer or your sisters."[39] He reminded George that it was especially crucial to appease Spencer, since his cannery could be counted on to provide steady income when Boas's museum funds were scarce. He also suggested that "the whole trouble lies with the meddlesome and nasty newspaper writers" who were, apparently, prone to exaggeration.

> You do not know how they are bothering us all the time, and how every thing they learn is twisted about in the papers so as to make it look exciting to the people. I suppose you remember the nasty figures and the horrible description of the dance that was in one of the newspapers, said to be written by me, but which was simply made up, and stolen out of my book. You may be quite sure that the same thing happened to the Smiths.[40]

The dispute was eventually patched up, and Hunt's collecting continued, but in 1900, Hunt was arrested while observing ritual performances. He wrote, "I am taken Prisoner in alert Bay for going to see Lawitsis tribe Winter Dance . . . and I was sent to Vancouver to be tried."[41] When he was fined $500, his brother-in-law Spencer bailed him out.[42]

George Hunt's correspondence reveals other unexpected challenges, including a concerning pattern of frequent deaths in his own household after he began working with Boas, beginning with the loss of his youngest son in a measles outbreak. In 1896, not long after George had surreptitiously spied on (and recorded for Boas) the last Winter Dance at Fort Rupert, his brother Robert drowned. Shortly after that, a cholera outbreak hit Fort Rupert, resulting in several dozen deaths. During the spring of 1899, Hunt's daughter died, and a few months later, his wife was desperately ill with dysentery. Tragic reactions to accidentally introduced diseases (cholera, measles, smallpox, etc.) were, sadly, routine.[43] In 1917, for example, Hunt personally witnessed the deaths of more than thirty people during a collecting trip. Some died just before he arrived; other informants passed away immediately after their interviews. During one trip to Blunden Harbour, Hunt reported, "I found lots of them sick with the Lagrip [grippe] and the same women I wanted to see Died and I help Buried her." At Revers Inlet, he found the same sickness, and "on the way Home I call into xomtasbe, also there got the sickness, and when I came Home, I got sick and I stay in Bed over two weeks."[44] A similar outbreak in Fort Rupert in 1918 killed Hunt's granddaughter and grandson.[45] In 1923, during a smallpox outbreak, Hunt wrote, "It was wonder I Did not get it also. for some of the People who Had the sickness stay in my house."[46] In the aftermath of every loss, Hunt asked Boas for more work, "for you know that I got a large family to work for."[47]

Unexpected deaths sometimes resulted in the loss of potential museum collections. In 1910 Hunt had contracted with an artisan named Mago to make a traditional broad box canoe, paying fifteen dollars in advance. After the canoe was finished, however, Mago accidentally drowned. Hunt learned that Mago had pawned the canoe for fifteen dollars, and it would cost an additional fifteen dollars to recover it. Making matters worse, while he was negotiating for the recovery of the canoe, he learned that the boxes and dishes collected from Koskemo for sale to George Gustav Heye had been stolen (and were likely then sold to another collector).[48]

Despite these losses and community concerns, Boas frequently asked Hunt to secretively excavate sacred sites and cemeteries to collect materials for the museum. In 1900, for example, Hunt excavated seven human skulls and a large collection of funerary objects (hats, images, dishes, masks) from graves in Koskemo.[49] In 1906 he discovered a Praying House at Nootka and a Whaler's Shrine / Washing House, each with human skulls and sacred objects.[50] Hunt informed Boas that the best time to collect would be in-between the whaling and fur seal seasons, when no one was around.[51] On another occasion, during a trip to Blunden Harbour, he was compelled to meet in a secret location, "where I got this story told to me in the woods, so as we are not seen by any Body. and he made me promise not to tell any Body about him telling it to me."[52]

Hunt was well suited for this kind of work, in part because he believed himself immune to supernatural forces and witchcraft. In an early, unsolicited recollection, Hunt told Boas that as a young man, while searching for a lost ox, he had discovered two *eg!enux* (medicine men) who had bewitched Chief Henak!alaso. Hunt crept into their camp, stole a box they were crying over, and brought it to the chief and his councilors so that it could be ritually destroyed. Chief Henak!alaso recovered his health only after the box was broken up, and he sent it away to be sunk in the ocean. The chief had been saved by his faith in the supernatural, but, Hunt explained, "as for myself I Don't Belive in the eka, that is How this eg!enux cant kill me," even though they had tried on several occasions. "That," he told Boas, "is How I was Well liked By the old chiefs."[53]

Yet, at times, death surrounded him. In December 1908 Hunt attended a large gathering of Kwakwaka'wakw people at Beaver Harbour. He had hoped to collect ritual data; instead, he was witness to the sudden and shocking deaths of twenty-seven chiefs from a fast-moving virus (apparently influenza). To grapple with this loss, the communities staged a Winter Dance at Fort Rupert that included the appearance of a Hamat'sa dancer and the ritual death and resurrection of a *tox'wet* dancer. Hunt described how this dancer was, apparently, "thrown into the fire and after she was Burnt up her Bones was taken off the fire and Put into another Box. which they carried into the wood." The ritual continued, with twelve men singing over the course of four nights, "ontill she came to life again."[54] The extremity of this ceremony echoes the extremity of grief expressed in many of Hunt's letters following sickness and death. Ritual dancers could be resurrected, but humans who had died could not be brought back. When reporting such losses, Hunt would close his letters by calling Boas "his only hope" and "his only friend in the world," while begging forgiveness for his temporary incapacity due to grief. On one such occasion, in 1911, Hunt requested the museum to return a life cast it had made of a beloved elder, G'omkenes, one of Hunt's "true friends" who had just died, so he could keep his face close at hand.[55]

Depending upon *Wi'oma*

In 1898 George Hunt provided folklorist John R. Swanton with an interpretation of the iconography of the totem pole that his mother, Anislaga, had erected at Fort Rupert.

At the top of this pole is Raven himself in the act of carrying off the moon in his mouth. The story told about this is the familiar northwest coast tale of the being at the head of Nass, who kept daylight and the moon in boxes in his house, and of how Raven stole these by assuming the form of a hemlock needle, letting himself be swallowed by that chief's daughter and being born again through her.[56]

This particular traditional tale also provides an apt metaphor for Hunt himself. Like Raven, he was intent on capturing treasures; not content with having been born to a chief's daughter, he also set out to marry one. Hunt's 1872 marriage to his first wife, Lucy Homikanis from Hope Island, was instrumental in ensuring his access to Kwakwaka'wakw knowledge. As the daughter of a high-ranking chief, Lucy was heir to several chiefs and to crucial bodies of knowledge; her children with George inherited this access. David, the eldest son, became head chief to the Sint'lam group of the Gwitala and the highest-ranked Hamat'sa dancer at Fort Rupert.[57] George was permitted to conduct potlatches and deliver occasional speeches as an auxiliary to his sons, but the Kwakwaka'wakw still regarded him as a cultural outsider. Hunt's position had actually inspired the renaming of an entire Kwakwaka'wakw tribal division as Gwitala, meaning "Northerners, Foreigners."[58]

Franz Boas was a foreigner of a different sort. He was assigned the Kwak'wala name Heiltsakuls, "the one who does the right thing," which apparently derived from his efforts to convince Canadian authorities to permit the practice of potlatch. Socially, he was positioned almost as a brother to Hunt, even though he was George's employer.[59] Boas made only twelve trips to the region over the course of forty-four years; on most of these occasions he was hosted by the Hunt family, who became his fictive kin.[60] Lucy would cook and serve his meals. Her daughter Emily and granddaughter Margaret would serve his tea and do his laundry. Boas paid special attention to George's sisters, and brought personal gifts for the Hunt women. In 1897, for example, Lucy added a note to George's letter to Franz: "My wife wishes me to thank you for the Silver Bracelet that you send her, for she say she will keep it and the gold ring till Death take her away from the World."[61] On the next trip, Boas brought shawls for Lucy and her daughter Emily.[62] During another visit, he brought copies of his books for George's sisters Annie, Sarah, and Jane.[63]

Lucy Homikanis Hunt was fluent in Kwak'wala, and the many references to her in George's letters suggest that she routinely reviewed the manuscripts he prepared for Boas, likely by hearing them read aloud. She frequently added personal notes of thanks for assisting the family, and sent warm wishes to Mrs. Boas and her children, in her dictated footnotes to George's letters. Although she was well versed in traditional language and knowledge, she was also interested in the trappings of modernity, and did not hesitate to let Boas know about her material desires and her willingness to pay for them. In 1900 George wrote:

> There was a man came to our house and he show my wife one of the Grapherphon [gramaphone] or talking machiens and after he finesh showing us let us here [hear] it. and my wife asked him What the Price was and he said $25.00 with 5 Roll. Now [she] May fancy to it, and asked me to write to you and see if you can get her one, then she will Pay you for it. of course she would like to have me calenders or Rolls you know what I mean that would come Handy.[64]

Sometimes, Lucy insisted that George should write about a particular topic. In 1906, for example, she convinced her husband to send a lengthy unsolicited manuscript on food harvesting, preparing, and cooking techniques. Boas complained, but George defended Lucy's choice, insisting that this was just as valuable as anything he had written on ceremonial practices. Yet it was much harder than writing stories, "for I got lots of Questions to ask from the old Peoples of things that I Dont know any about."[65] He reminded Boas of the difficulty: "And now you think that its Easy thing to study all the Diffrent ways of the Indian getting food and cooking them. now it is a Hard on my Head to Do it in the Right way."[66] In his *Ethnology of the Kwakiutl*, Boas offered token credit to Lucy, noting, "Much of the information in regard to cookery was obtained by Mr. Hunt from Mrs. Hunt," but he dismissed her status by characterizing her merely as someone who was "thoroughly familiar with the duties of a good housewife."[67]

In 1908 disease struck the Hunt household yet again. Lucy lingered in sickness for several months before passing away in April. Boas wrote to express his sympathy: "I have been thinking of you very often, and it must be hard for you to get accustomed to the loss of your dear wife."[68] George responded:

> This is about the Hardest thing I Ever got, that is to lose my Dear loving wife, who was a great Help to Both you and me in the work I have to Do for you. it is a great lose to me and my Poor children. . . . I am trying to get a tomb stone for her grave, for I want to work for her once more to get it. But I will never forget her.[69]

George was doubly bereft. Not only were he and his children emotionally adrift, but also he simply could not do the ethnographic work without Lucy's crucial assistance. He explained: "I am trying to Do the work for you, and I find that it is Hard without the Help I use to get from my Dead wife, for some times I would forget some thing in my writing then she would tell me. But now I got to get some one to tell me. and I have to Pay for it, so it come Hard for me."[70]

It surprised Boas to learn that Lucy had been an essential (albeit almost invisible) partner in the ethnographic project. She had participated in recounting, recording, and translating traditions that were virtually unknown to her husband. There is a large gap in the correspondence at this stage, and the extant letters reveal that Hunt nearly gave up on Boas altogether. He stopped collecting, stopped corresponding, and left Fort Rupert for several years, moving north to escape the memory of his loss. As soon as he returned, he wrote to Boas: "But now I see it is no use to try to live without working. so I made my mind to go to work for you again."[71] Hunt picked up where he left off by finishing up his wife's manuscripts on cooking.

At this juncture, if Franz Boas had been more familiar with Kwakwaka'wakw culture, he could have logically (and productively) turned to Hunt's sisters. Given that the lines of descent were reckoned matrilineally, and given the tight relationships among Kwakwaka'wakw women, Hunt's sisters inherited greater rights to cultural traditions and transmission than did their brother George. Did they wish to serve as informants? Perhaps so. Although they were soured by their early experience with the Smiths, they later spoke at length with Marius Barbeau, sharing details about their mother's kin and totem poles that their brother rarely spoke of. In some of his letters to Boas, George complained of having to hide his own copies of Boas's books from his sisters, who were quite keen to have them; he also felt compelled to hide his correspondence, notebooks, and texts he was working on.

Seven years after Lucy's passing, Hunt gleefully reported to Boas that he had a new wife, Tsukwani Francine. With her at his side, the letters flowed freely again. Like Lucy, Tsukwani was a *wi'oma*, a high-ranking Kwakwaka'wakw woman. George was actually Tsukwani's third husband in a chain of strategic couplings. She had first been married, against her wishes, to an elderly uncle on her mother's side, as a means of retaining his inherited rights. When he died, she took a younger man of lesser social standing. After finding him in love with someone else, she left him. "On the next day after that she was engaged to Mr. G. Hunt."[72] This relationship afforded George a renewed level of access to secret societies, since "the right to become a member of a secret society is acquired by marrying the daughter of an elder member and by subsequent introduction. . . . Great pain is taken that the societies are sustained by the right marriages."[73] In such a matrilineal and matrifocal system, it would be natural for the Hunt women to have a hand in George's choice of a new wife; Tsukwani, in fact, stated that George's eldest daughter, Emily Hunt Wilson, had arranged the match.

Tsukwani became a crucial partner in Hunt's most dramatic acts of cultural representation, his work for photographer Edward S. Curtis. Hunt recruited, hired, and directed Native artisans and actors for Curtis's popular 1915 documentary *In the Land of the War Canoes*. Tsukwani constructed costumes and acted in several scenes, and Hunt's daughter-in-law Sarah Abaya and granddaughter Margaret Wilson Frank (Emily's daughter) both portrayed the lead

Figure 4 Tsukwani Francine Hunt (George's second wife) with abalone shell ear ornaments, woven hat, and woven blanket, 1914. Titled by Curtis as "A chief's daughter—Nakoaktok." Photograph by Edward S. Curtis. Courtesy of the Library of Congress.

female character of "Naida."[74] This production also captured images of the ceremonies surrounding a traditional wedding, although it is unclear whether it was an actual marriage or a reenactment. Curtis photographed a wedding party arriving by canoe, with a bewinged husband (played by George Hunt) standing at the prow. He captured poignant images of Tsukwani in her wedding garb, seated on the ritual platform constructed for a highly ranked chief's daughter to be carried to her husband. Curtis also captured an evocative photograph of Margaret wearing her stepgrandmother's large abalone shell ear ornaments. In print, however, Curtis obscured personal and tribal identities, using images of a "chief's daughter" and "wedding party" to represent the generic culture, rather than specific individuals.[75]

The Hunts collected and arranged props for the documentary (including skulls and mummified human remains) and also posed for Curtis's Hamat'sa photographs. George Hunt's portrayals seem dangerously close to ritual transgressions, but he may have felt protected because the images and dances were creatively reinvented and removed from a traditional ritual context, or because his face was blackened. Curtis noted that Hunt had explicitly asked that his identity be concealed when the Hamat'sa images were published.[76] It is important to note that, as with the earlier Columbian Exposition in Chicago, Hunt and his neighbors were not naïve Natives doing traditional dances for the camera; they were savvy social actors actively engaged in re-creating, scripting, and performing specific renditions of culture intended for public consumption. At the time, and for decades thereafter, their performances of Kwakwaka'wakw culture came to be accepted as authentic representations of the "real" traditions.[77] Hunt later bragged to Boas that it was all done largely for show, and that Curtis knew virtually nothing about the Native stories behind the photographs.[78]

After working for Curtis, Hunt returned to Boas with the promise of providing even more previously unknown and inaccessible sacred knowledge through interviews with his new wife, Tsukwani. Before, he said, "all the names of the secret spirits was kept Back from you and I."[79] But now, he could even access Tsukwani's knowledge while she slept.

> I got her to Promise me that she will tell me all the Defferent nax'newalak!wes or PExEla spirits of the House and of the woods and of the sea. now there is some of these spirits names I did not know any thing about. some times while we are sleeping. my wife would start up and sing her PExEla songs. then . . . she would talk to the spirit, and she seems to get answer Back. next time the spirit comes to her I will write what she say to it.[80]

He insisted that his earlier knowledge was minimal, compared to what was now available, and he assured Boas, "The way things looks, she got lots of it

Figure 5 George Hunt dressed as a Kwakwaka'wakw Hamat'sa (cannibal dancer), 1914. Photograph by Edward S. Curtis. Courtesy of the Library of Congress.

yet to tell me."[81] He repeatedly emphasized the role that Tsukwani played in securing this unique information: "I Dont think theres any man got this great story. I Dont think I could get this, if I Did not take this wife I got now."[82] Heralding the discovery of more than forty different "secret spirits," Hunt fully acknowledged Tsukwani's role: "All these story these Indians would not tell you or me about it. ontill I took my wife."[83]

Legibility, Accessibility, and Productivity

Hunt's letters were, in general, polite and deferential, but he often felt over-worked or devalued by Boas. The frequency and content of their correspondence indicate that Boas expected Hunt to be at his beck and call virtually every year, between work at the cannery, hunting, or other jobs. Boas reassured him:

> If you are successful in getting good old material from out of the various places where the Indians used to hide it, we shall go on collecting; but if we cannot get the material, I shall not be able to get any more money for you. . . . So now, my dear friend, you know that the whole success of this work is in your hands, and that it depends only upon your efforts and your success in collecting and in writing, how long we are going to continue it.[84]

Boas demanded explanations whenever more than a few months passed without a letter, even if Hunt was needed elsewhere. In July 1899, for example, Boas demanded a batch of anticipated stories. Hunt replied, "I am trying to Write them as fast as I can," but Mr. Spencer needed him at the cannery. Even so, he assured Boas, "after I finish my Days Work then I set Down and Write."[85]

Boas appreciated Hunt's attention to detail, and his efforts to "make his descriptions as accurate as possible" through repetition and rechecking; he wrote, "On the whole, discrepancies are so few in number and the period of recording is so long that the information as such evidently deserves full confidence."[86] Boas also, apparently, appreciated Hunt's obsession with numbering every single page he wrote, in the exact sequence in which he created it.[87] Hunt did not always credit his own informants, however, and he complained when Boas demanded that he write quickly about things he knew nothing about. In many cases, Hunt expended considerable effort in securing knowledgeable informants, only to find that he could barely afford to pay them. At one juncture, Hunt's neighbors (knowing there was profit to be made in providing data) raised their rates. Hunt complained that five songs had cost him fifty cents each, more than the cost of paper and less than Boas was willing to pay Hunt to write them down. In the letter that accompanied a thick packet of songs and speeches made at a feast with full explanations for each one, Hunt explained, "I want you to know that these Indians wont tell or sing a song without they get Paid for it."[88]

Many of Hunt's letters to Boas contain frank assessments of his own productivity and reminders of their agreements and transactions. In 1899 Hunt went to some pains to explain the precise understanding.

> I don't know if you Remember that you asked me to Work for you last year for five months. that is to collect specimens and write the Histories of them. so I Did for

> I send you 260 Pages of Manuscript. Which is $13000 Dollars. and for my time
> in Buying specimens, is from the 15th May to the 20th June that bring me $85.00
> Dollars so that shows that I worked little less than three (3) months last year and
> now I am sending you the Bills for 166 Pages of manuscript for this year for I will
> try to fill out the other two months that is left out of the five, and another thing
> you will find in the stories, that there is Lots of thing that I am Buying now that
> we did not know any thing about Before.[89]

During the first seven years of their collaboration, Hunt's speed in collecting
data and the legibility of his handwriting steadily improved. Boas's handwriting, in contrast, was dreadful and nearly impossible to decipher, which explains
why Hunt often requested typewritten letters, "so as there will be no mistake
Between you and me."[90]

In the midst of this era of extraordinarily high productivity, George's first
wife, Lucy Hunt, became ill, and he hit an unanticipated dry spell that was
inconvenient for Boas's publication schedule. Boas might have encouraged
Hunt by offering a bit more money, but instead, he proposed that they rene-
gotiate the terms.

> I wonder why I do not hear from you at all. . . . I am also disappointed that you
> have not sent me any more writing. . . . I sent you quite a number of questions; and,
> on thinking over the matter, it occurs to me that perhaps the most satisfactory way
> would be if we agreed again, as formerly, on a payment for material that you may
> send per page. During the last seven years your writing has improved so much that
> of course the writing of a page takes much less of your time than it did formerly;
> and it seems to me that twenty cents a page would be a fair payment.[91]

Twenty cents per page was an enormous cut from the agreed-on fifty cents per
page, and Hunt penned an outraged response. He enumerated all the materials
required for writing: pads of writing paper, pencils, notebooks, envelopes, and
stamps. He explained that his handwriting was smaller, with more words on
a line, and that the paper was different, with more preprinted lines on a page.

> You get six or seven Pages more out of this Paper for the lines is close together. then
> those first Papers I us to write for you Because the lines was far apart. and I use to
> write Larger letters then what I am Doing now and therefor I think that twenty
> cents a Page is Rather too Low, for I can not Write fast Enough to make it Pay for
> there is to Big Drop from fifty cents to twenty.[92]

To drive his point home, Hunt reminded Boas that he had supplied a great
deal of new information that could not have been discovered otherwise. At the

most, Hunt could only write eight pages per day. At eight pages per day, he would only be paid $1.60, a fraction of what he could make for an equivalent amount of time spent at the cannery. Finally, after much back-and-forth, Boas agreed to pay one dollar for three pages (an average of $2.50 per day). Hunt agreed, but he insisted that, since each letter to Boas cost around thirty cents in postage, "the museum ought to Pay for the Paper and stamps."[93]

Boas also asked Hunt to serve as a census taker, by supplying a full accounting of every family and kinship network in the region.

> The best way to bring out all the other points that refer to this would be if you could give a regular census of Fort Rupert, naming the houses, in which the different people live, who live in there, how they are related, what their marriages are, and to what brother tribes they belong, and what their past and present names were. If you could include in this the people you knew and who died, it would be still better.[94]

At a later date, Boas sent surveyor's maps with instructions for Hunt to fill in Indigenous names of "all the places where the first of the various brother tribes came down," with both present-day and ancestral locales noted.[95] In the midst of this work, they haggled over payments for a map of tribal territories being produced for Edward Sapir, for the Geological Survey of Canada. Boas anticipated that this document might raise some suspicion among government authorities, and so he advised Hunt to mail it directly to Sapir (and to keep Boas's name out of it), so as to avoid crossing international borders. A month later, however, Hunt was challenged by the postmaster of Vancouver, who demanded to know who had sent these maps, what their intent was, and to also explain exactly how long he had been writing things for Boas. Boas contacted a friend in the Government Service to explain, and the postmaster released the maps, but there was still the question of how much to pay for the work. Boas suggested, "Perhaps the simplest way might be to count the names in such a way that about forty will equal a page. . . . I presume that means a trip to Knight Inlet, and presumably a few days work, but it is worth the trouble." When Hunt insisted that this rate was too low, Boas suggested a rate of one cent per name, including the cost of travel.[96]

Throughout their long collaboration, Boas appeared reluctant to fully acknowledge the importance and value of Hunt's efforts. In a 1913 publication, for example, Boas identified Hunt as the author of the manuscript, but he suggested that Hunt's fluency and writing system on the typewritten manuscript submitted for publication were of very poor quality. Boas asserted intellectual dominance by characterizing himself as Hunt's language instructor, editor, and proofreader, writing: "He was taught to write the language by Franz Boas in 1891, and by constant correction of his method of writing, the system of spelling applied in the present manuscript was gradually developed. Nevertheless the phonetics required revision, and everything written by Mr. Hunt up to 1901 inclusive has been revised by Franz Boas from dictation."[97]

In fact, their editing efforts were far more collaborative and organic than this statement might suggest. Both Hunt and Boas had learned the orthography of Kwak'wala (the Kwakwaka'wakw language) from the same instructor, Reverend Alfred J. Hall. Hunt had learned English and learned how to write in Kwak'wala when he was a youth at Hall's missionary school. The adult Boas, in his turn, had studied Hall's publication on "Kagiutl" grammar. As linguistic partners, Hunt and Boas were very well matched: Hunt's English spelling was inconsistent, but his fluency in Kwak'wala was excellent; Boas's English was excellent, but his Kwak'wala was never entirely fluent. As a result, whenever book manuscripts were being prepared for print, Boas would mail the draft text to Fort Rupert, asking Hunt to do any necessary editing and spelling corrections. The final manuscript would then be cleaned up by Boas for publication. The details of these editorial exchanges and negotiations are amply documented in letters and financial accounting on both sides. In the worlds of academia and public media, however, Boas wielded most of the power and gained most of the credit.

Over time, as other members of Hunt's family were enlisted to assist Boas, there were further revelations of secret knowledge and further losses of ritual objects. For example, in December 1921 Daniel Cranmer decided to defy the Canadian government by hosting a six-day-long feast potlatch at Village Island to mark his marriage contract to Emma Bell, giving away a large quantity of goods equivalent in worth to nearly thirty thousand Hudson's Bay wool trade blankets. The event was scheduled during the Christmas season, in hopes that the authorities would not notice, but spies informed on the family, and the Royal Canadian Mounted Police arrested and tried forty-five of the participants. They then tried to compel the chiefs to forfeit their regalia to escape prison. In the end, a large collection of elaborately carved masks, ritual tools, and clothing was confiscated.[98] Some of this ritual regalia was sold to the Victoria Museum / National Museum of Man in Ottawa. Thirty-five of the best objects were sold to George Gustav Heye at the Museum of the American Indian/Heye Foundation in New York City.[99] In light of earlier events, the rapid circulation of this confiscated regalia into museum collections seems a little too convenient. Was this a staged capture? Were collectors perhaps already waiting in the wings? Boas was unable to secure the return of the regalia, but he did help to facilitate Cranmer's release from custody; in what appears to be a reciprocal gesture, Cranmer then traveled to New York City to work with Boas for several years on translating Kwak'wala texts.

By the 1930s George Hunt's productivity started to wane. When asked to provide a new body of writings on dreams, shamanism, medicine, stars, and superstition, he complied, but he explicitly asked that his name not be attached to these particular writings. Hunt may have recognized, by this time, that he had outlived his ritual position as an assistant potlatch chief, since both his mother, Anislaga, and his beloved son David had passed on (in 1919 and 1928, respectively). As a result, his mother's Tlingit inherited rights and his first wife Lucy's Kwakwaka'wakw inherited rights had moved on to other family members. Since Hunt had no children with his second wife, there were no children to inherit Tsukwani's rights. The new delicacy of his social position may have alerted him to the dangers of violating ritual protocols.

During this time, George became jealous of other informants, such as Charles James Nowell (1870–1956), another Native man of mixed blood married to a high-ranking woman.[100] He continued to insist that Boas should not interview his sisters, even though they had begun sharing data with ethnographer Marius Barbeau from the National Museum of Canada. By way of explanation, Hunt insisted that only he spoke the "old-fashioned" version of Kwak'wala, and that his "youngest sister [Mary] Pretend to know the [old] Fashion language But I am half afraid She Dont know much."[101] Hunt was just as critical of other Kwak'wala speakers, claiming that few knew the "old-fashioned" ways of speaking. To illustrate his point, he observed that they typically used "one word for Every thing instead of useing the Defferent word for the Defferent [things]," and that "lots of the Indians comes and ask me the meaning of the words."[102] After hearing that Boas had visited a Kwakwaka'wakw woman, Ga'axsta'las Jane Constance Cook, Hunt warned that she "knows lots of things, of what she hears People talk about," but "her kwagut language is very short." Hunt told Boas, "I feels Proud that I know the old ways," but he also reported that Cook had charged he "made up lots of words."[103] Cook's contacts with Boas were brief, but she provided some key insights into Kwak'wala grammar that opened a window into what could have been a highly productive relationship. Boas did not follow up, and Cook did not appear to have had much interest in anthropological research. Her interests were more squarely focused on diplomatic negotiations and sovereignty. Most notably, she parlayed her skill at cross-cultural communication into important service for Kwakwaka'wakw people, by serving as a court interpreter for tribal chiefs making land claims before the McKenna-McBride Royal Commission.[104]

When George Hunt died in 1933, his son Johnnie wrote to Boas, requesting support for Tsukwani and funds for erecting a monument to his father. His father "was [a] great man for writing the Indian stories," he said, adding that Boas could not find another like him.[105] Boas expressed his sympathy, and offered to contribute a "small sum" to Mrs. Hunt, "if it is necessary," but he told Johnnie that he "could not possibly get the Museum or the University to help pay for the monument."[106] No monument to Hunt was ever constructed, but Boas did eventually agree to offer assistance to other members of Hunt's family, in exchange for their continuing work as Northwest Coast informants. Some family members also served as informants for Marius Barbeau. In a 1947 interview, Daniel Cranmer emphasized the fact that his knowledge did not originate with him; it all belonged to the women.

> I am entitled to a Tongas dance or whatever dance my wife gives me through our marriage. Her people would show me how to use it, had I an occasion to bring it out. The old Mrs. Hunt [Anislaga] used to attend dances, feasts, and potlatches. Her daughter, Mrs. Cadwallader, also did. They taught the Fort Rupert Kwakiutls lots of Tlingit songs, and I have learned them too. . . . They are dance songs, wild songs, in Tlingit. We don't understand the meaning of their words.[107]

Interviewing *Wi'oma* and *Witsatla*

As co-collectors, George Hunt and Franz Boas made a remarkable contribution to the ethnographic record of Northwest Coast cultures, but their work was shaped by limitations of geography and filtered by gender. There was an overemphasis on the tribal nations around Fort Rupert and Alert Bay, primarily because these were easier for Hunt to reach. The crucial roles of First Nations women, as cultural agents and owners of inherited cultural traditions, were obscured. Another level of filtering was introduced by the heavy emphasis on high-profile ceremonial activities and staged performances. Boas and Hunt persistently sought out objects, language, beliefs, and activities that denoted rank, prestige, and privilege rather than everyday survival. For example, Hunt devoted only one manuscript to the widespread fish ceremonialism (taboos, prayers, and rituals of preparation and discard) that constituted women's daily practice in Kwakwaka'wakw households.[108] Lucy Hunt, in her own way, apparently tried to address some of these oversights by providing data on essential life skills and foodways.

A small collection of manuscripts buried in the archives of the Committee on Native American Languages suggests that, given the chance, the First Nations women at Fort Rupert would have had a great deal to say if only George Hunt and Franz Boas had gotten out of the way. In 1930 Julia Averkieva, a Russian exchange student, accompanied Boas during his final field trip to Vancouver Island. During her six-month sojourn, Averkieva was warmly welcomed by the Hunt family and invited to potlatches and other social events.[109] She interviewed George's wife Tsukwani (identified as Mrs. G. Hunt), his daughter Mary (M. Hunt), his sister-in-law (Mrs. Sam Hunt), and his granddaughter-in-law (Mrs. B. Wilson). The resulting manuscripts—archived not in the Boas Papers but in the files of the Committee on Native American Languages at the American Philosophical Society—are brief but tantalizing. Tsukwani described Kwakwaka'wakw marriage and inheritance, puberty ceremonies, and techniques for blanket weaving. Mary spoke about Tlingit ideals of beauty, married life, and superstitions surrounding twins. George's first wife, Lucy Homikanis, resurfaced in Mary's memory of her mother; she recalled that "my mother was taking care of me for one year after my marriage. She did all of the important work of my husband's household." Mary also fondly recalled when her mother-in-law and sister-in-law both came to live with her, training her in the conduct of food preparation and hosting visitors in their community.[110] This pattern of female cohabitation and sharing of tasks (which was not uncommon in the region) is key in restoring a more accurate picture of the social relations of the Hunt households. If we were to gaze through the doors of the Hunt household, we would see not just a lone man at a writing desk but multiple generations of women as informants, witnesses, and perhaps even fact checkers for George Hunt's fieldwork. Their voices and perspectives have yet to be fully acknowledged and recorded in the anthropological records.

It seems especially ironic that Boas recorded these key social distinctions yet failed to seek out female informants. For example, in a 1921 article, Boas had noted that tribal names could only be inherited from one's wife's family: "The only names of the head chief of the numayms that can be given in marriage are the names which he obtains in marriage from his father-in-law, and also the privileges, for he can not give his own privileges to his son-in-law."[111] He also noted that women could assume the position of head chief in circumstances where there were no eligible men.

And when the head chief of a numaym has no son, and his child is a girl, she takes the place of her father as head chief; and when the head chief has no child, and the younger brother of the head chief (among the brothers of the man) has a child, even if she is a girl, then the head chief among the brothers takes the eldest one of the children of his younger brother, and places him or her in his seat as head chief of the numaym.[112]

In sum, among all the Northwest Coast First Nations, cultural narrations, songs, dances, names, and other physical and metaphysical cultural expressions were (and are) regarded as inherited privileges, replete with ritual responsibilities. Individuals could be shunned for speaking traditions outside of their tribe or rank. Hunt's present-day descendants are grateful for his efforts, yet they also have readily admitted to outside researchers that "Hunt made mistakes."[113] Later generations worked to reestablish the appropriate protocols for mediating knowledge through senior female authorities, and to recognize the appropriate means of earning and accessing rank by means of marriage and cultural roles rather than strictly through inheritance. Hunt's grandson Andrew Frank Everson recalled that his own status was inherited from his grandfather Andy Frank, who had married his grandmother Margaret in Alert Bay.

> Not long after this meeting, they wed and moved to Andy's home village of Comox. Largely because of Maggie's highborn status, Andy subsequently inherited the position of the old Pentlatch [*sic*] Chief Joe Nimnim after his death in 1940. . . . In 1972, several months after my grandfather had passed away, I was born and given the name Andy to represent reincarnate connections recognized by the old people. My widowed grandmother would even refer to me as her "little husband." I grew up spoiled by her, but aware of the responsibilities that are inherent when upholding the name and privileges of a late great man. I was raised to know that I was *from* Comox and that I was also Kwakiutl from Fort Rupert.[114]

In present generations, the Hunt family is well-known for respecting traditional protocols regarding male and female rank and responsibility. When Hunt descendant Lucy Mary Christina Bell interviewed family members regarding the protocols for cultural transmission, for example, she was "consistently told that my grandfather . . . said nothing without first being told what to say by my grandmother." Even today, the *wi'oma* exercise control over family boxes of treasures and traditions by placing individuals with restricted access into the social category of *witsatla*, meaning "you cannot reach into that box of treasures." In retrospect, among the Kwakwaka'wakw, both Boas and Hunt were actually *witsatla*; their access to tradition was enabled and mediated primarily through their association with privileged female insiders.[115]

Over time, as Northwest Coast objects began to return to communities, the memories of these losses softened, and new relationships emerged. The Kwakwaka'wakw regalia confiscated from Daniel Cranmer remained out of reach for another fifty years, until 1987, when the National Museum of Man (now the Canadian Museum of History) agreed to return the confiscated regalia. The repatriated objects were divided between the Kwagiulth Museum at Cape Mudge and the U'Mista Cultural Centre at Alert Bay, where some of them are on display today.[116] In 1997 Kwakwaka'wakw anthropologist Gloria Cranmer, Daniel's daughter and George Hunt's great-granddaughter, participated in a celebration of the centenary of the Jesup Expedition at the American Museum of Natural History. Boas's grandson Norman recorded her statement.

> We strengthen what is left of our culture after the white people did their best to destroy it. In that task we are more fortunate than most indigenous groups, because

we have a strong foundation to build on and for that we owe much to Hi_dzaKwal's (Franz Boas) and Kixitasu' (George Hunt). . . . I wonder how many people whom other anthropologists have studied have the same feeling of respect and affection that our people had and still have for Franz Boas?[117]

Today, the transcultural union of Anislaga and her husband, Robert Hunt, is recalled with pride by their descendants. The children of Lucy Homikanis and George Hunt, along with the progeny of George's sisters, remained in close contact with Northwest Coast traditions and many married into high-status Kwakwaka'wakw families. Members of the Hunt family are prominent in Northwest Coast art and cultural performance; there are sculptors, painters, jewelers, storytellers, and Chilkat blanket weavers, as well as anthropologists and filmmakers. In July 2013 more than five hundred Hunt descendants gathered at Fort Rupert for ceremonies of reunion. They welcomed neighbors who arrived by canoe, feasted on locally abundant seafood (prepared just as Lucy would have cooked it), and erected a magnificent new totem pole—made by master carver Calvin Hunt, decorated by other kin, and filmed by artist Corrine Hunt—to honor Anislaga.[118]

In sum, the Boas/Hunt publications should not be viewed as the primary authorities on Kwakwaka'wakw culture and language. Instead, these narrative reconstructions are rather like an open-ended shadow box, casting only partial light on the ethnographic encounter. Northwest Coast First Nations women can be seen, past the shadows cast by these men, living rich and complex lives outside these reconstructions. Like Anislaga's ancestral raven, they have the ability to transform themselves at will, and to reappear in subsequent generations, in ways that may not be recognized by one-dimensional observers.

3

Representing Modernity

Beulah Tahamont and Arthur Parker

> If I have had tragic moments it is because I brought them upon
> myself through mistaken loyalties and feelings of responsibility.
> Thus, I only kick myself hard and go forward to brighter goals.
>
> —Arthur Parker to Edna (Endeka) Parker Harrington,
> October 23, 1934

$\mathbf{A}$rthur Caswell Parker (1881–1955) was born at the Cattaraugus Indian Reservation, the son of Geneva Hortense Griswold, a missionary's daughter of Scots/English ancestry, and Frederick Ely Parker, Seneca and English. The Parker ancestry reads like a litany of famous Seneca royalty: great-uncle Ely Parker, aide-de-camp of General Grant; great-great-grandfather Handsome Lake, founder of the Handsome Lake religion; and, stretching even further back, lineal connections to Jikonsaseh and Hiawatha, key figures in the founding narrative of the Haudenosaunee Confederacy.[1] Beulah Tahamont (1887–1945), Parker's first wife, was born in Lake George, New York, into a community of gifted Abenaki herbalists, basket makers, actors, and models with ties to the First Nations reserve of Odanak (St. Francis), Quebec. The couple met in New York City, at the salon of Harriet Maxwell Converse. Beulah was, by all reports, an extraordinarily intelligent and beautiful young woman, educated at the Mission School at Sabrevois College in Montreal and fully fluent in three languages (Abenaki, English, and French). By the age of seventeen, she was already in demand as a model and Hollywood actress. Arthur was a divinity student at Dickinson Seminary and an editorialist and reporter for the New York *Sun* newspaper when he married Beulah in 1904. Almost immediately after their marriage, he was hired as field ethnologist for the New York State Library, before joining the staff at the New York State Museum of Natural History (formerly the State Cabinet of Natural History).[2] Arthur's star rose quickly, but his celebrated marriage ended in a stormy parting. Arthur (and his biographers) wrote Beulah out of the picture, but the real story is a bit more complicated.[3]

Representing Indians in the New York Indian Colony

The dropped threads of Beulah's life can be recovered by looking at the years before her marriage. The Tahamont family fluidly shifted between reservation, rural, and urban environments, tracing transnational connections from Quebec to New York City. Beulah's mother's cousin, Emma Mead (Abenaki and Oneida), was an "Indian doctor" with impressive skill at herbal medicine, and her ancestors Sabeal and Sebattis were famous Abenaki guides in the Adirondack Mountains. Her grandfather Elijah Tahamont Sr. was one of the first formally educated Abenaki Indians, having attended Dartmouth College. Her father, Elijah Tahamont Jr., was a graduate of Carlisle, where he became particularly adept at dramatic writing and performance. The younger Elijah adopted the stage name "Dark Cloud" while he and his wife, Margaret Camp, worked as film actors for D. W. Griffith's Majestic Film Company. Margaret went by the stage names "Dove Eye" and "Soaring Dove," and Beulah's stage name was "Prairie Flower."[4]

Beulah's younger sister, Bessie, was born in 1895, and a few years later, the family took up residence in the neighborhood around Broome Street, Spring Street, and West Broadway in New York City. In 1897 the *New York Times* reported that this quarter of mid-nineteenth-century homes, "half-commercial, half the abode of the poor," was occupied by the "New York Indian colony." Roughly one hundred Native people lived here, mostly Abenaki and Mohawk Indians from Upstate New York and Canada, working as day laborers, models, bead workers, and basket makers. They plied their trade for dress shops, craft dealers, and tourists. There were tailors like Lizzie Saylor, who crafted costumes and uniforms for the pseudo-Indian fraternal societies "such as the Independent Order of Redmen—headgear, belts, moccasins, and other insignia." There were herbalists like White Moon (Louis Smith), who was "the chief attraction of a traveling medicine show." There were models like "Thunder Cloud," whose "physical majesty" was so impressive that the artist who employed him had recently married him.[5] The *New York Mail and Express* reported that marketing their image was a crucial means of income.

> They dress, both men and women exactly as do their neighbors, and their native costumes are reserved for business purposes only. . . . Their red skins and this paraphernalia—their "Indianness"—are their capital. There are so few avenues of livelihood open to them that these they guard zealously, and to be snap-shotted [photographed for free] means to part perforce with what they feel is their one inalienable means of subsistence.[6]

They also mediated the value and circulation of their images, by insisting on payment for posing for sketches and photographs. One of the residents of the colony, an Adirondack native named Annie Fuller (stage name "Falling Star"), had been introduced to modeling by Harriet Maxwell Converse, who told her "she could probably earn more money by sitting still before an artist for five hours than she could by selling baskets for a week."[7]

In 1897 the *New York Times* reported that Elijah Tahamont had "won even more fame among the painters of Indian life than Thunder Cloud," due to being "of a more distinguished class, and of finer proportions."[8] He was selected as the perfect model for Frederic Remington's paintings and sculptures of western Plains Indians. A photograph of Tahamont, outfitted in full western Plains style regalia, was featured in a 1901 *San Francisco Call* article titled "Here Is the Most Perfect Indian Model in All America." The text read:

> If there were such a thing as a beauty show for men, few white men would stand any chance for the prize against a certain full-blooded American Indian now living in New York city. This man is Tahamont, a brave of the Abenaki tribe of Indians, who is regarded by artists as almost a perfect specimen of manly beauty, both in face and figure. . . . Tahamont is greatly in demand as an artist's model and receives, it is said, the highest price for posing paid to any male model. His face and figure are familiar to thousands who see the illustrations in the prominent weekly papers. E.W. Deming, De Conta [De Cost] Smith and Frederick Remington are among the well known artists who draw from him.[9]

In 1901 the *Boston Sunday Globe* announced that "Mrs. Tahamont, a Pure Blooded Member of the Abenaki Tribe, is Regarded as the Most Perfect Representative of her Race Now Living." Although the "original Indian people, together with their color and picturesqueness," were believed to be fast passing away, a matter of "genuine regret to the Indian painters and artists," they could seek out this famous model. "Possessing as she does superior mental gifts, an unusually characteristic Indian face, and varied beautiful Indian costumes, Mrs. Tahamont is looked upon as an ideal subject for illustrating."[10]

Technically, Margaret was not a "full-blood," since her father, John Camp, was of English/Irish ancestry, but from an artist's perspective, she looked like one. The family's popularity had a great deal to do with their phenotypically high-set cheekbones and sharp noses. Elijah displayed a "pure, full blood face, commanding figure and strong and characteristic features" that could, apparently, effectively represent virtually any Native group. The *Brooklyn Daily Eagle* reported, "The latest work on which his face appears was the Buffalo Fair Award Medal, where he posed for the two Indian figures representing North and South America united."[11]

An article titled "Handsome Indian and His Clever Daughter in Great Demand in New York Studios" described the appearance and eloquence of Margaret and Elijah's daughter.

HANDSOME INDIAN AND HIS CLEVER DAUGHTER IN GREAT DEMAND IN NEW YORK STUDIOS.

MISS BEULAH TAHAMONT. **DARK CLOUD.**

TWO FAMOUS INDIAN MODELS.

ONE of the most picturesque figures in the art studios of New York and Brooklyn, just now, is that of Dark Cloud, or Mr. Tahamont, the famous Indian model, who is considered the best all-around study or model of his race. He is much sought for by leading Indian illustrators and sculptors, for they find in Dark Cloud the best representative of the noble type of the Red Man. The main characteristics of Dark Cloud, which are prized by the artists, are his pure, full blood face, commanding figure and strong and characteristic features.

Mr. Tahamont is well educated and is a thorough student of Indian life and customs. He has designed all his own costumes from native material and they are true to life in every detail, full of vivid coloring and give to the artists striking opportunities for pro-ducing realistic effects. In stature Dark Cloud is six feet two inches; he weighs 150 pounds. He is a member of the Abenaki tribe, which has its reservation near St. Francis, Canada. He is looked upon as the most gifted one of his tribe. The latest work on which his face appears was the Buffalo Fair Award Medal, where he posed for the two Indian figures representing North and South America united.

Mr. Tahamont has an interesting family of a wife and two daughters. Beulah, the eldest, 16 years of age, is also in demand by artists for special roles. In Brooklyn she recently posed in the studio of Miss Isabel More Kimball, the well known sculptor at the Pratt Institute, for her last work, the life size Indian statue entitled "Weesonah." Beulah is straight as an arrow, with long, flowing black hair, and has unusually clear cut features. In bearing and appearance she is a type of the ideal Indian princess, and when dressed in her picturesque beaded garments presents a charming composition for pictorial work. She is a fine type of her race, both in beauty and refinement. When not in the studios she devotes her time to her books, and is remarkably fluent in English conversation.

She enjoys the distinction of being the first Indian girl to enter the public schools of New York City. She spent a term in the grammar grade and outstripped her white sisters in deportment and progress. She attended school for the first time two years ago, at the Indian mission college in Montreal, and at the close of her term she was second in a class of French Canadian girls. She was also confirmed in the Episcopal Church by the Lord Bishop of Montreal, and is the first young Indian girl of her tribe to join the church.

Figure 6 Beulah Tahamont and her father, Elijah Tahamont (stage name "Dark Cloud"), featured in the *Brooklyn Daily Eagle*, April 2, 1902. Photographer unknown.

Beulah is straight as an arrow, with long, flowing black hair, and has unusually clear cut features. In bearing and appearance she is a type of the ideal Indian princess, and when dressed in her picturesque beaded garments presents a charming composition for pictorial work. She is a fine type of her race, both in beauty and refinement. When not in the studios she devotes her time to her books, and is remarkably fluent in English conversation.

She enjoys the distinction of being the first Indian girl to enter the public schools of New York City. She spent a term in the grammar grade and outstripped her white sisters in deportment and progress. She attended school for the first time in Montreal, and at the close of her term she was second in a class of French Canadian girls. She was also confirmed in the Episcopal Church by the Lord Bishop of Montreal, and is the first young Indian girl of her tribe to join the church.[12]

The education and attributes of this young Native woman captured the media's attention, resulting in articles published in at least five newspapers across the country that year; each article added more tantalizing details. The *Salisbury Weekly Sun* out of North Carolina reported that Beulah had "unusual mental gifts for one of her race," and that her parents had surrounded her with "the most civilizing influences at their command," including music lessons.[13] In an article titled "Clever Indian Girl Honored," the *Spokane Daily Chronicle* made a prediction: "Beulah is a fine type of her race, both as to beauty and cleverness. . . . It is predicted that if she continues in her exceptional educational progress, Beulah is destined to become the cleverest Indian woman of today."[14] The newspapers missed an important human element in their rush to exoticize Beulah: this clever young Abenaki woman was then dating a young white man named Mark Raymond Harrington (who often went by M.R. or Ray), who was as keen as she was to make money promoting representations of Indians.

At the time, M.R. was working as an assistant in archaeology for Frederic Ward Putnam, collecting Native materials for both the Peabody Museum of Archaeology and Ethnology and Columbia University. He also had a sideline business buying and selling Indian artifacts for Covert's Indian Store on Fifth Avenue, conveniently located near the Waldorf Astoria Hotel, where some of the wealthiest patrons resided. For collectors like M.R., the New York Indian colony was a rich source of more than just tourist art and material artifacts; its residents were also eager to share traditional stories and historical traditions.[15]

M.R.'s ethnographic career started with a collection of Abenaki and Mohawk folktales that he and James Longfeather (a Mohawk resident of the New York Indian colony) hoped to publish.[16] After their book proposal was rejected, M.R. turned to academic journals, where he found immediate success. His first academic publication—"An Abenaki 'Witch-Story'" collected from

Figure 7 Mark Raymond Harrington in Native dress, in camp at Garoga, New York, 1905. Photograph by Irwin Hayden. Courtesy of Stephen Hayden.

Beulah Tahamont—was printed verbatim in the *Journal of American Folklore* in 1901. It describes a grim encounter in a burial ground.

> An old "witch" was dead, and his people buried him in a tree. . . . An Indian and his wife came along, looking for a good place to spend the night. They saw the grove, went in, and built their cooking fire. When their supper was over, the woman, looking up, saw long dark things hanging among the tree branches. . . . "They are only the dead of long ago," said her husband. . . . "I don't like it at all. I think we had better sit up all night," replied his wife. The man would not listen to her, but went to sleep. . . . When daylight came she went to her husband and found him dead . . . with his heart gone, lying under the burial tree, with the dead "witch" right overhead. They took the body [of the witch] down and unwrapped it. The mouth and face were covered with fresh blood.[17]

M.R. then published another version of the same story as told by Beulah's mother, Margaret. This time, the wife had a baby with her, and when she ran for help, she was pursued by the witch in the form of a fireball.

> When she was almost home, she looked over her shoulder, and saw a big ball of fire coming after her. It was the witch spirit trying to catch her! . . . She knew the

witch wanted to kill her, so she could not tell her story. The fire was gaining, closer and closer it came, and it was almost upon her when she saw her father's lodge just ahead. She rushed into the opening, and fell upon the mud floor.[18]

The mother and child were safe only after crossing the threshold into the sanctuary of kin and home. In both versions, after some initial confusion about whether the wife was a witch, people realized that a vampire spirit had stalked the family. They used fire to cleanse the site, burning the camp and the body of the dead witch, "so he could never bewitch or hurt another Indian."[19]

From an Indigenous perspective, this narrative is a deadly serious cautionary tale, with a relatively straightforward moral: do not disturb the dead, and listen to your wife. "Witches," within the frame of a story like this, represent forces with malicious intent that might manifest as human or "other-than-human"; in either case, they should not be provoked.[20] Given that Harrington was just starting out in anthropology at the time he collected these tales, one has to wonder what the Tahamont women were trying to tell him. Shortly after these articles were published, Beulah and M.R. ceased dating, but their parting was amicable; they remained friends, and behaved like family, for the entirety of their lives.

Field Training

Beulah Tahamont and Mark Raymond Harrington first crossed paths with Arthur Caswell Parker during visits to the salon of Harriet Maxwell Converse. Harriet (affectionately called "Aunt Hatty"), who had been informally adopted into the family of Seneca chief Red Jacket in 1878, had deep connections with the Seneca people. She was a longtime friend of Ely Parker, the Seneca informant who had assisted Lewis Henry Morgan, famous author of *League of the Ho-dé-no-sau-nee or Iroquois*. Converse was so devoted to the interests of her Seneca friends that in 1892, she was appointed as an honorary chief of the Six Nations and given the name Ga-ie-wa-noh, "The Watcher for the People."[21] During the early twentieth century, Seneca leaders used these ritual adoptions to enlist prominent white people as allies, but these honorary chiefs held no political power within the tribal nation or the Council of Chiefs.[22] Instead, they were expected to help guard against threats from state and federal authorities. The *New York Times* reported, "For many years Mrs. Converse has followed up legislation of their interest, visited with great frequency the reservation in the western part of the State, and kept a watchful eye on the Indians of New York City."[23]

Converse was also a close friend of Putnam, the Harvard Peabody Museum archaeologist who held a joint appointment at the American Museum of Natural History. In her effort to generate better relations on both sides, she served as an informal liaison for northeastern anthropologists interested in Indians. In Harriet's salon, aspiring researchers could meet with Mohawk storyteller James Longfeather, Abenaki actors Elijah and Margaret Tahamont and their two beautiful daughters, and other colorful residents of the New York Indian colony. She encouraged seasoned scholars such as Franz Boas, Harlan Ingersoll Smith, and George Hubbard Pepper to hob-nob with promising teen-agers such as Alanson Buck Skinner, Frank Gouldsmith Speck, and William Jones. One of her most regular visitors was young Arthur Parker; he was then attending Dickinson Seminary, but Putnam believed he had potential as an archaeologist. Parker was so entranced by Putnam that, in later years, he would claim to have attended classes at both Harvard and Columbia when, in fact, he had only listened to Putnam's lectures in Harriet's salon.[24]

Putnam encouraged Harrington to invite Parker to assist in a dig at a Montauk Indian burial site on Thomas Gardiner's property on Long Island. Parker was utterly charmed both by the work and by his new colleague. Harrington later recalled that Parker "was a divinity student at that time, planning to become a minister! However, I liked him, and invited him to go on an archaeological expedition with me to the Oyster Bay area on Long Island—and that changed his life!"[25] Those expeditions for the American Museum of Natural History "roused his interest to such an extent that he became an anthropologist himself."[26] Arthur quit college and enthusiasti-cally embraced the practice of archaeology. M.R. and Arthur worked side by side from 1902 to 1903, excavating Seneca human remains and artifacts at the Silverheels site at Cattaraugus Creek in western New York State, with funding provided by the Harvard Peabody Museum. Parker was so keen to rapidly elevate his status that, even though he was still learning the practice, he insisted that Putnam name him as a "co-laborator [*sic*]. I indeed dislike to be named an assistant."[27]

In 1903 Parker was adopted into the Seneca Bear clan at Tonawanda and given the name Gáwasowaneh (or Gawaso Wanneh), meaning "Big Snow Snake." This was a welcome mark of kinship, since, although he identified as Seneca, Parker had no status as a tribal member, being the child of a white women and a father of mixed Seneca and white ancestry. Parker was so eager to attain status that in his letters to Putnam, he (falsely) claimed that he was not just merely adopted but had been appointed as "chief" of the Bear clan.[28] Harrington was also given a Seneca name at this time, Hosaistuggéteh ("He carries a snake"), and he was admitted into the Hawk clan of the Tonawanda Seneca.[29]

During the same year, Parker and Harrington were also admitted into the Seneca False Face Society. Parker later recalled, jokingly, that the invitation came about after George Jimerson observed the two young men idly singing while moving their feet around, "simply to relax the tired muscles," and interpreted this as dancing. "Now you've got to join the False Face Company. . . . I saw your feet dancing. Now I've got to make a mask for you both."[30] Harrington's recollection of the same event was more serious, with an element of prophetic insight: "That night both young men dreamed of seeing Indians dancing. They told their dreams to an Indian friend named Don-dah [Tahahdondeh, George T. Jimerson], who was, indeed, startled. He later brought them two beautifully carved but grotesque wooden masks and taught them the dance step to go with the masks."[31]

These distinctions in reporting and interpreting a shared experience illustrate how each of these men continued to approach Native traditions over the course of their lives. Parker (perhaps due to his early religious training) remained forever skeptical of dreams, omens, and other so-called superstitions. He disdained the use of peyote among the members of the Native American Church, feeling it only encouraged pagan beliefs and behavior.[32] Harrington, on the other hand, eagerly embraced every opportunity (including ingesting peyote) to gain Indigenous insights, whether originating from waking or dream states, scientific research or visions, human or other-than-human encounters.

In 1903 Parker's new anthropological friends tried to persuade him to attend Columbia University to study with Boas, but he refused. Instead, he accepted a position as field ethnologist at the New York State Library. Later biographers suggested that Parker refused for financial reasons, being in need of a steady income to support his family.[33] In fact, there was an even more compelling reason for his refusal: Parker was grappling to come to terms with the death (and expectations) of his beloved "Aunt Hattie." In November 1903, while in the midst of preparations for a dinner date with the Tahamont family, Mrs. Converse unexpectedly suffered a stroke of apoplexy. She died in her home, "surrounded by the finest private collection of Indian relics in this country."[34] In the wake of her death, to honor her wishes, a match was made between two of the best and brightest Indians of their generation: Arthur Parker and Beulah Tahamont. They sealed the engagement just before the funeral, and committed to marrying the following spring.

Harriet Maxwell Converse's funeral was a dramatic cultural performance, scripted and staged for the bicultural community she belonged to. Arthur and Beulah were positioned as prominent mourners at a ceremony that wove together Episcopalian and Haudenosaunee traditions. The Episcopal Rev. Dr. Thomas H. Sill presided over the church service for the dead. Parker called Mrs. Converse "the Guardian Angel of the Indian. No Indian ever came to her for help that she did not give it." Seneca chief Cornplanter placed Converse's

Figure 8 Arthur C. Parker and Mark Raymond Harrington as young men, c. 1910. Photographer unknown. Image P.11342. Courtesy of the Braun Research Library Collection, Autry Museum, Los Angeles.

wampum insignia on the casket, and "while tears streamed down his face, he expressed grief in a few words of broken English, and then sinking back in his chair, buried his face in his hands and wept aloud."[35] Elijah Tahamont Jr., James Longfeather, William Crow, and Carlos Montezuma all delivered eulogies.[36] Joseph Keppler, the wealthy son of the *Puck Magazine* journalist of the same name, was selected to inherit the title of honorary Haudenosaunee chief and the wampum insignia that had been carried by Converse. Arthur Parker inherited Harriet's collection of important Iroquoian specimens, books, and manuscripts and saw, in them, a new opportunity to become an expert in all things Iroquoian.[37]

Marriage Unites Warring Tribes

Beulah Tahamont and Arthur Parker had a double wedding alongside two other residents of the New York Indian colony, Marie Toxuse (Huron) and Daniel LaFrance (Mohawk). The ceremony took place on April 23, 1904, at the Church of the Transfiguration in New York. This was the first modern American Indian "celebrity wedding" in North America; photographs of Beulah and Arthur were featured in articles with provocative headlines such as "Marriage Unites Abenaki and Seneca Tribes" and "Warring Tribes Are United by Romantic New York Marriage."[38] One article, "Romance of an Indian Maid," claimed that the spark of romance began when Arthur spotted a photograph of a teenaged beauty in Mrs. Converse's study. He asked, "Aunt Hatty, is this a picture of Beulah?" She replied, "Yes, Arthur, that is my little Abeniki, my little forest maiden." He insisted that he must marry her, and Harriet agreed then and there to make the arrangements.[39]

Their story dominated the American Indian news cycle for the entire spring and summer of 1904. Writers from newspapers and journals across the country reported tantalizing details about their looks, their credentials, and their dress. Beulah was described as "the star of her race, from her beauty and intelligence." To illustrate her allure, it was noted that she had been "already engaged to a paleface" (Harrington, who had, apparently, graciously stepped aside) before being swept off her feet. Arthur ("Chief Gawasawaneh") was proclaimed to be "the head of the Bear Clan of his nation," even though he was not a chief, and not the head of the clan that had just adopted him.[40] Another article correctly reported that Parker "was connected with field expeditions for the American museum of natural history" but falsely reported that he had "led an expedition for the Peabody Harvard museum" during the same time.[41] These factual errors mark the start of what became, for Parker, a lifelong habit of self-aggrandizing, claiming unearned titles so consistently that they appeared to be true. Since some of these accolades first appeared in articles printed in the New York *Sun*, where he worked as a reporter, he may have scripted the press releases himself.

Other events suggest that the Tahamont-Parker and Toxuse-LaFrance wedding may have been part of an elaborate publicity scheme to generate visibility for the New York Indian colony and the emergence of a new pan-Indian council. On November 27, 1904, the *Sun* was the first to break the news of a dramatic "Indian Council" meeting at Joseph Keppler's mansion estate, the first such gathering in the New York City area in several hundred years. The paper reported:

> Forty or Fifty Indians from various parts of the country met on Thanksgiving evening at the residence of Joseph Keppler of *Puck*, at Inwood-on-Hudson, and held a council

and performed their sacred dance. . . . They were called together by Chief Longfeather of the Mohawks. They met, if tradition is correct, near the spot where . . . Henry Hudson and his crew on the Half Moon fired upon the aboriginal Manhattanites gathered on the rocky promontory where Spuyten Duyvil Creek empties into the Hudson.[42]

This appears to be the only time that Arthur Parker appeared in public dressed in traditional Native clothing. Like the other attendees, he was "arrayed in buckskin clothing, decorated with wampum, beads and savage trinkets." The company, assembled in a line before the hundreds of non-Native visitors, was introduced by Chief Longfeather: "You of the Nation of the Morning Light, in your veins runs the blood of the men who once ruled Manhattan. So I give honor to you." Elijah and Margaret Tahamont stood in as representatives for the historical Abenaki, Mohican, and Lenni Lenape peoples. Indian delegates from Boston, Montreal, and Philadelphia also attended, hoping to "form a closer bond of union between the Indians of various tribes whose callings caused them to live in New York."[43]

The event included pageantry, oratory, dance, councils, and ritual enactments. The company engaged in "old time dances" to "rekindle the old Indian spirit that had slumbered too long," including "the violent exertions of the war dance." Then, they took off their regalia and donned modern suits and dresses to perform "the white man's dances," while a hired orchestra played the tunes of "civilized" music. The four newlyweds from the April wedding were dramatically presented to the company as exemplars of the remarkable progress the New York Indian colony had made in forging peaceful relations among disparate tribes. As Longfeather explained, "These tribes were anciently deadly enemies," but with these cross-tribal marriages, "ancient animosity has disappeared."[44] The language of this news release was, in fact, very close in tone to the earlier marriage announcements, leading one to suspect that the same author might have been involved.[45]

Speeches were given, including one from Parker reviewing Northeastern American Indian histories, traditions, ceremonies, and migrations. Then, there was a private council among the organizers and chiefs from other visiting tribal nations. The newspaper reported:

> The council proper was held in secret, but it may be said that during its season, the Indians took steps to protect their interests, political, commercial and social, against certain individuals and corporations that, posing as friends, seek to destroy them. A closer bond of union was formulated and a plan drawn up for mutual encouragement and assistance.
>
> Red Eagle discussed the causes that led to the weakening of the tribes with the era of the white man and pointed out how this must be changed, and that all Indians must forget tribal differences and stand simply as Indians and united.[46]

This large pan-Indian gathering must have been a remarkable spectacle. At one point, the young men came out in war dress to entertain council and public visitors with a mock battle evoking a colonial encounter from 1609. This show, "a battle with the spirits of the old Dutch voyagers and their captain, Henry Hudson," was enacted to "satisfy the spirits of the Manhattans who were killed by the bullets from the Half Moon, Hudson's ship." Toward the end of the gathering, Chief Deer from Philadelphia "paid a tribute to the life of Mrs. Converse," and Longfeather, "with his characteristic humor, brought down the house." "Three cheers and a war whoop" were given "for the good Chief Gyantwaka, Mr. Keppler."[47] Arthur Parker, as a representative for the New York State Library, promised to preserve a permanent record of the event in the state archives, but no reference to it survives there, or in any of his papers in Rochester; it may have been among the many manuscripts later lost to fire.

Archaeologist and Museologist

In her will, Harriet Maxwell Converse had designated Parker as executor of her estate, keeper of her papers, and custodian of her impressive collection of Native American artifacts. Just before she died, she had been in the midst of negotiating a deal with the New York State Library and the New York State Museum of Natural History to create a new American Indian Museum in the State Capitol Building, and she wanted Parker to manage it. The state was already in possession of the entire Lewis Henry Morgan collection, acquired during the 1840s with the assistance of Ely Parker. The state also had custody of a collection of Haudenosaunee wampum belts, gathered after Converse had negotiated the passage of Section 27 of the New York State Indian Law, which designated the state as an official Ho-sen-na-ge-tah (Wampum Keeper) on behalf of the Onondaga nation.[48] Melvil Dewey, state librarian and secretary of the New York State Board of Regents, was the acting curator of these Indian collections, but Converse suggested that an American Indian be recruited as a keeper. So, when the new commissioner of education, Andrew S. Draper, came into office, he interviewed Arthur Parker for the position of curator and ethnographic field-worker. The job would entail the following:

> Gathering information from the New York Indian reservations concerning the ceremonies, festivals, rituals, religious thoughts, songs, speeches, etc. of the tribes . . . [and] relics in the way of implements, dress, ornaments or manuscripts which would help to retain for future generations the best information as to the characteristics and customs of the Iroquois. . . . You must bear in mind your statements to me that your motive is to preserve information of your ancestors, and work earnestly to that end. . . . If you do so, it will be a real service to the history of the State.[49]

Parker wrote to his friend Joseph Keppler Jr., "When I read this I emitted several war yells and offered tobacco to my great clan totem!"[50] He responded to Draper with an enthusiastic yes. The job also offered an opportunity to supplement his museum salary by occasional trading in Indian artifacts.[51]

Parker was a strong proponent of both social evolutionary theory and Haudenosaunee exceptionalism. He believed that "savage" cultures were doomed to disappear unless they could evolve toward "civilization," and he positioned himself—as a well-educated, mixed-blood, acculturated Seneca—at the tip of the spear. His interest in museums was not focused on cabinets or exhibitions, which he found (during his early visits to the American Museum of Natural History in New York City) to be static and dusty. He sought out the "thrilling world back of the scenes," where scientists, hidden away "in remote offices down long halls," were engaged in making—and writing—far more interesting stories. He wanted in on that action. He wanted to collect those objects and tell those stories.[52]

Between 1904 and 1906, Parker, by his own reckoning, "conducted excavations and researches not hitherto equaled by one tenth by any other investigator." He collected jewelry, clothing, ritual objects, and other materials from living Native peoples, in addition to human remains and associated funerary objects (pottery, beads, artifacts) excavated from Seneca gravesites. Following Harrington's advice, he learned to time his collecting trips at moments (e.g., in-between harvest seasons) when sellers were so in need of ready cash that he could pay a low price. When selling those objects, he often retained at least 20 percent of the value as a personal commission.[53] Parker alerted the museum's director, John M. Clarke, that it was necessary to move quickly to secure the best objects.

> Often times while I am engaged in my regular work for the Department I am shown some very good specimens of Indian relics such as false faces, rattles, musical instruments, silver ornaments, games, baskets, etc. etc. Such things are becoming more rare every year, especially the older things, and are eagerly taken by collectors. . . . I have not purchased much nor have I told any of my friends who are collectors where these relics may be found for the reason that I wish the state to have the first opportunity to buy them.[54]

When Clarke raised concerns about private purchases and sales, Parker admitted that "in times past I have been in the habit of buying desirable relics . . . but I have always disposed of them to some scientific institution, never having made the business a matter of commerce."[55] Parker neglected to mention that he was profitably selling archaeological and ethnographic objects to private collectors Joseph Keppler and George Gustav Heye during this same time.[56]

Parker was an astonishingly prolific writer during his first decade of married life, clearly benefiting from the papers left to him by Harriet Maxwell Converse and the assistance of his wife, Beulah. In his first academic publication, "Secret Medicine Societies of the Seneca," for *American Anthropologist*, Parker acknowledged Beulah, although he did not mention her by name: "The writer, with the assistance of his wife, however, living with the 'pagans' and entering fully into their rites, discovered that the 'medicine lodges,' so far from having become extinct, are still active organizations, exercising a great amount of influence not only over the pagans but also over the nominal Christians."[57] Participant observation of this sort was crucial to the success of Parker's work, but (despite his Seneca ancestry) he was not automatically trusted. As he explained to Dewey:

> It takes a long time for the Indians to give their confidence to anyone and for some time, although they accepted my statements and gave me preveleges [*sic*], I was conscious of a certain reserve on their part. The trouble was the fact that I was brought up under mission influence. . . . I was much gratified, therefore, when the council of chiefs assured me through their chairman that after watching my movements and noting my methods they would give me their complete confidence in all matters and give me a place that only Mrs. Converse had enjoyed. My work immediately became easier and I am admitted to secret ceremonies that I was formerly barred from.[58]

Only through living at the reserve, developing relationships with the Faith-keepers at the Newtown Longhouse, and participating in their rites could he gather enough information to report on their doings. Religious discussions at home and in camp must have been interesting, since Arthur was a Congregationalist and former divinity student, and Beulah had been baptized in the Episcopal faith, yet here they were, together exploring "pagan" traditions.

Parker published more than sixty articles and three books during his decade of married life with Beulah, yet her name is barely mentioned in his correspondence, and credit for her assistance appears only once, in a single article. Given the gendered division in many Haudenosaunee communities, Beulah must have been a partner to this work, since there were some traditions that Seneca women would only share with another Native woman. There is no reason to believe that Beulah did not participate in Arthur's largest project during this time—"Iroquois Uses of Maize and Other Food Plants"—a work largely focused on foodways and horticulture. This publication brought together a wide range of source material: historical excerpts; ethnographic observations gathered by Converse, Harrington, and Speck; and snippets of interviews with "scores of Indians" from the Seneca, Cayuga, Tuscarora, Oneida, Onondaga, and Delaware tribal nations in New York State and Ontario. Parker also interviewed members of the New York Indian colony. The work is lavishly illustrated with drawings by Jesse Cornplanter and photographs of mortars, baskets, utensils, bowls, and so on in use by people wearing traditional clothing; most of these objects and clothes were purchased for the state collection.[59] It is difficult to believe that Arthur's "clever" young wife was sitting idly by while this material was being compiled, but Beulah's name does not appear in this work, and Arthur's field notes do not appear to have survived, so one can only speculate.[60]

Seneca Warnings

During their first few years together, while conducting ethnological and archaeological research, the Parkers traveled frequently, camping at dig sites and renting houses in multiple locations. The moves apparently took a toll on Beulah. In the spring of 1905, Arthur wrote to Keppler: "My Beulah does not seem able to stand the damp climate and changeable spring weather here and although she has been very well, now she is quite ill. . . . I am having every medical aid possible here, and await her recovery."[61] Later that year, her health had improved, and in mid-December, she gave birth to their first child, Melvil Arthur Parker, named for Melvil Dewey, the New York State librarian who had orchestrated Arthur's hire by the state.[62]

In 1906 Beulah's younger sister, Bessie (stage name "Bright Eyes"), moved in with the family at their home in Rensselaer, across the river from Albany, and enrolled in the local school. Arthur wrote to a friend that he was "giving her a little coaching she needs, she never having attended school for lack of opportunity beyond a few grades."[63] Beulah's parents periodically visited en route to Lake George or New York City, sometimes bringing venison from their hunting trips in the Adirondack Mountains.[64]

Beulah gave birth to their second child, Bertha, in August 1907, in camp at the Silverheels archaeological site near Sinclairville, New York. This outdoor locale (which would form an essential element of Bertha's origin story for years to come) was entirely unintended. Just two days earlier, Arthur had written to A. P. Chessman in Fredonia seeking to rent a furnished house, noting that they "have been camping most of the time but now require stabler quarters." Arthur requested lodging for (a very pregnant) Beulah, her sister, a nurse, and two-year-old Melvil, but he suggested, "I should not need the rooms for a longer period than six weeks."[65] Beulah's health appears to have stabilized once she was indoors. Later that year, in a letter to Putnam, Parker wrote: "Mrs. Parker read your letter with much pleasure and requests me to send her kindest wishes. . . . We have two little ones now and are very happy with them."[66] Both children had been given Seneca names: Melvil was Ga-nun-dai-ye-oh and Bertha was Ni-ye-wus-ah (Ye-wus), alternately spelled as Yeawas or Yewas.[67]

The extant correspondence suggests that Beulah was not particularly enthusiastic about participating in archaeological excavations of the dead. Traditionally, Seneca and Abenaki peoples alike regarded gravesites as inviolable; they believed that spirits of the dead remained with the body and might harm those who disturbed them.[68] Seneca friends had warned Arthur that breaches of spiritual protocols might be putting his family in danger, and at both the Ripley and Silverheels sites, ghosts had been spotted.[69] Seneca traditions also spoke of instances when ghosts and witches pursued not the perpetrators but their families: "Witches do not always injure people who have offended them but more often their children or other near relatives. This is done that the person they desire to punish may see an innocent person suffer for their offenses and so be tortured the more."[70] None of this was new information. When Parker and Harrington first dug into Seneca gravesites, they received warnings that very much resembled the Tahamont family's witch stories. Arthur recalled that Seneca people often came to the camp "to instruct Mr. Harrington and myself in the lore of the ancients."

> We were regaled with stories . . . of the whirl-winds, of the creation of man, of the death panther, and of the legends of the great bear, but in particular we were blessed with ample store of tales of vampire skeletons, of witches and of folk-beasts, all of whom had a special appetite for young men who dug in the ground for buried relics of the "old-time folks."[71]

Among the tale-tellers were a few Seneca Indians who worked as assistants to Parker and others, even though they feared that their interventions might provoke ghostly happenings. Parker was well aware of the fact that, in general, Seneca people did not condone archaeology on tribal lands. He noted, "The owners were horror stricken when the proposition was advanced," due to their desire to leave the bones of ancient ancestors undisturbed.[72] Yet he had no hesitation about continuing his excavations. In a 1907 letter to Tom Gardinier, the landowner at the Montauk burial site, Arthur jauntily announced: "We have been digging up old Indians for the last six weeks and are having great luck. We find lots of 'em too. . . . They are good Injuns too, for you know they say the only good Indian is a dead one."[73] Parker's attitude reflected more than just scientific detachment or disrespect for the dead; he ascribed his success in archaeology to divine intervention. During his second visit to the Ripley site, for instance, he wrote to Keppler of his "astonishing luck. . . . My trowel and shovel are veritable magnets. The most unique and beautiful things in clay and bone and stone seem drawn from the ground to them." He bragged, "You see the Great Spirit is giving me success."[74]

Despite his success in the field, Parker's family life was a mess. In late 1909, when Beulah became ill again, she took Melvil and went to stay with her parents at Lake George, leaving three-year-old Bertha with her father. Arthur's childhood friend and field assistant, Everett Russell Burmaster, helped to look after Bertha while Arthur worked.[75] Bessie also left, having been invited to live with Irene Van Cleef in New York City so that she could study art and the classics.[76] Parker may have been covering up for these abrupt departures when he told his landlord, R. G. Preston: "Owing to the ill health of Mrs. Parker and other reasons I have been obligated to vacate the house which I have hitherto occupied."[77]

In late September 1910, fifteen-year-old Bessie fell unexpectedly ill and suddenly died.[78] Arthur made arrangements for the school that Bessie had attended to install a memorial bas-relief of her in the classroom, but he was otherwise taciturn about this loss. It is not entirely clear where Beulah was at this time. In his correspondence with Keppler, Arthur claimed that Beulah had become unhinged, and that he had been forced to hospitalize her: "I write confidentially when I say that I sometimes fear for Beulah's mental health and I am never very sure what she may do to herself or to the rest of us. Last winter I had her in the hospital for some time."[79] Records of this supposed hospitalization have not yet surfaced; it is possible that she was still living with her parents, and that Arthur was covering up for her absence.

The year 1911 was much worse. In the middle of the night on March 29, the library wing of the New York State Capitol Building burned. Parker reported that most of the precious Lewis Henry Morgan and Harriet Maxwell Converse collections, along with about two hundred other "rare objects," went up in smoke.

> The famous Morgan collection of old Iroquois textiles and decorated fabrics went up in the first blast of flame, and the cases were burned to their bases. About 50 Morgan specimens were in the office of the archeologist of the museum for study purposes, and fortunately have been preserved. The Converse collection of silver articles was rescued intact. . . . None of the wampum belts of the Six Nations was injured. One of the odd features of the calamity was that hardly a single object connected with the ceremonies of the Iroquois totemic cults or the religious rites was injured. The hair of the 30 medicine masks that hung in a line across the westernmost cases was not even singed.[80]

Arthur wrangled his way through the wreckage, smashing open display cabinets while the blaze was still underway, "wielding a tomahawk passed down from a Seneca ancestor and using it as a fire ax as he rescued priceless Iroquois artifacts." In the rest of the library, among the collections of early Dutch and English colonial records, an estimated 500,000 books, 300,000 manuscripts, and more than 8,000 other artifacts in the collections were lost to the flames. Arthur was physically and emotionally devastated by this loss.[81]

Later that same year, Arthur and his daughter Bertha were camping at an archaeological field site when fire struck again. As Bertha later recalled, "a camp stove exploded," shooting out shrapnel and fiery sparks that burned and scarred her face. When Beulah learned about this accident, she returned to her husband just long enough to hand Melvil over to his father, pick up Bertha, and leave. By the spring of 1912, she and her parents, with Bertha in tow, were on their way to Hollywood. The famous marriage was over.[82]

Based solely on the evidence in Parker's letters, most historians have concluded that the marriage failed because Beulah was mentally ill, alcoholic, or otherwise flawed. Yet Beulah was wise to leave her husband, given his callous disregard for his family's health and disdain for traditional beliefs. There had been so many warnings, from so many encounters—with ghosts, unexpected deaths, and fireballs—that seemed like Abenaki witch stories come to life. Seneca and Abenaki traditionalists alike believed that other-than-human spirits might intervene if one repeatedly ignored spiritual warnings. These beliefs have persisted among Native peoples into the present, even among the most devout followers of Christian religions.[83] In any case, after Beulah left, Arthur never spoke her name publicly again. As a result, scholars who have studied the trajectory of Parker's life have largely ignored his first wife, while failing to consider that her efforts may have aided his rise to prominence, or that his actions may have caused her misfortunes. Some even pronounced her dead long before her time.

Two years after Beulah's departure, thirty-three-year-old Arthur was married again, on September 17, 1914, to a white woman half his age. Seventeen-year-old Anna Theresa Cooke, daughter of Inez and Dr. William Cooke, is said to have been a quiet, agreeable companion and talented musician.[84] According to Joy Porter, "Whether it was assisting on a dig, helping with installation of the Iroquois dioramas at the State Museum Building, or with design of the Fashion Hall at Edgerton Park, Anna was always a cherished companion and helpmate to her husband."[85] Parker arranged to have her adopted into the same Seneca Bear clan that had adopted him; she was given the Native name Yeiwano:t, meaning "Resting Voice."

Together, they raised Arthur and Beulah's son, Melvil, while rebuilding Arthur's precious museum, including the installation of his new exhibition *Indian Life Groups*.[86] These life-sized dioramas presented authentic representations of Native peoples from the past, cast in the likenesses of living Seneca individuals, clothed in regalia constructed by Native tailors and bead workers, and forever frozen in place.[87] In the *Sun*, and in a bulletin widely distributed to New York schoolchildren, Parker gleefully promoted this exhibition as a "magic window" through which museum visitors could view "a just picture of a people whose history, as he asserts, has been 'written by their enemies' and of whom there is no fitting record." He did not encourage interested visitors to engage with living Seneca people; instead, he promoted his museum as the best means to "perpetuate the memory of our remarkable aborigines," using archaeological and ethnological objects that represented all that was left of a supposedly "vanished culture."[88]

Red Progressives

Arthur Parker and Beulah Tahamont were more than just an ill-fated cross-tribal celebrity couple. They exemplified two dramatically different ways of embodying Indian identity during the early twentieth century: assimilated modernity versus cultural performance. Both were modern, both were Indian, but they chose very different forms of expression. For the Tahamont family, "playing Indian" offered unique opportunities to reclaim voice and visibility in public venues. Unlike the "show Indians" who were sometimes naïvely roped into performing for Wild West shows and then stranded somewhere without resources, the Tahamonts were resilient and self-reliant artists who made their own costumes and scripted their own roles.[89] Parker, however, disdained the wearing of Indian dress, whether show costumes or traditional garb. As an acculturated mixed-blood and an assimilationist, he believed it necessary to cast off past ways in order to prosper in the modern world. After the famous "Indian Council" meeting at Keppler's mansion in Manhattan in 1904, Parker never, apparently, appeared in "Indian dress" again. He preferred a suit and tie.

Like other educated Indians of his generation, Parker drew inspiration from his Indigenous heritage, but he aspired to transcend any perceived ethnic limitations by attaining prestige in white society.[90] In 1911 he joined a new organization that, he believed, would lift up an entire generation of Indigenous intellectuals: the Society of American Indians (SAI). Ideally, this new group would have no "show Indians"; it would be composed entirely of American Indian intellectuals. Parker joined a highly influential cohort of educated Native Americans that included John Napoleon Brinton Hewitt (Tuscarora), Gertrude Simmons Bonnin (Yankton Dakota), Charles Eastman (Lakota), Laura Cornelius Kellogg (Oneida), Angel Decora (Winnebago), Chauncy Yellow Robe (Sicangu Lakota), Francis LaFlesche (Omaha), Carlos Montezuma (Yavapai-Apache), Henry Roe Cloud (Winnebago), and many others. Most of them had been educated at Indian boarding schools like Carlisle Indian School and

Hampton Institute. Many of them had also pursued a college education, graduating from such august institutions as Harvard, Yale, Dartmouth, and Smith.[91]

In a 1912 newspaper editorial titled "Modern Red Indians," Parker asserted that the members of SAI represented "the nobler red men without the bloodthirstiness of their sires and their capacity for rum and mischief." Nearly half of the present population of American Indians had, according to Parker, already "intermingled with other races." He predicted: "Probably, as their native capabilities develop, and as they step freely into the walks of civilized life, they will tend more and more to lose their racial identity. Anthropologists say that the mixture of the red man with the white is a fortunate one and is no whit a mar to the racial excellence of either."[92] In other words, according to Parker's conception of race mixing, the loss of primitive markers of Indianness would benefit Native populations, and the incorporation of Indian blood would improve the white race.

SAI's Indigenous intellectuals aimed to transgress the inequalities and limitations of gender, race, and origin, via goals that embraced modernity and American citizenship. Sherman Coolidge, president of SAI, stated that the organization was designed to "promote and co-operate with all efforts looking to the advancement of the Indian in enlightenment which leaves him free as a man to develop according to the natural laws of social evolution" and to "promote citizenship and to obtain the rights thereof."[93]

As founding secretary for SAI, Parker promoted these goals through frequent editorials in the *Quarterly Journal of the Society of American Indians*. In a 1914 editorial, Parker urged all Indians to embrace modernity.

> Times have changed, the past has gone, the present is here, and points out the changes and advancement of the future. . . . Who are most healthy, most able, are most industrious, who are powers for good? Who are they who are best able to defend their people and who meet the white man on the same level? Are they the Indians who mourn over the past, who refuse to learn and who curse progress? No! Those who live best and who are happiest are those who know that a new day has come and that they must live in that day like the competent men of the surrounding [white] race do.[94]

Although this advice might, at first hearing, seem pragmatic and perhaps even enlightened, the drive to escape the past leaned dangerously close to the boarding school philosophy—"Kill the Indian; save the Man"—that led to wide-scale cultural erasures and societal disruptions from which Native communities are still recovering.

These "Red Progressives" became highly visible in public discourse, and they were often held up as examples of the success of assimilation. Much like

W. E. B. Du Bois's "talented tenth" of highly educated African Americans of the time, they were regarded by social reformers as admirable role models, compared to the masses of uneducated Native peoples who still clung to old ways and lived seemingly marginal lives. They strove to prove that, with sufficient education, Indians could match whites at every level of American achievement.[95]

Parker felt closer to the SAI members, as a community, then he ever had to his family or his anthropological colleagues. He developed very close relationships with Gertrude Bonnin (Zitkala-sa) and other Native intellectuals as they lobbied for or against common causes, and he vigilantly watched the shifts in representations of American Indians in the news, in politics, and in anthropological publications.[96] Although Parker editorialized about the value of mixed-race identities and proudly represented himself as an authentic *educated* Indian, he was a bit less certain about representing himself as an authentic *phenotype* of an Indian. In 1911 Arthur was invited by the Eastmans—Charles Alexander Eastman (Dakota) and his white wife, Elaine Goodale—to send a photograph of himself for inclusion in a gallery for the upcoming "Universal Races Congress" in London. Arthur declined, and in a letter to Elaine, he explained:

> At heart I am very much an Indian though in reality I am but a "quarter blood." However, though my Scotch-English ancestry is worthy of some boast I value more the greater royalty that comes down to me from my Indian fathers. Possibly I talk, think and write Indian so much and allow my "full blooded" Indian heart to beat so strongly at times that the public gets the impression that I am more of an Indian by blood than a view of my ancestral tree will warrant. . . . After these confessions if you still wish the photograph you may have it.[97]

This letter offers a fascinating self-assessment of Parker's identity and experience. He confessed, "My academic schooling never went much beyond the high school, supplemented by three years' study under the direction of Professor Frederick W. Putnam. The rest has been a matter of a little reading."[98] In other words, he had never graduated from college. Despite his bravado in asserting both his intellect and his Indianness in the museum world, Parker apparently felt he was not "Indian" enough to represent Seneca people on a world stage.

In 1917 Parker published what was intended to be a seminal text on Haudenosaunee traditions of governance: *The Constitution of the Five Nations*.[99] Yet, as J. N. B. Hewitt from the Smithsonian Bureau of Ethnology was quick to point out, this work was deeply flawed. Parker had included (without attribution) Duncan Campbell Scott's 1912 *Traditional History of the Confederacy of the Six Nations*, which, in turn, incorporated material borrowed from Horatio Hale's

Figure 9 Arthur C. Parker in "Rochester Portraits," illustrated by cartoonist Jack Moranz, n.d., in Arthur C. Parker Papers, A.P23, box 5, folder 10. Courtesy of the Department of Rare Books, Special Collections and Preservation, River Campus Libraries, University of Rochester.

1883 *The Iroquois Book of Rites.* In his scathing review in *American Anthropologist,* Hewitt lamented, "It is most unfortunate for the cause of truth that great institutions insist on publication at the expense of study and accuracy." Parker had, furthermore, failed to consult with Haudenosaunee leadership (evidenced by his uncritical reliance on a contested document produced by

Seth Newhouse) and had wrongfully suggested that traditional Longhouse ceremonies had died out. Hewitt noted: "The great religious festivals, all antedating the time of Handsome Lake, are today still in vogue on the Grand River reservation and elsewhere."[100]

Parker often dodged criticism by claiming to be operating only as an American citizen "without any tribal interests." In a frank letter to Rosa B. La Flesche, he noted his position.

> In working for Indian betterment I expect no profit from it. I can only incur criticism, suspicion and unjust remarks. The Senecas of a certain class will think that I am working to make citizens of them and this they have protested for 60 years. They wish to remain as they are, and to day the percentage of adult illiteracy in New York among the Indians is greater than in Oklahoma. In a movement of this kind I am injuring myself in a field which must be my life's work. Someone must sacrifice, however, before any good can ever be done.[101]

Parker embraced opportunities to politically represent Native peoples, writ large, as he rose to positions of increasing visibility and responsibility. In 1919 he was appointed as the New York State Commissioner on Indian Affairs, a post he held until 1922. The following year, the United States Secretary of the Interior appointed Parker as chair of the "Committee of One Hundred," a group selected to advise the Bureau of Indian Affairs (BIA). He also rose to prominence in the Masonic Order, reaching the thirty-third degree (Masonry's highest order) in 1924. Parker became one of the most visible and influential American Indians in the country, but, like the other Red Progressives, his actions were closely watched by traditional Native tribal leaders.

Parker's actions were also observed by his ex-wife's relatives, most notably Beulah's mother, Margaret Tahamont (Abenaki), who corresponded regularly with her cousin Emma Camp Mead (Oneida/Abenaki) in Indian Lake, New York. Emma was a successful businesswoman who rented resort rooms and hunting camps, ran a dry goods store, and made and sold herbal medicine.[102] She kept in close contact with her father's Abenaki kin and her mother's Oneida kin, and during the 1920s and 1930s, she monitored debates about pending Indian citizenship and land claims issues in New York State and across the country. Some of the traditional chiefs who were not fully fluent in English, or uncertain about how best to navigate American politics, turned to people like Emma for reports on the machinations of Parker and other BIA policymakers. Some of Emma's letters and notebooks read like espionage memos, hidden transcripts that reveal the extent to which Native people collaborated in monitoring real and potential governmental threats to independence and survivance. One entry, for example, notes that a girl working in an Indian Agent's office "overheard this conversation about talking to the officer from

Washington that the Six Nations were rich if they only knew the door to enter to get it."[103]

In 1923 the chiefs were especially nervous about the Wheeler Bill, which aimed to grant American citizenship to American Indians, and they feared that Parker, in his role as chair of the Committee of One Hundred, might be maneuvering to coerce the Haudenosaunee to settle land claims and accept American citizenship. Oneida Chief William Honyoust wrote to Emma about concerns expressed by the Six Nations Council of Chiefs, and their feeling that those who wished to become American citizens should relinquish tribal membership. William suggested a middle way: "Now for myself, I wish that we Indians would keep our tribal laws. If a person wants to become a citizen why he can be paid whole, while those that uphold the Indian laws can stay and be paid so much a year."[104] Chief Albert Shenandoah sought Emma's advice on how best to respond to Indian commissioner Warren Moorehead when he showed up asking questions about payments for land claims, as guaranteed in treaties. She cautioned Shenandoah to be very wary.

> When that man from Washington gets there be very careful what you say to him, and don't under any circumstances sign any sort of paper for him. If he asks what we want, tell him we only want just what belongs to us, according to the Treaties we have with the General Government of the United States. We want all our lands, and the money that is now in the U.S. Treasury that belongs to us. If he asks if we wish to become citizens of the U.S. tell him no, that you have no desire whatsoever to become a citizen. . . . Now we have never been conquered by the United States, therefore we are a Nation by ourselves.[105]

A few months later, in preparation for another meeting of the Council of Chiefs, Albert's wife, Minnie, asked Emma to check again: "Now Albert wants you to write to Arthur Parker. See if he don't know something what they are doing. He is gone all the week. I spose they are planning some scheme. I don't think they intend to hold any council again."[106]

The BIA administration, and most of the members of the SAI, thought that American citizenship would be a beneficial move, but the Haudenosaunee (rightly) feared it would interfere with tribal governance structures. The Indian Rights Association had insisted that the phrase "tribal rights and property" be included in the act to preserve some measure of Indigenous control, but once Native Americans were considered to be American citizens, there was no guarantee that they would retain control over tribal lands. Tribal leaders made their concerns known through various channels, public and private, and when the "Indian Citizenship Law" eventually passed on June 2, 1924, most of the New York State Haudenosaunee decided to opt out.[107]

Parker took personal credit for finessing state political relations with the Haudenosaunee. In a 1920 letter to his old friend Harrington, he said that he had gone to Washington to "have the Ongweoweh [Haudenosaunee] excluded from the provision of our general citizenship act making every Indian a citizen save our Iroquois. We won out and the bill passed saves us from extinction and the gobbling of the lands by the Ogden Land co."[108] Yet, it is critical to note that Parker and the other Red Progressives did not represent traditional leadership; they represented themselves.

In an important critique written decades later, Onondaga chief and Faith-keeper Oren Lyons, who knew Arthur Parker personally, summarized the problem of representation.

> The people who are involved in these pan-Indian movements are interesting and curious in their attitudes and relationships to their red brothers. The documentation, actions, and personal histories of these people are accessible to the American public because they have espoused the philosophy, social training, and religions of the white Americans. They are a product of Victorian America, with all the supremacist attitudes and convictions that afflicted the American people of that time. They mouthed in almost incredible naivete the "melting pot" theories, sentimentalities of the "good old red white and blue," and placed themselves at the head of the wedge of over-zealous missionaries assaulting the centuries-old religions and ways of life of the original peoples of this continent.[109]

Parker, Lyons asserted, was a perfect example of an educated pan-Indian who "lived an idealized romantic role of 'Indian' for his neighbors, evaluating solutions from this rarified atmosphere" and exerting power from "an elevated position of remoteness." Understandably, Haudenosaunee people were, and still are, suspicious of publicity-seeking Natives who might similarly override the wishes of traditional leadership.[110]

Adirondack Indians in Hollywood

Beulah Tahamont's life took a dramatically different turn when she left Arthur and followed her parents to Hollywood, with her daughter, Bertha, in tow. Little of the Tahamont family's correspondence has survived, but sources reveal that the family enjoyed immediate success in Hollywood. As featured performers in D. W. Griffith's company, the Tahamonts appeared in at least thirty-four silent movies and at least twelve feature films over the course of eight years. Under the stage name "Dark Cloud," Elijah Tahamont and his kin worked for American Mutoscope, Biograph, and Reliance. Margaret Camp Tahamont starred in *An Indian Love Story* (1914) and many other films whose names are now lost. Elijah Tahamont played roles that illustrated both the diversity of his acting skill and the appeal of pan-cultural "ethnic" casting. He appeared as "Shiek Achmed" in *The Dishonored Medal* (1914), "General" in *The Birth of a Nation* (1915), "Ethiopian Chieftain" in *Intolerance: Love's Struggle* (1915), "Joseph Brant" in *The Spirit of '76* (1916), and "Witch Doctor" in *The Woman Untamed* (1920), among many other roles.[111]

In 1915 Elijah was invited by Reliance Studios to compose a series of thematic screenplays. This was a rarity—giving an Indian actor creative control as a screenwriter—and Elijah embraced the opportunity to translate ancient oral traditions and contemporary experiences into dramatic interpretations. The *Brooklyn Daily Eagle* reported, "All of these subjects are based upon legends which Dark Cloud had from his ancestors by word of mouth. Many of them were handed down by oral tradition." His first screenplay—"The Race Love"—dramatized cross-racial attraction, a choice facing many modern Native peoples.

> It deals with the temporary love of White Dove, an Indian maiden[,] for Walton, a white man. . . . [The] white man and red appeal to the girl to choose between them. The white man pictures to the girl the cities and his people and the beauties of civilization. All these will be hers if she will leave her people and go with him. Upon the screen the marvels of modern civilization are thrown. When the Indian, Grey Crag, begins his plea the glories of Indian life are shown upon the screen. The beauties of nature, the grandeur of the mountains and forests are screened.[112]

The plot of the film is surprisingly postmodern, in that the Native female protagonist is presented as a character with options: instead of being manipulated by others, she considers carefully and strategically before choosing a path. In the end, the Indian maiden rejects civilization and chooses Grey Crag, lured less by the glorious scenery than by the desire to live with her own people. The *Ogden Standard* and other newspapers reported that Elijah's plots were eagerly welcomed as "a real service to the lovers of Indian legends and to the general public."[113]

In 1918 tragedy struck when Elijah Tahamont died in the Spanish flu pandemic. Due to the fame of the "Dark Cloud" name, Margaret, Beulah, and Bertha were still able to secure work with the support of other actors and agents in the Hollywood film community. Elijah's films remained in active circulation for another decade, feeding the public demand for images of Indians on the silver screen. Beulah appeared in at least two subsequent films: *Desert Gold* (1919) and *The Crimson Challenge* (1922).[114] To preserve their chosen livelihood, she and her mother joined with other members of the "War Paint Club" to promote the hiring of "full-blooded" Indians in place of the white and Mexican actors who were beginning to infiltrate Indian roles in film.[115] The Tahamonts were popular guests in Hollywood, accepting multiple invitations for dinners at other actors' homes, and each Christmas, the Actors' Association sent Margaret a massive fruit basket full of exotic offerings. The Tahamont women also found employment with Ringling Brothers Barnum and Bailey Circus, where teenaged Bertha played the starring role in a "Pocahontas" play.[116]

Perhaps the most useful skill the Tahamont women brought with them was the practice of Indigenous herbal medicine, learned from their kin in the Adirondacks of Upstate New York.[117] Emma Camp Mead had started packaging specific remedies for local and mail-order sales (under the label of "Camp and Company"), and Margaret often wrote to request these for personal use and sale. For example, in 1928 she and Beulah had a bad cough and lung inflammation, "but the medicine you sent just came in good time and it surely done us so much good and our coughs is cleared."[118] The cure was a decoction of chokecherry (*Prunus virginiana*), dried for use as both food and medicine. After interviewing local California Indians who also marketed herbal remedies, Margaret realized that this could be a lucrative sideline income, since, as she told Emma, "we have millions of floating population and those are the ones who are sick and needs medicines." There was only one hitch:

> We must have a license but the Indians out here get a permit from the Government to sell their medicines and I will know before long. An Indian told me he will help me to get a permit so I will not have to pay for a license. I have sold quite a lot of medicine without the doctors getting onto it and have done wonderfully good.[119]

In her subsequent letters to Emma, Margaret frequently requested eastern Indigenous plants like sweet fern (*Comptonia pergrina*) and "wild turnip"—jack-in-the-pulpit (*Arisaema triphyllum*)—while lamenting that California had so few of the plants she had known and used back home.[120]

Beulah had married again, to an Irish laborer named William O'Brien, but in 1928 she filed for divorce on the grounds of drunkenness and abuse. A sympathetic judge compelled O'Brien to pay $500 to cover all the lawyer's fees and court costs plus $12 per week alimony, barely enough to support Beulah, her widowed mother, and her teenaged daughter. Margaret wrote to Emma to share the news: "So she is free again. I don't know what she will do next. . . . Bertha is corresponding with her father, Arthur Parker. He is in Rochester. She tells me he wrote to her and told her he is going to France this summer."[121] The differences in their lives are poignant. Beulah Tahamont was starting from scratch, yet again, in California, and Arthur Parker was vacationing in France, just as the Great Depression was settling in.

Suddenly, Hollywood acting was no longer an option. The film industry was collapsing, and thousands of actors were stranded and starving. The Tahamont women took whatever jobs they could find to survive. Bertha cleaned houses, and Margaret and Beulah demonstrated ash-splint basket-making and sold their wares in theater lobbies whenever their pictures were being screened. Beulah had developed a drinking habit during a time when food was increasingly scarce since, as Margaret wrote, "one can always get a drink of whiskey when they can't get anything to eat."[122] In 1931 Beulah was married for a third time, to Thomas W. Filson, a railyard worker. The newlyweds headed out on their own to northern California to the gold mines; it was back-breaking work, but there was little else to be had. Margaret wrote: "They was working hard expecting to get a good haul. Their wives work like the men and she was good to me. But they came back here and all the trouble. . . . He could not get work any more than the thousands of men with starving families, so that was that."[123]

When Margaret retired, she was promised money from the Actors' Pension Fund, but it was withheld when she failed to provide a birth certificate. Ironically, at this juncture, American citizenship would have been a benefit rather than a burden, since it would have made her eligible for state benefits. But Margaret's transtribal (Oneida and Abenaki) and transnational identity did not neatly fit into any official category. She had been born in the United States, baptized in Canada, and resided in three different states, none of which recognized her as a legal resident, even though she owned property. Given the circumstances, the social service workers were willing to accept evidence from the family Bible, but that had been left in the hands of Arthur Parker, along with the rest of the Tahamont family's library.[124] Despite Bertha's pleas to her father, there is no evidence that the Bible was ever returned. Later that year, during the winter of 1934, both Margaret Tahamont and Emma Mead passed away within a few months of each other, and the letters between Los Angeles and Indian Lake stopped.

During the mid-1930s to 1940s, Beulah Tahamont remade her life, yet again, by accompanying her daughter, Bertha, on ethnographic field trips to other Native American communities across California, visiting Maidu medicine men, Paiute bear walkers, Pomo basket makers, and other elders, storytellers, and traditionalists, with the encouragement and support of the Southwest Museum of the American Indian, and her old friend (and former beau) Mark Raymond Harrington. Bertha Parker's field notes and publications (discussed in chapter 4) show that those California Indians, much like the Seneca elders Beulah had met decades before, welcomed and appreciated these Native women, and were more than willing to share their stories.

Some of Bertha's surviving letters include details about how Beulah spent her leisure time. For example, in 1945, when they took a camping trip in the mountains, Bertha wrote:

> Been up here at Fall River with the folks. We have camped out & how I have enjoyed it. The tall pines and cool streams add to our comfort. We have been out of touch with the outside world. . . . We did some mining and gathered Indian medicines, but mostly I rested. Tom [Filson] caught trout every day for us.[125]

These trips were refreshing, but also sad, since the mountains of California reminded her of the Adirondack home that she could never afford to return to.

Later that year, Beulah Tahamont Parker O'Brien Filson passed away, at the age of only fifty-eight. She was survived by her daughter, Bertha; her husband, Thomas; and her son, Melvil. An obituary in the *Mercury-Register* listed some of her accomplishments.

> A former actress, Mrs. Filson was known professionally as Beulah Darkcloud. She started her stage career as a child of four. She attended public schools and college in Montreal, Canada. Mrs. Filson's father, Chief Darkcloud, was brought to Hollywood in 1912 by D. W. Griffith. He starred in motion pictures and was well known as a lecturer on Indian lore, touring roadshow and circus circuits. As a young woman, Beulah Darkcloud was active in Los Angeles American Indian Clubs. She produced and directed many pageants, the most notable of which was "The Landing of the Pilgrim Fathers," one of the first plays produced in the Hollywood Bowl.
>
> Failing health as the result of a serious accident forced her to retire from professional life 17 years ago. Following her retirement she accompanied her daughter, Mrs. Bertha P. Cody, writer and associate in ethnology of S. W. Museum, on her ethnological expeditions, aiding in the collecting of data on the lore, mythology, and early history of the California Indians.[126]

Beulah Tahamont was not, as some Parker biographers have suggested, invisible or insignificant. During her youth, she was a stunning beauty with a brilliant mind and a gift for ethnology, but she was partnered to a husband who, apparently, despised her. When her husbands and Hollywood failed her, she did whatever she could to survive, eventually coming full circle to practicing ethnology alongside her daughter. Yet virtually no written documents in her own voice have survived. In the haste of her departure from Arthur, Beulah left her entire library behind, including books, research notes, medicinal formulas, and the Tahamont family Bible. Despite multiple requests, Arthur never returned any of Beulah's papers, and they do not appear to have been saved. The loss of these records is especially stark when laid alongside Arthur's voluminous works. Perhaps, at some day in the future, a trove of papers will resurface, written in Beulah's hand, recounting the missing pieces of her story.

Telling Stories

Two decades after his marriage to Beulah had failed, Arthur Parker began frankly discussing his feelings in coded letters to his best friend, Mark Raymond Harrington. Parker was racked by self-doubts and struggles with those who surrounded him: family, museum personnel, state officials, and tribal leaders. Other scholars who have seen these letters assumed that the two men were writing in some indecipherable or invented Native language. However, after laboriously sifting through all the possible Native languages they had contact with, I discovered a means to decode their texts. The two men used select phrases in the Chinook trade jargon—cribbed from a Chinook dictionary published in 1909, and adapted to their own idiosyncrasies of speech—as a secret language.[127] For example, in a 1927 letter (otherwise written in English) to Harrington, Parker included a coda with this phrase: "*Kwanasim tum tum konawe tillikuns mesatci pe konawe tillikums klatawa kopa diablo.*" In the Chinook trade jargon, that roughly translates to "At heart, all my relations are wicked and all my relations can go to the Devil."[128]

These letters contain several references to Beulah, including one in 1928 that coincided with the timing of Beulah's second divorce. Arthur acknowledged having received a letter from his daughter Bertha, but he feared that any attempt to communicate with her might "revive unhappy fears of my disloyalty and [create] excuses for further contact." M.R., who was then working in Nevada and California, had been in communication with Beulah, and he told Arthur that he was happily offering assistance to the Tahamonts, whom he regarded as old friends. Arthur thanked M.R. for assisting his ex-wife but warned him that "this course is fraught with danger, misunderstanding and perhaps tragedy."[129]

Parker wrote a similar series of letters to his sister, Endeka (who was, by then, married to Harrington), wherein he uncharacteristically admitted fault. Upon reflection, he realized that his courtship of Beulah had been a hasty mistake, borne from the desire to please his mentor, Harriet Maxwell Converse. He wrote:

> If I have had tragic moments it is because I brought them upon myself through mistaken loyalties and feelings of responsibility. Thus, I only kick myself hard and go forward to brighter goals. . . . Yes, I have had some hard things to bear. I do not

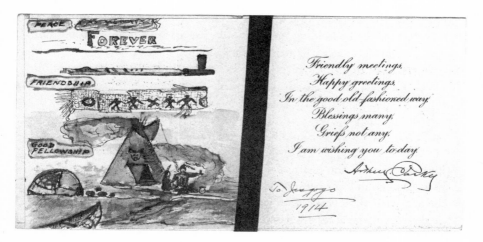

Figure 10 Card from Arthur Parker to Mark Raymond Harrington (Jisgogo), 1914. Illustration by Parker shows the two men in camp with a peace pipe, wampum belt, tipi, and canoe. Courtesy of the National Museum of the American Indian.

think of them much or ever dwell upon them, but I have a lingering feeling that I have had my share of terrible situations—and nobody to understand, nobody near to know or care, nobody to lend a hand because I couldn't tell. If I had been more of a coeard [coward] I could not have lived through it or borne up under the loads that came.[130]

In a later letter, he was distraught that his son, Melvil, had deserted from the Navy, abandoned his family, and gone to visit his mother, Beulah, so that he "might know the truth of things." Arthur refused to discuss "that ghostly shadow" of whom he had washed his hands, "even though it hangs over me—but I will have none of it." His only regret was the loss of connection with his daughter Bertha, whom he had "never ceased to adore." He lamented:

I was cursed but I have no longer the will to claim the curse because I pity or feel obligated. There is an end to endurance. . . . However, I can steel my heart . . . and everyone knows it who knows me. . . . I am just what I am, and nothing more and what if no one knows what I am or why? The centuries to come will not care when I am dust.[131]

In public, Parker kept up formal appearances, to such a degree that many of his museum colleagues were unaware of both his previous marriage and his lack of university credentials. For decades, Arthur had asserted having been both a student at Harvard and a Seneca chief, and had identified himself as "Dr. Parker," while holding no college degree or tribal leadership position whatsoever. His credentials were honorary rather than earned: a 1922 master's in science from the University of Rochester, and a 1940 doctorate from Union College. From a traditional Seneca perspective, claims of unearned status might be interpreted as acts of stealing power, and might invite corrective supernatural forces to intervene. In Haudenosaunee communities in particular, liars were universally shunned. Parker knew this when he wrote, "In fact the entire social life of the Indian is imbued with religious sentiment. He despises a liar and distrusts the man who offers too much to him. . . . A betrayal of confidence he never forgives."[132] Yet, in his biographical sketch for the *Masonic International Who's Who* (despite the request for a full accounting of all marriages), Parker listed only his second wife, Anna Theresa Cooke, and their daughter, Martha Anne. He made no mention of his first wife, Beulah Tahamont, or his children, Melvil and Bertha.[133]

Throughout his entire career, however, Arthur Parker never forgot his beloved mentor, Harriet Maxwell Converse. He made frequent recourse to files he had inherited from her work among the Seneca, often using these works to promote his own visions of Indigenous voice. In his editor's introduction to Harriet Maxwell Converse's posthumous *Myths and Legends of the New York State Iroquois*, for example, he scorned the scientific method of recording Native texts "with an exact translation interlined, word beneath word," claiming that "from the standpoint of literature it falls short."[134] Parker's dismissive attitude of linguistic anthropology was, in fact, a targeted criticism of work being done by Tuscarora scholar J. N. B. Hewitt, who was then engaged in a comprehensive project of recording Haudenosaunee folklore and language using precisely this approach for the Smithsonian Bureau of Ethnology. Hewitt's method was also preferred by anthropologists J. Dyneley Prince and Frank Speck, among many others, in large part because it preserved the sense of Indigenous ontologies embedded in word choices.[135] But, for Parker, pedantic texts of Native folklore were too inaccessible for the average reader; he wanted something more poetic.

Another approach, Parker suggested, might be to do away with all "picturesque eccentricities of expression" and rewrite these stories in modern English, but this might result in "florid, ocherous, recast and garbled folklore" (one suspects that he read many examples of this, given his biting critique). The most logical approach might be to simply record the unedited speech of bilingual storytellers in a mix of Indian and English, but Parker felt that this faulty brogue of "broken English" produced only a "grotesque caricature" that "fails to convey to our minds the ideas which exist in the mind of the native myth teller."[136]

For Parker, simple oral transmission would not do. First (he insisted), an intelligent and educated person must listen closely to the words of an American Indian storyteller. Then, the tale must be reinterpreted, while the listener/transcriber "attempts to assimilate the ideas of the myth tale as he hears it, seeks to become imbued with the spirit of its characters." The transcriber should then focus on "shutting out from his mind all thought of his own culture . . . momentarily transforming himself into the culture of the storyteller." Having done this, the listener should then make a new record of the story.

> The object is to produce the same emotions in the minds of civilized man which is produced in the primitive mind, which entertains the myth without destroying the native style or warping the facts of the narrative. If in the vernacular the ideas convey tragic, mysterious, or horrifying impressions, and the style is vigorous, metaphorical or poetic, the transcriber employs every consistent art to reproduce the same elements in his own language. . . . A myth tale recorded in this way is . . . the same living, sentient story, though dressed in the garments of another speech.[137]

Parker, in essence, was proposing what I would characterize as "literary spirit possession" or literary colonialism. He felt it necessary to pick apart the original story, consume its essence, and then spout it forth in one's own voice. The result would be a reanimated story that could then, presumably, survive on its own.

In essence, Parker believed that Indigenous traditions could not be entrusted to the memories of Indigenous knowledge keepers but should be filtered through the minds of educated outsiders. He identified Harriet Maxwell Converse as the ideal storyteller, claiming that her "great love for the Indians, her sympathetic nature, her scientific training and her psychic temperament" rendered her uniquely able to recover the soul of a story. Her "poetic mind schooled in all the arts of literature" was the perfect instrument. Her rendition "enables the reader to feel all that the red man felt when he listened to the ancient stories of his forefathers."[138] Converse was, admittedly, familiar with Seneca folktales, but she was also a spiritualist who believed that she could communicate with the dead. So, by promoting Converse as the perfect interpreter of Haudenosaunee traditions, Parker was directing his audiences to ignore living Haudenosaunee voices and, instead, to listen to her interpretations of the dead.

Converse left behind a rich body of work for Parker to reinterpret, and he may have similarly borrowed, or adapted, works left behind by Elijah Tahamont. For example, several early publications in the *Quarterly Journal of the Society of American Indians* attributed to Parker are authored by a writer identified as "Alnoba Waubunaki," which, quite literally, translates to "Abenaki person from

Abenaki land." Since Parker was inordinately proud of his Seneca ancestry, it would make no sense for him to claim a different tribal identity, let alone an Abenaki one. One article begins, "Long before 1620 the men of Dawn Land had heard of the pale invaders from across the big salt sea."[139] "Dawn Land" is the common translation of Wabanaki, Abenaki territory. The article employs Abenaki terms like Magwas (Mohawk), Chebi (an Arctic monster of story), and Manitou (Great Spirit), and it references names and incidents well-known to New England Algonkian Indians. The piece ends with a scathing critique of Puritanism, urging that "the self-repression, false sentiment, self-worship, self-consciousness, the false covering, shall be swept away."

> Though he made his own mistakes in thinking, the red man learned more error through the false things taught by the teachers of "civilization." In his natural desire for exhilaration he drained the poisoned cup and sold his birthright for more . . . yet shall the red man not be conquered. He shall live in his ideals. The river, the mountain, the valley, the lake, shall sing back the names he gave them.[140]

The article was accompanied by a poem, titled "My Race Shall Live Anew," with an evocative call to "Give freedom to the red man's mind!"[141] These texts, which would have made a compelling (if somewhat overdramatic) oratorical performance, bear little resemblance to Parker's other written works.

In 1926 Parker compiled a collection of Seneca stories in easy-to-read modern English, which he dedicated to Martha Anne, his daughter with his second wife, Anna Theresa Cooke. In the introduction to this book, *Skunny Wundy*, he fondly remembered the traditional storytellers of his youth.

> Into that home drifted many a visitor from the wilder parts of the reservation, visitors who lived back in the woods or on the hill where the long-house people dwelt, they who followed the old Indian customs and had grotesque masks and dances and who wore feathers and buckskins. Many of the Indian visitors stayed for supper and then sat around the fire to smoke. All the youngsters of the family would whisper to Grandfather asking if the visitor would not tell a story. And almost every time, he would.[142]

Historian George R. Hamell later explained the importance of the moral lessons embedded in these Seneca stories.

> Oral traditions—whether myths, legends, or folk-tales—are more than just "stories." They are the way by which a society communicates to its members the order and meaning to be found in the world around them. . . . The Iroquois do not live in a natural world, but in a social world. . . . They describe the social relations,

which exist between real human kinds of people and the other-than-human kinds of people, and the responsibilities each has for the other.[143]

Traditionally, Seneca stories provided a cognitive map of Indigenous thought-worlds, guidelines for respectfully navigating among humans and other-than-humans, and practical lessons for sustainability. One can only wonder how Parker's life trajectory might have shifted had he listened to the instructions embedded in the stories his Native relatives shared over the years.

In 1934, in a confessional letter to his sister, Endeka, Arthur admitted that much of his social and professional identity had been constructed from his own desires, entangled with the assumptions woven around him. He longed to return to the simplicity of his youthful years, when he was a simple "digger of the bone imps and sherds" alongside his old friend Mark Raymond Harrington. He told Endeka: "What are we, after all, but what people think we are—our real selves are covered by our own imaginings and we get a label. Thereafter we must live up to the label. It seems to mean everything and we are compelled to play the part."[144]

Over the course of a long career, Arthur Parker was inordinately successful, widely recognized as an accomplished archaeologist and museum educator, and credited with the preservation of Haudenosaunee cultural treasures. He amassed large collections and constructed influential exhibitions at both the New York State Museum and the Rochester Public Museum, and produced an impressive volume of publications. He fulfilled virtually every dream that he had ever desired, but he appears to have sacrificed the trust of his Seneca friends, the safety of his family, and the career potential of his talented first wife, Beulah, to get there.

4

Collaborative Kin

Bertha Parker and Mark Harrington

> Good worker, scientific turn of mind, considerable practical and
> theoretical knowledge of Southwestern archaeology. . . . Startling
> success in finding good things in the field.
>
> —Mark Raymond Harrington's description of Bertha Parker, 1931

Bertha Yewas Parker (1907–78), the only daughter of Arthur Caswell Parker and Beulah Tahamont, was literally born into archaeology. She first drew breath in a tent camp at the Silverheels site near Sinclairville in Cattaraugus County, New York, where her father was conducting excavations. After a stint in Hollywood with her mother and grandparents during her teen years, she landed in Nevada. There, she demonstrated an innate gift for scientific research, and gained important field experience while assisting her uncle, Mark Raymond Harrington, in archaeological excavations. Although she gained little recognition at the time, she was, apparently, the first professional Native American female archaeologist, and the first Native American female to serve as both an ethnologist and an archaeologist for a major museum, the Southwest Museum of the American Indian in Los Angeles. During the 1930s, Bertha made a groundbreaking discovery at a Paleolithic site at Gypsum Cave in Nevada, and published a number of research articles in *Masterkey*, the journal of the Southwest Museum. During the 1950s through 1970s, she served as a trustee for the Southwest Museum, while also consulting and acting in Hollywood, and co-hosting a KTLA TV show on Indian lore. She was married three times: first to a movie extra (Jose or Joseph Pallan); then to a paleontologist (James Thurston); and then to a movie star (Iron Eyes Cody), whose out-sized ego nearly eclipsed the memory of her professional career altogether.[1]

Mark Raymond Harrington (called by his friends both M.R. and Ray) (1882–1971) was born in Ann Arbor, Michigan, the son of University of Michigan professor and museum curator Mark Walrod Harrington. His mother, Martha Lowell Smith, had a touch of Mohawk ancestry, and this fragmentary Native heritage inspired a lifelong desire to accumulate Native kin. During his early teen years, while the family was living in Seattle, he socialized with Siwash

Indians and learned some of the Chinook trade jargon. When he was sixteen, the family relocated to Mount Vernon, New York. There, he began digging in Native sites along East Chester Creek and Pelham Bay, bringing his collections to Frederic Ward Putnam at the American Museum of Natural History for identification. Putnam was so impressed that he took young M.R. on as an assistant, sending him off in 1899 to gain professional training by working alongside Ernest Volk on Lenape sites in New Jersey. Harrington became so skilled at the "Putnam Method" of surveying, test pits, trenching, and so on (still routine in archaeological practice today) that he was asked to train many of Boas's and Putnam's students. Harrington completed a master's degree at Columbia with Boas in 1908, and until 1928, he worked as a curator, excavator, and collector for George Gustav Heye of the Museum of the American Indian/Heye Foundation. From 1911 to 1915, he also held an appointment in Philadelphia at the University Museum (now called the Penn Museum), as an assistant curator in the American section.[2] Throughout his life, Harrington was also an independent artifacts dealer, funding part of his research by trading in Indian goods. Like many of his colleagues, he also enjoyed "playing Indian": an early photograph shows him at an archaeological site with Irwin Hayden, outfitted in French and Indian War–era northeastern Indian dress and adornments, wielding tomahawks, and smoking pipes in front of their tents (see p. 53).[3]

Constructing Kin Networks

M.R. had a natural rapport with Native peoples, in part because he was fluent in so many Native languages and was such an entertaining guest. He appears to have occupied a crucial middle zone in collecting where, rather than manipulating people to steal tribal property, he encouraged people to make a little extra money by parting with items they no longer needed. On many occasions, his hosts would rush into their attics and storerooms immediately upon his arrival, "looking for 'old Indian things' to sell." Harrington had a fine sense of humor about being targeted as a strange "white man." At the Oneida community at Six Nations in Ontario, Canada, for example, he recalled eavesdropping on two girls chatting in Oneida: "Finally one of them said: 'See that Lasluni sitting in that chair? That's the kind of man I'd like to marry!' Now I knew that *Laslúni* was the same as the Mohawk *Raslúni*, from *asare*, 'knife,' *runi*, 'he makes,'—in other words, 'knife-maker,' referring to a white man. Since I was the only white man present, she meant me." He then politely interjected, in Oneida, "I'm sorry, but I already have a wife," at which point "both girls screamed and ran from the room."[4]

M.R. was eventually adopted by an elderly Turtle clan matron from that same Oneida community and given the name Jiskógo ("the Robin"). This, the first of many Native names he would be given over time, was "conferred in a full Long House ceremony, with speeches, songs, dances and feasting—the whole works!" When he left, the community held the formal ceremony of parting called "Pushing Off His Canoe," during which a chief intoned the hope that the "canoe would not strike any rocks or snags, but would bear me safely to my destination." Harrington wryly noted, "This although everybody knew I was going by rail."[5] While working at Ketchipauan, in Zuni homelands, he acquired another Native nickname.

> I had spotted some human bones dragged out by a badger from his hole . . . and with visions of the beautiful Pre-Spanish Zuni pots that might appear with such a skeleton—if I could find it—I started to burrow back into the bank, tracing the badger hole. The Zunis watched me with amusement. . . . It was then that Auste, with a chuckle, informed me that while the skeleton could evidently dig faster than I, and I had failed to catch up with it, I had shown such burrowing ability anyhow that he would confer up on me the name of To'nashi, "The Badger"—and To'nashi I have remained ever since.[6]

When conducting archaeology, M.R. was a determined researcher with an inclusive and egalitarian bent. He was willing to train virtually anyone who showed interest. He frequently brought his wife and child into the field with him, and he insisted on being accompanied by his two Native site managers, Pitt River Indians George and Willis Evans.[7] This stance occasionally drew criticism from colleagues. In a 1926 letter to Frederick Webb Hodge, George Gustav Heye (M.R.'s employer) complained that two white men had quit Harrington's team because they refused to work with women and children in camp, and they refused to take direction from Indians. Heye advised shaming M.R. by "reading the riot act, giving hell in general and ridicule (mostly the latter)"; instead, Hodge (who recognized the value and productivity of Harrington's work style) quietly encouraged M.R. to hire whomever he wished and make whatever arrangements he felt necessary to get the work done.[8]

Harrington, unlike some of his contemporaries, was notably generous about sharing intellectual credit with his workmen. While working at the Lost City site in Nevada, he had hired a local Native man, Leslie Sanchee (Zuni), to translate and excavate. After having rushed to send a report to *Scientific American*, Harrington realized that he had made an omission; he immediately wrote to editor A. A. Hopkins.

> In looking over the carbon of the article I find that I have forgotten to give credit to our two capable Pitt River Indians, George and Willis Evans, and to Leslie Sanchee, a Zuni Indian worker of ours. If you can slip in a sentence to give these three men

credit, with Mr. Turbyfill, for bearing the brunt of the heat and the dust in the caverns, I wish you would. They deserve it, because without their energy and grit those old salt-mines would never have been explored.[9]

As Harrington explained in one of his letters to Hodge, Native assistants were absolutely essential to the success of these digs: "I need one reliable man who knows the business—preferably a friend of mine who is an Indian—to be my right-hand man and second in command."[10]

Harrington lost his wife, Anna Johns, to respiratory illness in 1926. The following year, he received funding from George Heye's wife, Mrs. Thea Heye, to excavate near Pyramid Lake in Nevada. M.R. was seeking a nanny for his son, Johns Heye Harrington, at the very moment that his old friend Arthur Parker wrote seeking assistance for his sister, Edna (who preferred the name Endeka) Parker Carpenter. Endeka was in need of a divorce, and Nevada was the only state that could grant her one. Harrington replied, "Anything in my power that I can do for you or for Edna will be a privilege."[11] Since Endeka needed work, M.R. hired her to work as a secretary/tutor/nanny, but she quickly proved to be more than an ordinary helpmate. M.R. wrote to Arthur:

> She has a room here at the Indian Agency at Nixon and every morning she gives Mishaliku (Johns) his lessons and almost every afternoon she goes out to the digging where she helps me with measurements, etc., and in the evening we work on correspondence, articles, and stories. Endeka does not seem to mind working 14 or 15 hours a day, so I am getting a lot done.[12]

Together, they explored the caves at Pyramid Lake and, within a brief time, their fortuitous partnership evolved into much more. After working side by side through the fall season, M.R. and Endeka were married in early December 1927.[13]

The entangled kinship network of the Parkers and the Harringtons, which forms the framework of this particular chapter, bears some explaining. Around 1900 Mark Raymond Harrington, Arthur Parker, and Beulah Tahamont met in Harriet Maxwell Converse's salon. In 1904 M.R.'s girlfriend, Beulah Tahamont, became Arthur's first wife. Also in 1904 M.R. married Alma V. Cocks. Beulah and Arthur divorced in 1912, and in 1914 Arthur married his second wife, Anna T. Cooke. In 1916 M.R.'s wife Alma Cocks Harrington passed away, and in 1917 he married his second wife, Anna Johns; Johns passed away in 1926.[14] Around 1926 Beulah married her second husband, William O'Brien. At an unknown date in the 1920s, Arthur's sister, Endeka, married her first husband, Joseph Carpenter; in 1927 she divorced him and married M.R. Harrington.[15] Despite (or perhaps because of) these relationships, Arthur and M.R. remained close friends throughout their lives.

Figure 11 Endeka Parker and Mark Raymond Harrington beside petroglyphs at Valley of Fire, Overton, Nevada, c. 1929. Photographer unknown. Image P.47991. Courtesy of the Braun Research Library Collection, Autry Museum, Los Angeles.

As an example of just how close these families were, it was M.R. who, in 1929, rescued Arthur and Beulah's daughter, Bertha Yewas Parker, from a disastrous situation. Bertha and her mother had been working on the set of a Hollywood film, where Bertha fell in with a Hollywood extra, a Yuma Indian and self-styled "medicine doctor," Jose Pallan. In 1924, after Bertha got pregnant, she married Jose; their daughter, Wilma Mae (nicknamed Billie), was born on February 5, 1925. When Jose became abusive, Bertha sought a divorce, but Jose responded by kidnapping Beulah, Bertha, and Billie before crossing the border into Mexico. Family friend Julian Hayden later recalled the story of this rescue.

> Before we went to Nevada in early January of '29, Bertha had been kidnapped by Pallan and confined to a house of ill repute, from which Harrington had rescued her with the help of who? Law officers? This was the reason she went to Nevada with the museum party—and with Endeka Harrington, the sister of Arthur Parker, and Bertha's aunt, whom Harrington had married earlier. Sounds like a paperback novel, but to best of my belief, true, at least in broad outline.[16]

Picture the scene: Three beautiful Indian maidens are captured and confined in a Mexican whorehouse. Then, riding in on horseback with the sheriff at his side, comes anthropologist Mark Raymond Harrington. Then, the entire company escapes to the deserts of Nevada to do archaeology. The story sounds bizarre, but it happens to be true.

Practicing Indigenous Archaeology

Not long after their rescue, Beulah was escorted back to Los Angeles to pursue work in Hollywood, but Bertha stayed at the archaeological camp in the Nevada desert. The Harringtons provided room and board for her and her daughter, Billie, and in exchange, she was employed as a cook, expedition secretary, and assistant archaeologist. Despite her position as a young, non-university-educated Native American woman in a field typically dominated by white men, Bertha developed a surprisingly keen eye for archaeological discoveries, and she was welcomed as an important member of the crew. In the field, she worked alongside the men, as did her aunt Endeka.

Archaeology, at the time, was becoming increasingly professionalized; elite learned white men were considered to be both the holders of intellectual authority and the instructors of specialized knowledges and methods, and people of color often served as unskilled informants or laborers. Harrington, who felt that field experience was more useful than formal schooling, had a more fundamentally egalitarian approach to the production of scientific knowledge

Figure 12 Bertha Parker Pallan, Mark Raymond Harrington, and Irwin Hayden, in Nevada, c. 1929. Photograph by Milton Snow. Courtesy of the Museum of Northern Arizona.

in the field. He granted considerable autonomy to his crew members, inspiring collaborations that cross-cut race, class, and gender divisions. Most archaeologists hired single men; M.R. preferred to hire entire families, so that no one had to find work or housing elsewhere. He trained anyone who was able in the necessary skills, from excavating techniques to camp cooking, and encouraged every member of the crew, skilled or unskilled, male or female, white or Indian, to contribute whatever they could to the scientific project.

Evenings in the Nevada camp functioned as outdoor classrooms, where Harrington lectured on the foundational theories of anthropology and the scientific practice of archaeology.[17] In this sense, his practice foreshadowed the principles of the present-day practice of Indigenous archaeologies, by position-ing Indigenous and anthropological collaborators side by side, decolonizing relations in the field.[18] Although he never used this theoretical framing ex-plicitly, Harrington seems to have recognized that Indigenous knowledge had been imperfectly filtered through, and distorted by, Euro-centric perspectives and theories. By encouraging broader participation, Harrington shared his intellectual authority, and, as a result, recovered evidence that might have been missed by those with a solely Euro-American scientific bent.

In Nevada, Endeka and Bertha gained field experience that more than made up for any lack of classroom training. In a chatty report on life in the field, M.R. characterized Endeka as "always happiest and healthiest in camp, even though her active brain thinks up so many dandy things to do each day that her fingers cannot keep up with her program." He described Bertha (whom he typically called by her Seneca name Yewas) as "slender and willowy, with con-siderable pride in her boyish figure," and jokingly called her "Princess Never-eats." He noted that she actually worked two jobs: from early morning to mid-afternoon, she was the camp cook; and during the afternoons, she conducted independent archaeological research.

> She wields a skillful coffee-pot and frying pan, but I suspect she wishes the after-noons were longer, so she could put in more time digging in the ruin on the mesa. If you want to see her black eyes shine talk to her about archaeology, or watch her uncovering something choice. . . . Afternoon usually finds them digging on the mesa. . . . You could not keep them away from that ruin with a club.[19]

During the 1929 field season, Bertha discovered a Pueblo site that she named "Scorpion Hill." She started with field notes and measurements, and then proceeded very methodically, making a test hole to check for ground disturbance and collecting samples of pottery and flint to be examined by Harrington. With M.R.'s encouragement, the Evans brothers' wives, Jessie and Myrtle, offered to help out with the cooking and camp work so Bertha could continue this excavation on her own.

In her 1933 article for *Masterkey*, "Scorpion Hill," she recalled the details of this dig.

> Continuing with the test-pit previously commenced, I encountered a floor of adobe about two feet down. Following this I came to a wall built of alternate layers of sandstone slabs and large boulders set in adobe mortar and finely plastered over with adobe. The fragments of charcoal indicated that the room had been burned and that its roof had consisted of large beams covered with tules and arrowcane.

I uncovered about half the room that day. . . . After shoveling what seemed tons of "back dirt" from the previous day's digging, the room was completely bared. It was 8 feet 8 inches by 4 feet 6 inches in floor dimensions, and in the middle of the plastered floor was a break of 3 by 4 feet—the very break I had been told to look for, especially when a room had been burned, for this was indicative of a burial beneath.[20]

She excavated only a little more before backfilling in the interests of time. Harrington agreed that she should return for more comprehensive excavations at a future date, since the site was contiguous with "Lost City."[21]

In a popular article for *Desert Magazine*, Harrington described his egalitarian ethos. He readily credited the skill of a crew "composed almost entirely of American Indians!" He highlighted Bertha's qualifications as expedition secretary, noting that she "is the daughter of a distinguished Seneca . . . Arthur C. Parker."

Bertha, known to us as "Bertie," comes naturally by her archaeological interest, having been born in a tent on one of her father's expeditions. As secretary at Gypsum

Figure 13 Bertha Parker Pallan with black-and-white early Pueblo pot in situ, 1929, Overton, Nevada. Photograph by Mark Raymond Harrington. Image P.23222. Courtesy of the Braun Research Library Collection, Autry Museum, Los Angeles.

cave she took care of all dictation, typing, cleaning, repair and cataloging of specimens and often found time to work in the cave, worming her way into the most
inaccessible crevices, and usually returning with some real relic of the past.

My chief assistant was Willis L. Evans, a Pitt river Indian from northern California who had accompanied me on previous expeditions. He is the most resourceful
man I ever knew. Willis, now with the national park service, has distinguished
himself by discovering another ground sloth cave near the entrance of lower Grand
Canyon.

His brother Oliver served as assistant and his wife Jessie, a Shoshone from northern Nevada, was expedition cook, and a good one she was. She never lost her temper
when unexpected guests arrived for dinner, and what a test that is! Unofficial members of the party were Oliver's wife Myrtle, who is a Washoe, and several of Willis'
children. Our camp made quite an Indian village, with four tribes represented.[22]

M.R. noted that the only other "paleface" on site was Boston banker Alva
Morrison, for whom "no job was too dirty or difficult." With the Evans brothers directing operations, Morrison willingly donned "overalls and respirator
mask [for] delving in the dirtiest part of a dusty dry cave!" Most archaeologists
routinely hired Native peoples as laborers, but few were willing to level social
relations by assigning a wealthy banker to work as a digger.[23]

Julian Hayden, Field Man

In January 1929 the Harrington team was joined by M.R.'s old colleague from
the Peabody Harvard Museum, Irwin Hayden, in company with his seventeen-
year-old son, Julian. Young Hayden had little experience with archaeology, but
the fieldwork on Mesa House in Nevada proved inspirational. He was a great
"shovel man," a strong member of the field crew, and a prolific writer and
sketch artist who kept detailed field notes and records of his experiences. His
journals preserved a wealth of information about these Nevada digs: notes from
Harrington's educational lectures, remarks on the location and significance of
discoveries, descriptions of interactions among crew members, sketches of Bertha Parker, and antics in camp. Bertha made a powerful impression on Julian;
she was brilliant, hard-working, and beautiful, and he faithfully chronicled
every detail, praising her cooking and her scientific acumen alike.[24]

When the Nevada field season ended, the Harrington crew returned to
Los Angeles. During the summer of 1929, in-between his stints working on
excavations at Avila and Point Mugu for the Van Bergen-Los Angeles County
Museum, Julian initiated a romance with Bertha.[25] By early winter, she was
back in Nevada and he was at the Grew site in Arizona, but the two continued to correspond. Julian's letters to Bertha have not survived, but hers have,

preserving poignant reflections on their lives and perspectives. In a pragmatic 1929 letter, she discouraged him, writing, "You have your future, you are young and strong, and I hope you will take advantage of all that you can in knowledge, and forget me, in your efforts for higher education."[26] In a more poetic and romantic missive in 1930, she described the Nevada camp as it quieted down for the night.

> I took my chair and put it behind the tents outside of the wind-break and just gazed at far distant mountains of Arizona I could imagine you were sitting in a chair beside me, but it was only imagination. Then dust settled over the earth and the tiny bats started winging their way in search of food and the tiny cricket chorus started playing and the tiny twinkling stars were peeking through the fast disappearing light and I was alone just thinking of you darling mine and knowing that those same stars were looking down on you.
>
> Everything is quiet except the Indians were singing *Heigh oh whit ze neigh oh*. Uncle Ray is humming to himself while he is packing the Willis tangle and Aunt Deka is busily pecking as usual on the typewriter. Everyone else is quietly settled in their tents.[27]

Despite exchanges like these, there were serious tensions in their relationship. Bertha, who had burdensome family responsibilities, sought a stable marriage partner, but she felt disrespected by Julian's father, Irwin, who disdained her Indianness and regarded her more as a "maid" than a research assistant.[28] Julian was young, naïve, and (like his father) often headstrong. In some letters, she grew frustrated, responding to Julian's romantic entreaties by saying, "Do you think that all I have time for is writing letters?"[29] She also pointed out that M.R. never knew, when he jokingly called her "Princess Never Eats," that she was intentionally depriving herself of food so that her relatives could survive. It was necessary, she told Julian.

> Don't you realize that I have a mother and a little girl to look out for, and between studying so hard to finish school, that I have to find various means of earning money? You have no responsibilities and it doesn't matter if you miss a meal or two, but when you have hungry mouths to feed you have to put your nose to the grind stone. My health is all broken to pieces and I am far from strong because many times I went without meals so that Mother & Billie could have plenty, they didn't realize why I didn't eat any breakfast or dinner. Mother thought I wasn't hungry, but I knew we hardly had enough to carry on.[30]

From Bertha's perspective, Julian was out enjoying adventures around the world while she was starving. But in fact, he too was living hand-to-mouth, hitchhiking, and working odd jobs to get by. He responded to this letter by mailing her most of his paycheck even though he was nearly penniless himself.[31]

Bertha consistently found a safe harbor with the Harringtons, to whom she was both a surrogate daughter and a respected crew member. She drew a regular salary from the Southwest Museum, building her position up from field cook to expedition secretary to assistant archaeologist. She found her calling in archaeology and, for the first time in her life, foresaw a viable future.

> I am drawing a very excellent salary, lord knows I need it, and that is why I am hoping the expedition will stay out longer. . . . I have met so many lovely people of the scientific world, that I have learned quite a lot, they are all so nice to me, that I am very happy in my work, and the hard knocks make me appreciate it all the more.[32]

In 1930 Bertha met someone else, a field paleontologist who took an interest in her romantically as well as intellectually. As she explained in a letter to Julian, "His family isn't ashamed of me and he isn't. . . . Somewhere, some day Julian you will find a girl who will be your ideal and you will wonder why you were ever so silly over me."[33]

Julian and Bertha had a few more poignant meetings, but by the summer of 1931, they had both decided to move on. Julian later confessed to M.R. that it was nearly impossible to forget Bertha, writing:

> If she'd been any ordinary girl I reckon I'd be over it by this time but I was fortunate—or unfortunate—enough to be in love with and to have been loved by Bertie. And you know as well as I that Bertie is Bertie, the one and only, that there never was and never will be another girl like her in this world.[34]

He focused his energies on working other archaeological digs in the southwest, and in 1935, while working the Snaketown site, he met Helen Pendleton, who soon after became his wife.[35]

Julian Hayden parlayed all the techniques he had learned in Nevada into a profitable avocation, becoming a standout in southwestern archaeology while making his living as a contractor. Unlike his father, Irwin Hayden, who was Harvard educated, Julian was a "blue collar scholar" with no college training.[36] His work evidenced a perfect combination of Putnam's scientific method and Harrington's collaborative approach, mixed with a generous dose of dedicated shovel work. He constantly emphasized the importance of approaching research with an "open mind" free of both prejudice and hypothesis. "Preconceived ideas," Julian insisted, got in the way of discoveries; theories should be developed only after careful attention to material evidence and field observations, so as to avoid tainting results.[37] He consistently brought these principles and practices to his fieldwork, while disdaining the "New Archaeology" that relied heavily on lab-based statistical analyses, modern equipment, and textbook study. Julian was emphatically an "Old School" archaeologist and "shovel man" who believed "you don't learn how to use a trowel, you don't learn the textures of soils, from a book."[38]

Like his mentor Harrington, Hayden also appreciated the importance of developing reciprocal relations with local Indigenous peoples, and regarding them not just as cheap laborers or naïve informants but as knowledgeable intellectual collaborators. Stephen Hayden (Julian's son) attributed his father's cultural sensitivity to those early encounters in Nevada.

> I think that they (the whole lot of them) were probably the first Native Americans that Julian really got to know, and I think they left a strong and lasting impression— not only the love for Bertie, but the personalities of Endeka and Grandmother T[ahamont]. It was a good set up for some of his future work, recording the Pima Creation Myth, the Vi'ikita, and his friendship with Juan Xavier and other people of power.[39]

Julian Hayden was open to learning just about anything when, in 1935, he met up with Pima traditionalists Juan Smith and William Allison on the Gila River Reservation in Arizona. Over the course of several long nights, these otherwise close-mouthed traditionalists took a liking to Julian, and decided to share material that had never been recorded in print. This rare text, published as *The Hohokam Chronicles: The Short Swift Time of Gods on Earth*, consisted of "thirty-six distinct stories that begin with the creation of the universe and end with the establishment of the present-day village." Most importantly, it added living Pima voices to the ongoing archaeological debates (as yet unresolved by Frank H. Cushing, J. W. Fewkes, and others) over the origins of Pima-Papago-Hohokam tribal relations.[40]

Cave Explorers

During the three years of field seasons in Nevada, Bertha Parker continued her routine of making afternoon explorations, while recording her finds in small packets of handwritten field notes. Harrington praised her uncanny skill in spotting materials that others missed, at sites like the "Yewas Caves" that he named for her. In those caves, she found "the remnants of a bag made of yucca leaves" alongside a fragment of a pottery bowl, "cane arrows with wooden foreshafts and stone points hidden away in a deep crevice among the fallen rock," and "a piece of Indian hemp string in a crevice underneath a rock." At some sites, Endeka Harrington, Willis Evans, and Bertha Parker worked together as a team. At Bee Cave, Endeka discovered a rock shelter "in the conglomerate which yielded the greater part of a Paiute cooking pot," and Willis "found the bottom of a pot, perhaps the same one, in another pit." At the same site, they recovered an engraved stone "of the type known in the Moapa Valley as 'Paiute Maps'" and a "much weathered and primitive flint point."[41]

A later discovery, in the spring of 1930, drew international notice. The crew was working on the Gypsum Cave site, plowing through layers of fossilized dung identified by Professor Barnum Brown of the American Museum of Natural History as associated with the giant ground sloth, *Nothrotherium shastense*, a long-extinct inhabitant of the region during the Pleistocene era. The crew continued excavations, hopeful of finding the sloth itself, when Bertha's "keen eyes" spotted the skull lying in a layer above human artifacts. In an article for *Masterkey*, Harrington noted the remarkable opportunity this presented.

> It was not myself, but Yewas, alias Bertha Parker Pallan, our ambitious niece, who found the first sloth skull in the cave, the skull which Dr. Scherer has christened by "Gypsy Sloth," although Dr. Stock insists that it is a *Nothrotherium*. Bertie is expedition Secretary, but once-in-a-while she steals away to the Cave, trowel in hand, with her miner's light and dust-mask. . . . How she happened to stick her head under one rock in such a position that she could see the skull hidden under another I can't imagine, but she did it. . . .
>
> And because we have found in the same cave many things, mostly fragments of weapons, left by the earliest known human inhabitants of the Southwest, the Basket Makers, we agreed that here is probably the best opportunity for paleontologist and archeologist to work together on a single problem, North America's "Earliest Man."[42]

When Harrington promoted this find as evidence that challenged prevalent theories of ancient human occupation in the Americas, he knew that the team was treading on theoretically contentious ground. The entire archaeological profession was then entangled in fierce debates over the arrival of humans in North America, and over the supposed antiquity of American Indians. The "Bering Strait" theory of migration was in its infancy, and leading archaeologists across the continent were positioned to discredit every new "ancient" find. Harrington had, in fact, been warned by Frederic Ward Putnam to avoid having anything whatsoever to do with "Pleistocene Man in America—a subject taboo at that time." Putnam's recent article in *Science*, "indicating the association of man with the Ice Age mastodon," had been so scathingly criticized that he warned Harrington, "If you ever find anything that appears to be especially old, record it but don't interpret it, or you will get into serious trouble."[43]

Despite this warning, Harrington decided to meet the challenge head-on (so to speak). He sent the skull that Bertha had found to the California Institute of Technology (Cal Tech) for analysis. Dr. Chester Stock and Dr. E. L. Furlong immediately came out to visit the site, and were so excited that they offered funding for further excavations. Canadian paleontologist Dr. James Thurston was called in to verify the faunal remains. The find itself was remarkable enough, but it is notable that every man in the party respected Bertha Parker's skill as a field archaeologist. One might suggest that, as the niece of the field director, she received some kind of favoritism, but the first-person accounts suggest otherwise. In his field report, Dr. James A. B. Scherer of Cal Tech wrote:

> Harrington has with him, in addition to skilled Indian workmen, his wife and her niece, both of whom are experienced archaeologists. They, also, have Indian blood in their veins,—of distinguished lineage,—and perhaps this adds zest to the pursuit of their calling. At any rate, Bertha Pallan, the niece, made a sensational find in the cave before Harrington had time to do any digging at all. . . . A paleontologist would rather find a fresh ground sloth skull than its equal weight in gold nuggets. I shall never forget the enthusiasm with which Dr. Stock reported to me that the skull Mrs. Pallan had found was a very rare specimen of nothrotherium, and that he wanted me to go up to Gypsum Cave pronto.[44]

Scherer praised Bertha's other discoveries, noting the importance of "the many artifacts, or objects made by man's hands . . . [such as] pieces of beautifully twisted twine, made from yucca fiber, and certain small feathered objects" lying near the Pleistocene remains. The collaboration between Cal Tech and the Southwest Museum was touted as "the first known expedition where paleontologists and archaeologists have worked side by side from the very beginning of an undertaking of major scientific importance."[45] Bertha Parker Pallan was an essential member of the joint party; in addition to serving as expedition secretary, she assisted in digs and guided Thurston to other nearby sites to reexamine ancient faunal remains and artifacts.

The news made the headlines in papers across the continent. One of the first to report was the *Berkeley Daily Gazette*, in a lengthy article describing the Gypsum Cave discovery as potential proof of the "possible great antiquity of man on this continent," challenging the long-standing assumption that paleofauna had been "extinct for many thousands of years before the coming of man to America." After noting that the sloth skull had been "found under a large slab of stone by Mrs. Bertha Parker Pallan," the paper reported that further digging had revealed "the skeleton of a massively built ground-sloth [with] terrible claws, larger than those of any animal alive today." In addition, "within a few inches of the bones were found a piece of native cord made of

Figure 14 Original caption: "The sloth-finders." *Left to right*: Bertha Parker Pallan, Lyman Evans, and Myrtle (Mrs. Oliver Evans) at Gypsum Cave camp, Nevada, 1930. Photograph by Mark Raymond Harrington. Image P.22708. Courtesy of the Braun Research Library Collection, Autry Museum, Los Angeles.

yucca fibre and some small feathers bound with sinew, evidently either part of the trimmings of a prayer-stick or of some sort of headdress." The cave also held a large number of "darts hurled with the atlatl or dart thrower by the ancestors of the American Indians before the introduction of the bow and arrow. . . . Whether or not these darts were actually thrown at the ground-sloths still remains to be seen."[46]

The Associated Press released an illustrated article with a large feature photograph of Bertha. The same photo appeared in at least twenty newspapers across the continent, having circulated in "News of the Day in Pictures." The AP headline read: "Girl Leads Scientists to Nevada Prehistoric Find." The text clearly credited Bertha for the discovery, and gave her top billing alongside the team of scientists with doctoral degrees.

The keen eyes of BERTHA PARKER PALLAN (left) are credited with leading scientists exploring the Gypsum Cave, near Las Vegas, Nev., to the discovery of traces of prehistoric man estimated to be from 20,000 to 30,000 years old and far antedating any similar find ever made in the United States. Upper photo shows a group of scientists in the cave, left to right, Dr. Mark R. Harrington, Dr. J. A. B. Scherer, Dr. Chester Stock and Dr. E. L. Furlong. . . .

Miss Pallan, secretary of an expedition exploring the cave, detected the petrified remains of a giant ground sloth. Further investigation revealed traces of a campfire and ancient weapons which, the scientists declare, prove that men of "high intelligence" inhabited the cave from 20,000 to 30,000 years ago.[47]

In the press, as in his institutional reports, Dr. James A. B. Scherer, director of the Southwest Museum, praised this as "the most outstanding anthropological find ever made in the United States."[48] Over the course of the next year, virtually all the subsequent news reports highlighted not just the find but the novelty of the fact that a Native American woman had played such an important role.

To ensure proper verification and address any potential skeptics, Harrington then invited every scientist who expressed an interest to come and examine the Gypsum Cave site for himself. In January 1931, for example, Professor A. E. Jenks of the University of Minnesota arrived, ready to compare the Gypsum Cave materials to his recent studies of Paleolithic collections in North Africa and France. Jenks was poised to suggest what was then a very new theory: "He thinks man probably came to America from Asia over a Pleistocene land bridge during an inter-glacial period and that the American Indian is not descended from the Mongolian race but has developed here in this hemisphere entirely apart from it."[49]

Cave Explorers Are Married

All in all, the Gypsum Cave discovery had the potential to be a very dramatic contribution to Americanist archaeology. Harrington was especially pleased to have recruited Thurston, who, at the time, was considered the premier paleontologist on the continent. Trained by Charles M. Sternberg with the Geological Survey of Canada, Thurston had excavated dinosaur fossils in the Edmonton Formation, and served as a technician in zoology at the University of Alberta. He had accepted a position as a field collector for Cal Tech just a year before the sloth skull showed up, and he was the best man on the continent to analyze it.[50]

As it turned out, Thurston was also the best man for Bertha Parker. A little more than a year after they met, Bertha and James were married. The Parker–Thurston romance gained almost as much press as the Gypsum Cave discovery. The wedding announcement in *Masterkey* read:

Mystery, Revelations, Meaning—all these might be expected in the deep, dark, smelly depths of Gypsum Cave where once lurked a band of huge wooly ground sloths, clawsome and fearsome. But Romance? Who would expect to find that in such a place?

And yet, two members of our expedition discovered it there! Our own Bertha Parker Pallan, alias "Bertie," finder of the first and only perfect ground-sloth skull (not to speak of bushels of painted atlatl darts), was married July 3 to James E. Thurston, alias "Thirsty," ground-sloth hunter extra-ordinary to the California Institute of Technology, and finder of many other wonderful things in Gypsum Cave.

Whether the archeologists of the Southwest Museum and the paleontologists of "Cal-Tech" ever work together again, as a body, on the solution of a single problem, it is auspicious that Archeologist Bertie and Paleontologist Thirsty have decided to work out together the problems of life.[51]

Perhaps seeking to avoid the publicity that had accompanied her parents' celebrity wedding, Bertha arranged for a low-key private service at the Little Church of the Flowers, followed by a reception at "Ranchito Romulo," the San Fernando home of the Harringtons. The news of the wedding, however, made its way into newspapers across the West, due to the unusual circumstances of their meeting. An article titled "Cave Explorers Are Married: Caltech Paleontologist Weds Southwest Museum Worker" identified Bertha as the famous "girl archeologist [*sic*]," and noted, "the bride won distinction on that expedition through her discovery, in the depths of the cavern, of the skull of a strange extinct monster, the Ground Sloth Nothrotherium. . . . This find, the first of its kind, attracted world-wide attention."[52] Although Bertha had long been distant from her father, Arthur Parker, his fame made its way into her wedding announcements: "The bride also possesses the rare distinction of having been born on an archeological [*sic*] expedition while her father was State Archeologist of New York [*sic*]."[53]

When the Gypsum Cave digs in Nevada came to a close for the season, the entire party relocated to Los Angeles. Frederick Webb Hodge, the new director of the Southwest Museum, appointed Bertha Parker Thurston as head expedition secretary to catalog finds and write up reports, including the massive report on the Gypsum Cave site. The newlywed Mr. and Mrs. Thurston settled into what they hoped would be a stable family life, looking forward to spending their leisure time with Bertha's mother, Beulah, and her grandmother, Margaret Tahamont, who was still working in Hollywood films. In 1931 Margaret wrote to her cousin Emma Mead about the newlyweds: "They are happy. They have put their little girl in a Catholic School. She is six years old. She pays $35 a month for her board and tuition so I think it is the best place for her out here." Margaret also reported that Beulah had married again, and that she and her new husband, railyard worker Thomas Filson, had gone to northern California to pursue gold mining.[54]

All was well until February 1932, when tragedy struck. James Thurston suffered a sudden heart attack while lifting a rock at a research site, and he died on the spot.[55] Shortly thereafter, Bertha became very ill and had to take a leave from work; the Harringtons brought her to their home while she recovered. Later that year, the Southwest Museum, struggling against the general economic downturn, was considering layoffs. In a 1932 review of employees, Bertha Parker Thurston was described as follows: "Good worker. . . . Scientific turn of mind, considerable practical and theoretical knowledge of Southwestern archaeology, also Pleistocene paleontology. . . . Startling success in finding good things in the field."[56] Based on her past performance and future potential, Bertha was able to keep her job, at a time when so many in California were struggling to find work in the midst of the Great Depression. Sadly, in the aftermath of James's death, none of the members of the Gypsum Cave expedition, at the Southwest Museum or at Cal Tech, had the heart to continue without him. As a result, all research on the site stopped. The papers and ethnological materials remained in the Southwest Museum, and the sloth bones went to the California Institute of Technology, where they have remained, uncataloged, for decades. They have yet to be thoroughly examined.

Ironically, the Gypsum Cave discovery predated, by a little more than a year, the groundbreaking Clovis discovery made by Edgar B. Howard, archaeology research associate at the University of Pennsylvania Museum of Archaeology and Anthropology. In November 1932, after hearing that road crews had unearthed a cache of mammoth bones in Clovis, New Mexico, Howard visited the site and discovered carefully worked spear points lodged between faunal rib bones. The dating of the remains theoretically confirmed what was then a new hypothesis about the populating of the Americas: American Indians had migrated across the Bering Strait via a land bridge, after the Ice Age, following big game. Although this theory is still up for debate in archaeology, given the discovery of much older sites and evidence, Clovis is still considered to be highly significant.[57] The lithics universally described as "Clovis points" appear to be unique to the North American continent, and appear to date to a relatively narrow time zone (a few hundred years) approximately fourteen thousand years in the past. As described in a recent *Smithsonian* article:

> Clovis points are wholly distinctive. Chipped from jasper, chert, obsidian and other fine, brittle stone, they have a lance-shaped tip and (sometimes) wickedly sharp edges. . . . More than 10,000 Clovis points have been discovered, scattered in 1,500 locations throughout most of North America. . . . The near-simultaneous advent of Clovis points might represent the swift adoption of an improved technology by different groups, rather than the spread of one group. Still, most researchers believe

that the rapid dissemination of Clovis points is evidence that a single way of life—the Clovis culture—swept across the continent in a flash.[58]

Based on Howard's 1932 discovery, Clovis became the "gold standard" for proving the presence of ancient man in America, and for tracking the diffusion of Indigenous toolmaking (and toolmakers) across the continent. It was said to represent "the oldest unequivocal evidence of humans in the Americas, dating between 11,500 and 10,900 radiocarbon years before the present."[59] The concept of ancient people cohabiting with ancient beasts was omnipresent in regional Indigenous oral traditions, but these traditions were only considered to have been proven scientifically with the discovery of Clovis. Here was an opportunity where the team at the Southwest Museum could have blended archaeological with ethnological research, but for the fact that funding was running perilously short.

By April 1934, as the Southwest Museum was falling deeper into the economic downturn, Margaret Tahamont told her cousin Emma that Bertha "and all the others have got their salaries cut and don't know how long the museum will keep going."[60] When Bertha contracted a septic infection, Hodge queried whether she could continue to perform her job. In no uncertain terms, Harrington jumped to her defense, noting that she "had to fight against harrowing odds in every direction since she was a small child," and that she was still recovering from a recent operation, so "no wonder her work is falling off!"[61] He wrote a memo to the director stating that she was, in fact, indispensable to the museum.

> Bertha Thurston was one of the most useful members of the Gypsum Cave expedition and her work figured largely in the successful outcome of that project. When in good health her work at the Museum was most satisfactory as was her assistance in the preparation of the Gypsum Cave report. It is true that her interest lies along the lines represented by her title, "Assistant in Archaeology," rather than the routine typing and stenography, to which she has been restricted of late.[62]

Since all the men working for the museum had been routinely granted paid leaves of absence in matters of illness or emergency, Harrington insisted that Bertha should be afforded the same. Hodge agreed, and Endeka and M.R. brought her into their home to recover.

By June 1934 Bertha was back at work, and Howard decided to make a special trip to the Southwest Museum to meet with the Nevada team. The Clovis discovery had, by that time, gained an enormous amount of publicity, and it would have been timely to revisit the compelling evidence from the Gypsum Cave. Harrington arranged for Bertha to spend the day with Howard, and she graciously shared expedition sketches and field notes.[63] Howard must have found the material interesting, but there is no record that he ever followed up, perhaps because he was unwilling to unseat himself as the first person to locate evidence of the cohabitation of ancient humans and paleofauna in the southwest. Harrington never followed up either, for purely practical reasons: scientists at Cal Tech lost interest in the site after Thurston's death, and Harrington had found other high-paying archaeological work for the Army Corps of Engineers.

Research in the Hills and Deserts

Bertha Parker Pallan Thurston's career encompassed more than archaeology. At the Southwest Museum, she held positions as both assistant archaeologist and assistant ethnologist, and in 1933 she initiated a series of field trips to Native communities in the California hills. She was often accompanied by her mother, Beulah Tahamont Parker O'Brien Filson, to meet with Maidu medicine men, Paiute basket makers, Pomo bear maskers, and storytellers from both Maidu and Yurok communities. Small portions of Bertha's handwritten field journals and notes have survived, buried in the working papers of (and mistakenly attributed to) Mark Raymond Harrington. The error is obvious, because their handwriting is so unmistakably different, and because, after 1933, they worked on independent research in separate locales.[64]

One of Bertha's first published articles for *Masterkey* described her reexamination of the "Scorpion Hill" site that she had initially excavated in 1929. After a seven-hundred-mile drive across the desert, she and her mother found that local pothunters had looted the site. Disappointed but undaunted, Bertha organized other research projects. In June 1934 the two women visited "Box Canyon," where they had been warned that the "Indians down there has a language of their own," and that they had best be armed.[65] Intriguing as this sounds, apart from scant references in a letter to Emma Mead and Bertha's field notes, no records of their encounters with those people appear to have survived.

Bertha's field notes also reveal small but important details that illustrate her ability to distinguish between natural features and man-made constructions, and to recognize patterns of Indigenous occupation that might escape casual observers. In another section of Box Canyon, after spotting a "wind-eroded hole in boulder" alongside an "Indian cave dwelling," she returned to make observations such as the following:

> Can't date very well, desolate area, used only as a trail . . . so no Indian relics, mescal pits on ridges . . . old camp on inaccessible mesa, only one trail—was partly fortified

w breast wk [work] to command trail—covered w obsid & arrowheads—used to be magnesium spring . . . wind caves in soft sandstone.[66]

She also sifted local folklore for clues. At one locale, she heard of an old Indian who had filled a pot with gold, gone "away up canyon, hid until time for ceremony," but died before he could recover it. Her unnamed informant insisted the pot was still out there, hidden away under the "biggest rock," but he "couldn't tell which biggest, so dug none." Bertha's notes for that site include a plan to start measuring rocks. At Canebreak Canyon, her mother "found shattered olla among fragments." Near a cliff dweller site inhabited by what locals described as a "medicine man," Beulah "found half dozen ceremonial weapons (one encrusted with abalone shells) in reed quiver."[67] Every page of these notebooks is rich with tantalizing clues for future research: evidence of ancient lithic tool production, fortifications that bespeak old conflicts, abalone inclusions in ceremonial weapons, and sites with medicinal spring waters (not to mention that olla filled with gold).

Periodic notices in *Masterkey* would announce where Bertha Parker Thurston was going, where she had been, and what she had discovered. Her field notes, correspondence, photographs, and publications, when woven together, can be used to conceptually reconnect multiple communities and purposes. These field trips often included visits to her mother, jaunts to gather herbal medicines, surveys of potential archaeological sites, providing transportation for Native elders, and, when necessary, seeking out healing for herself.

One summer, she accompanied the stepdaughter of one of her informants to visit a Maidu medicine man, noting, "My mother and I decided that it would accomplish the double purpose of business and pleasure if we drove Alice to his place."[68] They met with Jim Stevens, who agreed to conduct an elaborate healing ceremony to address distinct injuries that each of the three women suffered from. Bertha's resulting article, "A Night in a Maidu Shaman's House," is so poetically written that a reader can practically hear the rattle and feel the wind blowing through the floorboards. Jim and his wife (called "Old Woman") were gentle and compassionate individuals, genuinely interested in the health of their visitors, going to some effort to perform a ritual intended to heal old wounds.

When morning came, Jim blessed each person, chanting in his native tongue, while he sprinkled water on our heads and gave us a sip of water from the cup he held in his hand; then he drank the remainder. He did this to cleanse us of any evil spirits that we might harbor. He next presented me with a very small basket, about two inches in diameter, which was his choicest possession, as "Old Woman" had made it for him many years ago. "Old Woman," not to be outdone, and to accomplish a double purpose, presented my mother with a larger basket. This was made by a Lake County Indian woman, who had given it to Jim for doctoring her.[69]

Acts of generosity like this typified long-standing patterns of reciprocity that cemented social relationships among Native peoples. In this case, there was also a self-serving purpose. Bertha explained: "Old Woman was jealous of this woman's weaving and gave the basket away so that she would not have it around for comparison with her own baskets."[70]

On a second visit, Jim and his wife fed Bertha and Beulah a stew with what appeared to be venison but was, upon closer inspection, "dear" meat (from a dog) and not "deer" meat. It might seem that the couple fed their visitors the family dog (food was scarce during the depression), but it is more likely that the meal was either a special offering for guests or part of a ritual practice.[71] A. L. Kroeber observed that some California Indians (even after missionary influence) routinely consumed dog meat.[72] From a Seneca perspective, great value was placed on dogs as potential carriers of messages to the beyond, and the killing and consumption of them was never done casually. In retrospect, Bertha considered the advice she had been given when preparing for her first meeting with Jim. She had been told to "bring him a fresh newspaper—don't expect them to feed you."[73]

The generous nature of these Maidu ritualists contrasts sharply with another informant, "an old Indian medicine man from northern California. For obvious reasons his name and tribe are omitted." In the article "How He Became a Medicine Man," she explains that "John" was a drunkard, raising a ruckus in church and cursing the minister, until the day he rode his horse "up into the hills" to nap under an oak tree. There, he was awakened by a ghostly visitor, who told him:

> You have the power to see things that are not meant for everybody to see, and can talk with the spirits from another world. All this time you have been wasting yourself on drink and bad habits . . . [they] walked a long way, then the man told me to face the east where the sun rises. This I did, and what do you think? I saw all my people that had passed on. . . . They all disappeared, and then I saw a great giant of a man standing by a big table. He had an arm about four feet long, and in his hand he held a huge knife just like a sword. Then I looked to one side and saw a pretty pool of clear water.[74]

The man with the knife cut out the hearts of "bad people" and threw them in the pool, where the water washed them clean and they were renewed. He told John to throw away his bottle, embrace his own power, and help his own people. John became a "good Christian" and also gained power as a "medicine man," noting that, now, "I have always had a home, tobacco, and food. Sometimes I run low, but my power is always with me and some way I get what I want."[75]

A subsequent story, "How a Maidu Medicine Man Lost His Power," links the transgression of spiritual protocols to the loss of magical powers. Bertha's informant answered her question: "You ask if a medicine-man can lose his power? Yes, it is possible. I was present when one of my friends lost his power in 1929."[76] The unnamed narrator recounted:

My friend was one of the best medicine-men we had around here, and he was young too, which made his power much stronger. He cured many people and his prophecies always seemed to come true. But he could not resist the ladies, and often he would resort to witchcraft. This of course was the beginning of his downfall.

Every time he held a ceremony to foretell events, he received warnings from them to behave, and each time he promised to obey. It was his duty to do good for others, and not harm by the use of sorcery. But he was tempted, and fell by the wayside.[77]

After marrying a much younger woman, the medicine man looked suspiciously younger; to the Maidu this dramatic change in appearance signaled that the man was stealing youth (as a form of power) from his wife. As a direct result, the spirits (which, Bertha noted, must remain unnamed) came after him in the form of a storm, and a sudden lightning bolt struck inside the house.

We rushed in to help and found him bleeding from the mouth. We then carried him outside and tried to revive him, but it was about an hour before he regained his senses. From that day to this he has had no power at all to cure people, although he still tries to doctor. The only power he still has is the ability to reach up behind his ear with his thumb, scratch, and produce fire and light his cigarettes. Too bad he will never retain his power, but it is a lesson well remembered by other medicine-men.[78]

These stories resonated with familiar Indigenous tropes: recourse to substances and actions (drink, medicines, prayer, etc.) that could poison or inspire visions, gifts (food, tobacco, shelter, etc.) offered to spirits or human agents, unexpected bodily dangers (drowning, burning, lightning, etc.) that could cause spiritual or physical transformations, and spirits seeking retribution.

Bertha was able to gather these stories and other unique kinds of information from her subjects, likely because they recognized her as a fellow Native. She was sensitive to cultural protocols and was willing to reveal or conceal names as necessary. The failed medicine man remained unnamed, but the Native women that Bertha interviewed often received editorial credit or co-authorship. One set of attributions identifies stories as follows: "by Bertha

Parker Cody, as Related by Mandy Wilson."[79] Another group of stories were presented "as told by Jane Van Stralen to Bertha Parker Cody."[80] This wording is subtle, but significant, since the naming of her collaborators coincided with Bertha's shift toward Indigenous activism, and her increased preference for working with living urban Native communities rather than deserted Native archaeological sites.

Hollywood Indians

During the 1930s Margaret, Beulah, and Bertha were among a growing group of educated urban Indians who built connections between Native Californian communities and the Hollywood Indian community in Los Angeles, where actors from different tribes across the country struggled to survive in a fantasy land far from home. A few years after Thurston's death, Bertha reconnected with an old friend from Hollywood, the famous actor Iron Eyes Cody, born Espera Oscar de Corti (1904–99). They had met years earlier when she was a teenager, and she finally agreed to marry him in August 1936. Mark Raymond Harrington was skeptical but supportive, and he notified Charles Amsden at the Southwest Museum: "Bertha will want to continue her Museum work. . . . We wish them every happiness."[81]

When Hollywood Indians started to meet with Maidu, Yurok, Pomo, and other Indigenous Californians, seeds were planted that would grow into a more widespread demand for Native peoples to recover sovereign tribal rights. Bertha positioned herself at the center of the Native rights movement in California, as hostess and co-organizer for the very first meeting of the California Indian Rights Association, held at the Southwest Museum. The 1939 meeting of the California Indian Rights Association at the Southwest Museum (a standing-room-only event) resulted in the passage of a resolution to convince the state legislature and U.S. Congress to establish an annual "Indian Day."[82] Perhaps not coincidentally, Arthur Parker had proposed just such an initiative decades ago through the Society of American Indians.

Bertha's new husband, Oscar, had an oversized ego and, by all accounts, was a braggart and a terrible flirt, but those who knew them personally say that they had a stable marriage, and that he supported Bertha's work at the museum (despite rumors to the contrary).[83] At museum events, Oscar appeared in a suit and tie, nearly unrecognizable without his feather headdress and wig. He was generous in finding jobs for Native American actors in Hollywood. For example, when the Actors' Guild restricted his public presentations (since they held the license for his persona of "Iron Eyes Cody"), he arranged for others to perform in his place. Neighbors recall that (despite the bizarre tales in his autobiography) he was kind to Beulah and Bertha, and was good to his stepdaughter, Wilma Mae (Billie).[84] Tragically, Billie died at the age of seventeen while hunting with her grandmother, when a rifle fired accidentally as she was climbing over a fence.[85]

After Billie's death in 1942, Bertha resigned from her job at the Southwest Museum, but she continued to serve as a consultant, and helped the Harringtons promote the Casa de Adobe renovation. Oscar started up a new consulting business called "Ironeyes Enterprise" and the couple served as technical advisers and wardrobe experts, including renting Native garments to the film studios. As recognized regional experts on Indians, they also collaborated on pageants and school programs, and hosted a popular California television program on Native American Indian history and folklore. The Codys were especially outspoken about concerns facing the other members of the "Hollywood Indian colony." In 1949, for example, in an article titled "Hollywood Tribe on Warpath; Seek More Wampum," Iron Eyes discussed rental bias in the housing market, and competition for work, explaining, "We'd like to see if there isn't something we can do about guaranteeing our people the right to keep their homes." Iron Eyes was one of the organizers of the newly formed Indian Citizens League that aimed to prevent evictions and ethnic biases in zoning. He told the reporter that mixed marriages were especially frowned upon in California; a local "white man, married to a redskin, has to pretend she's his maid so he can keep his house." Iron Eyes threatened to "hit the warpath in the local courts, to see if these laws can't be changed," and promised to use the profit from his recent appearance for Paramount on the Bob Hope picture *Paleface* to fund the effort.[86]

Despite the bravado, acting was not easy work; in one 1945 letter to M.R. and Endeka, Bertha wrote that Oscar would be away for months, and was expected to be on set "10 hrs a day 7 days a week again. They allow no time off."[87] By 1949 the Indian colony in Hollywood had diminished from "several thousand" to only about sixty people, "all of whom work constantly in movies," and competition was fierce. Since her ethnic beauty was a desirable commodity, Bertha went back into acting, and also posed for painters. In one instance, she posed for John Steele, for a painting of Kateri Tekakwitha (a seventeenth-century Mohawk convert) that still appears on Catholic prayer cards today.[88] The Codys also published several books on sign language, illustrated with photos of themselves demonstrating the signs.[89] When interviewed by the *Bakersfield Californian*, Bertha was identified as "the wife of one of Hollywood's best experts on Indian lore and a frequent movie technical advisor, [who] has been in movies ever since she was a papoose." The reporter noted that her grandfather Elijah Tahamont (a.k.a. Dark Cloud) was one of the most famous Indian actors in history, having appeared in D. W. Griffith's *Birth of a Nation* and *Intolerance*. Bertha told the reporter, "Most of the permanent

Figure 15 Bertha Parker in a white deerskin dress, during her years as a Hollywood actress. Photographer and date unknown. From Iron Eyes Cody and Collin Perry, *Iron Eyes: My Life as a Hollywood Indian* (New York: Everest House, 1982), following p. 98. Courtesy of Robert Tree Cody.

Indian residents of Hollywood today are professional actors . . . born and raised in show business," but "if they can't get enough real Indians locally," she confided, the studios did not hesitate to paint white actors in redface.[90]

The irony of this statement—non-Native actors in "Redface" being hired to replace Native American actors—cannot possibly have been lost on their friends. While the Hollywood world (and the film-going public) believed that Iron Eyes was American Indian, virtually all the Native peoples who knew and worked with him were aware of the fact that his birth family was Italian. Espera Oscar de Corti had changed his name and persona as a young man, and he was accepted as Native kin for reasons that are still poorly understood today.[91] Although he was obviously "passing," he was a savvy businessman who could secure good jobs in Hollywood films for Indian extras, at a time when work was otherwise hard to come by. When the studios bought his act, the entire Hollywood Indian community benefited.

During the early 1950s, Bertha and Oscar adopted two Native American boys of Maricopa-Dakota heritage. Robert and Arthur were coached in performing and powwow dancing by their father, and the family was especially active in events at the Indian Center, a gathering place for urban Indians who had relocated to Los Angeles.[92] Glenda Ahhaitty, who was a close friend of the family for decades, recalled their generosity, explaining that they

> usually had a freezer of turkeys, distributed food [at] various times of the year and assisted in the kitchen at community events in Indian families who had been moved here on relocation. When folks needed help they would go to their home for a few dollars to get them through. Jim Thorpe & Ira Hayes lived in the basement of her home in Echo Park for a time. . . . She ran her household. When she died Iron could not even find the keys to the freezer.[93]

Ahhaitty also recalled the family's sideline business of making and renting Indian costumes to Hollywood studios, noting, "Watching old movies I often see things that belonged to Iron and Birdie [Bertha's nickname] on various actors."[94] Iron Eyes was extraordinarily successful in Hollywood, but he was also generous, assisting American Indian actors who were down on their luck, and paying the funeral expenses for those who died destitute.

Bertha passed away in 1978, and a decade after her death, Oscar de Corti published a lurid account (largely ghost-written by Collin Perry) of their lives together that bore little resemblance to truth. His Hunter Thompson–esque narrative *Iron Eyes Cody: My Life as a Hollywood Indian* is packed with fact and fiction. His encounters with the rich and famous are mostly true, but the "Birdie" character in this book bears little resemblance to the real Bertha Parker.[95] Birdie and her mother, Beulah, are both cast as hard-drinking, hard-partying women at the center of Iron Eyes's life, even during the years when they were actually elsewhere. Innocent readers might assume that Iron Eyes was intimately involved with Bertha's archaeological career, but virtually every detail of those years in this book is a documentable falsehood. Iron Eyes was *not* married to Bertha in 1925; they did *not* go to Nevada together; she did *not* give birth to a baby girl when she was with him; and he did *not* accompany her on her trips to interview Maidu medicine men. Also (although this is a small point), she did *not* wear "knee-high moccasins" at the Gypsum Cave dig; she wore knee socks and work boots. Even the dates and details of the children's lives and origins were fictionalized. The only true depictions of Bertha in *Iron Eyes: My Life as a Hollywood Indian* appear poignantly near the beginning and the end: Bertha and Oscar did first meet as Hollywood extras around 1926, and he was at her side in the hospital when she died in 1978.[96]

Reading between the lines of this book, one finds that Iron Eyes reveals his motive: the book itself was a performance piece, a work of fiction very loosely based on his life.

> My story isn't really a reflection of Indians per se any more than the shenanigans of some white actors are a reflection of white Americans as a whole. Or, I don't know, maybe it is—you'll have to decide that one, depending on your politics or your view of America itself. I guess all I'm saying is that this is the story of my life and it's a story about Hollywood. The Indians who participated in acting out their role in the myth of the American West, including myself, *became* part of Hollywood.[97]

Iron Eyes Cody's "Indian" persona was firmly rooted in playing to the popular cultural stereotype, and so, as scholars of film have observed, his so-called biography must be seen as a farce, a piece of performance art scripted to titillate white audiences. As Michelle H. Raheja so astutely notes in *Reservation Reelism*, Cody was committed to performing "masculine redfacing" that fulfilled "his reader's desire for an authentic Native American subject." In public, and in front of the cameras, "Iron Eyes" acted like a hypersexualized wild man: that act brought in the biggest bucks. But at home—as is evidenced in Bertha's correspondence, family memories, and the annals of the Los Angeles Indian community—Oscar was gregarious, generous, and supportive of his wife, in whatever role she wanted, or needed, to play.[98]

Recognizing the First Female Native American Archaeologist

Even though Bertha Parker's ethnological and archaeological research tapered off over time, she remained active in the museum world. She was listed in the

1938 *International Directory of Anthropologists*, and she remained an active member of the Society for American Archaeology and the Southwest Archaeological Federation, and was secretary for the California Regional Archaeological Survey.[99] Later in life, her fame faded. Her public obituary correctly identified her as a writer for *Masterkey*, ethnologist, and archaeologist but also characterized her as apparently inextricable from the men around her: she was "Arthur Parker's daughter," "Harrington's niece," and "Iron Eyes Cody's wife."[100] Her brief death notice in the *Newsletter of the American Anthropological Association* identified her only as an assistant at the Southwest Museum.[101] She was not included in the supposedly comprehensive anthropology, ethnology, and archaeology section of the "field and career index" to *Women in Particular*.[102] Her gravestone names her only as "Mrs. Iron Eyes Cody."

This silence is notable, since Bertha appears to have been the most famous (perhaps even the first) female Native American archaeologist of her time. Perhaps the omissions were due to shifts in Bertha's public identity, her name changes, or some confusion between her Hollywood and museum personas. Her experiences in anthropology show that gender, race, education, and position were not as limiting as might be imagined. Despite a lack of university credentials, a young Native American woman could achieve scientific success and public acclaim in a white man's field by applying her hard work and innate curiosity.

In 2004 the Society for American Archaeology (SAA) posted a query to an academic chat list, H-Amindian, seeking to create a scholarship in honor of the first female Native American archaeologist, to complement the scholarship named for the first male Native American archaeologist, who, not coincidentally, happens to be Arthur C. Parker. Respondents proposed several Native women who received professional degrees during the 1960s, but all were latecomers to the discipline; I insisted that it was long past time to give Bertha Parker Pallan Thurston Cody her due.[103] Perhaps at some point in the future, the SAA will recognize Bertha as, if not the first Native American woman to put a trowel to ground, at least the first to be paid for doing so, and the first to have earned a professional appointment in archaeology and ethnography. She conducted her research with hard work and dedication, making discoveries and contributing insights that impressed the trained archaeologists around her. Like her mother, Beulah, she deserves to be remembered not just for her beauty or her associations with famous men but for her scientific skills and fierce determination to survive.

5

Resisting Red Power

Jesse Cornplanter and William Fenton

> Naturally, in an attempt to simplify and make things clear to others, I have probably omitted details that are all important to you.
>
> —William Fenton to Jesse Cornplanter, February 15, 1935

Cattaraugus Seneca artist Jesse J. Cornplanter (1889–1957) and anthropologist William Nelson Fenton (1908–2005) had an extraordinarily productive (and also contentious) relationship over the course of four decades. When they met in 1933, Cornplanter was a forty-four-year-old World War I veteran, wood carver, illustrator, and Longhouse traditionalist, who had already enjoyed several decades of working with Arthur Parker at the Rochester Public Museum (now the Rochester Museum and Science Center).[1] Fenton was a twenty-five-year-old Yale doctoral student eager to learn more about the Six Nations Haudenosaunee, starting with the Seneca.

The Fenton family's relations with Seneca people began during a bitter winter in the 1860s, when Fenton's great-grandmother Fanny Carr offered shelter to Seneca hunter Amos Snow and family. As a token of thanks, Mrs. Snow gifted Carr with a porcupine quill–embroidered burden strap to metaphorically "bind" the families in friendship. The Snows and other Seneca people subsequently paid regular visits to the family farm, situated between the Cattaraugus and Allegany Reservations. Young William was exposed to anthropology early on, through visits with archaeologists Warren K. Moorehead, Mark Raymond Harrington, and Arthur Parker when they passed through. The impressionable lad developed a taste for collecting, starting with the burden strap, two ceremonial wooden masks, and a string of wampum that became the foundation of an amateur "Indian collection" kept in the family attic.[2]

Fenton's college studies turned toward anthropology, and after graduating from Dartmouth in 1931, he began graduate study at Yale, working under the mentorship of Frank Speck from the University of Pennsylvania. At the encouragement of linguist Edward Sapir (who was then the Sterling Professor at Yale), Fenton returned to Allegany to conduct field research on ceremonial practices and social organization.[3] During the summer of 1933, his relationship with the Snow family was reawakened and reversed, in a sense, when Fenton became the one in need of shelter. He was allowed to set up a tent in the yard of Jonas Snow, Amos's son. That first field season was a blur: "I kept a journal, which is a miscellany of family life, medicines, rattlesnakes, turtles, drunks, feuds, friends, ball games, singing society sessions, mutual aid activities, and social dances at the longhouse. It was all quite confusing at first."[4] Fenton attended dances and ritual observances, and was permitted to accompany John Jimerson to the renewal of the "Little Water Medicine" rite, in part because he owned one of the few cars on the reservation and was willing to drive.[5]

By the year's end, members of the Coldspring Longhouse had decided to ritually adopt Fenton and bestow a Seneca name upon him. Here, it is important to reiterate that the Seneca practice of ritually adopting and renaming select outsiders served several Indigenous purposes. During the colonial era, names (and sometimes nicknames) were routinely given to both colonial officials and adopted captives to situate them within the Indigenous social system. According to present-day Seneca Faithkeeper G. Peter Jemison, the Seneca also used naming as a political strategy. During the nineteenth and twentieth centuries, adoptions marked certain people as acceptable visitors, formalized their position in the community within a specific family and clan, and, hopefully, instilled a sense of kin responsibilities that would encourage them to use their privileged positions in ways that would benefit the tribe. Thus, names were bestowed on well-placed white power brokers—Lewis H. Morgan, Harriet Maxwell Converse, Joseph Keppler, Mark Raymond Harrington, Frank Speck, and others—to encourage them to negotiate, advocate, and report on political discussions, legislation, and so on that might affect the Seneca. At the very least, the social obligations that accompanied Iroquoian naming included the expectation that adoptees would act in the best interests of their adopted clan and community.[6]

Out of recognition of the Fenton family's long friendship with the Snow family, Fenton was adopted by the Seneca Hawk clan and given Jonas Snow's boyhood name of Howan'eyao, meaning "He loses a game, or a wager." As Fenton later recalled, his new responsibilities included

> pledging his loyalty to them and his devotion in times of hardship. He must remember that whenever there are ceremonies at the Longhouse that he should contribute. . . . In following years, I would learn more of the obligations of clanship, its benefits, and demands. The name given me followed or preceded me wherever I went among the Iroquois people.[7]

The January 26, 1934, ceremony at the Coldspring Longhouse at Allegany included the requisite singing, dancing, and public greeting of the new clan

Figure 16 Anthropologist William N. Fenton photographing Seneca Indians at Coldspring on the Allegany Reservation. Photograph by R. E. Keene. Courtesy of the American Philosophical Society.

member. This adoption publicly marked Fenton as a welcome visitor and gave him a mediated level of inside access to traditional elders and activities there and elsewhere. Fenton's clan family at Allegany introduced him to adherents of the Handsome Lake tradition at Tonawanda, where he was welcomed as kin by members of that nation's Hawk clan.[8]

Geographically, the Haudenosaunee are conceptualized along an east-west orientation. The Mohawk are positioned at the "Eastern Door" around the Mohawk and Hudson Rivers, and the Seneca are positioned at the "Western Door" between Rochester and Niagara Falls. Fenton's appearance at the Western Door, at that moment in time, gave him a unique vantage point into the Iroquois League (Six Nations Haudenosaunee), writ large, in New York and Canada. Fenton stayed at Tonawanda from 1935 to 1937, during the Great Depression, serving as a community worker for the United States Indian Service. At first, he was eager to assist tribal peoples in adapting to modernity, as one of a cadre of young white scholars hired as community workers to help orchestrate Franklin D. Roosevelt's "Indian New Deal" program.[9] After realizing that many of the "old ways" had survived, Fenton used his residency at Tonawanda to develop his own research. In 1936, before Fenton had even completed his PhD degree, Yale agreed to publish his dissertation as a book, *An Outline of Seneca Ceremonies at Cold Spring Longhouse*.[10] From that moment in time, Fenton was recognized and accepted by academia as an expert on all things Haudenosaunee.

Jesse Cornplanter—Aboriginally Yours

At Tonawanda, William Fenton met the Seneca traditionalist, carver, illustrator, and singer who became his language tutor, cultural guide, and close collaborator: Jesse Cornplanter, Cattaraugus Seneca, the community's "resident intellectual."[11] As a child, young Jesse was first known by the traditional names of Ganondayeon? ("deserted village") and later Hayonwan?i:s ("he strikes the rushes"). He was exposed to anthropology as a teenager, by watching his father, Edward Cornplanter, working closely with Arthur Parker in recording the Code of Handsome Lake at Tonawanda in 1913. Jesse was an eager student who perfected his writing skills in the Newtown district school. As an adult, he became a man of many skills: carver of traditional masks, dancer, singer, showman, and illustrator. His natural gifts as a cultural intermediary enabled him to fill multiple roles, as "Keeper of the Faith" at the Newtown longhouse (a Wolf clan position inherited from his father), as a cultural performer with the "Indian Curio & Entertainment Company," and as manager of the Allegany Indian Lacrosse Team. He also served as an anthropological informant for several researchers, starting with Arthur Parker (Seneca) at the Rochester

Museum and John N. B. Hewitt (Tuscarora) at the Smithsonian Bureau of American Ethnology.[12]

Cornplanter was living at Tonawanda with his wife, Elsina Billy, when he first met William Fenton.[13] At the time, Cornplanter was a shell-shocked war veteran and traditionalist in search of academic allies who would help him put his thoughts to paper, his stories into books, and his carvings into museums. He welcomed Fenton as an ally; this was unusual, since "Indians usually complained about anthropologists." Cornplanter told Fenton:

> Much have been written and said but still not enough about the things worth knowing as regards to our people as they were or as they did in their days. I always said that you are the one person who can correct the errors made by students or historians regarding early history. I am pulling for you Old-Timer go to it. . . . My only regret is my inability to do the very thing you are doing due to a lack of proper education and training.[14]

Their correspondence began with mutual admiration of their common desire to collect Seneca knowledge that was presumed to be vanishing. Over the course of three decades, Cornplanter supplied Bill Fenton (and others) with stories, illustrations, songs, material culture, and a wealth of ritual Seneca knowledge. He created pen-and-ink drawings of clan activities, longhouse gatherings, and traditional objects for museum exhibits and publications. Cornplanter was a generous informant and a compulsive writer; he exchanged dozens of letters (many signed, "Aboriginally yours") with Joseph Keppler, Clark Wissler, Harold Conklin, Frank Speck, and other salvage anthropologists.

Researchers like Bill Fenton were so desirous of information that they would jump at opportunities to collect it from whomever offered; informants like Jesse were so in need of income that they would eagerly procure (or, when expedient, produce) whatever was desired for whomever could pay. There were minimal (if any) protocols in place for vetting the authenticity of materials or the trustworthiness of participants in exchanges that seemed, even at the time, to have been ethically questionable. Cornplanter was a Faithkeeper at Newtown, but that did not grant him unrestricted access to Haudenosaunee rituals and governance, or unrestricted permission to share or sell information. Fenton held an adoptive Seneca name and clan affiliation, but he had no cultural right to control the circulation of Seneca culture or property. The two men tussled over intellectual credit: Cornplanter wanted to be recognized as a source of Indigenous knowledge; Fenton desired intellectual control over his scholarship. Neither man held exclusive rights to Seneca knowledge, but each behaved as though they had free rein.

Although Fenton claimed to be a devout proponent for Native American cultural continuity, he was primarily focused on separating ancient from modern practices, collecting only what appeared (to him) to be "authentic." Following in the footsteps of his idols—Lewis H. Morgan, J. N. B. Hewitt, and Arthur Parker—he carefully maneuvered himself into a position as an Iroquois expert, while often serving as his own fact checker. As a case in point, Fenton's summary of Coldspring Longhouse ceremonies was based on data gathered from John Jimerson and Henry Red Eye at Allegany and Jesse Cornplanter and Elijah David at Tonawanda. After preparing his manuscript, Fenton "read it over" to Leroy Cooper, and then published it in an academic journal without re-contacting his original informants. He later wrote to Cornplanter that this was a routine and accepted practice in academia.

> I wished I could have had your censorship. It may not present the material as you see it. No two people see eye to eye, as you have often told me. Naturally, in an attempt to simplify and make things clear to others, I have probably omitted details that are all important to you. After all you know how much material I really have.[15]

This became a recurring pattern: once a piece was written, Fenton would circulate it for fact-checking, not to the Native peoples who had supplied the raw data but to his non-Native colleagues. Since some Native informants were unable to read English, Fenton would simply gloss the text verbally in person, or skip over them to find another reader. It was hard, however, for Fenton to avoid scrutiny by Cornplanter, who seemed to be in touch with everybody. Whenever Cornplanter complained (as he often did) and needed money (equally often), Fenton would offer payment as appeasement. For example, after admitting to having omitted important details from the Coldspring report, Fenton promised Cornplanter "a few bucks for answering the questions I sent." He reiterated their financial arrangements, knowing that other work was hard to come by: "I used to pay you 50¢ per hour, when I paid you. Therefore you ought to put in 16 hours of writing time for 8 bucks. I know I'm a tightwad, but everyone's pants are thin these days."[16]

Jesse Cornplanter was in a complicated liminal position. Seneca people still practiced traditional ways, but, as elsewhere across the continent, the marketing of Indigenous identity had become a crucial source of income. As he told Bill, "We are the subject of the prying eyes of so-called Science. Every 'ologist' comes to us."[17] Many Native families and individuals responded to that curiosity by strategically creating altered or "invented" versions of traditions to perform for white audiences.[18] Hewitt criticized one of Cornplanter's Seneca pageants as mere "show stuff," but, as Cornplanter explained, he was forced

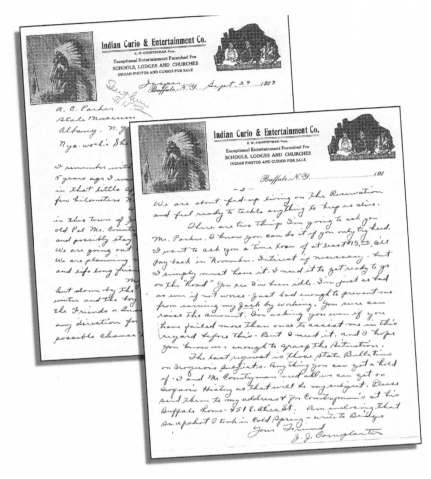

Figure 17 Letter from Jesse Cornplanter to Arthur Parker, September 24, 1923, requesting a loan of fifteen dollars to support his "Indian Curio & Entertainment" enterprise. Archived in the William N. Fenton Papers at APS. Photograph by Margaret Bruchac. Courtesy of the American Philosophical Society.

to construct a new version because traditional leaders had warned him against performing traditions publicly.[19]

Cornplanter also worked as an agent securing work for other Native peoples. In a 1942 letter to William Waller Edwards, he recommended Dwight Jimerson for constructing longhouses and bows, and praised the beadwork being done by Seneca women. He cautioned Edwards, however, against the lower-quality tourist art being produced by the Works Progress Administration (WPA) and Indian Welfare Association, denouncing "white folks who make a living off from the W.P.A. teaching Indians how to be Indians." Cornplanter, not incidentally, was one of the WPA's most prolific artists.[20]

In one exchange of letters in 1936, Cornplanter offered to share sketches and photographs of the ceremonial Seneca masks in his possession (often called "false faces"). Fenton refused, claiming they were rare, valuable, and sacred objects that had been entrusted to him personally. This is an odd refusal, given that Cornplanter had been so generous in assisting Fenton. He expressed appreciation for Fenton's "strong attachment to our own people," saying, "That is very good of you and no doubt you have felt within yourself the feeling of duty well done and all that sort of things." He insisted that he, as a Seneca traditionalist, had more rights to Seneca material than any white man, and he took especial offense at the insistence on signing an "Official or Affidavit form authorizing you to give out datas, sketches or any thing you have in your collection," since this would be tantamount to recognizing Fenton's ownership of the data. Cornplanter wrote: "Well if that is the case, I say Forget It! . . . I can get along some way without bothering about your Masks."[21]

Cornplanter further explained that this was an important Indian Arts and Crafts project sponsored by Arthur Parker as part of a regional cultural recovery effort. Cornplanter and his wife had specifically been hired to re-create lost arts, "things our ancestors made ages ago," working from photographs furnished by the Rochester Museum, and they were very much in need of traditional ritual objects to work from. He wrote:

> I did not expect my request for sketches would stir up so much agitation as it did. . . . You should lay us a visit and see for yourself the many wonderful things that are made here by us. I suppose according to your opinion, we are nothing but a cheap bunch of Copy-cats or at best Poor Imitators trying to make a living, anyway I don't give a Hoot what I am called. . . . There is one thing I resent, that is to be humiliated just because there happens to be a reason.[22]

The dispute became a moot point when WPA funding eventually diminished and the Seneca Arts Project ended around 1941.[23] By then, Cornplanter had other irons in the fire.

With the assistance of Nameé Price Henricks of Penn Yan, New York, Cornplanter was working on producing his own book of Seneca legends with stories and illustrations. Henricks, a minister's wife and social activist, was close to influential people, notably Arthur Parker at the Rochester Public Museum and First Lady Eleanor Roosevelt, and she kept watch for impending threats. Cornplanter wrote, "She seems to get what she fights for, she says the Roosevelts are intimate friends to her, as well as Gov. Lehman, she sees Comm. Collier in person. We are fortunate in having her as our adopted friend and fighter."[24] During the 1930s Henricks pressured state and federal agencies to secure work-relief projects, emergency supplies, road maintenance, and other projects, and she also worked to gain Roosevelt's support for the construction of the new community building on the reservation.[25] Henricks was adopted by the Tonawanda Seneca and regarded as a trusted ally who, Cornplanter made a point of telling Fenton, "does not care to even get publicity or credit for all she is doing for her chosen people."[26]

Preserving Culture

During the first few decades of his career, Fenton was a regular and welcome guest at events at Cattaraugus, Coldspring, Newtown, Six Nations Ontario, and other Haudenosaunee communities. He participated in "the doings" of midwinter festivals, Green Corn dances, feasts, and other community ceremonial events and recitations. In 1943, for example, Fenton was a guest at the Onondaga Longhouse in Ontario, where he witnessed Chief Logan, as head chief of the leading moiety, deliver the Ganeho'wi (a formal address of good words) on the second day of the "Green Corn Dance." In a series of unpublished letters to his wife, Olive, and his children, Betsey and John, he composed an engaging first-person account of every step of the gathering: chants, patterns of moieties exchanging the singing of songs, dancing, names of leaders, and even the taste of the "Indian boiled green corn bread" that he was given as a gift.[27]

These early letters capture a time when Fenton was a gracious and welcome participant observer of living Haudenosaunee traditions. In the early days, Cornplanter sometimes relied on Fenton's expertise. When requesting a translation of Seneca rituals for his own use, Cornplanter noted, "I would value that very highly as I know it to be authentic and from [a] good source."[28] Writing to William Waller Edwards, Cornplanter praised Fenton, writing, "The Government pays him a large salary for answering such questions . . . and believe me, he knows his Indians."[29] Cornplanter was also modest about his own limitations. For example, when Fenton sought information on traditional herbal remedies, Jesse said, "I know of many simple remedies used by my late mother," but when it came to ritual healing, "It is the women in many cases who are the Medicine People or healers. . . . I owe my life to this good medicine."[30]

Yet, as time went on, Cornplanter became more guarded and critical and Fenton became less generous. Rather than using his position as an intellectual gatekeeper to assist his adopted Seneca kin, Fenton used his privileged position to promote his own status and opinions. He claimed, "With Indians I have always been more prone to listen than to preach," but his correspondence with Native peoples adopted an increasingly paternalistic and officious tone. For instance, in 1945, when Reva Barse wrote to Fenton on behalf of a group of

Seneca mothers requesting research on women's traditional leadership roles and assistance with self-help organizations, he responded:

> Of one thing I am convinced: to succeed Indian organizations must be led by Indians. The Senecas have produced leaders in the past and they can produce them again. If you think your Society is worthwhile and work for its own ends, it will succeed. Things that people learn to do for themselves are what count. Study how others succeed in similar circumstances and act accordingly. You cannot return to the old Indian way of life. That is lost beyond recall. You can save what remains, and in working together you may achieve for yourselves some of the spirit of the old League and its ideals. . . . Good luck and courage.[31]

At first glance, a letter like this might seem encouraging, but the inference that the "old way of life" was "lost beyond recall" suggests no interest in preserving it. Instead, Fenton advised Haudenosaunee people to re-create their culture, even though he and his colleagues considered reinvented traditions to be, de facto, inauthentic. For Fenton, Indigenous antiquity and authenticity were inextricably linked; therefore, nothing "modern" could ever be considered to be truly "Indian."

Yet the Haudenosaunee were (and are) linked to long-standing living cultural traditions that, in many cases, depended heavily on ritual objects as crucial tools of continuance. In 1944, for example, fifteen strings of wampum were lost when the Longhouse at Newtown burned to the ground, and Cornplanter was tasked to find replacements. Knowing that wampum had been acquired by virtually every collector and museum in the northeast, Cornplanter wrote to Speck, Parker, Fenton, and other anthropological friends. Fenton did not respond directly; instead, he forwarded Cornplanter's letter on to Arthur Parker, writing:

> The sage of Tonowanda, *Hayon'wan'is' doisdowi*, Jess Cornplanter informs me that the Longhouse at Newtown lost its Six Nations' wampum a year or more ago when the house of its keeper James Crow burned to the ground. . . . On the presumption that the wampum was lost and that Jess is acting in good faith, I have written Speck and Heye and yourself as possible sources. Prof. Speck informs me that he procured wampum excavated from Seneca graves from the ghoul of Holcomb, N.Y., one Harry Schoff, archaeologist. . . . I have written Schoff an inquiry, stating the situation, that the value of such depends on the market, the interest of collectors in certain strings and their associated use, and that here is a chance for us to do something for the longhouse Indians who have helped us in the past.[32]

Fenton was willing to help, "if a reasonable price can be arrived at for that quantity of wampum," figuring that "the test of the Indians' good faith would

Figure 18 Jesse Cornplanter in Elison Park, Rochester, at the ceremony awarding the Seneca Silver Star to Joseph Keppler, 1937. Photographer unknown. Courtesy of Cornell University.

be their willingness to participate in the purchase."[33] Although the Seneca were very much in need of wampum, this particular deal fell through, likely because they were understandably reluctant to purchase stolen funerary objects that had been improperly removed in the first place.

In 1952 Fenton enlisted Cornplanter's help on a new project, compiling a complete set of Seneca ceremonial and dance songs. Fenton felt it would be a great experiment to offer a research subject free rein to record himself, so he shipped a tape recorder with instructions for collecting traditional songs and stories. After it arrived, Cornplanter complained bitterly about the difficulty of juggling drum, rattle, and microphone while managing the mechanics of the "dog-gone machine," and he railed at the assumption that he was expected to serve as Fenton's secretary. Cornplanter used his trusty Smith Corona type-writer to make his thoughts known in a letter to an old military pal, complaining, "I broke off with Bill Fenton on this Tape Recording of my songs that was to be made here some time this spring," since "he don't mean much to me as he is. . . . Life is too short to waste my time that way."[34] Cornplanter later agreed to continue the project, but he made his feelings about credit for the work known to Fenton: "Whats the matter Bill? A guilty conscience or have you forgotten your old Seneca Helper? . . . I should get full credit for my knowledge instead of just a mere small print in the bottom page."[35]

Cornplanter was also concerned about spiritual protocols; in a letter to Charles Bartlett, he admitted to having shared information that, in retrospect, should have remained secret: "You may not know it, but there are certain things that we can not do without we suffer some ill-effects as I have often told you. . . . I'm a sort of disloyal to my own tribe in exposing these songs to the public."[36] He also complained about being treated as a "novelty or curiosity," and asked:

> How many of the boys [anthropological collectors] are really interested in us Indians? How many? That is one reason I had a run-in with Prof. Tony Wallace of Philadelphia about making Tape Recordings for the records for some Science Research outfit, he wanted to pay me about 5 cents per song on this *Des wah dey-nyoh* and *Yeh ih ond dar tah*. I also told Dr. Fenton that he makes a sort of a joke about his work on us INJUNS and he makes money out of it at the same time. He tries to tell me that he is not, but he don't fool me one bit.[37]

Native informants were in a vulnerable, liminal position: they wished to profit from sharing valuable knowledge and skills, but it was difficult to do so without disrespecting tribal protocols, and they rarely gained fair recognition or recompense. In a letter to Charles E. Congdon, Jesse wrote: "I want to leave some of the things that I am and know," in the hopes that his Native kinfolk would say, "This man has done something during his life that not everyone can do. All those songs, rituals and speeches are preserved so that anyone can learn or study."[38] Cornplanter never achieved the level of respect that he desired, but his songs, artworks, and even his written words became collectible objects; most of his voluminous correspondence is now housed within William Fenton's papers.

In 1956, just a few months before his death, Jesse Cornplanter was dismayed to learn that his ancestral homelands had been targeted for destruction by the Kinzua Dam flood control project along the Allegheny River in Pennsylvania, just south of the New York State border. The president of the Seneca Nations drafted a letter to tribal citizens that read in part:

If the Kinzua Dam is constructed, it will destroy two-thirds of the Allegany Reservation and destroy the homes of over One Thousand Senecas in violation of the Treaty agreement made by the Federal Government, one hundred and sixty-three years ago. This mater effects [*sic*] every Seneca Indian, whether he has his home on the Allegany Reservation, the Cattaraugus Reservation or elsewhere. If the government is successful in its attempt to destroy the Allegany Reservation, it could likewise destroy Cattaraugus Reservation and the Treaty rights of all Senecas. . . . All of you unite and present a solid front in this fight to preserve your land and your Treaty rights.[39]

Cornplanter was specifically asked to translate this letter into the Seneca language, so it could be read aloud to "impress those that can't read nor realize the importance of that fact that this means more then the flooding of certain tracts of River lands, but it would be the first step to Abbrogate our Treaties with the government."[40]

When Bill Fenton was consulted for an expert opinion on the Kinzua Dam project, he suggested, at first, that tribal homes should be modernized and left in place; later, he supported relocation as an opportunity to encourage the Seneca to assimilate into the modern world and start anew. His press releases announced that this plan was welcomed by the Seneca Nation, but files in his own correspondence suggest otherwise.[41] In May 1957 head matron Mildred F. Garlow ("Geh Gwa Gar Dah Jeh"), writing on behalf of the "Mothers of the Seneca Nation of Alleghany and Cattaraugus Reservations," denounced those who aimed to "subvert our status and martyr us by drowning in the Kinzua Dam." Her letter read, in part:

We are not opposed to Progress, we marvel at your achievements, but when fraudulence within and without, threatens the life and property of our people, involves Congress and the State of New York, in the diatribe upon us, were you to concur upon the camouflage Appropriations requested on the part of the United States Army Corp of Engineers for a Million Dollar flood control and stream regulation Project. . . . According to scientific research, the topography along the River for construction of the Dam, demands a capitol and material expenditure that thwarts reason and justice, not only for the State and Federal Taxpayers, but the Civil liberties of the Seneca Nation. Lucrative gas and oil Wells, Homes, Villages, cultivated fields, woods and forests for Fuel, relocation for Public Funds and several years for redress.[42]

Garlow complained that the flood control project was a political gambit, intended primarily to help the New Deal politicians win elections, and she pointed out the sinister link between Indian relocations and the potential loss of tribal rights. Her fears were justified; there were, at the time, two bills pending in Congress for the termination of Haudenosaunee sovereignty: one for the Seneca (due to the Kinzua Dam project) and one for the other five nations in New York State—Cayuga, Mohawk, Oneida, Onondaga, and Tuscarora.

The push for Iroquois termination died in committee, but the Kinzua Dam project was approved, even though it violated the 1794 Canandaigua Treaty with the federal government. On August 31, 1964, Congress and the president approved the demolition of the Allegany Seneca community and the resettlement of 127 families.[43] In 1969 Fenton's old friend Richard Bell Congdon, the photographer who had assisted with the early research among the Allegany Seneca, wrote about the aftermath:

> The small hurts which happen to people in something like the Kinzua Dam never get written down just as no one knows the feeling of families left behind after a slave raid. I think of the sadistic glee with which the army engineers set fire to the Indian houses, the calculated campaign of deceit to both Indians and White in connection with the construction, the graft of the undertakers moving the cemeteries and the many little things which happen in every construction job of this sort. . . . Are you going to comment on this? It seems as though you are in a unique position to do so.[44]

The Kinzua Dam construction was devastating; the pain resonated through every Seneca community, far beyond Allegany. Faithkeeper G. Peter Jemison later recalled that many "elders wept openly" and some died prematurely of heartbreak.[45] After the houses were burned, Fenton suggested that an archaeological crew be sent in to salvage what was left, since these materials could contribute significantly to the state of archaeological research on the Seneca.[46]

Upstreaming or Backstreaming

For six decades, from the 1940s to the early 1990s, Fenton occupied high-level college and museum positions that enabled him to oversee virtually all scholarship on the Iroquois. He actively vetted students, faculty, conference participants, research grants, and publications having to do with any aspect of Six Nations Iroquois/Haudenosaunee research and scholarship. He served as the successor to J. N. B. Hewitt at the Smithsonian Bureau of American Ethnology, as the first president of the American Society for Ethnohistory, as a founder of the Iroquoian Conference, and as a Trustee of the Museum of the American Indian/Heye Foundation (MAI). In 1956 he was appointed director of the New York State Museum, and in 1968 he became a research professor at the State University of New York in Albany.[47]

Fenton published so extensively that he was widely recognized as the "Dean of Iroquoian Studies."[48] He mentored the next generation of Iroquoian scholars—including Elisabeth Tooker, Anthony Wallace, and Michael Foster, among others—and coached them on their interactions with the Haudenosaunee, while admitting that these relationships were increasingly fraught. In a 1969 letter to Foster, Fenton cautioned:

> I used to think that the Iroquois people were the greatest people on earth. They were most helpful and they taught me what it is to be an ethnologist. I worked with men who worked with Hewitt and Goldenweiser and some with Parker. These men were their models. It was something to measure up to. Now, the elected council demands that anthropologists appear, explain the study, and request permission to reside on the reserve. I did this and gained their assent. But I alienated the Old Chiefs. . . . It is just getting tough. There have been too many studies—some of them have been fly by night and bad—and the fear of commercialism is great.[49]

Despite these concerns, Fenton asserted his own intellectual authority, even though much of his research was rejected by Haudenosaunee people who accused him of misrepresenting culture and history, disclosing secret and sacred knowledge, and appropriating cultural property.[50]

Fenton invented the technique of "upstreaming," a comparative practice rooted in the theory that one could divine cultural continuity by examining what appeared to be authentic cultural practices in documentary records, and methodically constructing them into a continuous stream leading to the present. He collated historical information with data derived from interviews to produce texts that appeared to reflect an essentially unchanging cultural stability over time. Regna Darnell suggested that "the Iroquois themselves valued conservatism as critical to contemporary identity, so the fit between method and local uses was excellent." Yet Fenton was working during a time of dramatic social and political change amid a generational shift that made Native peoples wary of anthropological interference. Darnell put it this way:

> The patron-client relationships of anthropologist and "informant" were greeted with increasing suspicion by young Iroquois after the 1950s. Fenton's classic work was done at a time when Iroquois ceremonialists were worried about the potential loss of their knowledge and delighted in having someone who wanted to listen and to record it . . . [but] Fenton has been criticized by many Iroquois for revealing ceremonial knowledge that should remain secret . . . and for seeming to appropriate the knowledge shared with him.[51]

Fenton often justified his work by emphasizing the importance of capturing ancient (and therefore "authentic") traditions that were fast vanishing, while methodically denouncing present-day Haudenosaunee practices as modern (and therefore "inauthentic").

At one juncture, Fenton attempted to deconstruct the Deganawidah epic to discover the textual foundations of Haudenosaunee governance. Here, he picked up an argument that Parker and Hewitt left off four decades earlier. At issue was the question of source verification: Could the oral traditions be reconciled with colonial written traditions? In his 1949 publication "Collecting Materials for a Political History of the Six Nations," Fenton noted that two distinct categories of sources existed: "native traditions and rituals associated with the founding of the League, and accounts by European and American observers of their official relations with these forest diplomats."[52] Fenton focused on narrative survivals of the former, weighed against written observations of the latter. Fenton claimed that the works of two writers—Lewis H. Morgan's *League of the Ho-de-no-sau-nee or Iroquois* (1851) and Horatio Hale's *Iroquois Book of Rites* (1883)—were the most authoritative sources on Haudenosaunee ritual traditions and governance.[53] There were, however, geographical limitations: Morgan had focused primarily on the Onondaga and Tonawanda Seneca Nations; Hale had focused on Grand River, Ontario; and Fenton's research was located primarily among the Seneca. None of these effectively represented all the nuances of negotiating Haudenosaunee history and governance over time.

To assess these combined sources, Fenton applied upstreaming to position the collected data "against the tide of events."[54] He articulated his premises as follows:

> It rests on three premises. Major patterns of culture tend to be stable over long periods. We are too often taken in by the fallacy of assumed acculturation. Secondly, we proceed from what we know, concentrating on the most recent manuscripts first because they are apt to contain things familiar to us. Thus we can move from Newhouse to Asher Wright to Pickering and Kirkland, and to the eighteenth century writers. In this way can the sources be made to yield more than they apparently contain? Thirdly, we employ an ethnologist's preference for sources: those sources which ring true ethnologically merit attention.[55]

Apart from the insistence on written documentation of Indigenous cultures, there is a degree of inherent bias and subjectivity in this method that seems, in retrospect, to be glaringly Eurocentric. By assuming that Indigenous cultural patterns must be fixed and stable (rather than flexible and adaptive), Fenton could point to *any* evidence of fracture—even fracture resulting from colonial, missionary, or anthropological interference—as evidence of the supposed *instability* of Haudenosaunee culture over time. The lack of consensus around myths of the Confederacy's origins reflected a decaying oral tradition. The apparent "failure of the League chiefs to appear consistently as signers of treaties" was evidence of the "dissolution" of the league itself in the twentieth century. Fenton concluded that the Haudenosaunee "had confederated into a kinship state which never solved the problem of local autonomy and gradually eroded at the edges as marginal groups broke away and made their own agreements without clearing through Onondaga."[56]

Fenton's student, Anthony Wallace, took a somewhat different tack in his early research on the Haudenosaunee. In a 1958 article, "The Dekanawideh Myth Analyzed as the Record of a Revitalization Movement," he applied a retrospective psychological analysis to the historical circumstances that surrounded the emergence of the confederacy. Wallace suggested that the myth was not merely a story; it was "orally transmitted" as a "record of a reasonably ancient event"—an earlier revitalization movement that had enabled the Haudenosaunee to recover from traumatic warfare.[57] From this vantage point, the contemporary evidence of cultural revitalization and political activism could be seen as a marker not of decay, but of creative adaptation and regeneration in response to modern circumstances that had induced similar levels of psychological distress.

Haudenosaunee bands, councils, and communities during the early twentieth century were, of course, somewhat diverse in the specificities of their cultural and political practices, and influenced by local politics and personalities. But Fenton was not privy to the various conflicts and accommodations among traditional and elected chiefs, since many tribal leaders flatly refused to speak with him. He was willing to acknowledge the validity of the Six Nations at Grand River, Ontario, a locale "where the League was reconstituted after the Revolution to become the local government of the Six Nations Reserve down to 1924."[58] Yet he was reluctant to admit any contemporaneous evidence of similar political continuity in New York State, even when he was witness to evidence of Indigenous survivance and resistance. In a 1948 letter to his colleague Paul Wallace, he castigated educator Ray Fadden (Tehanatorens), one of the most ardent proponents of Haudenosaunee cultural survival, writing:

> Ray Fadden has evidently generated quite a propaganda machine against the legislation pending before the Congress affecting the New York Indians. . . . I do not think that the Congress will enact the legislation over the overwhelming opposition of the Indians, even though the opposition be unintelligent and misinformed. Regardless of what the folk think about their past, Fadden's thesis, albeit an old worn one, of the independent sovereignty of the Six Nations can scarcely be maintained, and he has probably chosen to forget that neither the Mohawk nor the St. Regis band participated in Ft. Stanwix and Canandaigua treaties, hence they receive no federal annuities.[59]

Fenton never relinquished his obsession with a centralized confederacy. In his article "The Lore of the Longhouse: Myth, Ritual and Red Power," he proclaimed, "The Red Power movement on the Six Nations Reserve is doomed to frustration," and he cruelly characterized the confederacy as a doomed but "fascinating relic of the stone age." For him, the "real" confederacy lived only in the past. He labeled the Oneida, Onondaga, Cayuga, Mohawk, Seneca, and Tuscarora nations as "structurally weak," adding that "they lack in executive authority, and chiefs enjoy great prestige but have no power."[60]

Given the force with which he held to these opinions, Fenton's ethnographic technique might more accurately be characterized as "backstreaming." In effect, he created present-day theories, and then extended them backward into the Indigenous past, relying heavily on written documents while eliminating from consideration any evidence (including the protests of living subjects) that did not fit his theories. In his mind, academic research was inherently more objective and reliable than any Indigenous tradition, and he was entirely unwilling to tolerate Indigenous critique.

In a telling exchange of letters concerning the 1980 Iroquois Conference, Fenton was dismayed to learn that Native leaders Duffy Wilson and Richard Hill had negotiated to move the last day of the conference to the new Native American Center for the Living Arts (the Turtle) at Niagara Falls, making it more accessible to Haudenosaunee attendees. Fenton told organizer T. Laird Christie of his "dismay" at the change of venue, complaining:

> It simply does not do to read an academic paper to an audience of mixed academics and Indians who are activists and emotionally involved in restructuring history to fit their ideas of the future. I have had two such experiences where I was asked to deliver a university lecture and prepared such only to be greeted by an audience that at the last minute included local Indians with particular axes to grind and who got terribly upset at formal analysis of events in their traditional past.[61]

Fenton's written works went far beyond mere "formal analysis" when he trended toward racially inflected diatribes against Indian activists who, he believed, were interfering with the practice of academic research. Whitfield Bell, who was then the librarian of the American Philosophical Society, agreed. He wrote, "The tension in anthropology of the American Indian now is between those of us who were scientifically trained and the so-called Native Americans who suffer from the genetic fallacy that one must have Indian blood to interpret Indian history and culture. This too will pass."[62] Gatekeepers at archives and museums did little to resolve these tensions. Instead, they tightened restrictions to keep Native activists out of their colleges and out of their collections. Fenton was uniquely well positioned to do so, since, among his other responsibilities, he served as the primary reviewer for Iroquoian graduate studies and research fellowships at APS and elsewhere.[63]

Resisting Wampum Repatriation

For decades, Fenton and other museum professionals kept a chokehold on sacred and patrimonial objects housed in museum collections, despite the fact that tribal communities needed these objects for the continuance of ritual practices and governance that were essential to cultural survival. In a letter to *Akwesasne Notes*, Fenton argued that anthropologists had no reason to be concerned with American Indian cultural survival. He wrote, "We are not social welfare workers and we cannot be expected to be. We need not be activists." He stated his case on wampum.

> I too believe that every society has a right to pursue its own destiny, but I do not believe that the descendants of the old Five Nations would be materially advanced by returning to them the wampum belts in the New York State Museum which were acquired by out-right purchase, by gift, and by deed of trust. Most of the belts are on permanent exhibition; they can be seen any weekday by anyone, and those that are in the vault can be seen by arrangement with very little notice.[64]

In fact, it was extraordinarily difficult to secure permission to view either the wampum in the vault or the documents in the files, as Rick Hill, Paul Williams, and other Haudenosaunee advocates learned when they attempted to conduct repatriation research.

As the "Red Power" movement gained strength, the chiefs stepped up their demands for the return of wampum belts housed at the Museum of the American Indian and the New York State Museum. Fenton responded by crafting an article titled "Red Power and Wampum"; the final version was titled "The New York State Wampum Collection: The Case for the Integrity of Cultural Treasures."[65] Fenton cruelly characterized Haudenosaunee chiefs as supposedly incompetent to manage their own cultural treasures; as proof, he expounded on histories of wampum theft. He insisted that wampum losses had resulted from Indigenous factionalism, political disorganization, relocation, and loss of traditions, and he theorized that sacred regalia had been privatized, which (so he claimed) made its sale to collectors appropriate.

In the same article, Fenton actually cited himself as a witness to the chiefs' complaints.

> The present Onondaga chiefs say that the wampum belts were loaned, and not sold to the state, and that they have records of the transaction which contradict the

printed record. The late George Thomas, then holder of the League Chieftain's title Thadodaho', is quoted in the *New York Times* March 25, 1967, as bemoaning how they had to go to Canada to borrow wampum, how it made him sick to see all they had at Albany, how some of it was locked up, that they were never invited to "read" the belts.[66]

Fenton countered these concerns by claiming that wampum ceremonialism was neither ancient nor Indigenous; he claimed it was "a product of the fur trade, and as such it is as American as apple pie."[67] Therefore (according to Fenton), Haudenosaunee attempts to repatriate colonial wampum belts would constitute thefts from American national patrimony and the intellectual commons.

At the time, Haudenosaunee elders and youth were struggling to recapture what had been lost through forced acculturation and anthropological collecting.[68] Yet, Fenton insisted, it was anthropologists, and not tribal leaders, who should be credited for Indigenous cultural survival. He named himself foremost among those who had "listened to the old people when the young Indian people ignored them," and claimed that his scholarly research had "fostered a revival of Indian culture among a new generation seeking an identity."[69] He patronizingly characterized repatriation as merely a "curious manifestation of the Red Power movement."

> The movement is nourished by such beliefs that the ancestors were bilked of their cultural treasures, that anthropologists exploited their grandfathers, growing rich and famous in their selfish careers at the expense of the poor Indians whom they studied, and that if the present generation of Indians (who read their books and monographs) could only recover these objects now in museums, the power and prestige of the Indian people would rise once more.[70]

This is an interesting list of charges, since cultural treasures *had* been stolen, Native informants *did* complain of exploitation, and anthropologists *did* build their careers on Indigenous knowledge.

Fenton insisted that the "myth-making" Iroquois Confederacy had actually ceased to function as a cohesive group during the early twentieth century.[71] He was joined in these opinions by other influential scholars, most notably William Sturtevant, Donald Colliver, and Philip J. C. Dark, fellow members of the Committee on Anthropological Research in Museums. In a 1970 letter to the American Anthropological Association, which was also reprinted in the *Indian Historian*, they claimed that the wampum at the New York State Museum did not record Haudenosaunee traditions; it only "commemorated largely political agreements arrived at with the Indians at Albany."[72] They argued that

Haudenosaunee requests to reclaim wampum for religious purposes were based on modern political desires rooted in reinvented traditions.

> We deplore the principle of returning such treasures to the acculturated descendants of the original owners lest a precedent be established. . . . The implication of such an act undermines the whole philosophy and practice of museology everywhere. . . . State property should not be legislated away lightly in the illusion of religiosity or as capital in the civil rights movement.[73]

In a letter to Warren A. Snyder, Fenton accused the Haudenosaunee of creative reinvention, asserting that "the Iroquois Confederacy as such has no existence at present except in the minds of a few members."[74] This was patently absurd. Fenton—who had built his entire career on studying the Haudenosaunee as a powerful and influential political and social confederacy—was now suggesting that the confederacy had effectively ceased to exist before he had even started.

Fenton's scholarly polemics were effective. He frightened museum curators into refusing Indigenous claimants and he won the admiration of colleagues who felt similar enmity toward Indians. When he felt under attack, those colleagues urged him on. For example, his former student Elisabeth Tooker, who was then a professor at Temple, praised his 1971 wampum article.

> I very much liked your wampum piece. It all needed saying. . . . If I had any quibble with it, it would be that I wish you had said less about the museums and more about "Red Man speak with forked tongue." But that might not be politic. . . . (I still have not gotten over the young people's witch hunting at the November A.A.A. meetings). Right on![75]

The "young people" who went "witch hunting" at the 1971 American Anthropological Association meeting included present-day tribal leaders and activists such as Oren Lyons (Onondaga), G. Peter Jemison (Seneca), Richard Hill (Tuscarora), Doug-George Kanentiio (Mohawk), and the late Vine Deloria Jr. (Lakota), each of whom had decided to confront white anthropologists on their own intellectual ground. Traditional leaders also came after Fenton. In 1971 the Onondaga Nation, in its role as host of the central council fire and ritual authority for the Haudenosaunee Confederacy, attempted to excommunicate Fenton from his adopted status among the Seneca.[76]

When Fenton delivered his paper "The Lore of the Longhouse" at the University of Buffalo, "the audience was largely comprised of Indians and they thought it too critical of their tradition."[77] He commiserated with his colleague Elisabeth Tooker, who agreed: "Between Deloria and the latest issue of *The*

Indian Historian I can only say that I regret the treatment the Indians are giving you."[78] In 1973 he made no comment when Edward Rogers, curator of the Royal Ontario Museum, was criticized by Haudenosaunee activists at that year's AAA meeting, later explaining, "I remained silent not wanting to draw fire on the wampum issue."[79]

Although Haudenosaunee voices were getting louder, few non-Native scholars were willing to jeopardize their academic careers by challenging Fenton. One exception was Fenton's younger colleague Anthony Wallace, who was then chair of the Department of Anthropology at the University of Pennsylvania. Wallace was emotionally moved by the Haudenosaunee complaints. He wrote:

> I have reason to think that some time soon one of the Indian groups concerning itself with the Iroquois wampum is going to ask me to make a statement. . . . Times have changed and if the State were now to find it possible to return the belts . . . it would be an action welcomed not only by many Indians but by many who are not Indians.[80]

Fenton regarded this as a personal betrayal; he felt "like the bottom had dropped out of everything," and threatened to reveal "damning information" about the Haudenosaunee "that I won't put on paper."[81]

Fenton's "damning information" consisted of his opinion that the wampum sales by individual tribal members had been legitimate. As he told Tooker, he "was very much tempted to silence our Mohawk friend to ask him where he was when I was learning from the old men before they sold off all of the belts which they now claim were stolen or confiscated."[82] He speculated that Haudenosaunee people only wanted their wampum belts back so they could cash in on the lucrative antiquities trade by reselling them. Yet, after combing through decades of correspondence, lawsuits, and public pleas from tribal leaders, including documents in Fenton's own archives, I have found nothing that supports these inferences. Some individuals *were* designated as "keepers" of wampum belts, but that designation did *not* signify personal ownership of tribal property; they were custodians, not owners.[83] When unscrupulous tribal members *did* sell patrimonial wampum belts, there is no evidence whatsoever that they received permission from their nations or tribal councils to do so.[84]

With their wampum belts missing, Native artisans resorted to experimenting with other materials to replace shell beads. Ray Fadden constructed glass bead reproductions to use in teaching Haudenosaunee youth; those are still on display at the Six Nations Indian Museum in Onchiota, New York.[85] Guy Spittal, of the Iroqrafts Shop at Six Nations in Ontario, was first to witness the use of a new and unexpected material.

During the recent "Convention" we had visitors from Alleghany who told us that the Lewiston Tuscarora were trying to start their own L.H. [Long House] but were unable to find the necessary wampum to get it going. Necessity is a well known mother. The other evening I went to invite your old friend Bill [Jake] Thomas down here to preach for a dead feast. He was busy making strings of wampum from sections of black and white insulation.[86]

Examples of those plastic wampum beads, meticulously cut from insulation tubes (with the electrical wires removed), can be found in reproduction wampum belts housed in the Canadian Museum of History today. Although Fenton disdained objects like this as mere reproductions, it is important to note that—with sufficient ritual intentions—plastic, glass, and other materials could be imbued with the same ceremonial significance as shell.[87] Even so, tribal nations were desperately hoping to recover the originals.

At one juncture, members of the MAI Collections Committee seriously discussed the prospect of selling their wampum collection to avoid returning it to tribal nations. In 1977 Terry Doxtator (who was then studying at Trent University with Cayuga Chief Jake Thomas) wrote to Edmund Carpenter requesting an inventory of MAI wampum and offering to share information proving the belts had been stolen from their Six Nations keepers.[88] Carpenter responded, "I have no special knowledge concerning the subject which interests you," and suggested the young man conduct research elsewhere.[89] Carpenter forwarded Doxtator's letter to Fenton, noting, "My reply may have ended the matter," and proposing a plan for the sale of the very belts that Doxtator was inquiring about.

If the Heye trustees consider selling the eleven wampum belts to Canada, I suggest that the price be no lower than 250,000. This is well within the range of prices they are currently paying. Last week they paid 275,000 US for six Northwest Coast pieces. . . . How rare are these belts? Really, not all that rare. . . . I have seen some fine ones on the market recently, including one that came from the Fort Williams Museum in upstate New York, and some extra-fine ones that Dr. Dockstader let go. . . . It's the history of the Brantford belts which makes them important.[90]

In 1985 Carpenter told fellow MAI committee member George Abrams, "If MAI has good title, the trustees don't have the legal right to give these belts to anyone. Legally they can sell or trade them at market value," while stating, "Personally, I'd like to see these belts returned to their *traditional* owners for use, and favor a trade with the National Museum of Canada"; this was the National Museum of Man (NMM), now the Canadian Museum of History.[91] Abrams shared Carpenter's letter with Fenton, who conditionally agreed but expressed his concern that repatriation would be unwise, since (in his opinion) "the reserve is so cut up into factions that it is difficult to identify and evaluate claimants."[92] William Fenton made inquiries to Michael Foster, Iroquoian ethnologist at NMM, and shared his reply with MAI director Roland Force, stating:

> The chiefs do keep pretty much to themselves, particularly regarding their traditional symbols. If they get their belts back they are going to want full control over their use. Would there be some way to legally bind them as owners with some kind of proviso that if ever, in their collective judgement, it appeared they could not among themselves provide reasonable safeguards they would return them to MAI as custodians? . . . I would doubt they would try very hard to get the belts back unless there are a few strings attached (no pun intended).[93]

These concerns could easily have been assuaged if museum professionals had only communicated directly with the Haudenosaunee Standing Committee on Burial Rules and Regulations (HSC). This consortium of Iroquoian chiefs, community leaders, and lawyers, guided by the Council of Chiefs and Clan Mothers, is dedicated to facilitating consulting, collections research, and repatriation on behalf of Haudenosaunee nations in the United States and Canada.[94] Fenton received regular communications from the HSC, but he refused to provide provenance data that could have assisted with accurate object identification and repatriation. When his assistant Mary Druke conducted extensive research on wampum in museum collections, he never offered to share her findings with the Haudenosaunee.[95] In fact, during a museum consultation with Onondaga lawyer Paul Williams, who was working on behalf of the Six Nations and the Union of Ontario Indians, Fenton intentionally hid the relevant wampum provenance records.[96] Fenton often used Seneca phrases in his correspondence, sometimes ending letters by appealing to the Haudenosaunee ideals of "Peace (Skennon), Civil authority (gasas'densha), Righteousness (Gaihwio), and the Great Law or Commonwealth (Gayanesha'go'wa)."[97] Yet there is little evidence that he truly adhered to these ideals.

Fenton often attempted to control academic discourse by blocking Haudenosaunee people from presenting at academic conferences. In a 1980 letter to Edward Lehman, executive officer of the American Anthropological Association, he asked that two accepted panels on Native American issues be rejected, since Native presenters (in his opinion) "have no qualifications as scholars to address a learned society of anthropologists," and the rhetoric of "Iroquois militants" was unwelcome. Fenton vaguely threatened legal action if their museum proposals on repatriation would "result in my not being able to pursue my profession."[98]

When Martin Sullivan became director of the New York State Museum (NYSM) in 1983, the public discourse shifted dramatically. Sullivan "was startled to find that with the position went the title of Ho-sen-na-ge-tah, or wampum-keeper," and that the 1908 agreement brokered by Harriet Maxwell Converse had "conferred that title in perpetuity on the director of the State Museum and his successors!"[99] After meeting with a delegation from Onondaga, Sullivan suggested to the commissioner of education that they stop arguing and start cooperating. He realized that the original non-Indian authors of the wampum agreement had clearly taken unfair advantage, since "Onondaga signers had very little command of the English language or of Anglo-American legal practices, and were not likely to have given the kind of informed consent to the transaction that modern legal standards would require."[100]

Despite the existence of what appeared to be an 1898 bill of sale to the state for wampum, the NYSM lawyers and administrators agreed to repatriate many of the wampum belts in the collection to Onondaga. Sullivan recalled:

> The Board of Regents displayed sensitivity and flexibility in their willingness to admit oral testimony from Onondaga sources; to consider the impediments of language and cultural differences that influenced the written agreements of a century ago; and to focus on common interests rather than property rights. The Onondaga chiefs, through their readiness to enter into pragmatic discussions instead of dwelling on grievances of long standing, created a climate of partnership that has continued to grow.[101]

The successful negotiations at NYSM had a ripple effect on other wampum claims. As plans emerged for the dissolution of the Museum of the American Indian (MAI) into the new National Museum of the American Indian (NMAI), Haudenosaunee activists tried to move quickly to recover tribal patrimony before the collections moved to Washington, D.C. In 1989 MAI trustees finally agreed to recognize eleven wampum belts associated with the Six Nations at Grand River as tribal patrimony, and agreed to repatriate them.[102] Publicly, Fenton claimed responsibility for having effectively facilitated this repatriation, but privately, he encouraged Elisabeth Tooker to conduct further research. In a subsequent article, she proved that the recently repatriated wampum belts had been misidentified, implicitly supporting Fenton's contention that tribal leaders could not tell one wampum belt from another.[103] Closer examination of the provenance records, however, reveals that tribal leaders were misled by museum officials who had introduced some of the very errors that Tooker corrected.

The founding of NMAI was a source of great anxiety for Fenton, in large part because so many members of the museum community agreed that Native

Americans should be appointed to board, management, and curatorial positions at the new museum.[104] Fenton complained to Edmund Carpenter that "Indian activists are coming out of the woods and all want to be trustees and/or director."[105]

He was particularly incensed at NMAI's new Repatriation Policy, which served as a precursor to the Native American Graves Protection and Repatriation Act in designating certain objects as sacred or patrimonial.[106] In a letter to attorney Barber Conable, chair of the MAI Trustees, Fenton outlined his objections.

> There is a fundamental philosophical conflict between rational science embodied in the Smithsonian charter "for the increase and diffusion of knowledge" and the religiosity inherent in the NMAI Repatriation Policy. The policy places restrictions on the scientific use of the collections and the publication of research results that are antithetical to the freedom of research and in conflict with the act that chartered the SI [Smithsonian Institution].
>
> Native Indians and their descendants have been in the business of selling religious objects to collectors and museums for more than a century, and much of the information about these objects that are now deemed "sacred" has been in the public domain for more than a century. Nor are native people reliable custodians of their own history.[107]

Fenton was correct in his assertions that *some* Native peoples had sold sacred objects in the past, but it was absurd to suggest that the wrongdoings of some negated the rights of all. In his criticism, Fenton chose to willfully ignore the interferences of collectors (including himself) and museums, despite having intimate knowledge of exactly how tangled those accessions had been.

As new tribal leaders came on the scene and old informants passed away, William Fenton became increasingly alienated from the Haudenosaunee, and he was no longer welcome at some of his old research sites. Yet, even after his death in 1995, William Nelson Fenton continues to cast a long shadow, retaining a surprisingly high degree of influence in academic scholarship. The sheer volume of his publications—and the reiterations of these in museum exhibitions, school curricula, and popular history—is such that he is still widely regarded, even by many Haudenosaunee people, as an authoritative source.[108] He did remarkable recovery work in museums and mentored several generations of scholars, but he often deployed his research and his influence as political tools to resist Indigenous sovereignty. If this seems too harsh a judgment, one need only examine his correspondence, which reveals a messy narrative of fraught relations wrought with obvious bias. In this light, Jesse Cornplanter's voice still resonates: "I value your friendship Bill. But I've got to protect myself."[109]

6

Indian Stories

Gladys Tantaquidgeon and Frank Speck

In my earlier years, I perhaps wasn't aware of the fact that time was going by so rapidly. . . . Many of our old people were dying and their knowledge went with them. Something had to be done.

—Gladys Tantaquidgeon, 1983

Frank Gouldsmith Speck Jr. (1881–1950), born in Brooklyn and raised in Hackensack, New Jersey, was the eldest of three children born to Frank Gouldsmith Speck Sr. and Hattie L. Staniford.[1] As a youth, he enjoyed sojourns into the forests and swamps of New Jersey and rural southern New England during family vacations. Speck entered Columbia University in 1899, and received his master's degree in 1905 under the tutelage of John Dyneley Prince and Franz Boas, while conducting fieldwork among the Mohegan Indians in Connecticut. He came to the University of Pennsylvania (Penn) as a Harrison Fellow in 1907, and was the first student to graduate with a Penn PhD in anthropology in 1908. From 1909 to 1913, he held a joint appointment as an instructor in anthropology and as an assistant in ethnology at the University Museum (now the University of Pennsylvania Museum of Archaeology and Anthropology, or Penn Museum). In 1913 he was appointed as an assistant professor and designated anthropology department chair, a position he held continuously until 1949.[2] Speck was perhaps the most prolific ethnologist of his generation, with more than three hundred publications, including books, scientific monographs, and articles. Over the course of five decades, he worked with Indigenous informants from Algonquin, Cherokee, Mohegan, Naskapi, Nanticoke, Penobscot, and other Native nations in the eastern United States and Canada. Speck amassed thousands of Indigenous objects, contributing to collections at the Victoria Museum (now the Canadian Museum of History), Denver Art Museum, Museum of the American Indian (now NMAI), and Peabody Essex Museum, among others.

Gladys Iola Tantaquidgeon (1899–2005) was the third of seven children born to Mohegan Indians John Tantaquidgeon (also spelled Quidgeon) and Harriet Fielding at Mohegan Hill in Uncasville (Norwich), Connecticut. As

Figure 19 Delaware Indian Witapanóx'we (James Webber) posing with Frank G. Speck. Photograph staged by Frank G. Speck, c. 1930. Graphics # 4173. Courtesy of the American Philosophical Society.

a child, she was trained in Indigenous knowledge by Mohegan sociocultural authorities, including Nehantic elder Mercy Ann Nonesuch Mathews, medicine woman Emma Baker, and one of the last fluent Mohegan speakers, her great aunt, Fidelia Fielding.[3] In 1919, at the age of twenty, Gladys became the first American Indian to attend anthropology classes at the University of Pennsylvania, and from 1919 to 1933, she worked as a research assistant for professor Frank G. Speck. During her time at Penn, she accompanied Speck on field expeditions to many Native nations, published a series of research articles, and completed a book on Algonkian ethnobotany. In 1931 Gladys, her brother Harold (1904–89), and their father, John, cofounded the Tantaquidgeon Indian Museum in Uncasville, Connecticut. The family was devoted to teaching Mohegan history and culture, in local and regional venues.[4] In 1934 Gladys was hired by the Bureau of Indian Affairs to survey New England tribal nations, and in 1935 she was recruited to serve as a community worker on the Yankton Sioux Reservation in South Dakota. From 1938 to 1947, Tantaquidgeon was an "Indian Arts" specialist for the Federal Indian Arts and Crafts Board. Gladys also served as secretary to the Algonquin Council of New England, an organization devoted to publicizing the survivance of eastern Native nations.[5] In recognition of her accomplishments, she was awarded honorary doctorates from both the University of Connecticut (1987) and Yale University (1994).

Encounter at Fort Shantok

Frank Speck's interest in Mohegan culture was sparked one midsummer evening in the summer of 1900, while camping at Fort Shantok, when he crossed paths with three Mohegan teenagers: Edwin Fowler, Roscoe Skeesucks, and Burrill Tantaquidgeon. Speck (then nineteen years old) invited the trio over for a smoke; they struck up a conversation and invited him to stay around for a while.[6] Edwin's aunt, Cynthia Fowler, who ran an informal boarding house, offered Frank a place to stay for a few days.[7] In a letter to his mother, Hattie Speck, Frank wrote:

> I have a room with the common old-fashioned bedstead with a mattress of down. The food is very plain but solid and very abundant. I had some Indian baked beans last night. . . . Then there is a young Indian just my age, Ed Fowler, who is a nephew to Mrs. Cynthia Fowler; he is in the room next to me, while Theo Cooper, Alonzo's crippled brother is in the same [room]. So you see there is enough company here. Theodore's mother is here to take care of him and she is a perfect type of the old-fashioned big-boned, Indian squaw, very kind but very pleasant.[8]

This undated letter, housed in the archives of the American Philosophical Society in Philadelphia, survives only in fragments; a few segments are missing, but the remaining pieces, when fitted together, take on the shape of a trapezoidal box, rather like a folded birch-bark *mokuk*, suggesting that the letter may have been designed as a puzzle. On one page, Speck expressed the hope that his mother has "arrived home safely," suggesting that she had dropped him off, before traveling home without him. On another page, a line reads, "love to all until Friday," indicating that he expected to reunite with his family later that same week.[9]

The letter reports that Frank's new friends took him around to reconnoiter the Mohegan landscape, and that ferryman John (also called Alonzo) Cooper and his wife invited him out for a ride on the Watch Hill Ferry. When Sunday came around, the minister at the Congregational Mohegan Church was out of town, and so, in lieu of services, the young men visited another place sacred to the tribe:

> Skeesucks, Tantaquidgeon and I went over to Cochegan rock the largest boulder in the district heavily wooded and stands up like a great baseball 60 or 70 feet high.

To climb up, one must chin up a tree and then wobble over to a ledge of rock about 4 inches wide, then it is a climb and pulling up to the top. There is a stone chair up top.[10]

Cochegan Rock, a massive glacial erratic weighing seven thousand tons, is one of the largest boulders in New England, and one of the most significant cultural landmarks in Mohegan territory. The location was used during the mid-seventeenth century as a gathering place by Uncas, the first chief of the Mohegan tribal nation.[11]

During this sojourn, Frank Speck made a preliminary field study of this Native community, noting, "There are more Indians here than I thought, and ma[ny] are fullbloods." He recorded "the names of 76 Mohegans and there are some more," and observed, "There is very little Negro blood in the tribe, less than any Eastern tribe."[12] He met one of the tribal elders, Fidelia Ann Hoscott Smith Fielding (1827–1908), also called Jeets Bodernasha ("Flying Bird"). Fidelia, the widow of William Fielding, was said to be the last fluent speaker of the Mohegan-Pequot language. Tribal members later recalled that she "was not too friendly toward non-Indians," but, "she welcomed Speck and that was the beginning of a friendship which resulted in her telling him legends and words in the Mohegan language which he later published."[13] Frank's "discovery" of Fidelia Fielding, as it happens, was especially fortuitous: his interviews with her supplied the text for his first academic publications and launched his ethnological career.

Speaking in Mohegan

Speck, who was then a student at Columbia University, reported his discoveries to his professor, linguist John Dyneley Prince, who was fascinated to hear that Mohegan-Pequot (a language thought to be already dead) was still being spoken. Prince introduced Speck to his colleague Franz Boas, and they directed the young man to collect whatever information he could. Over the next few years, Speck conducted a series of interviews with Fielding, who lived with a female companion in an old timber frame house on Mohegan Hill. Fielding was in the habit of occasionally recording thoughts and observations in small notebooks (also described as "diaries"), which she loaned to Speck. These papers were, as it turns out, quite remarkable. Fielding was literate and fluent in both Mohegan and English, and she was using an orthography that, Speck deduced, had been collaboratively devised by "white men and educated Indians who tried to write the Pequot language while it was still a living idiom."[14] At a time when many Algonquian languages were fading away, Fielding was still speaking and writing in Mohegan.

In 1903 Speck published five articles based on Fielding's texts, including "The Remnants of Our Eastern Indian Tribes" in the *American Inventor*, two short articles for the *Papoose*, and "A Pequot-Mohegan Witchcraft Tale" in the *Journal of American Folklore*.[15] In his introduction to the latter, he presented Fielding and an unnamed woman (erroneously identified as her sister) as "the sole members of the community at Mohegan who retain a complete knowledge of the ancient tongue."[16] In another article co-authored that same year with Prince, titled "The Modern Pequots and Their Language" and published in *American Anthropologist*, Speck intimated that the language was not quite dead: a "revival of interest" was already underway, a number of tribal members had passing knowledge, and "even the children are able to use a few native words."[17]

A subsequent article with Prince, however, painted a gloomier picture. Prince wrote:

> There is always something strangely pathetic about a dying language, especially when, like the Mohegan-Pequot idiom, the dialect exists in the memory of but a single living person. Mr Speck has obtained two connected texts and most of the following words and forms from Mrs Fidelia A. H. Fielding, an aged Indian woman resident at Mohegan, near Norwich, Conn., who has kept up her scanty knowledge of her early speech chiefly by talking to herself.[18]

Strictly, this was not true, since there were others who had at least passing familiarity with the language: James H. Rogers knew the numeric system; one informant spoke both Mohegan and Ojibwe; and at least four others spoke a little Mohegan—Hannah Dolbeare, Lester Skeesucks, Emma Baker, and Amy Cooper.[19] Even so, English was rapidly becoming the dominant tongue for Native communities across the region. The distinction, according to Prince, was that few Native peoples were left who "can talk Indian *consecutively*."[20] However one might choose to interpret the relative vitality of the language community, one thing was certain: with these articles, Speck and Prince had firmly staked their claim to capturing what little was left of the Mohegan language, while signaling that there was little left for anyone else to discover.

One of Speck's 1904 articles—"A Modern Mohegan-Pequot Text"— grappled with the linguistics of folklore, in a discomforting experiential anecdote that retains the character of a folktale, with its references to omens and shape-shifting. Speck may have interjected some inadvertent cultural interpretations, since he altered Fielding's orthography throughout—including changing the spelling of her Mohegan name, from Jeets Bodernosh-shor to Dji-ts Bud-unacu—to conform with linguistic conventions of the time. In this text, a Native woman (likely Fielding) travels away from Mohegan into an eerily depopulated landscape just outside the urban seaport town of New London. There, she comes face-to-face with a white woman offering false comfort. Speck's translation captures Fielding's speech patterns, as follows:

> An old Indian woman goes to sell brooms at New London (Conn.). It becomes very dark. Where is she going to stay? She sees a house. She thinks, "Perhaps I can stay there tonight." I go rap! rap! on the door. A white woman comes and opens the door. I know her. She says, "Come in"; she smiles. I say, "Can I stay here tonight?" The white woman says, "Yes! Are you not hungry? I made some bread and cheese, can you eat some?" "I am not hungry tonight. I will eat if I live in the morning." The white woman says, "You must not say that you saw me here." (She did not wish it to be known that she was a witch.)
>
> Then I put down my back-basket, and then I lie down. I go to sleep. Early I arise. There is nothing (to be seen) of the house; it is all a great stone. Then I find my bread and cheese (to be) a great cold piece of cattle dung and a white bone. Horrors![21]

From a purely narrative perspective, this text accurately reflects the fear and caution that traditional Native elders tended to display around strangers (including curious white folks). The story also followed a familiar Mohegan (and English) folkloric motif, by warning travelers against consuming strange substances when visiting different lands.

Speck's cultural interpretation is sparse, but he did include a few notes on distinctly Algonquian linguistic expressions. For example, the word *numunu'di* ("basket") combines the central concept of *muu'ndu* ("mystery") with the Algonquian first-person singular possessive, *nu*, and an inanimate suffix: "the whole meaning 'my basket,' cognate with idea of unknown inan[imate] contents." Speck then notes a practical observation and categorical distinction that Algonkian Indians make, not just about baskets but about external appearances: "Indians of the east designate a basket or its contents as objects which betray nothing of their internal character by their outside appearance or shape, hence the psychological analogy with God, or mystery."[22] Speck had already learned that, for Algonkian people, considerable power might be perceived within apparently inanimate objects.[23]

In their conversations, and in her diary, Fielding bluntly shared her opinions on the undercurrents of race hatred in everyday social relations in New England. In an entry for May 6, 1904, she referred to the New London encounter, writing about "that stone where the witches come. . . . Perhaps it is cold, then will they want a fire to warm their hands. Then will they divide their money that they could steal. Then the people think those people are good because they have money." Here, she felt compelled to clarify the difference between these moneyed folks and the Mohegan: "Poor Indian! He has not money, he has not anything because he cannot steal, lie!"[24] In his explanation of this text, Speck wryly noted:

> Like most Indians of the East, she never forgot to lament the political and moral injuries done her race by the whites. Her most cordial feelings toward me during the time of our friendship were occasionally interrupted by outbreaks of racial antipathy on her part reawakened by the memory of the Yankees, whose name she derived from the active verb denoted in the first syllable of the word.[25]

Speck's unexpected success in recovering a dying language rapidly made him a star in the world of salvage anthropology. By the time Speck's master's studies were done, Professor Prince was recommending him for a research fellowship at the University of Pennsylvania, identifying him as a "most careful and talented investigator." In the letter, Prince identified Fielding, falsely, as the "last survivor of the Mohegan-Pequots," while praising Speck as "a very accurate recorder in Algic philology," noting, "I was able to place nearly every word, of this obsolescent dialect, by comparison with other eastern Algonquian languages which I have studied as a side issue."[26] This accomplishment sounds impressive, but it must be seen, more rationally, as a qualified success. Speck's early work did not actually evidence linguistic or cultural fluency in Mohegan. The material he discovered was "new" to the academic world, but it was "old" to the Mohegan community.

By 1905 Speck concluded that "the last morsel of obtainable linguistic and ethnological material concerning this important and little known group of Algonkian had been secured and published."[27] He handed Fielding's diary to Prince, but shortly thereafter, the book was lost forever when Prince's house went up in flames. Fielding passed away in 1908, but her influence on Speck had by no means ended. Around 1918, her adopted son, John Cooper (who had, by then, taken on the surname of Fielding), handed Speck additional texts that included historical data, migration stories recorded by Emma Baker and Lemuel Fielding, cultural data, geographical names and legends, and maps, in addition to Fielding's diary entries from 1902 to 1905.[28] Inspired to revisit his Mohegan research, Speck adapted this material into a publication for the Bureau of American Ethnology titled *Native Tribes and Dialects of Connecticut*.[29]

The book was welcomed by the academic world for the insights it offered into the Mohegan world, even though parts of it veered into Eurocentric stereotyping. Speck included a character sketch of Fielding, written from a social psychology perspective, that critically assessed her eccentricities. Both her "religious fanaticism" and "native superstition" were identified as natural by-products of having "a cast of mind and appearance typically Indian." He wrote:

Her home in later years was a place of solitude amid the brush and pasture land of the old Mohegan settlement. Here she tended a tiny garden, alone except for the companionship of creatures of her imagination and an occasional stray dog, a fox or deer appearing in her clearing, always bearing to her sensitive mind some augury or omen. Her atmosphere was that fairyland of giants, dwarfs, will-o'-the wisps, ghosts, and haunts. . . . In this respect she portrayed a phase of the old New England Indian paganism in her anthropomorphic concept of *Ma'undu, di'bi,* and other monsters of the intangible world.[30]

This description paints Fielding as an odd recluse; yet, from a traditional Mohegan perspective, she was perfectly sane, grounded in a profoundly Indigenous world, fully cognizant of the importance of maintaining balanced relations among human and other-than-human beings. As her niece Gladys later recalled:

The most interesting part of Fidelia's life that I recall was that she knew about the Little People who live in the woods, the Makiawisug. On one occasion there was a family dinner and meeting in the old parsonage, half a mile down the road from here. At one point, she told one of the relatives that she was stepping outside for a minute to talk to the Little People. . . . Some of the younger family members regarded her as "quite different" (and they laughed, but I did not). She used to visit my parents because they did not ridicule her.[31]

Fielding served a crucial role in Mohegan society, as the inheritor of sociocultural traditions passed on by Martha Uncas. As someone who "bridged pre-reservation and post-reservation Mohegan society," she was not lonely; she was simply a loner who preferred to keep her own company.[32]

The diary entries from 1902 to 1905 clearly show that Fielding socialized on her own terms. Joseph Ray did chores for her, and Roscoe Skeesucks came by to visit. She walked to New London to peddle brooms and baskets, and she foraged for herbal medicines in the surrounding forests and meadows. She regularly walked out to pick up mail at Muddy Cove; one can only wonder who she corresponded with. There were periodic shopping trips to Palmertown and Norwich, which she called "Landing," recalling the history of the site as a trading locale with colonial settlers. Some Sundays, she attended services at the Mohegan Church, afterward visiting the Tantaquidgeons, Fowlers, and others on the hill. She occasionally complained of having too little money or food but always counted herself better off than Theodore Cooper, the lame "pitiful boy" and younger brother to her adopted sons. Frank Speck is mentioned only once in these diaries: a single note records a visit from "Mr. Speck" during which nothing remarkable happened.[33] All of these seemingly mundane activities and phenomenological experiences were guided by and interwoven with Indigenous kinship, deep knowledge of local oral traditions, ecological understandings reflected in patterns of resource gathering, and carefully negotiated relations with the other-than-human residents of Mohegan homelands.[34]

Speck theorized that Fielding's fluency was indicative of the durability of oral tradition. When he compared her Mohegan to the Pequot terms collected in 1764 by President Ezra Stiles of Yale University, he was surprised to see linguistic stability with "practically no deviation from the Mohegan given here, even after the wide lapse of 158 years."[35] He assumed that Fielding was an anomaly, but literacy was relatively common in southern New England's Native communities during the eighteenth and nineteenth centuries, especially among Christian Indians like Mohegans Samson Occum and Joseph Johnson.[36] The Tantaquidgeon family had long been literate; they "lived in the old Tecoomwas-Hoscoat homestead where a young Missionary teacher held Sabbath and Day School classes for Mohegan children in 1827."[37] Fielding had learned Indigenous knowledge (medicinal, spiritual, ecological, linguistic, etc.) from her grandmother Martha Shantup Uncas (1761–1859), and her mentor Emma Baker (1828–1916), a bilingual tribal historian who may have taught her Mohegan orthography.[38]

By the time Frank Speck showed up, however, Native children were being pressured to conform to English language and customs, and elders were reluctant to share their language and cultural traditions with vulnerable youth. He noted that few people were "taking any pains whatsoever to master her speech, a fact which she knew and lamented so frequently." Speck recalled that she placed intense emphasis on teaching her orthographic system, having "dictated at different times during her life, her words to me, so that most of them had been recorded."[39] Given the vulnerability of the language, it is entirely possible that Fielding tapped Speck to function as a sort of ghostwriter, a vehicle for recording Mohegan traditions that might otherwise have been lost. Perhaps her diaries were composed as part of an informal tutoring strategy. It is doubtful that she intend these writings to be published, especially since they contained both personal notes and prayers. Regardless, Speck recorded and published most (if not all) of what Fielding shared with him, leaving a record that preserved her utterances in print.

Fictive Kin: Raised by Indians?

Frank Speck had such an innate skill in learning Indigenous languages that many people assumed he had Indian blood, and that he had spent his childhood living among Indians. In his early publications, as noted, Speck stated unequivocally that he first met Fidelia while he was a student at Columbia

University. Yet his colleagues and biographers later embraced (and appear to have originated) the myth that young Frank, as a sickly child, was sent away to live with the Mohegan Indians and was raised by Fidelia Fielding.[40]

In fact, Frank Speck's early years were spent in Brooklyn, New York, with his parents, Frank G. Speck Sr. and Hattie L. Staniford, and two siblings, Gladys H. (born 1890) and Reinhard S. (born 1891).[41] Frank Speck Sr. worked as a bookkeeper before prospering on the Cotton Exchange; city directories from 1889 to 1894 list him as a broker residing at 328 First Street.[42] The 1892 New York State census lists Frank Speck Jr. (then age eleven) as a student living at home at the same location.[43] During the summer, the family often took sojourns in the country, visiting Fish's Eddy, a rural retreat just north of Brooklyn, and rural Connecticut.[44] The children also attended summer camp, as evidenced in a letter sent by Frank from a camp in Summitville, in the lower Catskill Mountains.[45]

Around 1898 the Speck family relocated to Hackensack in Bergen County, New Jersey, to escape the congestion of urban New York City. Frank Sr. commuted to his workplace in Manhattan by train, and Hattie managed the household with the assistance of a young German immigrant woman, Anna Muller, who was employed as a live-in servant.[46] Seventeen-year-old Frank Jr. (hereafter simply called Frank) enjoyed rambles in the forests and swamps of Hackensack, exploring the salt marshes by canoe. He collected "a library of books on natural history and Indians, which he kept in a little summer house on his father's property."[47] In 1899 Frank entered Columbia University, where, at his father's urging, he had been considering a degree in business. During the following summer, on his first break from Columbia, Frank took that jaunt to Fort Shantok, where he first made contact with the group of teenaged Mohegans who would become his lifelong friends. On December 5, 1902, Frank Sr. passed away unexpectedly in Manhattan; by all accounts, this was a devastating loss.[48] In subsequent years, although he traveled frequently, Frank Speck was rarely alone; at home and in the field, he was always surrounded by an extensive network of familial and academic kin and company.

In 1908, after having been awarded the Harrison Fellowship at the University Museum, Frank married Florence Insley (1884–1979) from Rockland County, New York. Frank and Florence shared a house in Philadelphia with another former Columbia graduate student, Edward Sapir, recipient of the 1909 Harrison Fellowship.[49] When Sapir left to assume a new post as head of the Canadian anthropology division at the Victoria Museum in Ottawa (now the Canadian Museum of History), Frank brought his mother and younger siblings to Philadelphia. There, they employed Gussie Giles, a thirty-six-year-old "Mulatto" woman (of mixed African and Native American ancestry) from South Carolina, as a live-in nanny and maid.[50] The extended family lived together in Philadelphia until 1912, when Frank's mother and siblings moved back to Hackensack, New Jersey.[51] Frank and Florence then bought a house at 103 Cornell Avenue, in Swarthmore, Pennsylvania, where they raised three children: Frank Staniford (nicknamed Billy, born 1917), Alberta Insley (born 1923), and Virginia Colfax (born 1925).[52] The family also kept a summer home on the Annisquam River at Cape Ann on the north shore of Massachusetts, inherited from Frank's father, and located a few miles away from his brother Reinhard's dairy farm in Rockport.

One possible source for the myth of Frank Speck's Mohegan upbringing can be traced to a letter he wrote to Professor Prince in 1938, recalling how, in the aftermath of his father's death, he had gravitated to Prince as a substitute father figure. Frank had been "an eager youth open to influence that would mold my future," and was charmed by the possibility of future research adventures.

> Before you was a youth whose early life, as well as ancestry, were imbedded in the history of the New Amsterdam-New York region and Hudson Valley, by land and sea, from aboriginal and colonial times. Something in his make-up was calling him in one direction while circumstances of the age were pressing in another. . . . And so he came to dream of some day being like you, in the high light of activity in letters, in glimpsing within the recesses of alien minds and cultures, to impart through the magic of languages the golden treasures of such knowledge to others like himself, looking for principles of guidance in humanistic research. That student was myself.
>
> Then one day you took me to Boas and told me that there was where I belonged. Another star was added to my firmament. . . . Then you bestowed upon me the privilege of sharing your literary honors by signing me as collaborator in the publication of my heritage pittance in Mohegan. You lifted me to the dignity of co-author in the company of a savant, giving me a share of your status without the asking. . . . This was my beginning.[53]

Years later, researchers would point to several phrases in this letter as supposed evidence of Speck's Indian origins: Did his family roots in "aboriginal and colonial times" in the Hudson Valley denote Mahican ancestry? Did his "heritage pittance in Mohegan" signal Mohegan kin?

Speck never found any verifiable blood or genealogical ties to any Native ancestors, though he longed to think it might be possible. Carl Weslager observed that Frank "liked to be told that he resembled an Indian and was very pleased one day when I said he looked like one of the Nanticoke mixed bloods."[54] Frank's son, Frank Staniford Speck, observed similar longings: "He lived a life imagining he was an Indian. It was romantic."[55] His daughter Alberta recalled, "My father wanted to be an Indian so badly. He and my mother were interested in genealogy, but they could never find any Indian ancestry."[56] Over time, Speck's colleagues surmised that he *must* have been raised by Indians, since he so readily understood their philosophies and was so eager to associate with them.[57] There is no evidence that Speck ever actually *claimed* to have been raised by the Mohegans, but he does not appear to have discouraged his colleagues from guesswork. He likely found these stories amusing.

Speck's Penn students John Witthoft and Loren Eisely appear to have been the chief contributors to the legend of Speck's fictive kin. The stories became so compelling with retelling that they demonstrate the circuitous manner in which romantic speculation can morph into fact. Where did he get that natural ability for learning Indian languages? Why else would a wealthy white boy consort with Indians? They even imagined Mrs. Fielding as a schoolmarm, although there is no evidence that she ever served as such. Speck never explained, so his colleagues filled in the blanks.

Horace Beck recalled that Speck once said "as a child he had had an Indian woman as a nurse," but there was no mention of her name.[58] Eiseley heard that when young Frank was "in ill health, he had been entrusted to the care of an old Mohegan woman," who acted like a "foster mother."[59] Was this woman one of the live-in housekeepers hired by the Specks? Was she a local herbal medicine peddler? Witthoft claimed that the Speck family was "proud of their Dutch and Mahican ancestry" and had long been close friends with Mrs. Fielding. So, when Frank's "childhood health was precarious" and "family and physicians began to fear for his life," he was whisked away to Mohegan where (so the story goes), little Frank flourished.

> As Frank's health improved with a good rural life and loving care, he learned to converse in Pequot with Mrs. Fielding. His lessons in the country school were supplemented by her reading and spelling lessons in the literary form of John Eliot's Bible. She inspired him with her love of nature and her knowledge of woodcraft, and showed him endless botanical curiosities recognized in the lore of the herbalist. . . . If Speck's family traditions made the historic past of his Mahican ancestors seem near and recent, Mrs. Fielding brought him into the reality of Indian civilization within his own time. Her love for him was a demonstration of the true character of the aboriginal peoples; his love for her remained as an abiding knowledge of the true state of affairs in history and as a knowledge of true human values.[60]

In this highly romanticized version, it was Fielding, not Prince, who inspired Speck to pursue anthropology so that he could recapture his supposed childhood at Mohegan.

The presumed veracity of this fanciful tale only increased after Speck's death in 1950, when Witthoft's account was uncritically incorporated into the official finding aids and background notes for Speck's papers at the American

Philosophical Society (APS), the University of Pennsylvania Archives, the University Museum (now the Penn Museum), and other supposedly authoritative archival institutions. The APS background note states, for example, that Speck was "a fragile and sickly child" who, from 1888 to 1894, was placed "in the care of family friend Fidelia Fielding," who "tutored him in nature, natural history, English literature, and Mohegan language and literature."[61] None of this is verifiable. Adding to the confusion, four decades after Speck's death, Witthoft embellished the story in a commemorative volume edited by Speck's grandson, Roy Blankenship. Blankenship had no personal experience with Speck's fieldwork or Native informants (he was only six when Frank died), but he embraced the idea of Native kinship, regarding his grandfather as "more Indian than white man."[62]

Oddly, although Speck's colleagues all *assumed* Speck to be related to the Mohegan, none of them sought verification from the Mohegan people who actually knew him, including the members of the Tantaquidgeon family who outlived him. Apart from the fantasy of a white boy raised by Indians, there are other problems with this fictive kin relationship. John Witthoft, who promoted the characterization of Fidelia Fielding as a simple Indian mother adopting a sickly white boy, apparently imagined the Mohegan community to be full of little sick boys, pointing to the evidence of the disabled lad who lived with Cynthia Fowler. Such a characterization assigns an odd pathology to sickness within a community where, as Melissa Tantaquidgeon Zobel puts it, "disability was not seen as such." From a Mohegan perspective, it would have made no sense whatsoever to separate an individual from their culture of origin for the purpose of healing. To the contrary, healing was best effected by embedding one even more deeply within one's culture, and applying appropriate Indigenous pharmacological, physical, and spiritual interventions to encourage some restoration of balance or accommodation to both the individual, and the community, relations.[63] This is not to say that white people had no access to Indian medicine; during the nineteenth century, Native peoples routinely peddled herbal medicine to their white neighbors.[64] By the 1890s, however, there was such a deep racial divide in Connecticut, and Fielding had such a deep dislike of white people, that it would have made no sense for her to invite a sick white boy to live with the tribe.

More to the point, the suggestion that Frank Speck's skills emerged from his fictional Indian upbringing obscures the contributions of the real Indians who collaborated with him. The Mohegans were not naïve primitives; they were skilled recordkeepers who (being literate) kept both oral and written records of their encounters, now preserved in the tribal archives. The records show that Fielding did adopt two boys, but they were both Mohegan: John Leach and Alonzo (John) Cooper, both sons of Effie Cooper.[65] Members of the Tantaquidgeon family recall that Speck had been "vacationing with his family in Niantic, Connecticut," when he first visited Fort Shantok, about fourteen miles to the north. Elders recalled, "Everyone liked the personable young student and he was made welcome in all Mohegan homes."[66] It was Burrill Tantaquidgeon who had encouraged Frank "to meet his aunt Fidelia Fielding and record the language from her. I do not know how he did it. Fidelia didn't like many people."[67] Some recall Fielding as having been a rather cross-tempered woman who "hated white people, she even hated other Indians." Yet she enjoyed visiting with Frank, perhaps because, as Gladys Tantaquidgeon later noted, "his theories were in their formative stages. He was to participate in a give-and-take relationship with her people."[68]

Those early encounters evolved into lifelong friendships, marked in other ways. Burrill's baby sister, Gladys (who was only one year old when Frank first showed up), grew up to become a close friend and research assistant, and rather like a surrogate daughter to Frank.[69] Their brother Harold was especially fond of Frank, whom he described as "one of the greatest. He was a man's man and was comfortable with those from all walks of life. He walked in my moccasins and I walked in his."[70] Roscoe Skeesucks gave Frank a tattoo, after Frank had admired (and photographed) the line drawing of a thunderbird with a man's head (copied after Chief Uncas's signature) inscribed on Roscoe's left forearm. On Frank's forearm, Roscoe inscribed the letter *S* with a snake's head, marking the Mohegan nickname that Fielding had given him: Skook-een ("Snake Man").[71] Frank Speck visited many times over the years, as Gladys recalled:

> One summer while in Mohegan he visited me at a Boy Scout camp where I had built, with the help of Scouts and Counselors, a Mohegan Village. He had planned to stay overnight and the camp director said that he would prepare sleeping quarters in one of the cabins but Speck preferred to stay in my longhouse. A painting he did of that Village scene is one of our prized possessions.[72]

Gladys's niece, Jayne Fawcett, told me personally of her delight at meeting Frank Speck in person when she was a small child in the 1940s; smiling widely, she recalled that "everybody loved Frank" as the most welcome non-Native visitor to Mohegan Hill.[73]

Several elements of the myth of Frank Speck's Mohegan adoption likely emerged from the experiences of another generation, when there actually *was* a "Frank Speck" who spent part of his childhood living with Indians. This was Frank's son, Frank Staniford Speck (whom Mohegan people also called Frank, but who went by the family nickname of Billy). For most of his childhood, this boy was surrounded by Indians. At the Speck family home in Swarthmore, the young boy and his sisters lived for months at a time with the Mohegans

Gladys Tantaquidgeon, her brother Harold, and their friend Jerome Roscoe Skeesucks. Skeesucks boarded with the Speck family for about a year while he was taking art lessons (under Frank's sponsorship) at the Pennsylvania Academy of Fine Arts in Philadelphia.[74] Other house guests included Tlingit Indians Louis and Florence Shotridge, the Delaware medicine man Witaponox'we, a honeymooning Nanticoke couple, and the Penobscot dancer Molly Spotted Elk. Frank Staniford Speck recalled that Molly kept a trunk of clothes at the house, and that she "would appear and disappear at our house when I was quite young. She slept on the sofa, or upstairs in the room where Gladys had stayed. There was nothing regular about her coming and going."[75] There were many, many other Native guests over the years.

In 1919 a young and sickly "Frank Speck" was indeed sent to live with the Indians. Three-year-old Frank Staniford and his mother, Florence, contracted the flu during the horrific Spanish influenza epidemic, and they left Philadelphia for several months. Carl Weslager recalled the incident.

> Her physician prescribed sunshine and rest. Her husband lost no time in putting Florence and the boy aboard a train for Indian River [Nanticoke homelands in southern Delaware]. There, in the healthful pine air, mother and son lived among the [Nanticoke] Indians, thriving and growing stronger. Speck came down from Philadelphia by train each Friday to spend the week-end with his family.[76]

The boy and his mother were nursed back to health by Nanticoke elders Howard and Eliza Ann Johnson, who were old family friends.

In another parallel to the myth, there is the fact that sometimes during the summers young Frank Staniford Speck lived in Connecticut with the Mohegans. When Frank and Florence were away doing field research, they left all three children—Frank, Alberta, and Virginia—to be looked after by the Tantaquidgeon family on Mohegan Hill. Gladys recalled:

> One year when the Specks were going to be away for several months their three children lived with our family. Frank Jr. attended a local Elementary school and Alberta and Virginia were taught by our sister Ruth. A small building in our yard (now a garage) served as the schoolroom. Harold served as custodian. They had fun playing with Mohegan girls and boys and going on picnics.[77]

Often, both families—Specks and Tantaquidgeons—would spend part of the summer together living in "The Wigwam," which was not a rustic Indigenous structure but a wooden "summer cottage" built beside the Annisquam River in Cape Ann, Massachusetts.[78] Frequent visitors included local archaeologist N. Carleton Phillips, Ernest Dodge from the Peabody Essex Museum, Ralph

Figure 20 Three Mohegan men—Chief Matagha, Harold Tantaquidgeon, and Mr. Ross (holding bow and arrow)—standing beside sixteen-year-old Frank Staniford Speck (*second from left*) in front of the Tantaquidgeon Indian Museum, Montville, Conn., 1932. Photograph by Frank G. Speck. Courtesy of Tantaquidgeon Indian Museum.

Dexter from Kent State University, and dozens of Native visitors, some of whom stayed in a tipi set up in the backyard.[79] Gladys recalled those summers at the cottage as "learning vacations" amid a "menagerie of artists, professors and assorted Algonquian Indians."[80]

Frank Staniford Speck, like his father, also engaged in field research among the Indians during his late teens. From 1934 to 1936 (when he was seventeen-to-nineteen years of age), he accompanied his father on research trips to visit Six Nations people in Ontario, Innu in Labrador, Cherokee in South Carolina, and Penobscot in Old Town, Maine. Some travel expenses were paid by Penn research grants; father and son covered the rest by collecting material for the Museum of the American Indian, Denver Art Museum, Penn professor Samuel Weiler Fernberger, Samuel Pennypacker, and others.[81]

In 1936, when Speck was preparing to finally publish his monograph *Penobscot Man*, he revisited Old Town, with his nineteen-year-old son in tow to assist.[82] In the introduction to the book, Speck recalled that he had been "little more than a boy" when he started that work in 1911; this was a slight exaggeration, since Speck was, in 1911, twenty-nine years of age. He dedicated the book to his primary informant, Newell Lyon, and begged forgiveness from critics who had moved beyond the intimacies of personal relationships with their informants to practice more detached studies in the field. The text of his dedication must have added fuel to the rumors that Speck had been raised by Indians. He wrote:

> The moving reason for my actions in releasing these records now lies in what they mean as documents of the thoughts and actions of old Indians at a time when, as little more than a boy, I traveled and camped with them by day and by night, watched them and wrote down their verbal offerings drawn from experience and memory going back to their own youth and childhood.[83]

With all this in mind, it is entirely possible that some of the Speck family stories became tangled together over time, and that some people, reaching back in memory, confused one story for another, and mistook Frank Staniford Speck (the son) for Frank Gouldsmith Speck Jr. (the father), since both Franks spent so much of their lives among Indians.

Founding a Department

In 1907, when Prince and Boas recommended Frank Speck for the George Lieb Harrison Research Fellowship at the University of Pennsylvania in Philadelphia (Penn), Boas allowed Speck to finish his doctorate at Penn rather than Columbia. In 1908 Speck's dissertation "Ethnology of the Yuchi Indians" was approved and immediately accepted for publication as a book.[84] From 1909 to 1913, Speck held dual appointments as both an assistant in ethnology at the University Museum and an instructor of anthropology for the university.[85] He was not, as is often suggested, the original founder of the Department of Anthropology at Penn.[86]

The teaching of anthropology at Penn actually began in 1886, when Daniel Garrison Brinton (1837–99), professor of ethnology and anthropology at the Academy of Natural Sciences in Philadelphia, was hired as a professor of archaeology and linguistics at Penn.[87] By 1891 instruction in archaeology was also being offered at Penn via the University Archaeological Association and the new Department of Archaeology and Paleontology. In 1892 Brinton drafted a proposal for a formal Department of Anthropology at Penn that would merge these disciplines, arguing: "We erect stately museums, we purchase costly specimens, we send out costly expeditions, but where are the universities, the institutions of high education, who train young men how to observe, how to collect and explore in this branch?"[88] Brinton requested that the university establish "an autonomous department with faculty, laboratories, museums, and fellowships," but the proposal was not embraced by the administration.[89] Instead, efforts focused on the construction of the new University Museum, and the first phase was completed in 1899. Brinton passed away in that same year; his courses remained on the books, even though there was no one to teach them.[90] Although Brinton's vision failed to come to fruition in his lifetime, in 1986 the Penn Department of Anthropology celebrated "A Centennial for Anthropology at the University of Pennsylvania" with commemorative events, academic conferences, and a new publication on Brinton.[91]

In 1904 George Byron Gordon, the University Museum's assistant curator of archaeology and ethnology, revived Brinton's proposal with an imperialist angle, arguing that elite white men should be trained, not just as scientific observers of different cultures but as future state administrators.

> The need in America for men highly trained in Anthropology has been greatly increased by the acquisition of territories inhabited by people in the lower stages of development. The administration of these territories can best be accomplished by men with a scientific knowledge of the qualities that are peculiar to these lower stages and an intelligent insight into the institutions and antecedents of the people with whom they will have to deal.[92]

Penn provost Charles C. Harrison approved an undergraduate curriculum with lecture courses in prehistoric archaeology, American archaeology and ethnology, ethnology of Europe, peoples of the Pacific, somatology (biological anthropology), primitive arts, primitive society, and primitive religions, in addition to a hands-on course in museum methods.[93] Gordon recruited Speck to teach the introductory course.

> I do not wish to dictate to you how the course shall be conducted. It is simply designed to be a course covering in a general way the whole field of Anthropology as it is taught at the present time in the American Universities. I shall probably give the first part myself dealing with the biological side of anthropology. After that you will be expected to take up ethnography giving an outline of the whole field. After that the subject of linguistics. . . . Then the history of different systems of writing. . . . Then the origin and early development of the aesthetic arts and industrial processes. . . . Then the origin and early development of social institutions.[94]

A 1908 letter signed by Dean Herman V. Ames established the new Department of Anthropology and approved raising Gordon from instructor to assistant professor. Speck was appointed in his dual position as museum assistant and university instructor, and Edward Sapir, that year's Harrison Fellow, was also appointed as a part-time instructor of linguistic anthropology.[95] At first, the trio worked well together, and they all enjoyed the resources of the University Museum, which had a substantial collection of ethnographic material. Gordon had arranged for wealthy collector George Gustav Heye "to place on deposit in this Museum his entire collection of many thousand objects." When the collection was moved to Philadelphia, Heye also paid for the appointments of Mark Raymond Harrington as assistant curator and George H. Pepper as acting curator to manage it.[96]

Tensions arose in 1910, when Dean Fisher instructed the group to elect a department chair, and Gordon selected himself.[97] Speck and Sapir were fiercely opposed, going so far as to accuse Gordon of having fabricated administrative correspondence. Sapir left Penn, accepting a position as head of anthropology for the Geological Survey of Canada, and work at the Victoria Museum.[98] In that same year, the museum's Board of Managers appointed Gordon as the new University Museum director. His overlapping appointments generated confusion that persists to the present day.[99]

Speck was never, as some sources suggest, "fired" from the museum and "rehired" by the university.[100] Instead, he held dual appointments until 1912, when his full-time faculty appointment in anthropology enabled him to leave his half-time post in the museum. He told Sapir, "I am now no longer an attache of the Museum, only Asst. Prof. in Dept. so I am partly relieved of G.B.G. [Gordon] opprobrius control."[101] Over the next few years, the two exchanged dense correspondence full of complaints about Gordon, who had reappointed himself as department chair. Things were so difficult that Tlingit ethnologist Louis Shotridge (who had just arrived in 1912) almost left, "on account of general dissatisfaction with Gordon. . . . He is pretty well peeved with this place."[102]

A century later, Penn professor Igor Kopytoff tried to explain the enmity between Gordon and Speck, stating: "There are many anecdotes about the feuding between them. The question of how many of them are true . . . is the kind of problem that collectors of oral tradition face." Kopytoff insisted that Gordon had been "opposed to the formation of a regular academic department within the college—an indication of his view that there was an inherent conflict between the missions of museums and of academic anthropology."[103] The truth, however, is that Gordon very much wanted an academic department, and he intended to run it. Kopytoff also reported a bizarre anecdote that had acquired local popularity.

> In his campaign to dislodge Speck, Gordon supposedly put a padlock on the bathroom on Speck's floor, depriving Speck of its use. Speck solved the problem by opening and using his window—the dribbling on the Director's window below

quickly resulted in a key being conveyed to Speck. Apocraphyl or not, the story is consonant with Speck's personality.[104]

This tale makes no sense, given the abundance of toilet facilities in the museum, and it is logistically nearly impossible, given the locations of their respective offices and the depth of the director's window sill. Why would a promising young man make such a serious breach of social protocol? Kopytoff attributes this bad behavior to Speck's "Native American descent" and his obvious preference for associating with Indians.[105] This is, however, a troubling conflation of social nonconformity and racial stereotyping. It is undeniably true that Speck preferred the company of his Native informants to some of his university colleagues, but the question of which group was better behaved is open for discussion.

The truth is that Gordon had become increasingly "despotic and unreliable," demanding absolute domination over junior faculty while failing to fulfill academic responsibilities. He insisted that Speck collect ethnographic materials for the museum but refused to provide field research funding.[106] He demanded to publish research that Speck had promised elsewhere. Then, during the summer of 1913, he forced Speck to vacate his office to make room for new research fellows.[107] Speck told Sapir, "GBG has dispossessed us of our office & thrown out my library, insults me and presumes to meet my classes and dictate policy in courses."[108] Making matters worse, Gordon had confiscated Speck's nearly complete *Penobscot Man* book manuscript and locked it in the museum vault. Speck was subsequently allowed to access it, with advance permission, but the manuscript was not allowed to leave the custody of the museum until after Gordon's death in 1927. Parts of it, in fact, are still housed in the Penn Museum archives today.[109]

Gordon further retaliated by moving the skeletal material used for teaching physical anthropology to the Wistar Institute, and he placed the museum library under lock and key, rendering it nearly inaccessible to students and faculty.[110] In the midst of these troubles, Heye (who was every bit as authoritarian and high-strung as Gordon) packed up his entire collection and returned to New York City, taking curators Harrington and Pepper with him.[111] Speck was responsible for the teaching of ethnology, but he had limited access to the museum, even to the objects he had collected. Over time, his office and his homes became substitute museums, filled with ethnographic objects from many corners of the world.[112]

After Speck moved his office to College Hall, he assumed the position of chair of the Department of Anthropology. Gordon continued teaching part-time for a few years, but by 1918 Speck was the sole anthropology faculty member left standing. Speck taught courses at all levels until 1923, when he

Figure 21 Frank G. Speck Jr. in his office in College Hall at the University of Pennsylvania, 1937. Photograph by Ted Stone. Image # UARC20080922002. Courtesy of the Collections of the University of Pennsylvania Archives.

hired his former graduate student A. Irving Hallowell. Enrollments in anthropology courses averaged ninety-seven undergraduate and thirty-five graduate students each year, an impressive number.[113] Speck served as department chair for nearly four decades, stepping down just a few months before he passed away in 1950. When former students Loren Eiseley, John Alden Mason, John Witthoft, and Sam Fernberger drafted a brief history of the department, they retrospectively decided that "Dr. Speck should be considered as the founder of anthropology at the University of Pennsylvania."[114] In essence, they chose to define a "department" as an autonomous entity operating separately from the University Museum, which, interestingly, is precisely what D. G. Brinton had originally proposed in 1886.[115]

Crossing Color Lines

During an era of extreme racial prejudice and social stratification, Speck demonstrated a remarkable ease in crossing boundaries and an egalitarian acceptance of differences. His colleagues observed that "race and color meant nothing to Frank Speck. He treated people of all races without prejudice. . . . Black people were not welcomed in Virginia restaurants where white people ate, but Speck took the dark-skinned mixed bloods into restaurants to eat with him."[116] Speck fraternized with African American herbalists on the streets of Philadelphia, Lenape men in the New Jersey Pine Barrens, and Montagnais guides in the wilds of Labrador.

His predilection for what he called "bedside ethnology" (rather than "door-step" or "kitchen-table" encounters) separated him from scholars who maintained both social and scientific distance from their subjects.[117] This physical closeness, which included living and camping with informants, gave him access to data that other researchers might miss. It also enabled him to gain working fluency in a number of Algonquian and Iroquoian dialects. His student Edmund Carpenter recalled that Speck was masterful at code-switching.

> When his host hunted, he hunted; when they spoke, he replied in their language; and thus he came to know what symbols meant and where value lay. He was completely, happily at home in each of these cultures, so much so he could switch from one to another, from language to language, the way a train switches tracks. This never failed to astonish me.[118]

Loren Eisely described Speck as a "magician"; he saw him as "a man of extraordinary mental powers and a formidable personality," who readily embraced and absorbed Indigenous beliefs and practices.[119]

Speck's experiences with Fidelia Fielding made him especially attentive to the urgency of working with elderly Native people who were carriers of dying traditions. In 1914, for example, he requested three weeks' leave midsemester to make an immediate trip to Canada to work with one such informant.

> François Neptune, an old Indian whom I had the good fortune to chance upon recently, [is] the sole survivor of the band of Algonkians speaking the dialect of the Wawenock. This band disappeared, according to history, from the coast of Maine about 1727. Accordingly the dialect is on the verge of extinction. I have found it to be related to Penobscot which I have been studying for a number of years; consequently the cognate material which can be obtained from Wawenock will be particularly valuable for correlation.[120]

As J. Alden Mason would later observe, Speck seemed destined for this work.

> Speck remained all his life true to his first love, the Indians of the eastern seaboard from Labrador to the Carolinas, and mainly the Algonkians and Iroquois. Distant pastures were no greener for him. He knew all the disappearing half-blood groups

of Connecticut, Long Island, Delaware, and everywhere else in his chosen field, and knew the individuals personally; he went back to visit them time and time again, wringing from them the last memories of by-gone days.[121]

There are many reports of the warmth with which Speck's Native informants greeted him. Ernest Dodge, who had accompanied Frank to a Bear Ceremony at Six Nations in Ontario, was impressed by the "successful ritual of psychotherapy" but equally impressed at witnessing "Frank at his very best as a sympathetic and knowledgeable genius." Dodge knew they would never have been welcome had it not been for Speck's "long and close relationship with the participants."[122] On one return visit to Nanticoke, after two decades away, Carl Weslager reported that everyone recognized him: "His fame had been inherited by a generation that had never seen him. 'I've heared my grandfather and grandmother talk about you,' one of the youngsters said. Those who remembered him were genuinely pleased to see him again."[123]

During his trips into the field, Speck was particularly attentive to cultural protocols of gift-giving and reciprocity. For example, in 1913 he held a "potlatch" giveaway to repay his friends at Bear Island in Temagami, Ontario, for their assistance. He told Sapir:

> Last night I gave this band a little feast and they gave us a dance in the bush. Almost 150 Inds. came & we were the only white people permitted on hand, although there are a half dozen or so on the island. The ceremony opened with a round dance, a kind of "reverser." Then I had soft drinks passed around, & a Duck Dance followed, very pretty figure to it. Then they gave a Bear Dance "*Magwace*." Then my "potlatch man" passed around bags of candy, cakes, peanuts, pipes & tobacco. Then another old man gave a solo dance while they were eating & I followed with a little speech which the chief translated in stentorian basso-relievo, & another round dance wound up my "potlatch." Needless to say my speech was a little complimentary & they gave me a good "Migwetc!" shout.[124]

Events like this explain some of the unusual notations in Speck's research accounts at the University Museum; he was the only Penn professor to include a line item for bulk purchases of candy and tobacco when he went into the field.[125]

At the same time, Speck's correspondence reveals the social inequalities that characterized many of these ethnographic encounters. Some informants were artisans eager to sell old tools and new work. Some were Faithkeepers or chiefs, who strove to mediate anthropological relations in ways that could help their kin and communities. The most vulnerable informants were the elderly, infirm, lonely, and desperate. When Mohegan elder Cynthia Fowler was starving, Speck purchased the single thing of value she still owned—a strand of wampum beads. When the Delaware medicine man Witapanox'we was ill and impoverished, Speck helped out his old friend by purchasing his ritual regalia, feathers and peyote wands.[126] Some Native people were so desperate they gave Speck permission to sell ritual regalia. For example, in 1941 Speck wrote to Frederick H. Douglas at the Denver Art Museum about a collection of Peyote equipment, pawned by Jacob Goodshot of Pine Ridge, who, with his Passamaquoddy wife, "came into contact with me over a year ago and borrowed $25 to cover an emergency. He left this outfit with me to cover the loan." Speck eventually sold the outfit to Douglas, since "Goodshot was under economic stress [due] to the sickness of his child."[127] Collectors were sometimes warned about unscrupulous individuals attempting to sell cultural heritage. For example, when John Buck, son of a Mohawk chief, was looking for easy cash, Speck purchased his collection of Haudenosaunee ritual masks, ostensibly to preserve them. Many of these objects, however, remain trapped in museum collections today.

Like most collectors of his time, Speck's expeditions were often geared toward profit as much as research. When his Penn research funds fell short, he covered expenses by snapping up valuable objects as "investments" for sale to museums—the Denver Art Museum, Museum of the American Indian, Victoria Museum, Peabody Essex Museum, and so on—or to wealthy independent collectors such as Samuel Pennypacker and Samuel Fernberger. Examples of these transactions fill the pages of his 1912–49 collecting journal.[128]

Edmund Carpenter observed that, at times, Speck behaved like "a surrogate tribal elder, bridging the gap of a missing generation." Unlike other collectors who engaged in "subterfuge designed to gain the confidence of tribal sages," Speck respected and admired Indigenous knowledge-keepers as "noble minds" and "aristocrats of culture."

> Many trusted him, more than they trusted their own children. . . . He preserved treasures and truths from certain loss, and did so at personal expense, thanked only by dying elders. He encouraged surviving customs; re-awakened dormant ones; returned ritual objects to anyone who would use them, guard them; sent quills and beads to women, wampum to men, urging both to keep their arts and rituals alive.[129]

Statements like this, when compared to the evidence in field notes and correspondence, suggest that some collections were handled rather like an Indian pawn shop. Speck would purchase objects whenever they were available (especially when his informants seemed desperate to sell), and sometimes loan or give them back as needed.[130] This was quite unusual for the time. Collectors were rarely willing to consider returning or recirculating items to anyone other than another collector or museum.

At heart, it seems that Frank Speck was an opportunist and a sort of ethnographic shape-shifter, willing to participate in whatever strategic fictive kinship would offer him the best access to desired material or data. Native people welcomed him because he was generous, kind, and nonjudgmental. He allowed his white colleagues to imagine that he had Native ancestry or Native kin, perhaps as a means to explain his desire to cross social color lines, or avoid compliance with white social norms. While navigating these transcultural borders, Speck was often accompanied by Indigenous guides. For more than a decade, one of his closest companions was his Mohegan research assistant, Fidelia Fielding's great niece Gladys Tantaquidgeon.

Indian Girl in Philadelphia

During Speck's early visits to Mohegan, when Gladys Tantaquidgeon was only a small child, he recognized a spark of precociousness and made an audacious promise: "When I get married I'll come back with my wife and take you away with me."[131] During her first visit to the University of Pennsylvania, when she was only ten years of age, Gladys was photographed in tribal regalia with her hair braided, and heralded in the local newspaper as proof of the survival of a supposedly vanished Indian tribe.[132] When Gladys returned to Philadelphia in 1919, as a college student of twenty, she assumed far less stereotypical attire, presenting herself as a thoroughly modern Native woman in professional dress with a fashionable hair bob.[133]

Speck arranged to have Gladys formally admitted to the university as a family member (with a full tuition waiver), listing her college address as the Speck family home, at 103 Cornell Avenue in Swarthmore, Pennsylvania, and her home address as Mohegan Hill, Norwich, Connecticut.[134] Tantaquidgeon was a unique student at Penn, in several respects. Although she was registered in the College Courses for Teachers program, all her classes—one English course and at least twelve anthropology courses—were taken in the School of Arts and Sciences, which, at the time, did not accept women.[135] The schools were segregated by gender, and most of the women on campus were enrolled in the School of Nursing; the College of Liberal Arts for Women (founded in 1933) did not yet exist.[136] Tantaquidgeon was the first Native American student (and perhaps also the first female student) specializing in anthropology. She was more than a student, serving also as a secretary, cultural liaison, and research collaborator with Professor Speck.[137] Despite her many roles, she tended to be quiet and unassuming. Loren Eiseley recalled her as "a pleasant, attractive Indian girl [who] occupied the desk by the door" in Speck's office.[138]

From 1924 to 1926, Speck also sponsored another Native student at Penn, Molly (Dellis) Spotted Elk (Penobscot).[139] At this juncture, the two women became minor celebrities, announced in the local newspapers as "the first Indian women to enter the University of Pennsylvania."[140] Gladys and Molly were invited to live at International House, a dormitory originally designed to help foreign students acclimate to life in America.[141] Recognizing that they were seen as exotic outsiders, the two teamed up to educate and entertain their classmates by founding the "American Indian Club" at International House and organizing a regular "American Indian Nite" event in mid-January in Houston Hall.[142] Molly, who had performing experience from her time with the Penobscot Band on Indian Island, gave recitals and also participated in larger productions: "When the Music League of Philadelphia gave its famous Pageant on Franklin Field in 1925, this young Indian scholar [Molly] led 150 Indians in one of the episodes of that Pageant."[143] Few records of that event appear to have survived, but the Indian contingent must have made an impressive picture.

Speck was the first Penn professor to regularly invite Native Americans into the classroom as guest lecturers. For three weeks in 1914, for example, he "had an Indian informant employed at my own expense for the benefit of the department," and in 1915 he hosted Mrs. Ida White Cloud, "a Mohawk Indian," and "Mr. Gabe Paul, ex-chief of the Penobscot tribe," to speak on their respective cultures.[144] Frank's son recalled that he apparently "had arranged through the faculty club to provide a place for one Indian student a year at the university," and he also welcomed Native people to audit courses, whether or not they had been formally admitted.[145]

Edmund Carpenter recalled that Speck's office was always in action: "Students, friends, colleagues, Indian delegations, visiting scholars, strangers, all assembled there daily."[146] He and his students rushed to collect endangered Indigenous cultural traditions, languages, and other data: "Like volunteer firemen, everyone sought to prevent the destruction of something precious. Traditions, languages, entire cultures were threatened. Get into the field; publish; get on to the next job."[147] William Fenton recalled that Speck's schedule was frequently interrupted.

> No academic appointment, no learned gathering, no university functions took precedence over the visit of an Indian colleague, the summons of an Indian council, or the call to attend a ceremony. . . . Speck did not covet academic honors; rather, he valued the good opinion of his Indian friends equally with the esteem of his colleagues among academicians.[148]

Many of Tantaquidgeon's research experiences at Penn began with chance encounters with other Native people in Speck's office. One day, Delaware/

Lenape medicine man James Webber, traditionally called Witapanox'we (meaning "Walks with Daylight") serendipitously dropped by just as a donor from the Pennsylvania Museum and Historical Commission was offering to support research on local Native people. Tantaquidgeon recalled Speck's exclamation at the time, "The Lord sent Witaponoxwe."[149] Although he lived in Oklahoma, far from traditional Lenape territory, Witapanox'we provided a wealth of information.[150] The Historical Commission paid Tantaquidgeon to work with Witapanox'we, and she and Speck recorded detailed information on the Big House Ceremony, medicinal knowledge, masking rituals, and other eastern traditions that bore strong similarities to Mohegan tribal practices. The commission also paid Tantaquidgeon's travel expenses for research visits in 1931 to the Onondaga Nation in Syracuse and to the Cayuga and Delaware communities located at Six Nations in Ontario.[151]

Tantaquidgeon and Speck sought data on traditional medicinal practices, folklore, and so on during joint trips to Maine, Labrador, Newfoundland, and Six Nations communities in Ontario and Quebec.[152] The photographs from these trips are scattered throughout the university archives, publications, and family papers. In a still photograph, Gladys can be seen standing alongside a group of Nanticoke chiefs on the steps of the Delaware State House in 1922. In a film clip from 1930, she is walking out the door of the Hudson's Bay post in Labrador, shyly waving at the camera. In a photo album from 1931, Frank and Gladys are alternately posing in front of the various longhouses at the Six Nations reserve in Canada; alternate pages in the same album feature her sketches of the interiors of each longhouse.[153] Frank also encouraged other researchers to work with Gladys. In 1933, for example, he suggested that young William Fenton consider collaborating, since "Miss Tantaquidgeon has some collections of data on Cayuga herbology and ceremonial therapeutics. I would accordingly suggest that you continue arrangement of your Waugh notes on herb medicines and that we try to sit together later on."[154] Fenton, however, never followed up.

During the course of their long academic partnership, Speck was more prolific than Tantaquidgeon, but they were mutually supportive. The evidence of this can be found in snippets of correspondence, photos, fieldwork, and manuscript notes. Several sets of Speck's lecture notes in the Penn archives bear notes in her handwriting at the top. One manuscript at APS attributed to him, but written by Tantaquidgeon, describes Mohegan and Pequot archaeology, ecology, medicinal traditions, and wampum making. During the spring of 1927, he (perhaps they?) gave lectures on oral traditions of the Giant Beaver, on "Birds Regulating Human Affairs," on "Smoking as a Rite," and on Catawba medicinal knowledge. In the text for a May 9, 1927, lecture on Native American religion, Speck insisted, "To write a book on the religion of any tribe

Figure 22 Gladys Tantaquidgeon interviewing Wampanoag interlocutors at Aquinnah, Mass., c. 1928. Photograph by Frank G. Speck. Courtesy of the Phillips Library, Peabody Essex Museum.

of people is a task which obviously should never be attempted by anyone who professes to limit himself to scientific method."[155] He emphasized the importance of collaborating with Native traditionalists, rather than attempting to impose academic theories. Speck often engaged with contentious issues of identity and sovereignty that are still relevant today. His passionate advocacy for his research subjects practically flies off the page.

Speck's archived papers, scattered into multiple institutions, contain other bits of evidence revealing Tantaquidgeon's work as an editor, a research assistant, and a teaching assistant. After he had persuaded the University Museum to unlock his *Penobscot Man* manuscript, Speck enlisted Tantaquidgeon for the task of retyping and editing it. Her distinctive handwriting is clearly visible in handwritten edits and notes throughout the text; his notes to her, in an equally distinctive hand, are written in the margins. The distribution of these edited pages says as much about their patterns of work as it does about the accidents of archiving: some pages are housed at Penn, some are at APS, and some are at Mohegan. One note on a page with ink blurred by rain says, "Glad—the Thunder Beings were here tonight." When *Penobscot Man* finally did go to press in 1940, Speck formally thanked Gladys Tantaquidgeon in the introduction.[156]

Remaining Indian

Over time, Frank G. Speck became increasingly sensitive to issues of representation that threatened the very survival of the tribal communities he researched. For example, in Canada, while Speck was conducting research for the Victoria Museum, he learned that First Nations communities were being forced out of their traditional hunting and fishing territories by American sportsmen. Chiefs William Berens and Aleck Paul, among others, begged Speck to plead their case to Canadian authorities. In consultation with his old friend Edward Sapir, Speck developed a possible solution. Using data derived from interviews, combined with patrilineal demarcations of hunting territories, Speck worked with tribal leaders to create a new map of tribal lands that would "prove" Indigenous ownership.[157] In academic publications and in the popular press, Speck argued that the Algonquin, Ojibwe, and other bands were not roving nomads; they were "keepers of the game," who practiced "farming" of wild fauna, hunting within fixed territories, policing boundaries, and inheriting responsibilities in the male line.[158] Chief Aleck Paul from Bear Island, Temagami, testified that each family maintained a "family hunting ground, which would be parceled out among the sons when the owner died. . . . Each family had its own district where it belonged, and owned the game."[159]

Speck was fully aware that, traditionally, these territories were communally, rather than individually, managed. Algonkian people adhered to the ontological construction of wild animals as "other-than-human" kin, and they recognized certain spirits as "masters" of the game who would mediate human access to this wild harvest.[160] By transmuting those animal "masters" into human "keepers," and by placing responsibility within families of man rather than families of animals and spirits, Speck conceptually secularized hunting practices into a modern model that (apparently intentionally) fit the restrictions of the 1876 Indian Act, wherein land ownership, hunting rights, and chiefly title were vested conspicuously in men.[161]

The Robinson-Huron treaty had, after all, promised hunting and fishing rights to the Teme-Augama Anishinaabe at Bear Island, but Ontario had refused to set aside a reserve. First Nations people were forced to depend, in part, on income derived from working as guides and fire rangers for the non-Native hunters, tourists, settlers, and surveyors who sought to displace them.[162] Chief Paul explicitly told Speck:

You can write this down for me. . . . What we Indians want is for the Government to stop the white people killing our game, as they do it only for sport and not for support. We Indians do not need to be watched about protecting the game, we must protect the game or starve. . . . When the treaty was made, about sixty years ago, the Government said, "You Indians own the game. . . . These Indians need to have their rights in the land recognized and protected as much as the new settlers."[163]

With this in mind, Speck's informants were not "primitives" stuck in the past; they were savvy people in a modern world, using ancient logics to respond to the forces around them. In a world where power can be conceptually invested in spoken words (e.g., ritual speech) and in apparently inanimate objects (e.g., wampum), written words on paper could become a powerful weapon for cartographically reclaiming territory. Later scholars, however, attacked this research by insisting that patrilineal hunting lineages were an artifact of the fur trade, and not a true reflection of Indigenous lifeways.[164] Ironically, those scholarly arguments inadvertently supported governmental attempts to claim unceded Indigenous territories as federal lands. The First Nations land tenure struggle in Canada continues today, and is not yet resolved.

In Delaware, Speck tackled a different problem that was equally rooted in settler colonial power dynamics, land claims, and ethnic prejudice. The Nanticoke people in Delaware, of mixed Native American and African American ancestry, were subjected to scorn and marginalization on all sides. During their first visit to Indian River, Frank and Florence Speck recognized them as Indigenous. They were "among the first whites to treat the Indian River folk as equals," and the first white visitors to stay overnight at Howard and Eliza Ann Johnson's home. From that time on, "Frank and Florence Speck were treated as close relatives," and the families often exchanged gifts.

Their bags always contained presents for their Indian friends: candy, cakes, fruit, clothing, dolls and toys. When, after each visit, the time came to return to Philadelphia, the Specks found their hosts pressing gifts upon them in return. They were frequently laden with shoe boxes full of corn meal; fresh eggs packed in baskets; hams; sweet potatoes; green vegetables; butter; homemade molasses, and other country delicacies.[165]

Speck repaid Nanticoke hospitality in more than just material ways. In 1922 he facilitated the founding of the Nanticoke Indian Association of Delaware, intended to help the group gain visibility as Indigenous people and establish legal status vis-à-vis the state of Delaware.[166] In the long run, the corporate model of Indian organization may have been a flawed strategy, only because the

Bureau of Indian Affairs placed so much emphasis on the western reservation model as a marker of federal recognition.

One of the best contributions Speck made to the Nanticoke was to encourage revitalizing cultural performances that could, sometimes literally, dance traditions back to life. He helped to reawaken the Nanticoke Thanksgiving "powwow" tradition at Indian River.

> Under the guidance of their benefactor, Dr. Speck, they made costumes, strings of beads, and feather headdresses. He taught them the steps of simple Indian dances and the words to Indian songs. . . . Native ceremonial rites, like the Indian language, had been dead in Delaware for over a century, as all admitted. The purpose was patently to revive the Indian individuality by attaching some aboriginal practices to their own denuded cultural framework. It was a perfectly valid method of procedure from a sociological viewpoint.[167]

Dozens of Penn students and faculty attended these annual events. The "uninformed whites living in Indian River Hundred," however, expressed puzzlement; they "could not fathom why these mixed-bloods assumed Indian garb once a year and dressed conventionally at other times."[168] That powwow tradition continues today and, ironically, ill-informed white observers still express occasional puzzlement about the ethnic identities of the participants.[169]

In 1922 Speck returned to his Connecticut Mohegan research with renewed vigor, spending "much time with the elders in an effort to learn about and preserve any and all references to early life and customs."[170] This time, he also encouraged Gladys Tantaquidgeon to combine traditional Mohegan teachings with her new ethnographic insights, and began promoting her as a public speaker and researcher. When Speck published Fidelia Fielding's diaries, in his *Native Tribes and Dialects of Connecticut*, he gave Tantaquidgeon prominence by including one of her first research articles, "Mohegan Medicinal Practices, Weather-Lore, and Superstitions," as an addendum.[171] He also encouraged her to publish materials collected during their trips to Nanticoke in her 1931 "Report on Delaware Ethnobotanical Investigations."[172]

In 1923 they answered Thomas Bicknell's invitation to join the Algonquin Indian Council of New England (AIC), an intertribal Algonkian organization that included representatives from Massachusetts, Merrimack, Kennebec, Mohegan, Pequot, Narragansett, Niantic, Nipmuc, Passamaquoddy, Penobscot and Wampanoag communities.[173] The group organized pan-Indian powwows across the region and held regular meetings at the Haffenreffer Museum in Bristol, Rhode Island. Speck served as an advisor to the group, and Tantaquidgeon was elected as secretary of the AIC.[174]

In a special issue of *Science News-Letter*, Speck highlighted Tantaquidgeon's research at Mashpee and Aquinnah as the nearly miraculous discovery of a hidden cultural complex.

> Little known to the outside world, happy in their fishing and seafaring life, they have evaded the prying interests of investigators who have hitherto remained ignorant of the meaning of the legends preserved in the closets of memory of the older generation. Sedulously refusing to communicate legendary secrets to the questions of the white aliens their reserve has been at last penetrated by one of their own race, a young Indian girl, Gladys Tantaquidgeon, who has just returned from Gay Head with a host of treasures of legend and folk-lore to be woven into a scenic epic . . . like a tapestry.[175]

With wry humor, Speck played to his audiences' expectations, depicting Tantaquidgeon as an "Indian maiden" who "loosened their tongues." What emerged, however, was a sophisticated assemblage of oral traditions inextricably connected to the Wampanoag landscape, not mere fragments but "a connected story of their ancient and imposing legends to be admired and studied."[176]

Tantaquidgeon recognized the oral traditions she heard at Aquinnah as part of a regional cultural complex that was linked to the world she knew at Mohegan, inhabited by little people and giants who were alive in more than memory.

> The Giant Moshup was very much alive in the tales related by my informants. Moshup through his magic power could lure whales ashore and cook them over a huge fire at the top of the cliffs. . . . Then there was "Little Granny Squannit" whom no one ever saw, but it was believed that she lived along the shoreline. It was customary, when going out gathering plants, fishing or hunting to leave some bread and meat in a small basket somewhere along the shore for "Granny" to ensure "Good Luck."[177]

She published her research on Wampanoag basketry and herbal medicine in the pages of *Indian Notes*, but much of the folklore she collected still remains unpublished. Her personal papers include a book-length draft manuscript on Wampanoag oral traditions; Speck's handwriting is visible throughout, in the form of helpful comments, editing suggestions, and insights.[178]

The Tantaquidgeon Indian Museum holds other materials from Speck, including objects he donated to the museum, photographs, his original watercolor paintings of the Wigwam Festival and Boy Scout Camp, and prints of his articles and books (all autographed to Gladys). The copy of his article

"Birdlore of the Northern Indians" is signed "To Gladys, from a 'words-dorf' like herself." His files, in turn, hold some of Tantaquidgeon's unpublished work, including early notes on Algonkian Indian plant medicines that were mistakenly attributed to Speck.[179]

Tantaquidgeon's research on motifs in Algonkian Indian basketry was particularly significant in that she illuminated decorative motifs that were not merely made for tourists: "The Mohegan-Pequot designs show an unaffected style, free from the kind of thing one finds upon objects constructed to satisfy the taste of Europeans," pointing to "a purity of native style suggestive of antiquity." She conducted methodical comparative research on other Algonkian basketry, seeking evidence of "expression communicating a feeling on the part of the long deceased artist in respect to magic or the portrayal of some natural phenomenon." Tantaquidgeon identified distinctive design elements, composites, florals, and other markers denoting spiritual, territorial, and kinship relations that went far beyond mere decorations.[180]

Around this time, there was a significant shift in Frank Speck's collecting practices. In the earlier years, he had sold a number of Mohegan items—Fielding's diaries and mush paddle, Skeesucks's carvings, Fowler's wampum, and more—to Heye.[181] By the late 1920s, however, he started sorting out Mohegan materials for deposit at the Tantaquidgeon household, where Harold was building a bark lodge and a stone museum.[182] When the Tantaquidgeon Indian Museum opened to the public in 1931, it was full of materials that the Tantaquidgeons and Specks had collected together, during trips to Massachusetts, Labrador, Maine, Ontario, and elsewhere. A birch-bark canoe from Indian Island, snowshoes from Newfoundland, and masks from Delaware were displayed alongside hundreds of Mohegan objects, including carvings from Roscoe Skeesucks, baskets from John Tantaquidgeon, and tribal regalia (including clothing, beadwork, and headdresses). On the first page of the museum's guest register, Frank Speck's signature was placed right between his old friends Burrill Fielding and Harold Tantaquidgeon.

In retrospect, Speck was clearly grooming his Mohegan collaborators to take his place. In a 1934 letter to Edward Rogers at the New London Historical Society, he identified Gladys Tantaquidgeon as the most authoritative source for Mohegan history and culture.

I am glad to be able to say that Miss Gladys Tantaquidgeon of Mohegan Hill Place is the successor to my interests in Conn. Indian life. . . . She is now an authority in this field and, as you may imagine, greatly in need of finding an outlet for her experiences and data. It should prove a chance for her to use her talent and her profession, and for you to secure invaluable help in your literary scientific undertaking. I am quite serious about this and happy in being able to refer you to one

Figure 23 Gladys Tantaquidgeon and her brother Harold in traditional Mohegan regalia, c. 1929. Photograph by Frank Speck Jr. Courtesy of Tantaquidgeon Indian Museum.

so near and also so well equipped for service in a line which needs to be carefully considered in view of its permanency as a published source. . . . There are some interesting things to be done with New England Indian life accounts and Miss T. is still in possession of material which will prove a valuable contribution to folk-lore, legend and comparative customs.[183]

Rogers, who was "much impressed" with this praise, immediately booked Tantaquidgeon for a talk, and found her to be brilliant and engaging.

During that same year, on Speck's recommendation, Tantaquidgeon was hired by the Bureau of Indian Affairs to conduct a survey of northeastern tribes. Soon after, she went west to assist Rosebud Sioux Indian families on South Dakota reservations. She also worked with the Federal Indian Arts and Crafts Board, endeavoring to improve economic conditions and bolster community identity by recovering and re-centering traditional artistry and ceremony by teaching and promoting traditional arts. She also "invited accomplished Native American artists to come and teach, and exhibited the art in museums across the country." This work was more than merely artistic: "Sacred ceremonies were often part of art production in Native American cultures, and Tantaquidgeon was instrumental in winning back the right to perform rituals such as the Sun Dance, which had been banned from reservations by federal authorities."[184]

Even while she was out west, Tantaquidgeon continued her research on eastern Native nations. In a 1938 letter to Frank Speck sent from the Sherman Institute, she wrote, "Things seem to have been going 'old Algonkian' lately and this evening we have been talking Delaware and Shawnee ethnology," including queries about "silk ribbon applique." Her new Shawnee friend, Pierrepont Alford, shared a story that appeared to mingle earth-diver and earth-shaper origin traditions: "Shawnee originated after deluge. Grandmother sent animals down to get piece of earth and all failed but crawfish. Grandmother took earth and rolled it and it got bigger and bigger and then made forms—male and female."[185] Buried in her uncatalogued papers are notes for these and other unpublished research projects.

In 1941 Tantaquidgeon's cumulative ethnobotanical research was published as a book-length manuscript, titled *A Study of Delaware Indian Medicine Practice and Folk Beliefs*, later republished as *Folk Medicine of the Delaware and Related Algonkian Indians*.[186] In the foreword, Donald A. Cadzow, state anthropologist for the Pennsylvania Historical Commission, praised Tantaquidgeon's dual training, noting that "she had the advantage of association in childhood with her grandmother and other old women versed in tribal traditions of plant and herbal medicines," as well as sound "training in comparative ethnobotany and lifelong interest in Algonkian nature-curing."[187] Newspaper articles similarly celebrated the novelty of an author who was both an Indian and an anthropologist.[188]

Gladys Tantaquidgeon returned to Mohegan Hill in 1947, just a few years before her mentor, Frank Speck, passed away in 1950. For six decades, until her own passing at the age of 106, she served her nation in various capacities, including Vice Chair of the tribal council, tribal Medicine Woman, and curator of the Tantaquidgeon Indian Museum. For much of that time, she and her brother Harold collaborated to educate thousands of museum visitors, work with local Boy Scout troops, lecture for historical societies, host events, and otherwise promote Mohegan history and culture, receiving a great deal of attention over the years, even though they were often misidentified as the "last of the Mohegans." Gladys Tantaquidgeon's research was key in the Mohegan Tribe's successful bid for federal recognition, granted in 1994, since much of the necessary evidence of the tribe's continuing government-to-government relationship with state and federal authorities was preserved in her archives.[189]

In 2001, after Melissa Jayne Fawcett published the biography *Medicine Trail: The Life and Lessons of Gladys Tantaquidgeon,* the University of Pennsylvania finally publicly recognized Tantaquidgeon. An article in the School of Arts and Sciences newsletter, titled "Running Against Time," highlighted her efforts in ethnological research, her publication of *Delaware Indian Medicine Practice and Folk Beliefs,* and, especially, the founding of the Tantaquidgeon Indian Museum.[190] Over the course of her very long life, Gladys Tantaquidgeon made some remarkable choices for an educated Indian. Most Native American people raised in traditional ways were reluctant to leave the security of their tribal communities. Those who did leave typically lost touch with traditional languages and lifeways, through force or through acculturation, and rarely returned home. Tantaquidgeon benefited from having both a traditional upbringing and a college education, without having to endure the trauma of boarding school. "Remember to take the best of what the white man has to offer," she was fond of saying, "and use it to still be an Indian."[191]

Ironically, despite the dense evidence of Tantaquidgeon's long-term collaboration with Speck, minimal mention of her is preserved in the guides to the Frank G. Speck Papers in various archives. Although she was a groundbreaking Indigenous ethnologist and museum anthropologist, she remains largely invisible in the annals of anthropology. Her invisibility can be attributed, in part, to the persistence of the myth that Frank G. Speck was adopted by Fidelia Fielding. By attributing Speck's familiarity with Mohegan culture and skill in anthropology to his supposed experiences as a young child, and to a woman long dead, his colleagues overlooked his living Mohegan collaborators, even when they were standing right in front of them.

Conclusion

Restorative Methodologies

[These objects] have been mislocated and mishandled and abused, and are trying to find themselves again. They come back to us as these broken people. But when they are made whole again, when they're given a place to be, we can heal each other.

—Fred (Kabooniishin) McGregor, 2017

When I first envisioned this project, I thought that Native informants might have been trying to *Indigenize* American anthropologists by teaching them the cultural protocols of respectful engagement. After nearly a decade of reading the correspondence, I came to realize that, in many cases, they were simply seeking ways to *manage* them. Indigenous gatekeepers and informants observed the actions and motivations of the "other-than-Indian" persons who came into their worlds, and attempted to mediate contacts with these strangers in ways that might prove the most beneficial and least harmful. When outside researchers appeared, there were multiple possibilities for collaboration or rejection. Some encounters were brief: a person could sell a few old things, pose for a photograph, share a story, and then the stranger would move on. There might even be short-term work opportunities: guide a hunter, carry a load, work on an archaeological site, rent a room, cook for the camp. Tourists were relatively easy to manage; they came and went quickly and bought what was offered. Lengthier encounters required different strategies.

The first few Native people who chose to learn and apply anthropological methods—the first *Indigenous* anthropologists—walked a difficult path. They walked two roads simultaneously, but, like the old adage that suggests one cannot travel with a foot in two canoes, it was not easy. To navigate that path, they had to forge long-term relationships with white anthropologists, while maintaining connections with their communities of origin. The case studies in this book illustrate the complexities of those relationships. George Hunt, for example, relied heavily on the status of his wives, Lucy Homikanis and Tsukwani Francine, to ingratiate himself with Franz Boas. Arthur Parker distanced himself from his first wife, Beulah Tahamont, as a means to more effectively assert control over his research and attain an elite position in the museum. Mark Harrington was an accommodating soul who welcomed Native researchers as equals and used his position to help promote Beulah and Arthur's daughter, Bertha Parker. Jesse Cornplanter, a traditionalist who demonstrated his culture through performance, asserted his authority through dense correspondence, including scathing critiques of William Fenton. Frank Speck and Gladys Tantaquidgeon adapted to racial and intellectual divides by, in effect, adopting each other as kin, enabling each of them to assert and maintain authority in their respective communities.

Ironically, and fittingly, anthropological collectors preserved the evidence of these complicated relationships (even the bad relationships) by archiving their papers in elite locales that, until relatively recently, were quite difficult for non-academics to access. The correspondence is literally scattered. Arthur Parker and Mark Harrington's letters are in at least four different museum archives in New York, Washington, and Los Angeles. Frank Speck's correspondence is deposited in archives in nine different locations (at last count), including Colorado, Connecticut, Maryland, Massachusetts, Ontario, and four locations in Philadelphia (including three different archives at the University of Pennsylvania). Indigenous field notes and publications were routinely, and inadvertently, concealed by indexing processes that identified them as works by their non-Native collaborators. For example, Bertha Parker's field notes were hiding in Mark Harrington's papers, and Gladys Tantaquidgeon's field notes were mixed into some of Frank Speck's field notes (and vice versa). Jesse Cornplanter's correspondence was everywhere until William Fenton (in what might be considered an act of possession in itself) collected and collated it into his own academic archives.

These kinds of cataloging erasures were not only enacted with Native people—they were also routine with regard to female researchers of any ethnicity. As Nancy Parezo discovered, early ethnologist Matilda Coxe Stevenson had been forced to publish her early work at the Smithsonian Bureau of Ethnology under her husband's name. Missing copies of her papers were cataloged with John P. Harrington's work in the National Anthropological Archives: "He had removed her name from the copies, cut them up, and interspersed them with his own."[1]

To locate this evidence, it was necessary to travel to each of these archives, and to review each document in its original form, rather than rely on transcriptions (or even microfilm). The handwriting in original letters can be traced to particular individuals, and even early typewriters left distinctive marks. Each written document is an artifact that informs some part of the larger picture; yet if it is misunderstood or miscataloged, it could function as a tool of erasure. This was especially the case during the early twentieth century, when many

Indigenous people were not fluent in English, had no access to anthropological publications, and were not invited to proof (or even see) what was being written about them. Sometimes, a simple transcription, edited with a few keystrokes here and there, could serve to render an informant nameless, or an assistant invisible. Craft an anecdote that is oddly compelling, and everyone will want to hear it. Repeat a theory often enough, and it may take on the weight of fact. Transcribe a story borrowed from an Indigenous informant and put your name on it, and it becomes your own. Ironically, the evidence of cultural appropriation was often preserved (sometimes even bragged about) in papers that white researchers must have assumed Indigenous descendants would never be allowed to access. The recovery of these records fundamentally changes our understanding of the on-the-ground relations that shaped the field of anthropology.

Those early anthropologists cast a long shadow. Anthropology, after all, was not a neutral science; it was an activist project that fetishized and commodified Indigenous objects, cultures, and bodies, while positioning Euro-American scientific thought and practice as neutral and normative. As members of privileged societies, white scientists wielded significant power and influence. Their theories did not exist in a solely intellectual realm; they exerted real power in the real world, by conceptually positioning ethnographic "others" (and visions of the lived pasts and possible futures of their subjects) in roles from which, in some cases, they have not yet escaped.[2] They depicted virtually all Native peoples of North America as inherently naïve, uneducated, primitive, and helpless to resist the inevitable fading away of traditions and assimilation into mainstream (white) society. They circulated anthropological discoveries and theories (which could be classed as "scientific stories") in ways that marginalized Indigenous knowledges while praising the value of scientific research. The benefits to researchers were considerable; the costs to the anthropologized have yet to be fully measured. Long after the researchers passed away, their early publications continue to exert authority over the Indigenous communities they studied.

It is easy to assume that collectors performed a great service by capturing and preserving what was about to be forever lost. Yet a surprising number of the letters exchanged between anthropologists and their Indigenous collaborators sway between collegial friendship and fierce argument. "Talking back" may seem to be a modern trend, but Indigenous gatekeepers expressed resistances to colonizing modes of anthropological research in ways that are still relevant today.[3] Their intellectual contributions remain largely invisible in the annals of anthropological theory and practice, even though their words are archived within the papers of famous anthropologists. If we recognize these Indigenous interlocutors as major contributors to the discipline (much as we do long-dead anthropologists), we might better understand the logic of their engagement, and the ferocity of their determination to preserve something of themselves in the written record. With these thoughts in mind, what is most needed is a restorative approach to relationships, a dialogical response to the recovery of missing stories.[4]

At many ethnographic museums, just such conversations are now underway. The National Museum of the American Indian, guided by a Native American director and a team of Native American curators, has been carefully examining the status of collections and engaging in unusual exhibition strategies that foreground the concerns of contemporary Native communities.[5] Scholars to the north are still coming to terms with the political and theoretical isolation of Canadian First Nations peoples as "others" in narratives of Canadian nationhood and in museum representations.[6] In this new era of "Truth and Reconciliation," Canadian museums are moving in multiple ways to improve their relations with living communities.[7] Comparable efforts are taking place elsewhere, as Indigenous peoples worldwide aim to refute invented histories, reclaim their patrimony, and reshape the images constructed by outsiders. These new configurations of identity and possession are increasingly defining and shaping landmark legislation in cultural property, internationally, while also increasing attention to Indigenous human rights, and the urgency of preserving regional heritage sites.[8]

Object Considerations

Critical assessments of the museum enterprise took a sharp turn in the second half of the twentieth century, as curators were forced to grapple with the protocols and practices of repatriation, and to reexamine records from the early years of collecting. Those early collections often suffer from physical scattering and conceptual disorganization; as a result, significant objects (e.g., photographs, ritual regalia, cultural heritage) may appear to be unidentified or unidentifiable. Exhibit cards and provenance papers rarely recorded the context of collecting, the identities of informants, or the choices that resulted in some items being sent to museums, and others to private collections. Institutional memories were shaped not by Indigenous memories but by new theories and hypotheses. Museological notions of authenticity were produced by "ethnographic rescues" that required the removal of objects from living communities.[9] Over time, as those objects were handled by generations of curators, faculty, students, and others, new stories and new interpretations emerged, and ontologies shifted. Museum exhibitions trained audiences to look through, but not behind, the glass and to accept the representations and arrangements laid out for them as "authentic," even in the absence of Indigenous context.

It seems obvious, but necessary, to state that anthropological desires and selective collecting practices also shaped the relative degrees of visibility of specific tribal nations and categories of objects in museum collections.[10] Objects that had been considered, in Indigenous communities, as potentially powerful living agents of ritual expression were rendered mute, if not dead.[11] The more dramatic and highly decorated objects (e.g., feather headdresses, beaded clothing, jewelry, weapons, ritual objects) found especial favor in exhibitions, and those still tend to be fetishized and highlighted today. Objects that seemed, to the non-Native observer, to be common or utilitarian (e.g., rocks, tools, undecorated clothing) were regarded as less exotic and less interesting, even though they may have been considered significant and powerful. Indigenous ontologies and sensitivities were poorly understood, and often ignored. As a result, some objects gained prominence in the museum, some stories transformed their listeners, some tribes became desirable research subjects, and some did not. Do the relative degrees of visibility in the museum correspond to relative degrees of visibility and political sovereignty today? Is there a correlation between having been an uninteresting research subject in the past and being politically marginalized today? These questions deserve further consideration.

North American museums were not, as they were assumed to be, safe repositories for Indigenous artifacts. They were showcases designed to educate, but they also validated the authenticity and exotic beauty of Indigenous artifacts. Wealthy antiquities collectors desired some of that for themselves. There is, in fact, a direct linkage between the collecting of Indigenous objects for museums, the removal of objects from museums, and the emergence of the multimillion-dollar American Indian Art Market. The most notorious case implicated Museum of the American Indian (MAI) director Frederick Dockstader in the removal of at least eighty thousand objects from collections for sale to Douglas Ewing, James Economos, and other art dealers who then resold these objects to private collectors.[12] At the time, William Sturtevant, curator of ethnology at the Smithsonian, complained that "to many scholars, selling privately any work from a primitive group is like selling a baby for adoption on the black market. . . . The object's roots, its history, its vital statistics disappear."[13] In 1974 MAI trustee Edmund Carpenter tipped off the New York State Department of Law, and state attorney general Louis Lefkowitz launched a full investigation into the "surreptitious, wasteful and fraudulent exchange transactions between the museum and certain Indian-artifact dealers and collectors" at MAI.[14] The 1975 court case—*Lefkowitz v. The Museum of the American Indian Heye Foundation*—led to the removal of the director and most of the trustees, and the museum was closed for restructuring.[15] With only a few exceptions, the objects removed from MAI were never recovered; they remain in private hands, periodically resurfacing at art auctions.

In 1989 and 1990, respectively, the U.S. federal government enacted two new pieces of legislation—the National Museum of the American Indian Act (NMAIA) (Public Law 101-85) and the Native American Graves Protection and Repatriation Act (NAGPRA) (Public Law 101-106)—each of which was intended to facilitate the identification and repatriation of four Indigenous categories of material: human remains, funerary objects, sacred objects, and items of cultural patrimony.[16] NMAIA transferred the remaining MAI collections to the new National Museum of the American Indian, under the control of the Smithsonian Institution. The museum's repatriation policy explicitly aims to "support the continuance of ceremonial and ritual life among Native American peoples, to foster and support the study by Native Americans of their own traditions, and to forge consensus among the Museum and Native American communities while accounting for and balancing the interests of each."[17]

In the nearly three decades since, hundreds of museums and tribal nations have engaged in consultations, and thousands of materials have been returned. As of September 2016, the repatriations via NAGPRA include the remains of 57, 847 Native individuals, 1,479,923 associated funerary objects, and 243,198 unassociated funerary objects (including many small items) that had been excavated from gravesites; in addition, museums have repatriated 5,136 sacred objects, 8,130 objects of cultural patrimony, and 1,662 objects that are classified as "both sacred and patrimonial."[18] The increased awareness of cultural sensitivity has also inspired some museums to create separate curatorial spaces for sacred and patrimonial objects, thereby concealing them from public display and allowing for traditional curatorial practices and ceremonial treatment.[19]

Yet there are some rather large loopholes and unintended consequences. NMAIA applies to only one museum, and the NAGPRA legislation applies only to collections currently housed in federal institutions and museums (also schools, libraries, etc.) that receive federal funding. Objects that left these museum, even when they constitute tribal patrimony, receive no consideration under either law. Private museums, private individuals, auction houses, and international collectors and museums are (legally, if not ethically) free to operate beyond the reach of these laws.[20] Some scholars have suggested that this freedom is necessary to support research. As a case in point, when MAI trustee Edmund Carpenter created the independent Rock Foundation, his explicit goal was to ensure that "the collection isn't subject to the Repatriation Bill."[21]

Also, although these laws dictate the sharing of museum data, tribal nations rarely have full access to or knowledge of documentation, especially when related objects and collections are housed in different repositories. The NAGPRA and NMAIA object categories—"sacred" and/or "patrimonial" and/or "funerary"—are often determined not just through consultation but through the chance preservation of contextual evidence.[22] What rituals were enacted when those objects were in use? Who permitted that excavation? Where is the proof of tribal identity? Were those things personal property or national patrimony? Who decided then? Who decides now? When Native nations and museums disagree, museums retain the final say. With all this in mind, it seems fair to ask if federal attempts to facilitate repatriation have actually *restored* respect for Indigenous patrimony writ large, or merely *legislated* respect for a few protected (and museologically accepted) categories of Indigenous materials.

Similar concerns are now being raised in document repositories.[23] At the American Philosophical Society, the new Center for Native American and Indigenous Research (CNAIR) has developed consultations and digital sharing initiatives to enable the distribution of copies (digital surrogates) of linguistic recordings, photographs, and other documents to Native nations, especially in cases where the originals are too fragile to travel.[24] Although this archive does not curate objects, it does curate crucial knowledge about objects. There is important cultural data in the voluminous correspondence of George Hunt and Franz Boas. There are notebooks—such as those compiled by Frank Speck—that record both monetary values and insights into Indigenous object ontologies. There are also audio recordings (are these not objects?) that could inform language recovery projects today. There is a surprising volume of sensitive material that was never meant to be shown to outsiders. CNAIR defines "culturally sensitive" as follows:

> "Materials that are culturally sensitive" means any indigenous material that depicts a tribal spiritual or religious place (e.g., kiva or Midewiwin map), object (e.g., Iroquois masks), belief or activity (e.g., Cherokee sacred formulae). A spiritual or religious activity may include prayers, ceremonies, burials, songs, dancing, healings, and medicine rituals. The definition of "culturally sensitive" may include any other definition provided in writing by a specific tribe with respect to any indigenous materials held by APS depicting that tribe's culture or from which the materials originate. APS will then determine whether the tribe's definition falls within the spirit of the definition set forth herein.[25]

Although this sounds relatively straightforward, in practice, CNAIR staff must negotiate exactly how these protocols will be applied for the appropriate sharing of digital data to the appropriate tribal communities. Which communities are the appropriate claimants? Which documents are sacred? In all these museums, I would add: How can we move from legal arguments over classifications and work together toward the more humane goals of reconciliation and restoration?

Reverse Fieldwork

This situation calls for what I identify as "reverse ethnography" and "reverse fieldwork," which is crucial to the practice of restorative methodologies. Restorative methodologies entail, at minimum, cross-walking through archives to track objects and their related stories (even the false or fishy stories) through the locales and tribal nations represented in collections. This research goes well beyond routine identifications and classifications (e.g., distinguishing between "art" and "artifact," or sorting "authentic" from "inauthentic" objects).[26] As a case in point, an unusual collection of Indigenous objects at the Penn Museum (including Delaware peyote ritual tools and Haudenosaunee masks) was cataloged as a donation from Samuel Pennypacker, one of Speck's wealthy students. The records of transactions between Pennypacker and Speck are vague and incomplete (consisting of a few file folders of postcards and miscellaneous notes), but taken together they suggest that Speck served as an intermediary between his rich friend and Native people in need of money. Pennypacker never sold the items he got from Speck; instead, he kept this select collection in a dedicated "Indian Room" in his mansion outside Philadelphia. The collection remained intact until 1968, when Pennypacker's widow donated the objects to the Penn Museum.[27] It is therefore impossible to trace the origins of any of these objects by relying on Pennypacker as a source; one must understand the social entanglements to trace them back to Speck and his informants.

There are, of course, logistical challenges to cross-collections research. It can be extraordinarily difficult to link the data in disparate card catalogs, databases, storage locations, and other indexing structures and practices. Internal museum memories, even flawed memories (especially when fixed on erroneous exhibit labels), may take on the veneer of fact; with increased time and distance, disconnections and misinterpretations tend to multiply. To address these challenges, I suggest that we retrospectively examine the relations among participants at each moment of acquisition, and map the cartography of object circulation. It is especially helpful (in many cases, necessary) to do this research while consulting with contemporary Indigenous interlocutors who hold tribal information relevant to those historic objects. By using this approach, I have found (despite warnings from skeptical curators) that it is often possible to resolve some of the mysteries surrounding object provenance and meaning. Although we can never altogether re-create those early encounters, we can draw closer to understanding the original context of collecting these objects that now represent a shared past.

In museums, the recovery of object memories can begin with simple, open-ended conversations, as a precursor to formal consultations. The social rituals

Figure 24 A collection of postcards among the Frank G. Speck Papers in the Penn Museum Archives, documenting some of Speck's travels and sales of objects to his former student and benefactor, Samuel Pennypacker. Photograph by Margaret Bruchac.

of formal repatriation consultations are often such that individual participants feel obligated to speak for a particular nation, protect an institutional memory, assert positional power, or argue a fine legal point. In such polarized settings, consensus can be an elusive goal. Informal conversations, in contrast, encourage more relaxed social interactions; when participants are more at ease, memories and insights are more likely to surface. This discursive approach removes the obligation to speak *for* a particular position, and encourages participants to speak *with* one another. So, for example, while chatting about a random piece of documentation, a curator might suddenly recall a collector's name, a bit of correspondence, or a related object. A single detail in one collection could solve a long-standing mystery in another. One might find an uncataloged note beside a seemingly unrelated and unidentifiable object, and, *Voila!* a lost file may resurface that ties them together. One might turn over an early nineteenth-century ash-splint basket (as I did one day at Historic Deerfield) and discover the name and tribal identity of the heretofore unknown artisan (Sophie Watso, Abenaki) written underneath. One might even pick up a rock that is significantly more powerful than it appears. In general, objects that were meaningful remain meaningful, even if their stories appear to have been lost or distorted.

To demonstrate the potential success of reverse fieldwork, in 2014, with funding from the Penn Museum, I set out on what was dubbed "The Wampum Trail," a project that began with a survey of a single category of objects: wampum belts.[28] In company with two student research assistants, Lise Puyo and Stephanie Mach, I physically retraced the path of Frank Speck's travels during the 1910s and 1920s through New England, Canada, and New York among various Haudenosaunee and Algonkian communities. We fine-tuned methods for tracking the circulation of Indigenous objects by delving into the collections at multiple museums and archives. The survey (which continues to the present day) includes, but is by no means limited to, the following: Canadian Museum of History (CMH), Harvard Peabody Museum of Archaeology and Ethnology, McCord Museum, National Museum of the American Indian (formerly MAI), New York State Museum, Peabody Essex Museum, Rochester Museum and Science Center, Rock Foundation, Royal Ontario Museum, and (of course) the University of Pennsylvania Museum of Archaeology and Anthropology. This work also necessitated reconnecting with tribal descent communities and heritage centers, including the Mashantucket Pequot Tribal Museum and Research Center, Tantaquidgeon Indian Museum, Deyohahá:ge Indigenous Knowledge Centre at Six Nations, and the Seneca Art and Culture Center at the Ganondagan State Historic Site, among many others.

Along the trail, we successfully located four wampum belts that had been purchased by Frank Speck in 1913 after having been secretly removed from the custody of the Kanesatake Mohawk Nation (Oka). These belts had followed a tangled path through multiple hands. Two were sold to the Victoria Museum (now CMH) and two to MAI (now NMAI).[29] One of the belts at MAI was sold by Dockstader in 1974 to an art dealer, who immediately sold it to another art dealer, who sold it to another collector, whose children later placed it for sale at Sotheby's. My research revealed multiple moments of "strategic alienation" that obscured identifying data and fractured chains of custody.[30] One of most poignant clues came in the form of a letter from Florence Speck (written to Edmund Carpenter twenty-two years after her husband Frank had passed away) hidden away in the uncataloged correspondence files of the New York State Museum. She wrote:

The Indians have been trying to buy back the wampum belts which Frank had bought from a man in Canada. I was with him when we went there. . . . I carried the belts in a dark green bag, like all the students carried with their books. Later on we took the beaded belts to the State Museum [NYSM] at Albany and gave them for safe keeping. The Indians have been trying to get them back but Frank always said, they would sell them again and they are safe there.[31]

Carpenter and Fenton had minimal knowledge of this case, since the wampum belts in question had no relationship to the collections in the New York State Museum. So, they dismissed her request for assistance as delusional, and filed the letter without responding.[32]

Yet Kanesatake chiefs persisted, and the memory of these particular removals came down, through several generations, to Condoled chief Curtis Nelson, who testified in 2009:

> There is no knowledge or oral tradition in which Kanesatake or the Haudenosaunee Confederacy authorized this Wampum Belt to leave its community, or be presented to any other individual or entity. It is known that Frank Speck wrongfully purchased this Wampum Belt and other Wampum items from a French man named J.B. Delay who was married to a Kanesatake woman. People at Kanesatake and other Mohawk communities at Grand River Territory tried to get all the stolen Kanesatake Belts returned but were not successful at that time.[33]

In 2014 and 2017, as a direct result of restorative research, two of those wampum belts were finally repatriated to Kanesatake, and the other two are soon to follow. The research on these removals confirmed my original premise: the lack of provenance data for many of the objects captured in museums represents not the absence of Indigenous knowledge but the influence of physical dislocations and flawed identifications that separated Indigenous objects from Indigenous histories.

Wampum belts thus served as a paradigmatic example of a highly valued object that was much in demand by ethnologists, historians, state officials, museums, and art dealers, and that was susceptible to being deployed in new interpretations that, in effect, made these objects strangers to themselves. By tracking the collectors, in addition to conducting detailed provenance searches, I was able to trace how Indigenous objects had been conceptually transformed from tribal heritage to private property, and from sacred objects to collectible art. Individual items had been stripped of context and scattered among different museums, often without clear records of tribal identities and symbolic meanings. In virtually every museum, curators and scholars had then devised idiosyncratic (and often flawed) interpretations based on speculative and incomplete data.

With the wampum research, we often found that data housed in one museum shed light on objects in another museum. Meticulous attention to materiality was also required, since minute construction details in each of the

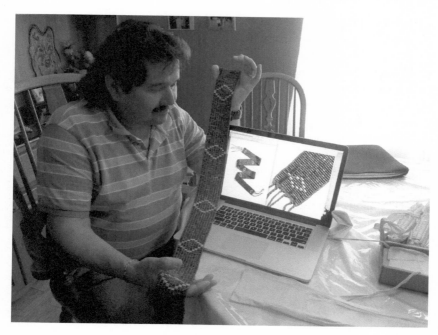

Figure 25 Kanesatake Condoled Chief Curtis Nelson holds a Six Nations wampum belt that was improperly removed from tribal custody for sale to Frank Speck in 1913. On the computer screen is a Five Nations wampum belt that was part of the same removal. Both belts have been recently repatriated and restored to their traditional use. Photograph by Lise Puyo for the Wampum Trail. Courtesy of Margaret Bruchac.

more than eighty historic wampum belts examined (thus far) revealed crucial information about Native artisans, sources of shells, weaving materials, and modes of repair and curation.[34] In a small collection at the Royal Ontario Museum, we discovered that Speck had been on a "Wampum Trail" of his own, collecting comparative samples of wampum from many different tribal nations in an effort to pin down details of its historic manufacture and circulation.[35]

I also learned that when Frank Speck died in 1950, he left behind a large collection of Indigenous objects stored at his home in Swarthmore, his office at Penn, and his summer cottage in Annisquam. His intentions for the disposition of these (as communicated to his son, Frank Staniford Speck, and his daughter-in-law, Louise Barrett Speck) were recalled, four decades later, in a 1992 letter from Louise. She told John L. Cotter at the Penn Museum about the chaos that had followed Speck's death. His office was plundered of his best books, and some Native items had disappeared, even though Frank had left explicit instructions.

As for Indian artifacts, F.G. had mentioned that he thought many things should be returned to the Indians for their museums. . . . We actually received very little but in every case we donated them to the Denver Art Museum and Peabody Museum at Salem. We had a small house and no knowledge of how to properly care for museum objects. . . . We enjoy our Indian friends and are deeply interested in their welfare, but are mindful of our dear friend, Ruth Underhill's remark that it is now time to turn over the management of Indian affairs to the Indians, help them, when it is requested, and rejoice in their success.[36]

When stories like these are recovered, they cast a different (and not always flattering) light on the circumstances of collecting. Conversations about the objects entangled in those earlier encounters and transactions, however, need not devolve into litigious arguments about the past. Instead, museums should engage in conciliatory communication with related Indigenous communities in the present day. The practice of restorative research is thus more than the mere study of museological methods. By critically questioning the speculations contained in secondary sources, by reexamining the social relations of collecting, and by collaborating with Indigenous knowledge bearers, we can develop more nuanced awareness of object ontologies, and better understand exactly why, and to whom, these Indigenous objects and histories matter.

Relating and Reconnecting

Looking back, the partnerships in this book illustrate the social dynamics of ethnographic collecting as a complicated discursive dance with intricate steps, moving through a vast web of connections across Indian Country. Despite colonizing tropes and romantic fantasies of the lone vanishing Indian, Native informants, in many cases, called the steps of the dance. Indigenous anthropologists, as our intellectual foremothers and forefathers, actively engaged in assisting or resisting the anthropological process, operating from within situated strategies of survivance. Research about them is absolutely necessary to reverse fieldwork, which requires a good bit of travel, going back to the archives and going back to Indigenous communities, to collect more stories about anthropologists.

Each of the historic partnerships I examined were selected, as indicated at the outset, based on the density of correspondence, the length of contact, and the volume of material in major museum collections. Not all these individuals were professionals, or equally influential, but they were all actively engaged at the ground level for more than three decades. Their partnerships represent important shifts that continue to ripple through the discipline today. So, for example, by studying George Hunt in a region where kinship is matrifocally constructed, we can see how the economic machinations of acquisitive men obscured the knowledge carried by Indigenous women. In Bertha Parker's archaeology, we can glimpse an Indigenous archaeologist poised at a groundbreaking moment of discovery who suddenly vanishes from sight due not to gender bias but to personal tragedy.

By applying contingent methodology to all these field relations, we can also illuminate the very different social identities that anthropologists assumed in the field. Arthur Parker gained what appears, in retrospect, to be undue credit for his Indigenous identity, given his unusually fraught relations with his relatives and his tribal nation. William Fenton's adoption was (if we listen to Seneca Faithkeepers today) an utter failure; he manipulated his informants, removed tribal property, and misrepresented tribal leaders in public. He embraced the name without accepting the attending social responsibilities. Anthropologists such as Frank Speck, on the other hand, were important allies against the historical erasures of antiquarian histories. As a result, the Tantaquidgeon Indian Museum became a repository for materials that not only preserved the tribal history but also bolstered the Mohegan case for federal recognition. One might even suggest that anthropological visibility and federal status are linked, since the neighboring tribes that lacked comparable museums (e.g., Schaghticoke, Paugusset) and suffered from historical erasure still lack federal status today.[37]

In sum, if we are ever to understand the issues and contests that surround American Indian collections in museums today, we must revisit the past. Effective object identification cannot be accomplished unless and until we untangle museological interferences and false constructions. Here is where Indigenous (rather than legalistic) protocols could be applied to repatriation practice to facilitate better relationships, to repair broken relations as well as broken connections. Like the Haudenosaunee rituals of condolence that were designed to guide grieving or conflicted parties out of conflict and toward clear-mindedness, collaborative models of repatriation research could improve museum relations with Indigenous claimants.[38] As Fred (Kabooniishin) McGregor—an Omaamiiw-ininii (Algonquin) Anishinaabe from the Kitigan Zibi community—has suggested, some of the objects that went missing are rather like the Indigenous children who survived residential schools: "They have been mislocated and mishandled and abused, and are trying to find themselves again. They come back to us as these broken people. But when they are made whole again, when they're given a place to be, we can heal each other."[39] No matter what they have been through, they are still part of our shared history. Even if they appear to be strangers, we are still kin.

As the efforts of multiple institutions and tribal nations in recent decades illustrate, there is enormous healing potential in processes of collaborative cultural recovery. Many of my colleagues in museum anthropology are encouraging one another to move beyond one-way acts of "repatriation" to multidirectional acts of "reconnection," as a means to correct some of the errors that resulted from antiquarian disconnections and salvage anthropology.[40] They are also more consciously seeking new approaches, beyond pro forma adherence to legal protocols of repatriation practice, to repair broken relationships. These efforts are about far more than merely returning objects to their source. When we revisit those early encounters, and reexamine the stories their participants told, we can begin to recover some sense of the social worlds these people moved through. We might then recognize that the stories we tell one another—about specific objects, museums, and collections—have become other-than-human agents with lives of their own. By reexamining the on-the-ground relations and collaborations that generated early ethnographic collections, we can reconceptualize the role of those Indigenous informants who shared Indigenous knowledge and material in what they hoped would be a lasting and reciprocal relationship, rather than a one-way trip to the museum.

Notes

Preface and Acknowledgements

1. Richard White ran the North Labrador Live Fox Depot in Voisey's Bay and a trading post in Nain. See "Richard (Dick) White's Trading Post," accessed May 10, 2017, http://www.heritage.nf.ca/articles/society/richard-white-trading-post.php. At the time we met, Winston was working on a book about his father, drawing on family memories, and on letters to Frank Speck, which are archived at the American Philosophical Society and the Phillips Library, Peabody Essex Museum.

Introduction

Chapter epigraph: A. Irving Hallowell, "Ojibwa Ontology, Behavior and World View," in *Culture in History: Essays in Honor of Paul Radin*, ed. Stanley Diamond (New York: Columbia University Press, 1960), 23.

1. Hallowell, "Ojibwa Ontology, Behavior and World View."

2. Frank G. Speck, "Game Totems Among the Northeastern Algonkians," *American Anthropologist*, n.s. 19, no. 1 (1917): 18.

3. Lisa T. Brooks, *The Common Pot: The Recovery of Native Space in the Northeast* (Minneapolis: University of Minnesota Press, 2008).

4. Roy Harvey Pearce, *Savagism and Civilization: A Study of the Indian and the American Mind* (Baltimore: Johns Hopkins University Press, 1953).

5. Rayna Green, "The Indian in Popular American Culture," in *Handbook of North American Indians*, vol. 4, *History of Indian-White Relations*, ed. Wilcomb E. Washburn (Washington, D.C.: Smithsonian Institution, 1988).

6. Edward Said, *Orientalism* (New York: Pantheon, 1978), 2.

7. Linda Tuhiwai Smith, *Decolonizing Methodologies: Research and Indigenous Peoples* (New York: St. Martin's, 1999).

8. Alejandro Haber, "This Is Not an Answer to the Question 'Who Is Indigenous,?'" *Archaeologies: Journal of the World Archaeological Congress* 3, no. 3 (2007): 218.

9. Donald L. Fixico, "Ethics and Responsibilities in Writing American Indian History," in Natives and Academics: Researching and Writing About American Indians, ed. Devon A. Mihesuah (Lincoln: University of Nebraska Press, 1998).

10. Amy Den Ouden, "Locating the Cannibals: Conquest, North American Ethnohistory, and the Threat of Objectivity," *History and Anthropology* 18, no. 2 (2007).

11. For a longer discussion of ethnographic labels, see Audra Simpson, "On Ethnographic Refusal: Indigeneity, 'Voice,' and Colonial Citizenship," *Junctures 9* (December 2007).

12. Gordon Day, "Note on St. Francis Nomenclature," *International Journal of Linguistics* 16, no. 4 (1959).

13. During the late 1700s to late 1800s, the Six Nations Iroquois also maintained political relationships with the members of the Seven Nations alliance, a cross-cultural

group of seven Christianized Algonkian and Haudenosaunee bands situated along or near the St. Lawrence waterway. David Blanchard, "The Seven Nations of Canada: An Alliance and a Treaty," *American Indian Culture and Research Journal* 7, no. 2 (1983).

14. Daniel N. Paul, *We Were Not the Savages: A Mi'kmaq Perspective on the Collision Between European and Native American Civilizations* (Black Point, Nova Scotia: Fernwood, 2006).

15. Colleagues who participated in this brainstorm included Jameson Brant, Lisa Brooks, Barb Gurr, Doug George Kanentiio, Drew Lopenzina, Daniel Mandell, Tim Powell, Cheryl Savageau, Siobhan Senier, Paulette Steeves, Laura Adams Weaver, and Melissa Tantaquidgeon Zobel, to name just a few. One popular title was "Sleeping with the Enemy," but that would be a very different kind of book.

16. Françoise Dussart, personal communication, October 28, 2010.

17. Marilyn Strathern, *Audit Cultures: Anthropological Studies in Accountability, Ethics and the Academy* (New York: Routledge, 2000), 186.

18. Hallowell, "Ojibwa Ontology, Behavior and World View," 25.

19. Ibid.

Chapter 1

Chapter epigraph: Clifford Geertz, "Thick Description," in *The Interpretation of Cultures: Selected Essays* (New York: Basic Books, 1973), 5.

1. Shepherd Krech III and Barbara Hail, eds., *Collecting Native America, 1870–1960* (Washington, D.C.: Smithsonian Institution Press, 1999).

2. See, for example, Lewis Henry Morgan, *Ancient Society; or, Researches in the Lines of Human Progress from Savagery Through Barbarism to Civilization* (New York: Henry Holt, 1877).

3. Donna Haraway, "Teddy Bear Patriarchy: Taxidermy in the Garden of Eden, New York City, 1908–1936," *Social Text* 11 (Winter 1984–85).

4. Sergei Kan, *Strangers to Relatives: The Adoption and Naming of Anthropologists in Native North America* (Lincoln: University of Nebraska Press, 2001).

5. David L. Browman and Stephen Williams, eds., *Anthropology at Harvard: A Biographical History, 1790–1940* (Cambridge, Mass.: Peabody Museum Press, 2013), 274.

6. See Lewis Henry Morgan, *League of the Ho-dé-no-sau-nee or Iroquois* (Rochester, N.Y.: Sage, 1851). See also Morgan, *Ancient Society*.

7. W. H. Holmes, "The World's Fair Congress of Anthropology," *American Anthropologist* 6, no. 4 (October 1893).

8. Putnam's statement from December 25, 1895, is cited in Browman and Williams, *Anthropology at Harvard*, 245–46.

9. On cultural relativism and historical particularism, see Franz Boas, *The Mind of Primitive Man* (New York: Macmillan, 1911), 928. See also Franz Boas, "On Alternating Sounds," *American Anthropologist* 2, no. 1 (1889).

10. Nicholas B. Dirks, "Franz Boas and the American University: A Personal Account," *Proceedings of the American Philosophical Society* 154, no. 1 (2010): 33.

11. George W. Stocking Jr., "Afterward: A View from the Center," *Ethnos* 47, nos. 1–2 (1982).

12. Franz Boas, "Some Principles of Museum Administration," *Science* 25, no. 650 (1907), 928. See also Franz Boas, "Race Problems in America," *Science* 29, no. 752 (1909).

13. Boas, "Some Principles of Museum Administration," 928.

14. Regna Darnell, *Invisible Genealogies: A History of Americanist Anthropology* (Lincoln: University of Nebraska Press, 2001), 41.

15. Harriet Maxwell Converse [unattributed], "A Woman Elected a Chief of the Six Nations," *Journal of American Folklore* 5, no. 17 (April–June 1892).

16. Lewis Henry Morgan, League of the Ho-dé-no-sau-nee or Iroquois, xi. For a fuller discussion of Ely Parker's influence on Lewis Henry Morgan, see Elisabeth Tooker, "Lewis H. Morgan and the Senecas," in Strangers to Relatives: The Adoption and Naming of Anthropologists in Native North America, ed. Sergei Kan (Lincoln: University of Nebraska Press, 2001).

17. Browman and Williams, Anthropology at Harvard, 246.

18. Jones's diary entry is quoted in Henry Milner Rideout, *William Jones: Indian, Cowboy, American Scholar, and Anthropologist in the Field* (New York: Frederick A. Stokes, 1912), 41.

19. For biographical summaries of Jones, see Rideout, *William Jones*; and Browman and Williams, *Anthropology at Harvard*, 258–62.

20. William Jones, "Some Principles of Algonkin Word Formation," *American Anthropologist*, n.s. 6, no. 3 (1904).

21. "The Diary of William Jones: 1907–1909," Robert F. Cummings Philippine Expedition, unpublished manuscript in the Field Museum Library, Field Museum of Natural History, Chicago, Ill.

22. Franz Boas, "William Jones Obituary," *Southern Workman*, May 1909, 263.

23. Michael Ames, *Cannibal Tours and Glass Boxes: The Anthropology of Museums* (Vancouver: University of British Columbia Press, 1992), 3.

24. Patricia Pierce Erikson, "Decolonizing the Nation's Attic," in *The National Museum of the American Indian: Critical Conversations*, ed. Amy Lonetree and Amanda J. Cobb (Lincoln: University of Nebraska Press, 2008).

25. Philip J. Deloria, *Indians in Unexpected Places* (Lawrence: University Press of Kansas Press, 2004).

26. For a fuller discussion of museum representations of the Indigenous, see George Stocking Jr., ed., *Objects and Others: Essays on Museums and Material Culture* (Madison: University of Wisconsin Press, 1985). For additional case histories of collecting Indigenous materials for natural history and ethnology museums, see Krech and Hail, *Collecting Native America*.

27. Curtis Hinsley, *The Smithsonian and the American Indian: Making a Moral Anthropology in Victorian America* (Washington, D.C.: Smithsonian Institution Press, 1994).

28. Deloria, *Indians in Unexpected Places.*

29. Margaret M. Bruchac, "Lost and Found: NAGPRA, Scattered Relics, and Restorative Methodologies," *Museum Anthropology* 33, no. 2 (2010): 137–38.

30. Ann McMullen, "Reinventing George Heye: Nationalizing the Museum of the American Indian and Its Collections," in *Contesting Knowledge: Museums and Indigenous Perspectives*, ed. Susan Sleeper-Smith (Lincoln: University of Nebraska Press, 2009), 71. See also Ira Jacknis, "A New Thing? The NMAI in Historical and Institutional Perspective," *American Indian Quarterly* 30, nos. 3 & 4 (2006).

31. Harrington to Dockstader, March 3, 1967, Museum of the American Indian/Heye Foundation Records, 1890–1989, Series VI: Collectors, box 232, folder 3, NMAI.

32. See, for example, James Clifford, "Identity in Mashpee," in *The Predicament of Culture: Twentieth-Century Ethnography, Literature, and Art* (Cambridge, Mass.: Harvard University Press, 1988).

33. James Scott, *Domination and the Arts of Resistance: Hidden Transcripts* (New Haven, Conn.: Yale University Press, 1990), 27–28.

34. Pierre Bourdieu, *Language and Symbolic Power*, trans. Gino Raymond and Matthew Adamson (Cambridge, Mass.: Harvard University Press, 1991).

35. See, for example, Charles Briggs and Richard Bauman, "'The Foundation of All Future Researches': Franz Boas, George Hunt, Native American Texts, and the Construction of Modernity," *American Quarterly* 51, no. 3 (1999). See also Akhil Gupta and James Ferguson, eds., *Anthropological Locations: Boundaries and Grounds of a Field Science* (Berkeley: University of California Press, 1997).

36. Michelle H. Raheja, *Reservation Reelism: Redfacing, Visual Sovereignty, and Representations of Native Americans in Film* (Lincoln: University of Nebraska Press, 2010).

Chapter 2

Chapter epigraph: Hunt to Boas, March 4, 1898, Franz Boas Papers, Series I: Correspondence, George Hunt, folder 1, APS. An early and very condensed version of this chapter was published as "My Sisters Will Not Speak: Boas, Hunt, and the Ethnographic Silencing of First Nations Women," *Curator: The Museum Journal* 57, no. 2 (2014): 153–71.

1. Franz Boas, "Beiträge zur Erkenntniss der Farbe des Wassers" [Contributions to the understanding of the color of water] (PhD diss., University of Kiel, Germany, 1881).

2. Franz Boas, diary, December 23, 1883, quoted in Douglas Cole, "'The Value of a Person Lies in His Herzensbildung': Franz Boas' Baffin Island Letter-Diary, 1883–1884," in *Observers Observed: Essays on Ethnographic Fieldwork*, ed. George W. Stocking Jr. (Madison: University of Wisconsin Press, 1983), 33.

3. For an overview of Boas's early work, see Briggs and Bauman, "'The Foundation of All Future Researches.'" See also Robert H. Lowie, *Biographical Memoir of Franz Boas 1858–1942* (Washington, D.C.: National Academy of Sciences, 1947).

4. Franz Boas, diary, June 12–13, 1888, in Cole, "'The Value of a Person Lies in His Herzensbildung.'"

5. Douglas Cole, *Captured Heritage: The Scramble for Northwest Coast Artifacts* (Vancouver: University of British Columbia Press, 2011), 156.

6. Franz Boas and George Hunt, "The Jesup North Pacific Expedition: Kwakiutl Texts," issued in 3 vols. in the *Memoirs of the American Museum of Natural History* (New York: G. E. Stechert, 1902–5).

7. Judith Berman, "George Hunt and the Kwak'wala Texts," *Anthropological Linguistics* 36, no. 4 (1994). See also Regna Darnell, "The Pivotal Role of the Northwest Coast in the History of Americanist Anthropology," *British Columbia Studies*, no. 125/126 (Spring/Summer 2000).

8. Judith Berman, "Unpublished Materials of Franz Boas and George Hunt: A Record of 45 Years of Collaboration," in *Gateways: Exploring the Legacy of the Jesup North Pacific Expedition, 1897–1902*, ed. Igor Krupnik and William W. Fitzhugh (Washington, D.C.: Smithsonian, 2001), 181.

9. For discussion of the Hunt family relations, see Marius Barbeau, *Totem Poles: According to Location*, vol. 2 (Ottawa, Ontario: National Museum of Canada, 1950), 651.

10. Marius Barbeau, "Totem Poles: A By-Product of the Fur Trade," *Scientific Monthly* 55, no. 6 (1942): 510–11.

11. Marius Barbeau, "Totem Poles: A Recent Native Art of the Northwest Coast of America," *Geographical Review* 20, no. 2 (1930): 262–63.

12. Barbeau, *Totem Poles: According to Location*, 651–52.

13. Franz Boas, *Contributions to the Ethnology of the Kwakiutl*, Columbia University Contributions to Anthropology 3 (New York: AMS, 1925); and Franz Boas, *The Social Organization and the Secret Societies of the Kwakiutl Indians*, Smithsonian Institution, Report of the U.S. National Museum, 1895 (Washington, D.C.: Government Printing Office, 1897). For a contemporary discussion of inherited rights to family treasures among members of the Hunt family, see Lucy Mary Christina Bell, "Kwakwaka'wakw Laws and Perspective Regarding 'Property'" (master's thesis, University of Victoria, British Columbia, 2005).

14. Barbeau, *Totem Poles: According to Location*, 651–52.

15. Boas, *The Social Organization and the Secret Societies of the Kwakiutl Indians*, 556–57. See also Barbeau, *Totem Poles: According to Location*, 654.

16. Michael Ames, "How to Decorate a House: The Renegotiation of Cultural Representations at the University of British Columbia Museum of Anthropology," *Museum Anthropology* 22, no. 3 (1999).

17. Daniel Cranmer, George Hunt's grandson-in-law, quoted in Barbeau, *Totem Poles: According to Location*, 661.

18. Boas, *The Social Organization and the Secret Societies of the Kwakiutl Indians*, 335. See also Franz Boas, *Ethnology of the Kwakiutl, Based on Data Collected by George Hunt* (Washington, D.C.: Smithsonian Institution, 1921).

19. For more examples of Boas's general reluctance to engage with Native women as authorities, see Steffen Bohni Nielsen, "Civilizing Kwakiutl: Contexts and Contests of Kwakiutl Personhood, 1880–1999" (PhD diss., University of Aarhus, Denmark, 2001).

20. Boas to Hunt, February 3, 1899, Franz Boas Papers, Series I: Correspondence, George Hunt, folder 2, APS.

21. Boas to Hunt, June 8, 1906, Franz Boas Papers, Series I: Correspondence, George Hunt, folder 7, APS.

22. Ronald P. Rohner, ed., *The Ethnography of Franz Boas: Letters and Diaries of Franz Boas Written on the Northwest Coast from 1886 to 1931*, trans. Hedy Parker (Chicago: University of Chicago Press, 1969), 188.

23. Berman, "George Hunt and the Kwak'wala Texts," 491.

24. Franz Boas, *Kwakiutl Ethnography*, ed. Helen Codere (Chicago: University of Chicago Press, 1966), xxix–xxx.

25. Boas to Hunt, September 17, 1918, Franz Boas Papers, Series I: Correspondence, George Hunt, folder 19, APS.

26. Hunt to Boas, November 5, 1895, Franz Boas Papers, Series I: Correspondence, George Hunt, folder 1, APS.

27. Hunt to Boas, June 10, 1918, Franz Boas Papers, Series I: Correspondence, George Hunt, folder 19, APS.

28. Hunt to Boas, November 21, 1926, Franz Boas Papers, Series I: Correspondence, George Hunt, folder 36, APS.

29. Hunt to Boas, March 21, 1906, Franz Boas Papers, Series I: Correspondence, George Hunt, folder 7, APS.

30. Hunt to Boas, June 10, 1918, Franz Boas Papers, Series I: Correspondence, George Hunt, folder 19, APS.

31. Ibid.

32. See Paige Raibmon, "Theatres of Contact: The Kwakwaka'wakw Meet Colonialism in British Columbia and at the World's Fair," *Canadian Historical Review* 81, no. 2 (2002). See also Aaron Glass, "A Cannibal in the Archive: Performance, Materiality, and (In)Visibility in Unpublished Edward Curtis Photographs of the Kwakwaka'wakw Hamat'sa," *Visual Anthropology Review* 25, no. 2 (2009).

33. Hunt to Boas, March 21, 1907, Franz Boas Papers, Series I: Correspondence, George Hunt, folder 9, APS.

34. Boas conducted extensive studies of these specific beliefs, published in such texts as *The Social Organization and the Secret Societies of the Kwakiutl Indians* (1897) and *The Religion of the Kwakiutl Indians*, Columbia University Contributions to Anthropology 10 (New York: Columbia University Press, 1930).

35. Hunt to Boas, March 4, 1898, Franz Boas Papers, Series I: Correspondence, George Hunt, folder 1, APS.

36. See Harlan Ingersoll Smith, *Archaeology of Lytton, British Columbia* (New York: AMS, 1975), originally published in *Memoirs of the American Museum of Natural History*, vol. 2, pt. 3 (New York: G. P. Putnam's Sons, 1899).

37. Hunt to Boas, January 10, 1899, Franz Boas Papers, Series I: Correspondence, George Hunt, folder 2, APS.

38. Ibid.

39. Boas to Hunt, February 3, 1899, Franz Boas Papers, Series I: Correspondence, George Hunt, folder 2, APS.

40. Ibid.

41. Hunt to Boas, March 15, 1900, Franz Boas Papers, Series I: Correspondence, George Hunt, folder 19, APS.

42. Hunt to Boas, March 27, 1900, and April 28, 1900, Franz Boas Papers, Series I: Correspondence, George Hunt, folder 19, APS.

43. These observations emerged from my survey of the entire stream of nearly forty years of correspondence between Franz Boas and George Hunt, from 1895 until Hunt's death in 1933.

44. Hunt to Boas, May 31, 1917, Franz Boas Papers, Series I: Correspondence, George Hunt, folder 14, APS.

45. Hunt to Boas, August 5, 1918, Franz Boas Papers, Series I: Correspondence, George Hunt, folder 18, APS.

46. Hunt to Boas, September 7, 1923, Franz Boas Papers, Series I: Correspondence, George Hunt, folder 32, APS.

47. Hunt to Boas, July 23, 1899, Franz Boas Papers, Series I: Correspondence, George Hunt, folder 2, APS.

48. Hunt to Boas, March 29, 1910, Franz Boas Papers, Series I: Correspondence, George Hunt, folder 11, APS.

49. Hunt to Boas, October 10, 1900, Franz Boas Papers, Series I: Correspondence, George Hunt, folder 3, APS.

50. Hunt to Boas, March 21, 1906, Franz Boas Papers, Series I: Correspondence, George Hunt, folder 7, APS.

51. Ibid.

52. Hunt to Boas, January 31, 1917, Franz Boas Papers, Series I: Correspondence, George Hunt, folder 14, APS.

53. George Hunt, "Oka to Henak!alaso," manuscript, n.d., box 125, folder W 1a.8, Ms # 910, Committee on Native American Languages Papers, APS.

54. Hunt to Boas, May 14, 1909, Franz Boas Papers, Series I: Correspondence, George Hunt, folder 11, APS.

55. Hunt to Boas, November 19, 1911, Franz Boas Papers, Series I: Correspondence, George Hunt, folder 11, APS.

56. John R. Swanton, "Explanation of the Seattle Totem Pole," *Journal of American Folklore* 18, no. 69 (1898): 108–10.

57. See Boas, *Ethnology of the Kwakiutl*, 788–92, 976–1002. See also Hunt to Boas, October 4, 1913, Franz Boas Papers, Correspondence, APS.

58. Berman, "George Hunt and the Kwak'wala Texts," 486–87. For further discussion of the resonance of these relations in the present day, see Frank Everson, "Renegotiating the Past: Contemporary Tradition and Identity of the Comox First Nation" (master's thesis, University of British Columbia, 2000).

59. These renditions of Boas's Kwak'wala names come from Boas, "The Indians of British Columbia," *Journal of the American Geographical Society* 28, no. 3 (1896); and Rohner, *The Ethnography of Franz Boas*, 33.

60. Darnell, "The Pivotal Role of the Northwest Coast," 34.

61. Hunt to Boas, December 1, 1897, Franz Boas Papers, Series I: Correspondence, George Hunt, folder 1, APS.

62. Hunt to Boas, October 10, 1900, Franz Boas Papers, Series I: Correspondence, George Hunt, folder 3, APS.

63. Hunt to Boas, April 12, 1908, Franz Boas Papers, Series I: Correspondence, George Hunt, folder 10, APS.

64. Hunt to Boas, January 9, 1900, Franz Boas Papers, Series I: Correspondence, George Hunt, folder 3, APS.

65. Hunt to Boas, March 9, 1906, Franz Boas Papers, Series I: Correspondence, George Hunt, folder 7, APS.

66. Hunt to Boas, January 18, 1907, Franz Boas Papers, Series I: Correspondence, George Hunt, folder 9, APS.

67. Boas, *Ethnology of the Kwakiutl*, 45.

68. Boas to Hunt, June 11, 1908, Franz Boas Papers, Series I: Correspondence, George Hunt, folder 10, APS.

69. Hunt to Boas, June 18, 1908, Franz Boas Papers, Series I: Correspondence, George Hunt, folder 10, APS.

70. Hunt to Boas, September 18, 1908, Franz Boas Papers, Series I: Correspondence, George Hunt, folder 10, APS.

71. Hunt to Boas, March 29, 1910, Franz Boas Papers, Series I: Correspondence, George Hunt, folder 11, APS.

72. Unpublished interview with Mrs. G. [Tsukwani Francine] Hunt, "Kwakiutl Autobiography" (1930), box 2, folder U 7b.5, Committee on Native American Languages Papers, APS.

73. Franz Boas, "Field Notes of Dr. Franz Boas on his trips to British Columbia," box 130, folder B61, Committee on Native American Languages Papers, APS.

74. For a full discussion of the process of making this film, including the names of the participants photographed, see Bill Holm and George L. Quimby, *Edward S. Curtis in the Land of the War Canoes* (Seattle: University of Washington Press, 1980).

75. See photograph of Tsukwani Francine Hunt titled "A chief's daughter—Nakoaktok" (1914), in Edward S. Curtis Collection, LC-USZ62-52204, no. 3567, Library of Congress, Prints & Photographs Division, published in Edward S. Curtis, *The North American Indian*, vol. 10, *The Kwakiutl* (Cambridge, Mass.: Plimpton Press, 1915), 364. See also photograph of Margaret Wilson Frank wearing the same abalone shell ear ornaments, titled "Tsawatenok girl, Kwakiutl Indian" (1914), in Curtis Collection, published in Curtis, *The North American Indian*, facing p. 90.

76. Glass, "A Cannibal in the Archive," 133.

77. For a fuller discussion of the documentary *In the Land of the War Canoes*, see Florence Curtis Graybill and Victor Boesen, *Edward Sheriff Curtis: Visions of a Vanishing Race* (Boston, Mass.: Houghton Mifflin, 1986).

78. Hunt to Boas, December 15, 1919, and June 7, 1920, Franz Boas Papers, Series I: Correspondence, George Hunt, folder 11, APS.

79. Hunt to Boas, December 22, 1916, Franz Boas Papers, Series I: Correspondence, George Hunt, folder 13, APS.

80. Ibid.

81. Hunt to Boas, December 12, 1916, Franz Boas Papers, Series I: Correspondence, George Hunt, folder 13, APS.

82. Hunt to Boas, February 10, 1917, Franz Boas Papers, Series I: Correspondence, George Hunt, folder 14, APS.

83. Hunt to Boas, January 31, 1917, Franz Boas Papers, Series I: Correspondence, George Hunt, folder 14, APS.

84. Boas to Hunt, May 1, 1901, Franz Boas Papers, Series I: Correspondence, George Hunt, folder 3, APS.

85. Hunt to Boas, July 23, 1899, Franz Boas Papers, Series I: Correspondence, George Hunt, folder 1, APS. Even lengthier complaints about the speed of production

appear in letters from Hunt to Boas on January 23, 1906, March 9, 1906, October 7, 1916, and February 4, 1920. Hunt frequently requested more money to pay informants; see, for example, Hunt to Boas, March 9, 1906, September 18, 1908, October 27, 1908, and October 12, 1920, Franz Boas Papers, Series I: Correspondence, George Hunt, various folders, APS.

86. Boas, *Ethnology of the Kwakiutl*, 451, 467.

87. All those pages have been reshuffled in the archives since, but they could (with sufficient time and patience) be dated based on the style of handwriting and the sequential numbers assigned to them.

88. Hunt to Boas, June 10, 1918, Franz Boas Papers, Series I: Correspondence, George Hunt, folder 17, APS.

89. Hunt to Boas, February 18, 1899, Franz Boas Papers, Series I: Correspondence, George Hunt, folder 1, APS.

90. Hunt to Boas, April 21, 1907, Franz Boas Papers, Series I: Correspondence, George Hunt, folder 9, APS.

91. Boas to Hunt, December 19, 1906, Franz Boas Papers, Series I: Correspondence, George Hunt, folder 7, APS.

92. Hunt to Boas, January 18, 1907, Franz Boas Papers, Series I: Correspondence, George Hunt, folder 9, APS.

93. Hunt to Boas, November 30, 1907, Franz Boas Papers, Series I: Correspondence, George Hunt, folder 9, APS.

94. Boas to Hunt, May 12, 1919, Franz Boas Papers, Series I: Correspondence, George Hunt, folder 19, APS.

95. Hunt to Boas, February 16, 1931, Franz Boas Papers, Series I: Correspondence, George Hunt, folder 43, APS.

96. Hunt to Boas, July 8, 1918; Boas to Hunt, July 27, 1918, Franz Boas Papers, Series I: Correspondence, George Hunt, folder 18, APS.

97. Franz Boas, "Sketch of the Kwakiutl Language," *American Anthropologist* 2, no. 4 (1900): 708.

98. Martine J. Reid, ed., *Paddling to Where I Stand: Agnes Alfred, Qwiqwasut'inuxw Noblewoman*, trans. Daisy Sewid-Smith (Vancouver: University of British Columbia Press, 2004), 196.

99. Many of these items have since been repatriated. See U'Mista Cultural Society, "The History of the Potlatch Collection," U'Mista Cultural Centre, accessed November 1, 2017, https://www.umista.ca/pages/collection-history.

100. For more information on Nowell, see Clellan S. Ford, *Smoke from Their Fires: The Life of a Kwakiutl Chief* (New Haven, Conn.: Yale University Press, 1941).

101. Hunt to Boas, June 9, 1930, Franz Boas Papers, Series I: Correspondence, George Hunt, folder 41, APS.

102. Hunt to Boas, March 15, 1930, and June 9, 1930, Series I: Correspondence, George Hunt, folders 41 and 42, APS.

103. Hunt to Boas, February 17, 1931, Franz Boas Papers, Series I: Correspondence, George Hunt, folder 43, APS.

104. For more information on Jane Cook, see Leslie A. Robertson and Kwagu'l Gixsam Clan, *Standing Up with Ga'axsta'las: Jane Constance Cook and the Politics of*

Memory, Church, and Custom (Vancouver: University of British Columbia Press, 2012).

105. J. Hunt to Boas, September 26, 1933, Franz Boas Papers, Series I: Correspondence, Johnnie Hunt, folder 1, APS.

106. Boas to J. Hunt, October 5, 1933, Franz Boas Papers, Series I: Correspondence, Johnnie Hunt, folder 1, APS.

107. Barbeau, *Totem Poles: According to Location*, 660.

108. Berman, "Unpublished Materials of Franz Boas and George Hunt," 183.

109. A few notes on this trip appear in Julia Averkieva and Mark A. Sherman, *Kwakiutl String Figures* (Seattle: University of Washington Press; New York: American Museum of Natural History, 1992).

110. Unpublished interviews with Mary Hunt, "Kwakiutl Autobiography" (1930), and Mrs. G. [Tsukwani Francine] Hunt, "Kwakiutl Autobiography" (1930), box 2, folder U 7b.5, Committee on Native American Languages, APS.

111. Boas, *Ethnology of the Kwakiutl*, 824.

112. Ibid.

113. Berman, "George Hunt and the Kwak'wala Texts," 509.

114. Everson, "Renegotiating the Past," 7–8.

115. Bell interviewed Ann Brotchie, Lucy Smith, and Colleen Hemphill at Gwa'Sala-'Nakwaxda'xw Reserve, among others. See notes throughout Bell, "Kwakwaka'wakw Laws and Perspective Regarding 'Property.'"

116. U'Mista Cultural Society, "The History of the Potlatch Collection."

117. Peter M. Whiteley, "Commemorating Boas" (paper presented at the Colloquium on Collaborative and Engaged Anthropology, American Museum of Natural History, April 1, 2008), 14–15. See also Norman Boas, *Franz Boas: A Biography* (Mystic, Conn.: Seaport Autographs Press, 2004).

118. Marina Dodis, "Anislaga Commemorative Totem Pole," August 7, 2013, accessed December 10, 2014, https://vimeo.com/70460990. Corrine Hunt and Marina Dodis also recorded a video tribute to Anislaga; see "Anislaga," 2013, accessed December 10, 2014, http://www.indiegogo.com/projects/anislaga.

Chapter 3

Chapter epigraph: Arthur Parker to Edna Parker Harrington, June 3, 1934, Museum of the American Indian/Heye Foundation Records, 1890–1989, Series VI: Collectors, box 231, folder 3, NMAI. This and other confessional letters were preserved in Mark Raymond Harrington's papers after Arthur's sister, Edna (also known as Endeka), passed away.

1.   Parker's family ancestry is outlined in his c. 1930 biographical sketch for the *Masonic International Who's Who*. See Arthur C. Parker Papers, Collection A.P23, Family Ephemera, box 5, folder 3, RCL.

2.   The State Cabinet of Natural History (1855–70) was formerly the State Cabinet of Curiosity (1842–55). See "History of the Museum," New York State Museum, accessed November 1, 2017, http://www.nysm.nysed.gov/about/history.

3. There is virtually no information on Beulah in Joy Porter, *To Be Indian: The Life of Iroquois-Seneca Arthur Caswell Parker* (Norman: University of Oklahoma Press, 2001), 54. Even in the most comprehensive Parker biography—Chip Colwell-Chanthaphonh, *Inheriting the Past: The Making of Arthur C. Parker and Indigenous Archaeology* (Tucson: University of Arizona Press, 2009)—Beulah is characterized as "elusive in the historical record" (118).

4. Family information is drawn from multiple sources, including census records and correspondence in the uncataloged Emma Camp Mead Papers, Indian Lake Historical Society, ILM. See also Lynn Woods, "A History in Fragments," *Adirondack Life* (November/December 1994).

5. Cromwell Childe, "The Indians of New York City," *New York Times*, September 12, 1897.

6. Anonymous, "New York Indians: Lives of Members of That Race in the City; Their Annual Migration to the Reservations; How the Indians in the City Are Employed," originally published in the *New York Mail and Express*, reprinted in the *Los Angeles Times*, April 10, 1904.

7. Anonymous, "Falling Star: The Indian Beauty Who Died Last Week," *Sun* (New York), February 5, 1903.

8. Childe, "The Indians of New York City."

9. Anonymous, "Here Is the Most Perfect Indian Model in All America," *San Francisco Call*, February 10, 1901. This text is reprinted in Thomas M. Charland, *Les Abénakis d'Odanak* (Montreal: Editions du Lévrion, 1964), 65.

10. Anonymous, "Beautiful Indian Model," *Boston Sunday Globe*, May 12, 1901.

11. Anonymous, "Handsome Indian and His Clever Daughter in Great Demand in New York Studios," *Brooklyn Daily Eagle*, April 6, 1902.

12. Ibid.

13. Anonymous, "Indian Girl in New York School," *Salisbury* (N.C.) *Weekly Sun*, January 31, 1901.

14. Anonymous, "Clever Indian Girl Honored," *Spokane Daily Chronicle*, March 15, 1901.

15. Mark Raymond Harrington, "Reminiscences of an Archeologist: II," *Masterkey* 37, no. 1 (1963): 25.

16. Mark Raymond Harrington, "College Essays," Museum of the American Indian/Heye Foundation Records, 1890–1989, Series VI: Collectors, box 231, folder 3, NMAI.

17. Mark Raymond Harrington, "An Abenaki 'Witch-Story,'" *Journal of American Folklore* 14, no. 54 (1901): 160.

18. Mark Raymond Harrington, "Witchcraft Story," *Journal of American Folklore* 15, no. 56 (1902): 63.

19. Ibid.

20. See, for example, multiple warnings in George S. Snyderman, "Witches, Witchcraft, and Alleghany Seneca Medicine," *Proceedings of the American Philosophical Society* 127, no. 4 (1983).

21. Statement regarding Harriet Maxwell Converse from Onondaga Castle, September 18, 1891, Museum of the American Indian/Heye Foundation Records, 1890–1989, Series VI: Collectors, box 231, folder 5, NMAI.

22. This liminal status of honorary chiefs like Harriet Maxwell Converse and Joseph Keppler was confirmed in discussions with Seneca Faithkeeper and Repatriation Officer G. Peter Jemison and other members of the Haudenosaunee Standing Committee on Burial Rules and Regulations. This information emerged during consultations about Keppler's "horns" (a strand of wampum affixed to a document) archived in the collections of the Rochester Museum of Science and Industry.

23. Childe, "The Indians of New York City."

24. Anonymous, "Harriet Maxwell Converse," *New York Times*, September 12, 1897. For a discussion of Arthur Parker as one of "Putnam's boys," see Browman and Williams, *Anthropology at Harvard*, 265–69.

25. Harrington to Fenton, September 30, 1967, William N. Fenton Papers, Series I: Correspondence, box 15, APS.

26. Harrington, "Reminiscences of an Archeologist: II," 25. See also Colwell-Chanthaphonh, *Inheriting the Past*, 80–83.

27. Parker to Putnam, June 12, 1903, Frederic Ward Putnam Papers, Correspondence, box 17, folder 5, HUA.

28. Parker to Putnam, August 24, 1903, Frederic Ward Putnam Papers, Correspondence, box 17, folder 5, HUA.

29. Mark Raymond Harrington, "Reminiscences of an Archeologist: IV," *Masterkey* 37, no. 3 (1963).

30. Arthur C. Parker, *The Indian How Book* (New York: George H. Doran, 1931), 61–62.

31. Marie Harrington, *On the Trail of Forgotten People: A Personal Account of the Life and Career of Mark Raymond Harrington* (Reno, Nev.: Great Basin Press, 1985), 32.

32. Thomas C. Maroukis, *The Peyote Road: Religious Freedom and the Native American Church* (Norman: University of Oklahoma Press, 2004), 53–54.

33. Hazel W. Hertzberg, "Nationality, Anthropology, and Pan-Indianism in the Life of Arthur C. Parker," *Proceedings of the American Philosophical Society* 123, no. 1 (1979): 54–55. See also Porter, *To Be Indian*, 57; and Colwell-Chanthaphonh, *Inheriting the Past*, 122.

34. Anonymous, "Chief of Red Men," *Detroit Free Press*, November 22, 1903.

35. Anonymous, "Indians Mourn for Friend," *San Francisco Chronicle*, November 23, 1903.

36. Anonymous, "Indians Mourn at Converse's Bier," *New York Times*, November 23, 1903.

37. Since Parker was then a reporter for the *Sun* (New York), it is likely that he authored some of the laudatory news articles that had appeared during Converse's lifetime, as well as the reports and obituaries that spread her postmortem fame. Newspaper articles about her funeral are archived in Joseph Keppler Jr. Iroquois Papers, Collection 9184, Series II: Correspondence, box 1, folder C6.A, CUL.

38. Anonymous, "Marriage Unites Abenaki and Seneca Tribes," *Boston Globe*, July 27, 1904; Anonymous, "Warring Tribes Are United by Romantic New York Marriage," *Post-Standard* (Syracuse, N.Y.), July 11, 1904.

39. Anonymous, "Romance of an Indian Maid," *Pittsburgh Daily Post*, July 31, 1904.

40. Anonymous, "Warring Tribes Are United by Romantic New York Marriage."

41. Anonymous, "Romance of an Indian Maid."

42. Anonymous, "Indian Council in Town," *Sun* (New York), November 27, 1904. Curiously, Parker was identified in this news article as bearing the Native name "Star Shaft."

43. Ibid.

44. Ibid.

45. See, for example, Anonymous, "Warring Tribes Are United by Romantic New York Marriage."

46. Anonymous, "Indian Council in Town."

47. Ibid.

48. See Onondaga Nation v. Thacher, 29 Misc. 428 (Sup. Ct. Onondaga Co. 1899), aff'd, 53 A.D. 561 (4th Dept. 1900), aff'd, 169 N.Y. 584 (1901); New York State Indian Law § 27, NY L.1899, c. 150; amended L.1971, c. 960, eff. June 25, 1971; repealed 1992.

49. Draper to Parker, November 4, 1904, Arthur C. Parker Papers, Collection A.P23, Family Ephemera, box 5, folder 1, RCL.

50. Parker to Keppler, November 24, 1905, Joseph Keppler Jr. Iroquois Papers, Collection 9184, Series II: Correspondence, box 2, folder P2, CUL.

51. Ibid.

52. Arthur C. Parker, "Where Questions Are Answered," *Museum Service*, December 1953, 163. For a fuller discussion of Parker's evolving museum career, see Stephen W. Thomas, "Arthur Caswell Parker: 1881–1955; Anthropologist, Historian and Museum Pioneer," *Rochester History* 17, no. 3 (1955).

53. Porter, *To Be Indian*, 57–58.

54. Parker to Clarke, December 31, 1905, Office of the New York State Archaeologist, Correspondence, box 1, folder 4, NYSM.

55. Parker to Clarke, February 10, 1906, Office of the New York State Archaeologist, Correspondence, box 1, folder 4, NYSM.

56. See, for example, Parker to Heye, January 4, 1905, Office of the New York State Archaeologist, Correspondence, box 1, folder 11, NYSM.

57. Arthur C. Parker, "Secret Medicine Societies of the Seneca," *American Anthropologist*, n.s. 11, no. 2 (1909): 161.

58. Parker to Dewey, April 7, 1906, quoted in William N. Fenton, "Introduction," in *Parker on the Iroquois*, by Arthur C. Parker (Syracuse, N.Y.: Syracuse University Press, 1968), 12–13.

59. Arthur C. Parker, "Iroquois Uses of Maize and Other Food Plants," *New York State Museum Bulletin* 144 (November 1, 1910).

60. Among the unpublished material in the Parker Papers are notes on herbal medicine collected from Beulah's relatives in the Adirondacks. See "Notes while at John Kennedy's, 1905," Arthur C. Parker Papers, Collection SC13604, Notes, box 1, folder 32, NYSL.

61. Parker to Keppler, April 16, 1905, Joseph Keppler Jr. Iroquois Papers, Collection 9184, Series II: Correspondence, box 2, folder P2, CUL.

62. Census takers and Parker's biographers have often incorrectly spelled Beulah and Arthur's son's name as "Melville."

63. Parker to Fannell, December 19, 1906, Office of the New York State Archaeologist, Correspondence, box 1, folder 9, NYSM.

64. Ibid.

65. Parker to Chessman, August 28, 1907, Office of the New York State Archaeologist, Correspondence, box 1, folder 3, NYSM.

66. Parker to Putnam, December 27, 1907, Frederic Ward Putnam Papers, 1717.2.1, box 17, HUA.

67. The children's names are first mentioned in a letter from Arthur Parker to Edward Cornplanter, December 7, 1908, Office of the New York State Archaeologist, Correspondence, box 1, folder 3, NYSM.

68. On Seneca witchcraft folklore, see Matthew Dennis, *Seneca Possessed: Indians, Witchcraft, and Power in the Early Republic* (Philadelphia: University of Pennsylvania Press, 2010), 94.

69. For the Silverheels ghost sightings, see Harrington, "Reminiscences of an Archeologist: IV," 116. Parker's account of the Ripley site, interestingly, makes no mention of ghosts.

70. See Arthur Parker, "Excavations in an Erie Indian village and Burial Site at Ripley, Chautauqua Co., N.Y.," *New York State Museum Bulletin* 117 (December 1907).

71. Arthur C. Parker, *Seneca Myths and Folk Tales* (Buffalo, N.Y.: Buffalo Historical Society, 1923), xix–xx.

72. Parker to Clarke, November 18, 1905, Office of the New York State Archaeologist, Correspondence, box 1, folder 4, NYSM.

73. Parker to Gardinier, July 11, 1907, Office of the New York State Archaeologist, Correspondence, box 1, folder 23, NYSM.

74. Parker to Keppler, July 27, 1906, Joseph Keppler Jr. Iroquois Papers, Collection 9184, Series II: Correspondence, box 2, folder P2, CUL.

75. Details of this separation are recounted in a letter from Bertha Parker Cody to Rebecca Burmaster Wiley, February 8, 1965, shared with the permission of Rosie Wiley, Everett Burmaster Papers, private collection.

76. Anonymous, "Bessie Tahamont," *Warrensburgh News* (Lake George, N.Y.), September 23, 1909.

77. Parker to R. G. Preston, May 31, 1910, Office of the New York State Archaeologist, Correspondence, box 1, folder 5, NYSM. The Parker family appears in the 1910 census as living in Albany, New York. Bureau of the Census, *1910 United States Federal Census* (Washington, D.C.: National Archives and Records Administration, 1910), page 8A, ED 0045, image 522, NARA microfilm publication T624_920, FHL no. 1374933.

78. Anonymous, "Bessie Tahamont."

79. Parker to Keppler, September 23, 1911, Joseph Keppler Jr. Iroquois Papers, Collection 9184, Series II: Correspondence, box 2, folder P2, CUL.

80. Arthur C. Parker, "Fate of the New York State Collections in Archaeology and Ethnology in the Capitol Fire," *American Anthropologist* 13, no. 1 (1911): 171.

81. Chris Carola, "1911 Capitol Fire Commemorated in NY," *Huffington Post*, March 3, 2011.

82. Bertha Parker to Rebecca Burmaster Wiley, February 8, 1965, courtesy of Rosie Wiley, Everett Burmaster Papers, private collection. Bertha's recollection of the accident was also shared with Julian Hayden; see "Notes on 'Iron Eyes' Cody's autobiography, '*My Life as a Hollywood Indian*,'" Julian Hayden Papers, private collection.

83. Snyderman, "Witches, Witchcraft, and Alleghany Seneca Medicine," 277.

84. Colwell-Chanthaphonh, *Inheriting the Past*, 133.

85. Porter, *To Be Indian*, 222.

86. Arthur's son is nearly invisible in Parker's records; his name rarely appears in correspondence, but he is living with the family in the census records. See Arthur C. Parker, Albany Ward 10, Albany, N.Y, in Bureau of the Census, *1920 United States Federal Census* (Washington, D.C.: National Archives and Records Administration, 1920), page 1A, ED 48, image 1062, NARA microfilm publication T625.

87. On the Indian dioramas, see Anonymous, "Looking Back into Indian New York," *Sun* (New York), December 17, 1911.

88. Arthur C. Parker, "The New York Indians," *University of the State of New York Bulletin to the Schools* (November 15, 1915).

89. For discussion of the dangers of being duped by promoters of Wild West shows, see Chauncey Yellow Robe, "The Indian and the Wild West Show," *Quarterly Journal of the Society of American Indians* 2, no. 1 (1914). To situate the Tahamont family among other Hollywood Indians, see P. Deloria, *Indians in Unexpected Places*, 76, 78. See also Katie Ryder, "Hollywood Indian," *Paris Review*, August 1, 2013, http://www.theparisreview.org/blog/tag/margaret-tahamont/.

90. For a general discussion of the class, education, and representational distinctions of Parker's generation, see Lucy Maddox, *Citizen Indians: Native American Intellectuals, Race, and Reform* (Ithaca, N.Y.: Cornell University Press, 2005).

91. For an overview of the complex relationships among the members of the SAI, see Hertzberg, "Nationality, Anthropology and Pan-Indianism." For a more indepth discussion of the psychologies and strategies of SAI, see Chadwick Allen and Beth H. Piatote, eds., *The Society of American Indians and Its Legacies: A Special Combined Issue of SAIL [Studies in American Indian Literature] and AIQ [American Indian Quarterly]* 25, no. 2 (2013).

92. Arthur C. Parker, "Modern Red Indians," *San Francisco Call*, October 12, 1912.

93. Sherman Coolidge, "The Function of the Society of American Indians," *Quarterly Journal of the Society of American Indians* 2 no. 3 (1914): 187.

94. Arthur C. Parker, "The Editor's Viewpoint: A Survey of the Problem—Its Elements and Its End," *Quarterly Journal of the Society of American Indians* 2, no. 4 (1914): 22.

95. For a broader discussion of this pan-Indian movement, see Hazel W. Hertzberg, *The Search for an American Identity: Modern Pan-Indian Movements* (Syracuse, N.Y.: Syracuse University Press, 1971). See also Frederick Hoxie, ed., *Talking Back to Civilization: Indian Voices from the Progressive Era* (Boston, Mass.: Bedford, 1971);

and Joane Nagel, *American Indian Ethnic Renewal: Red Power and the Resurgence of Identity and Culture* (Oxford: Oxford University Press, 1997).

96. For further discussion of the intellectual goals of SAI, see Robert Warrior, "The SAI and the End(s) of Intellectual History," *Society of American Indians and Its Legacies: A Special Combined Issue of SAIL [Studies in American Indian Literature] and AIQ [American Indian Quarterly]* 25, no. 2 (2013).

97. Parker to Mrs. Charles A. Eastman [Elaine Goodale], February 14, 1911, Office of the New York State Archaeologist, Correspondence, box 1, folder 5, NYSM.

98. Ibid.

99. Arthur C. Parker, *The Constitution of the Five Nations*, New York State Museum Bulletin 184 (Albany: University of the State of New York, 1916).

100. J. N. B. Hewitt, "North America," review of *The Constitution of the Five Nations*, by Arthur C. Parker, *Traditional History of the Confederacy of the Six Nations*, by Duncan Campbell Scott, and *Civil, Religious and Mourning Council and Ceremonies of Adoption of the New York Indians*, by William M. Beauchamp, *American Anthropologist* 19, no. 3 (1917): 433, 438.

101. Parker to La Flesche, November 27, 1911, Office of the New York State Archaeologist, Correspondence, box 1, folder 5, NYSM.

102. An early version of the research in this section appeared in Margaret M. Bruchac, "Indian Lake Is the Scene You Should Make: Emma Camp Mead, Indian Doctor/Entrepreneur/Activist/Fashion Plate" (paper presented at the Native American History: Current and Future Directions symposium in honor of Neal Salisbury at Smith College, Northampton, Mass., March 5, 2009).

103. Notes from an undated bank memo notebook, Emma Camp Mead Papers, ILM.

104. Honyoust to Mead, June 5, 1923, Emma Camp Mead Papers, ILM.

105. Mead to Minnie and Albert Shenandoah, July 31, 1923, Emma Camp Mead Papers, ILM.

106. Shenandoah to Mead, November 17, 1923, Emma Camp Mead Papers, ILM.

107. The 1924 Indian Citizenship Act was passed by the 68th Congress on February 22, 1924, and signed into law by Calvin Coolidge on June 2, 1924 (43 Stat. 253. ante, 420). Charles J. Kappler, ed., *Indian Affairs: Laws and Treaties*, vol. 4, *Laws* (Washington, D.C.: Government Printing Office, 1929).

108. Parker to Harrington, January 16, 1920, in Museum of the American Indian/Heye Foundation Records, 1890–1989, Collectors, box 231, folder 12, NMAI.

109. Oren Lyons, review of *The Search for an American Indian Identity: Modern Pan-Indian Movements*, by Hazel W. Hertzberg, *New York History* 53, no. 1 (1972).

110. Ibid.

111. Elijah's first films resulted from his collaborations with director David W. Griffith and cinematographer Billy Bitzer in a series of Western films shot in eastern settings, including *The Broken Doll*, filmed in Coytesville, New Jersey, in 1910; and *The Song of the Wildwood Flute* with Mary Pickford and Mack Sennett, filmed near Fishkill, New York, in 1910. For the full filmography, see IMDB, "Dark Cloud," filmography of Elijah Tahamont, accessed May 20, 2016, http://www.imdb.com/name/nm0167144/.

112. Anonymous, "Motion Picture Notes," *Brooklyn Daily Eagle*, May 28, 1915; Anonymous, "An Indian Writes Photoplays," *Ogden (Utah) Standard*, May 22, 1915.

113. Anonymous, "An Indian Writes Photoplays," *Ogden Standard*.

114. Ryder, "Hollywood Indians."

115. Wade Werner, "Indians Make Place for Selves in Films, Oust Painted Extras," *Cumberland Evening Times*, September 27, 1927.

116. Tahamont to Mead, April 28, 1933, Emma Camp Mead Papers, ILM.

117. Fragments of this knowledge were preserved in a small collection of notes archived in Arthur Parker's papers. See "Notes while at John Kennedy's, 1905," Arthur C. Parker Papers, Collection SC13604, Notes, box 1, folder 32, NYSL.

118. Tahamont to Mead, September 14, 1931, Emma Camp Mead Papers, ILM.

119. Ibid.

120. Tahamont to Mead, January 4, 1928, Emma Camp Mead Papers, ILM.

121. Tahamont to Mead, n.d. [1928], Emma Camp Mead Papers, ILM.

122. Tahamont to Mead, January 8, 1934, Emma Camp Mead Papers, ILM.

123. Ibid.

124. Ibid.

125. Bertha Parker to Harrington, n.d. [c. 1945], Southwest Museum of the American Indian, Correspondence, box 1, folder 28, BRLC.

126. Anonymous, "Obituary: Beulah Filson," *Mercury-Register* (Oroville, Calif.), January 4, 1946.

127. The version of Chinook that M.R. and Arthur used is very close to that found in George C. Shaw, *The Chinook Jargon and How to Use It* (Seattle, Wash.: Rainier Printing Company, 1909).

128. Parker to Harrington, March 6, 1927, Museum of the American Indian/Heye Foundation Records, 1890–1989, Series VI: Collectors, box 232, folder 1, NMAI.

129. Parker to Harrington, c. 1928, Museum of the American Indian/Heye Foundation Records, 1890–1989, Series VI: Collectors, box 232, folder 1, NMAI.

130. Parker to Edna Parker Harrington, June 3, 1934, Museum of the American Indian/Heye Foundation Records, 1890–1989, Series VI: Collectors, box 232, folder 1, NMAI.

131. Parker to Edna Parker Harrington, October 23, 1934, Museum of the American Indian/Heye Foundation Records, 1890–1989, Series VI: Collectors, box 232, folder 1, NMAI.

132. Harriet Maxwell Converse, *Myths and Legends of the New York State Iroquois*, ed. and annotated Arthur Caswell Parker, New York State Museum Bulletin 125, Education Department Bulletin 437 (Albany: University of the State of New York, 1908), 135.

133. Arthur Parker, c. 1930 biographical sketch for the *Masonic International Who's Who*. See Arthur C. Parker Papers, Collection A.P23, Family Ephemera, box 5, folder 3, RCL.

134. Parker, "Introduction," in Converse, *Myths and Legends*, 12.

135. See, for example, J. Dyneley Prince and Frank G. Speck, "Glossary of the Mohegan-Pequot Language," *American Anthropologist*, n.s. 6, no. 1 (1904).

136. Parker, "Introduction," in Converse, *Myths and Legends*, 12.
137. Ibid., 13.
138. Ibid.
139. Alnoba Wabunaki, "With the Passing of Puritanism the Red Man Comes," *Quarterly Journal of the Society of American Indians* 2, no. 2 (1914).
140. Ibid.
141. Alnoba Wabunaki, "My Race Shall Live Anew," *Quarterly Journal of the Society of American Indians* 2, no. 2 (1914).
142. Arthur C. Parker, *Skunny Wundy: Seneca Indian Tales* (1926; repr., Syracuse, N.Y.: Syracuse University Press, 1994), 9–10.
143. George Hamell, "Introduction," in Parker, *Skunny Wundy*, xv–xvii.
144. Parker to Harrington, June 3, 1934, Museum of the American Indian/Heye Foundation Records, 1890–1989, Series VI: Collectors box 232, folder 1, NMAI.

Chapter 4

Chapter epigraph: Mark Raymond Harrington, "Confidential Personnel Information," 1931, Southwest Museum of the American Indian, Correspondence, box 1, folder 21, BRLC. A brief summary of this research appeared in Margaret M. Bruchac, "Breaking Ground in the 1930s: Bertha Parker, First Female Native American Archaeologist" (keynote lecture for the Sixth Annual Regina Herzfeld Flannery Lecture on the Cultural Heritage of Native Americans at Catholic University, Washington, D.C., April 9, 2014).

1. Bruchac, "Breaking Ground in the 1930s."
2. For an overview of Harrington's work for Putnam, see Browman and Williams, *Anthropology at Harvard*, 63–65.
3. The Irwin Hayden photo album from 1905 is in the Julian Hayden Papers, private collection.
4. Mark Raymond Harrington, "The Knife-Maker Understood," *Masterkey* 39, no. 2 (1955): 61.
5. Mark Raymond Harrington, "Reminiscences of an Archeologist: VI," *Masterkey* 38, no. 3 (1964): 107–8.
6. Mark Raymond Harrington, "Ruins and Legends of Zuni Land," *Masterkey* 3, no. 1 (1929): 15–16.
7. The names of Harrington's assistants routinely appear in census records. Due to their travels, they sometimes appear in two locales in the same year. See, for example, Mark R. Harrington, Los Angeles, Calif., in Bureau of the Census, *1930 United States Federal Census* (Washington, D.C.: National Archives and Records Administration, 1930), p. 1A, ED 682, roll 162, image 188.0, NARA microfilm publication T626. See also Mark R. Harrington, Las Vegas, Clark, Nev., in *1930 United States Federal Census*, p. 3B, ED 8, image 258.0, roll 1296, NARA microfilm publication T626. The Las Vegas census includes Bertha Parker, James Thurston, three Zuni Indians, and Willis and Jessie Evans with their three children, all in residence at the same camp.

8.   Heye to Hodge, May 22, 1926, Southwest Museum of the American Indian, Correspondence, box 1, folder 21, BRLC.

9.   Harrington to Hopkins, February 11,1926, Museum of the American Indian/ Heye Foundation Records, 1890–1989, Series VI: Collectors, box 231, folder 12, NMAI.

10. Harrington to Tupeyashi (Hodge), July 29, 1926, Southwest Museum of the American Indian, Correspondence, box 1, folder 21, BRLC.

11. Harrington to Parker, March 9, 1927, Museum of the American Indian/Heye Foundation Records, 1890–1989, Series VI: Collectors, box 232, folder 11, NMAI.

12. Harrington to Parker, November 27, 1927, Museum of the American Indian/Heye Foundation Records, 1890–1989, Series VI: Collectors, box 232, folder 11, NMAI.

13. Parker to Harrington, December 20, 1927, Museum of the American Indian/Heye Foundation Records, 1890–1989, Series VI: Collectors, box 232, folder 11, NMAI.

14. Details on Harrington's four wives can be found in notes from his fourth wife, Marie Harrington, in Museum of the American Indian/Heye Foundation Records, 1890–1989, Series VI: Collectors, box 229, folder 16, NMAI.

15. The details of these marriages are collated together from scattered references throughout the Parker and Harrington correspondence.

16. Julian Hayden, "Notes on 'Iron Eyes' Cody's autobiography, '*My Life as a Hollywood Indian*,'" Julian Hayden Papers, private collection.

17. Harrington's lectures and the activities in camp were referenced in the detailed diaries of Julian Hayden during his work on the site in 1929; these diaries are now located in the Julian Hayden Papers. They were also noted in some of Bertha Parker's letters to Hayden.

18. For discussion of the influence of cross-cultural collaboration in the field of Indigenous archaeology, see George Nicholas, *Being and Becoming Indigenous Archaeologists* (Walnut Creek, Calif.: Left Coast Press, 2010), and Margaret M. Bruchac, Siobhan Hart, and H. Martin Wobst, eds., *Indigenous Archaeologies: A Reader in Decolonization* (Walnut Creek, Calif.: Left Coast Press, 2010).

19. Mark Raymond Harrington, "In Nevada with Our Expedition," *Masterkey* 2, no. 6 (1929): 22.

20. Bertha Parker Thurston, "Scorpion Hill," *Masterkey* 7, no. 6 (1933): 174.

21. Ibid., 177.

22. Mark Raymond Harrington, "Man and Beast in Gypsum Cave," *Desert Magazine* 3, no. 6 (1940): 3.

23. Ibid.

24. These and other details about the Nevada field camp are preserved in the Julian Hayden Papers, private collection.

25. Correspondence with Stephen Hayden and Diane Boyer, March 1, 2017.

26. Parker to Hayden, November 20, 1929, Julian Hayden Papers, private collection.

27. Parker to Hayden, April 16, 1930, Julian Hayden Papers, private collection.

28. Parker to Hayden, November 25, 1929, Julian Hayden Papers, private collection.

29. Parker to Hayden, November 12, 1930, Julian Hayden Papers, private collection.

30. Ibid.

31. Correspondence with Stephen Hayden and Diane Boyer, March 1, 2017.

32. Parker to Hayden, November 12, 1930, Julian Hayden Papers, private collection.

33. Parker to Hayden, May 25, 1931, Julian Hayden papers, private collection.

34. Hayden to Harrington, December 12, 1931, Julian Hayden Papers, private collection.

35. Julian D. Hayden, *Field Man: Life as a Desert Archaeologist*, ed. Bill Broyles and Diane E. Boyer (Tucson: University of Arizona Press, 2011), 59.

36. Todd W. Bostwick, review of *Field Man: Life as a Desert Archaeologist*, by Julian D. Hayden, *Kiva* 77, no. 3 (2012): 15.

37. Hayden, *Field Man*, 226.

38. Ibid., 234.

39. Correspondence with Stephen Hayden, April 9, 2012.

40. For Hayden's transcription of the Pima tradition, see Donald Bahr, Juan Smith, William Smith Allison, and Julian Hayden, *The Hohokam Chronicles: The Short Swift Time of Gods on Earth* (Berkeley: University of California Press, 1994).

41. These details are preserved in the notebooks for Clark County, Lincoln County, and White Pine County Reconnaissance, S1–6, in the Mark Raymond Harrington Papers, box 3, BRLC.

42. Mark Raymond Harrington, "The Gypsy Sloth," *Masterkey* 3, no. 8 (1930): 15.

43. Mark Raymond Harrington, "Reminiscences of an Archeologist: III," *Masterkey* 37, no. 2 (1963): 66. For a detailed discussion of the controversy over these early discoveries, see David J. Meltzer, *The Great Paleolithic War: How Science Forged an Understanding of America's Ice Age Past* (Chicago: University of Chicago Press, 2015).

44. Dr. James A. B. Scherer of the California Institute of Technology, "Gypsum Cave" report, Mark Raymond Harrington Papers, box 49.12, BRLC. Related manuscripts, notes, and published articles can also be found in boxes 48.1–49.13, BRLC.

45. Ibid.

46. Anonymous, "Bones of Man and Extinct Beasts Found Together in Arizona Cave," *Berkeley Daily Gazette*, April 17, 1930.

47. Anonymous, "Girl Leads Scientists to Nevada Prehistoric Find," *Oakland Tribune*, May 20, 1930.

48. Ibid.

49. "Gypsum Cave Notes," Notebook for Nevada Reconnaissance, Mark Raymond Harrington Papers, box 3 S5, BRLC.

50. The summary of Thurston's career is from Stephen M. Rowland, "The Career of James E. Thurston and the Extinction of the Professional Field Collector in North American Vertebrate Paleontology" (paper delivered at the Geological Society of America Annual Meeting, Denver, Colo., October 28–31, 2007).

51. Mark Raymond Harrington, "A Gypsum Cave Romance," *Masterkey* 5, no. 2 (1931): 49.

52. Anonymous, "Cave Explorers Are Married: Caltech Paleontologist Weds Southwest Museum Worker," July 7, 1931, unattributed newspaper clipping found in Julian

Hayden's files. This same text appeared in *Nevada State Journal,* July 7, 1931, with the headline "Cave Explorers of Nevada Wed."

53. "Cave Explorers of Nevada Wed."

54. Tahamont to Mead, September 14, 1931, Emma Camp Mead Papers, ILM.

55. Rowland, "The Career of James E. Thurston."

56. Harrington, "Confidential Personnel Information."

57. For a discussion of the arguments for and against the antiquity of Indigenous peoples in the Americas, in light of the Bering Strait theory and the Clovis discovery, see Meltzer, *The Great Paleolithic War.*

58. Charles C. Mann, "The Clovis Point and the Discovery of America's First Culture," *Smithsonian Magazine,* November 2013.

59. Ibid. See also Michael R. Waters and Thomas W. Stafford Jr., "Redefining the Age of Clovis: Implications for the Peopling of the Americas," *Science* 2315, no. 5815 (2007).

60. Tahamont to Mead, January 8, 1934, Emma Camp Mead Papers, ILM.

61. Harrington to Teluli (Hodge), April 18, 1934, Southwest Museum of the American Indian, Correspondence box 1, folder 21, BRLC.

62. Ibid.

63. Harrington to Teluli (Hodge June 21, 1934), Southwest Museum of the American Indian, Correspondence box 1, folder 21, BRLC.

64. See, for example, Bertha Parker, "Notes on Box Canyon," Mark Raymond Harrington Papers, box 257, folder P. 47921x, BRLC. See also Southwest Museum of the American Indian, Correspondence, box 1, folders 21, 23, and 28.

65. Tahamont to Mead, June 15, 1934, Emma Camp Mead Papers, ILM.

66. Parker, "Notes on Box Canyon."

67. Ibid.

68. Bertha Parker Thurston, "A Night in a Maidu Shaman's House," *Masterkey* 7, no. 4 (1933): 111.

69. Ibid., 115.

70. Ibid.

71. Bertha Parker Thurston. "A Rare Treat at a Maidu Medicine-Man's Feast," *Masterkey* 10, no. 1 (1936).

72. A. L. Kroeber, "A Mission Record of the California Indians," *University of California Publications in American Archaeology and Ethnology* 8, no. 1 (1908).

73. Parker, "Notes on Box Canyon."

74. Bertha Parker Thurston, "How He Became a Medicine Man," *Masterkey* 8, no. 3 (1934): 80.

75. Ibid., 81.

76. Bertha Parker Thurston, "How a Maidu Medicine Man Lost His Power; Related to Bertha Parker Thurston by a Maidu Indian Herbalist," *Masterkey* 9, no. 1 (1935): 28.

77. Ibid.

78. Ibid., 29.

79. Bertha Parker Cody, "A Maidu Myth of the First Death; by Bertha Parker Cody, as Related by Mandy Wilson of Chico, California," *Masterkey* 13, no. 4 (1939); Bertha Parker Cody, "A Maidu Myth of the Creation of Indian Women; by Bertha Parker Cody, as Related by Mandy Wilson, Maidu Indian of Chico, California," *Masterkey* 13, no. 2 (1939).

80. Bertha Parker Cody, "Yurok Fish-Dam Dance; as Told by Jane Van Stralen to Bertha Parker Cody," *Masterkey* 16, no. 3 (1942); Bertha Parker Cody, "Yurok Tales: Wohpekumen's Beads, as Told by Jane Van Stralen to Bertha Parker Cody," *Masterkey* 15, no. 6 (1941).

81. For the timing of Bertha's marriage to Iron Eyes Cody, see Harrington to Amsden, August 13, 1936, and Harrington to Teluli (Hodge), August 27, 1936, Southwest Museum of the American Indian, Correspondence box 1, folder 21, BRLC. Iron Eyes later said about Bertha's Native name: "'Yewas' means 'hard to get' in Indian. (She was, too . . .)." See Virginia MacPherson, "Hollywood Tribe on Warpath; Seek More Wampum," *Bend (OR) Bulletin*, September 30, 1947.

82. Harrington to Teluli (Hodge), September 18, 1939, Southwest Museum of the American Indian, Correspondence box 1, folder 21, BRLC.

83. Colwell-Chanthaphonh suggested that Cody was "horribly unsupportive of her work" (*Inheriting the Past*, 173), based on the narrative in Iron Eyes Cody and Collin Perry's *Iron Eyes: My Life as a Hollywood Indian* (New York: Everest House, 1982), most notably 43, 78–83, 103–10. For insights into the reality of Oscar and Bertha's relationship from the perspective of a close family friend, see Glenda Ahhaitty, "Re: Beulah Tahamont Parker and Bertha Parker Cody (Native archaeologist)," comment on H-Amindian Discussion Logs, *Humanities and Social Sciences Net*, April 10, 2005, http://h-net.msu.edu/cgi-bin/logbrowse.pl?trx=vx&list =h-amindian&month=0504&week=e&msg=s24774OBPj1kIq542Urr3Q&user =&pw=.

84. Ahhaitty, "Re: Beulah Tahamont Parker and Bertha Parker Cody."

85. On Billie's accidental death, see note in Julian Hayden Papers, private collection. See also Anonymous, "Pallan Girl's Death Held an Accident," *Mercury-Register* (Oroville, Calif.), July 25, 1942.

86. MacPherson, "Hollywood Tribe on Warpath."

87. Bertie (Bertha Parker Cody) to Uncle Ray (Harrington), July 31, 1945, Southwest Museum of the American Indian, Correspondence, box 1, folder 28, BRLC.

88. Prayer card of "Blessed Kateri Tekakwitha," painted by John Steele, original printed by the Noteworthy Company, Amsterdam, N.Y., 1980.

89. Iron Eyes Cody and Ye-Was [Bertha Parker Cody], *Sign Talk in Pictures* (Hollywood, Calif.: H. H. Boelter Lithography, 1958).

90. Patricia Clary, "Hollywood Film Shop," *Bakersfield Californian*, June 18, 1949.

91. Iron Eyes Cody's true ethnic identity was publicly exposed after his death. See Amy Waldman, "Iron Eyes Cody, 94, an Actor and Tearful Anti-Littering Icon," *New York Times*, January 5, 1999.

92. See "Whispering Winds," *Talking Leaf* 1, no. 4 (1951): 2; also 1, no. 5 (1951): 2, Indian Center of Los Angeles, BRLC. On Robert Tree Cody, see Tish Leizens, "A

Man Called Tree: The Stepson of Iron Eyes Cody Is a Commanding Pow Wow Presence," *Indian Country Today Media Network*, April 2, 2013. Arthur William Cody served with the U.S. Marines in Vietnam and died in 1996 from the aftereffects of exposure to Agent Orange. Robert "Big Tree" Cody is a prominent and skilled Native American wooden flute player and recording artist.

93. Ahhaitty, "Re: Beulah Tahamont Parker and Bertha Parker Cody."

94. Ibid.

95. Julian Hayden, who knew them both, made a point-by-point refutation of Oscar's lies about Bertha in an unpublished memo, "Notes on 'Iron Eyes' Cody's autobiography, '*My Life as a Hollywood Indian*," in the Julian Hayden Papers, private collection.

96. Cody and Perry, *Iron Eyes*, 110.

97. Ibid., 43.

98. For a careful analysis of Iron Eyes's performative style, see Raheja, *Reservation Reelism: Redfacing, Visual Sovereignty, and Representations of Native Americans in Film*, 111–21.

99. *International Directory of Anthropologists* (Washington, D.C.: National Research Council, 1938), 284.

100. Anonymous, "Bertha Parker Cody," *Masterkey* 53, no. 1 (1979): 38.

101. "Death Notices," *Newsletter of the American Anthropological Association* 20, no. 6 (1979): 5.

102. Kali Herman, *Women in Particular* (Phoenix: Oryx Press, 1984).

103. Margaret Bruchac, "First Female Native American Archaeologist," comment on H-Amindian Discussion Logs, *Humanities and Social Sciences Net*, April 10, 2005, http://h-net.msu.edu/cgi-bin/logbrowse.pl?trx=vx&list=h-amindian&month=0504&week=b&msg=5dXeUDYDuKgR%2BWm0Nqugjw&user=&pw=. Nearly a decade later, Bertha did receive mention in David L. Browman's *Cultural Negotiations: The Role of Women in the Founding of Americanist Archaeology* (Lincoln: University of Nebraska Press, 2013), 127–29.

Chapter 5

Chapter epigraph: Fenton to Cornplanter, February 15, 1935, William N. Fenton Papers, Series I: Correspondence, box 8, folder 1, APS. An early version of this research appeared in Margaret M. Bruchac, "Resisting Red Power: Scholarly Domination of Haudenosaunee Representation" (paper presented at the Native American and Indigenous Studies Association Conference, Sacramento, Calif., May 19, 2011, read by Alyssa Mt. Pleasant in my absence).

1. The Rochester Museum and Science Center also houses the privately owned Rock Foundation collection.

2. Fenton's biographical recounting of his early Seneca relationships can be found in William N. Fenton, "He-Lost-a-Bet (*Howanˀneyao*) of the Seneca Hawk Clan," in *Strangers to Relatives: The Adoption and Naming of Anthropologists in Native North America*, ed. Sergei Kan (Lincoln: University of Nebraska Press, 2001), 81–82.

3.   For a summary of Fenton's career, see Regna Darnell, "William N. Fenton (1908–2005)," *Journal of American Folklore* 120, no. 475 (2007).

4.   Fenton, "He-Lost-a-Bet," 84.

5.   Ibid.

6.   Information on Seneca adoption practices is from an interview with G. Peter Jemison, Christine Abrams, Jere Cardinal, and others at a private meeting of the Haudenosaunee Standing Committee on Burial Rules and Regulations, May 15, 2015. On the Native practice of naming anthropologists, see also Kan, *Strangers to Relatives*.

7.   Fenton, "He-Lost-a-Bet," 82.

8.   Ibid., 81, 92.

9.   Under the "New Deal," President Roosevelt developed work relief, agricultural support, and emergency aid programs to assist recovery from the Great Depression. For the effects of these programs on Haudenosaunee people, see Laurence M. Hauptman, *The Iroquois and the New Deal* (Syracuse, N.Y.: Syracuse University Press, 1981).

10.   William N. Fenton, *An Outline of Seneca Ceremonies at Cold Spring Longhouse* (New Haven, Conn.: Yale University Press, 1936).

11.   Fenton, "He-Lost-a-Bet," 93.

12.   For an overview of Jesse Cornplanter's early years, see William N. Fenton, "'Aboriginally Yours': Jesse J. Cornplanter, Hah-Yonh-Wonh-Ish, the Snipe," in *American Indian Intellectuals of the Nineteenth and Early Twentieth Centuries*, ed. Margo Liberty (Norman: University of Oklahoma Press, 2002).

13.   Fenton, "He-Lost-a-Bet," 96.

14.   Fenton to Cornplanter, February 14, 1936, William N. Fenton Papers, Series I: Correspondence, box 7, folder 2, APS.

15.   Fenton to Cornplanter, February 15, 1935, William N. Fenton Papers, Series I: Correspondence, box 7, folder 1, APS.

16.   Ibid.

17.   Cornplanter to Fenton, January 8, 1935, William N. Fenton Papers, Series I: Correspondence, box 7, folder 2, APS.

18.   For a discussion of the complicated role of "show Indians" amid the larger theme of "playing Indian," see Deloria, *Playing Indian*. For a discussion of the popular "Wild West" shows and pageants organized by Buffalo Bill, which increased demand for performing Indians, see Joy Kasson, *Buffalo Bill's Wild West: Celebrity, Memory, and Popular History* (New York: Hill and Wang, 2000).

19.   Cornplanter to Fenton, October 2, 1934, William N. Fenton Papers, Series I: Correspondence, box 7, folder 1, APS.

20.   Cornplanter to Edwards, January 28, 1942, William N. Fenton Papers, Series I: Correspondence, box 7, folder 2, APS.

21.   Cornplanter to Fenton, December 8, 1936, William N. Fenton Papers, Series I: Correspondence, box 7, folder 1, APS.

22.   Ibid.

23. For a full discussion of WPA at the Rochester Public Museum, see Laurence H. Hauptman, "The Iroquois School of Art: Arthur C. Parker and the Seneca Arts Project, 1935–1941," *New York History* 60, no. 3 (1979).

24. Cornplanter to Fenton, December 19, 1936, William N. Fenton Papers, Series I: Correspondence, box 7, folder 1, APS.

25. Laurence M. Hauptman, "Eleanor Roosevelt and the American Indian: The Iroquois as a Case Study," *Hudson Valley Regional Review* 16, no. 1 (1999): 4. See also references to Henricks in Hauptman, *The Iroquois and the New Deal*.

26. Cornplanter to Fenton, December 19, 1936, William N. Fenton Papers, Series I: Correspondence, box 7, folder 1, APS.

27. Fenton to Olive, Betsey, and John Fenton, September 18–20, 1943, William N. Fenton Papers, Series I: Correspondence, box 12, APS.

28. Cornplanter to Fenton, October 2, 1934, William N. Fenton Papers, Series I: Correspondence, box 7, folder 1, APS.

29. Cornplanter to Edwards, January 28, 1942, William N. Fenton Papers, Series I: Correspondence, box 7, folder 2, APS.

30. Cornplanter to Fenton, November 18, 1940, William N. Fenton Papers, Series I: Correspondence, box 7, folder 2, APS.

31. Fenton to Reva Barse, March 23, 1945, William N. Fenton Papers, Series I: Correspondence, box 2, APS.

32. Fenton to Parker, June 8, 1944, William N. Fenton Papers, Series I: Correspondence, box 27, APS.

33. Ibid.

34. Cornplanter to Perry, January 11, 1952, William N. Fenton Papers, Series I: Correspondence, box 8, folder 6, APS.

35. Cornplanter to Fenton, March 1, 1952, William N. Fenton Papers, Series I: Correspondence, box 8, folder 6, APS.

36. Cornplanter to Bartlett, November 26, 1956, William N. Fenton Papers, Series I: Correspondence, box 8, folder 8, APS.

37. Ibid.

38. Cornplanter to Congdon, May 3, 1954, William N. Fenton Papers, Series I: Correspondence, box 7, APS.

39. Jesse J. Cornplanter, "Attention Seneca Indians," typed document, c. December 1956, William N. Fenton Papers, Series I: Correspondence, box 8, folder 8, APS.

40. Cornplanter to Bartlett, December 23, 1956, William N. Fenton Papers, Series I: Correspondence, box 8, folder 8, APS.

41. Press release from assistant commissioner for the New York State Museum and Science Service, New York State Education Department, June 18, 1957, William N. Fenton Papers, Series I: Correspondence, box 26, APS.

42. Garlow to Fenton, May 4, 1957, William N. Fenton Papers, Series I: Correspondence, box 13, APS.

43. Bruce Elliott Johansen and Barbara Alice Mann, *Encyclopedia of the Haudenosaunee (Iroquois Confederacy)* (Westport, Conn.: Greenwood, 2000), 188.

44. Congdon to Fenton, February 17, 1969, William N. Fenton Papers, Series I: Correspondence, box 6, APS.
45. G. Peter Jemison, "Sovereignty and Treaty Rights: We Remember," *Akwesasne Notes*, n.s. 1, nos. 3–4 (1995).
46. Press release, New York State Education Department, June 18, 1957.
47. Anthony F. C. Wallace, "The Career of William N. Fenton and the Development of Iroquoian Studies," in *Extending the Rafters: Interdisciplinary Approaches to Iroquoian Studies*, ed. Michael K. Foster, Jack Campisi, and Marianne Mithun (Albany: State University of New York Press, 1984).
48. Darnell, "William N. Fenton," 74, 75.
49. Fenton to Foster, April 16, 1969, William N. Fenton Papers, Series I: Correspondence, box 13, APS. Fenton was directing Foster's graduate field study at the University of Pennsylvania, for his dissertation project, "Formal Speaking on the Six Nations Reserve," funded by APS.
50. See, for example, William N. Fenton, *The False Faces of the Iroquois* (Norman: University of Oklahoma Press, 1987); and William N. Fenton, *The Little Water Medicine Society of the Senecas* (Norman: University of Oklahoma Press, 2002). For a similarly sharp critique of Fenton, see Jose Barreiro, "Fenton, William N.," in *Encyclopedia of the Haudenosaunee Confederacy*, ed. Bruce Elliott Johansen and Barbara Alice Mann (Westport, Conn.: Greenwood, 2000).
51. Darnell, "William N. Fenton," 74.
52. William N. Fenton, "Collecting Materials for a Political History of the Six Nations," *Proceedings of the American Philosophical Society* 93, no. 3 (1949): 233.
53. See Morgan, *League of the Ho-de-no-sau-nee or Iroquois*; Horatio E. Hale, *The Iroquois Book of Rites* (Philadelphia, Penn.: D. G. Brinton, 1883).
54. Fenton, "Collecting Materials," 233.
55. Ibid., 236.
56. Ibid., 238.
57. Anthony F. C. Wallace, "The Dekanawideh Myth Analyzed as the Record of a Revitalization Movement," *Ethnohistory* 5, no. 2 (1958).
58. Ibid.
59. Fenton to Wallace, January 29, 1948, William N. Fenton Papers, Correspondence, box 37, APS. Fadden was the secretary to the Akwesasne Mohawk Counselor Organization, and founder of the Six Nations Indian Museum in Onchiota, New York.
60. William N. Fenton, "The Lore of the Longhouse: Myth, Ritual and Red Power," in "Anthropology: Retrospect and Prospect: A Special Issue in Honor of Regina Flannery Herzfeld," *Anthropological Quarterly* 48, no. 3 (1975): 144.
61. Fenton to Christie, July 23, 1980, William N. Fenton Papers, Series I: Correspondence, box 6, APS.
62. Bell to Fenton, August 5, 1980, William N. Fenton Papers, Series I: Correspondence, box 1, APS.
63. Fenton's correspondence, archived at APS, contains many examples of his reviews, letters, and critiques of students, scholars, and Native American writers. Bell specifically asked Fenton to review all Iroquois studies applications and research at APS.

Bell to Fenton, August 5, 1980, William N. Fenton Papers, Series I: Correspondence, box 1, APS.

64. Clipping of Fenton's letter to *Akwesasne Notes* (Winter 1970), William N. Fenton Papers, Series I: Correspondence, box 33, APS.

65. William Fenton, "The New York State Wampum Collection: The Case for the Integrity of Cultural Treasures," in *Proceedings of the American Philosophical Society* 115, no. 6 (1971).

66. Ibid., 438.

67. Ibid., 437.

68. Some of the personal experience of this revival was reported by Tuscarora scholar Richard W. Hill, in "Regenerating Identity: Repatriation and the Indian Frame of Mind," in *The Future of the Past: Archaeologists, Native Americans and Repatriation,* ed. Tamara Bray (New York: Garland, 2001).

69. William Fenton, "Red Power and Wampum," draft manuscript, William N. Fenton Papers, Series III: Works by Fenton, box 10, folder 13, APS.

70. Ibid.

71. Fenton to Warren A. Snyder, April 17, 1970, William N. Fenton Papers, Series I: Correspondence, box 32, APS.

72. William C. Sturtevant, Donald Colliver, Philip J. C. Dark, and William N. Fenton, "CARM Concerned at Proposed Wampum Return," *Anthropology News* 2, no. 4 (1970): 4.

73. Ibid. See also William C. Sturtevant, Donald Colliver, Philip J. C. Dark, William N. Fenton, and Ernest S. Dodge, "An 'Illusion of Religiosity,'" *Indian Historian* 3, no. 2 (1970).

74. Fenton to Snyder, April 17, 1970, William N. Fenton Papers, Series I: Correspondence, box 32, APS.

75. Tooker to Fenton, April 1, 1972, William N. Fenton Papers, Series I: Correspondence, box 35, APS.

76. Fenton to George Abrams, April 29, 1971, William N. Fenton Papers, Series I: Correspondence, box 1, APS.

77. Fenton to Tooker, October 29, 1970, William N. Fenton Papers, Series I: Correspondence, box 35, APS.

78. Tooker to Fenton, July 23, 1970, William N. Fenton Papers, Series I: Correspondence, box 35, APS.

79. Fenton to Rogers, January 18, 1973, William N. Fenton Papers, Series I: Correspondence, box 29, APS.

80. Wallace to Fenton, November 25, 1970, William N. Fenton Papers, Series I: Correspondence, box 37, APS.

81. Fenton to Wallace, December 5, 1970, Fenton Papers, Series I: Correspondence, box 37, APS.

82. Fenton to Tooker, January 18, 1973, Fenton Papers, Series I: Correspondence, box 35, APS.

83. For historical understandings of wampum keepers, see Hale, *The Iroquois Book of Rites.*

84. This was confirmed through consultations with Onondaga lawyer Paul Williams and other members of the Haudenosaunee Standing Committee, who have been working on wampum repatriation cases for four decades. See also Hill, "Regenerating Identity."

85. Photographs of these belts were made available in Tehanetorens [Ray Fadden], *Wampum Belts of the Iroquois* (Summertown, Tenn.: Book Publishing Company, 1999).

86. Spittal to Fenton, December 11, 1961, William N. Fenton Papers, Series I: Correspondence, box 32.

87. For a discussion of the use of these plastic beads in a ritual context, see Stephanie Mach, "On the Wampum Trail: Balancing Traditional and Museological Care of Wampum," *Beyond the Gallery Walls* (blog), University of Pennsylvania Museum of Archaeology and Anthropology, August 11, 2014, accessed November 1, 2017, https://www.penn.museum/blog/museum/on-the-wampum-trail-balancing -traditional-and-museological-care-of-wampum/.

88. Doxtator to Carpenter, August 2, 1977, William N. Fenton Papers, Series IIa: Subject Files, box 11, Wampum, APS.

89. Carpenter to Doxtator, August 12, 1977, William N. Fenton Papers, Series IIa: Subject Files, box 11, Wampum, APS.

90. Carpenter to Fenton, August 12, 1977, William N. Fenton Papers, Series IIa: Subject Files, box 11, Wampum, APS.

91. Carpenter to Abrams, August 16, 1985, William N. Fenton Papers, Series IIa: Subject Files, box 11, Wampum, APS.

92. Fenton to Carpenter, August 19, 1985, William N. Fenton Papers, Series IIa: Subject Files, box 11, Wampum, APS.

93. Ibid.

94. Richard W. Hill Sr. chaired the HSC during the 1980s; Christine Abrams is the current acting chair of the HSC. The group works closely with Onondaga tribal lawyers, the Grand Council of the Haudenosaunee (Six Nations Iroquois) Confederacy, and committee representatives from the Cayuga, Mohawk, Oneida, Onondaga, Seneca, and Tuscarora nations and bands in both the United States and Canada. The HSC also coordinates and assists with repatriation claims under NAGPRA. See Haudenosaunee Confederacy, "Haudenosaunee Repatriation Committee," accessed June 30, 2016, http://www.haudenosauneeconfederacy.com/hrc.html.

95. Mary Druke's notes are in William N. Fenton Papers, Series I: Correspondence, box 3, and in William N. Fenton Papers, Series IIb: Subject Files, Iroquois Documentary History Project, APS. Fenton also relied on Sally M. Weaver, "The Wampum Case," in *The History of Politics on the Six Nations Reserve* (Brantford, Ontario: Records and Council Minutes, Indian Office, 1973).

96. Notes from the MAI's Curatorial Council also record Fenton's attempts to discredit Williams rather than consult with him. See William N. Fenton Papers, Series IIa: Subject Files, Museum of the American Indian/Heye Foundation, boxes 6 and 8, APS. See also Paul Williams, "Wampum of the Six Nations Confederacy at the Grand River Territory: 1784–1986," in *Proceedings of the 1986 Shell Bead*

Conference: Selected Papers, ed. Charles F. Hayes (Rochester, N.Y.: Research Division of the Rochester Museum and Science Center, 1989).

97. Fenton to Barse, March 23, 1945, William N. Fenton Papers, Series I: Correspondence, box 2, APS.

98. Fenton to Lehman, November 3, 1980, William N. Fenton Papers, Series IIa: Subject Files, box 11, Wampum, APS.

99. Martin Sullivan, "Return of the Sacred Wampum Belts of the Iroquois," *History Teacher* 26, no. 1 (1992): 9–10.

100. Ibid., 13.

101. Ibid.

102. William N. Fenton, "Return of Eleven Wampum Belts to the Six Nations Iroquois Confederacy on Grand River, Canada," *Ethnohistory* 36, no. 4 (1989).

103. Elisabeth Tooker, "A Note on the Return of Eleven Wampum Belts to the Six Nations Iroquois Confederacy on Grand River, Canada," *Ethnohistory* 45, no. 2 (1998).

104. For an overview of NMAI, see Amy Lonetree and Amanda J. Cobb, *The National Museum of the American Indian: Critical Conversations* (Lincoln: University of Nebraska Press, 2008).

105. Fenton to Carpenter, June 8, 1989, William N. Fenton Papers, Series I: Correspondence, box 5, APS.

106. On NMAIA, see Smithsonian Institution, National Museum of the American Indian Act, Public Law 101-185 (November 28, 1989), appendix F, accessed November 10, 2017, http://nmai.si.edu/sites/1/files/pdf/about/NMAIAct.pdf. On NAGPRA, see United States Department of the Interior, National Park Service, Native American Graves Protection and Repatriation Act, Public Law 101-601, 25 U.S.C. 3001 et seq. (November 16, 1990).

107. Fenton to Conable, October 26, 1991, William N. Fenton Papers, Series I: Correspondence, box 6, APS.

108. Fenton's penultimate work on the Haudenosaunee remains widely popular. See William N. Fenton, *The Great Law and the Longhouse: A Political History of the Iroquois Confederacy* (Norman: University of Oklahoma Press, 1998).

109. Cornplanter to Fenton, March 1, 1952, William N. Fenton Papers Series I: Correspondence, box 8, folder 6, APS.

Chapter 6

Chapter epigraph: Melissa Jayne Fawcett, *Medicine Trail: The Life and Lessons of Gladys Tantaquidgeon* (Tucson: University of Arizona Press, 2000), 151.

1. Speck's faculty record at the University of Pennsylvania, in the alumni archives, indicates that he was born on November 8, 1881, in "Brookline, NY." This spelling reflects the pronunciation of the original Dutch name of Breukelen, which morphed into Brockland and Brookline before becoming Brooklyn.

2. For a brief summary of Speck's career, see J. Alden Mason, "Frank Gouldsmith Speck, 1881–1950," *University Museum Bulletin* 15, no. 1 (1950). For an obituary

and full bibliography, see A. Irving Hallowell, "Frank Gouldsmith Speck, 1881–1950," *American Anthropologist* 53, no. 1 (1951).

3. Melissa Fawcett Sayet, "Sociocultural Authority in Mohegan Society," *Artifacts* 16, nos. 3–4 (1988).

4. Melissa Fawcett, "The Role of Gladys Tantaquidgeon," in *Papers of the Fifteenth Algonquian Conference*, ed. William Cowan (Ottawa, Ontario: Carleton University, 1984).

5. For an overview of Tantaquidgeon's life, see Fawcett, *Medicine Trail*. For a brief history of the Mohegan nation, see Melissa Jayne Fawcett, *The Lasting of the Mohegans: The Story of the Wolf People* (Ledyard, Conn.: Pequot Printing, 1995).

6. That summer, Speck met Edwin Fowler (1881–1959), age nineteen; Jerome Roscoe Skeesucks (1884–1950), age sixteen; and Burrill Tantaguidgeon (also called Quidgeon) (1888–1958), age twelve. Data from private Mohegan tribal genealogical records, courtesy of Melissa Tantaquidgeon Zobel.

7. The 1900 Montville U.S. census records show Cynthia Fowler (1849–1928) as "head of household" with Theodore Cooper (1883–1904) listed as a "boarder." See Cynthia Fowler, Montville, New London, Conn., in Bureau of the Census, *1900 United States Federal Census* (Washington, D.C.: National Archives and Records Administration, 1900), ED 0456, roll 149, NARA microfilm publication T623, FHL no. 1240149.

8. Speck to Speck, n.d. [after 1897], Frank G. Speck Papers, Subcollection I, Series II: Biographical Material, box 20, APS.

9. Ibid.

10. Ibid.

11. Cochegan Rock originated in Labrador, and was carried southward by glaciers to its present location roughly seventeen thousand years ago, remaining in place when the glaciers receded. Richard Curland, "Historically Speaking: Montville Is Home to Largest Boulder," *Bulletin* (Norwich, Conn.), July 1, 2012; Jeff Holtz, "Mohegans Buy Rock Sacred to Tribe," *New York Times*, July 8, 2007.

12. Speck to Speck, n.d. [after 1897], Frank G. Speck Papers, Subcollection I, Series II, Biographical Material, box 20, APS.

13. Gladys Tantaquidgeon, "Frank Speck," unpublished reminiscence in the Gladys Tantaquidgeon Papers, TIM. Reprinted as Gladys Tantaquidgeon, "An Affectionate Portrait of Frank Speck," in *Dawnland Voices: An Anthology of Indigenous Writing from New England*, ed. Siobhan Senier (Lincoln: University of Nebraska Press, 2014).

14. Regarding her orthography, see Prince and Speck, "Glossary of the Mohegan-Pequot Language."

15. Frank G. Speck, "The Remnants of Our Eastern Indian Tribes," *American Inventor* 10 (1903); Frank G. Speck, "The Last of the Mohegans," *Papoose* 1, no. 4 (1903); Frank G. Speck, "Mohegan Traditions of 'Muhkeahweesug,' the Little Men," *Papoose* 1, no. 7 (1903); Frank G. Speck, "A Pequot-Mohegan Witchcraft Tale," *Journal of American Folklore* 16, no. 61 (1903).

16. Speck, "A Pequot-Mohegan Witchcraft Tale," 104.

17. Frank G. Speck and J. Dyneley Prince, "The Modern Pequots and Their Language," *American Anthropologist*, n.s. 5, no. 2 (1903).

18. Prince and Speck, "Glossary of the Mohegan-Pequot Language," 18.

19. Frank G. Speck, *Native Tribes and Dialects of Connecticut: A Mohegan-Pequot Diary*, Bureau of American Ethnology Annual Report 43 (Washington, D.C.: U.S. Government Printing Office, 1928), 224.

20. J. Dyneley Prince, "Last Living Echoes of the Natick," *American Anthropologist*, n.s. 9, no. 3 (1907).

21. Frank G. Speck, "A Modern Mohegan-Pequot Text," *American Anthropologist*, n.s. 6, no. 4 (1904).

22. Ibid., 474.

23. Frank G. Speck, "Primitive Religion," in *Religions of the Past and Present: A Series of Lectures Delivered by Members of the Faculty of the University of Pennsylvania*, ed. James A. Montgomery (Philadelphia, Penn.: J. B. Lippincott, 1918).

24. Speck, *Native Tribes and Dialects of Connecticut*, 245.

25. Ibid., 225.

26. Letter of recommendation for scholarship at the University of Pennsylvania by John Dyneley Prince, 1907, Frank G. Speck Papers, Subcollection I, Series II: Biographical Material, box 19, APS.

27. Speck, *Native Tribes and Dialects of Connecticut*, 204.

28. Ibid.

29. Speck initially deposited Fielding's remaining diaries at the Museum of the American Indian/Heye Foundation in New York City; they are now archived in the Native American Biography Vertical File, Collection 9242, Division of Rare and Manuscript Collections, Carl A. Kroch Library, Cornell University, Ithaca, N.Y.

30. Speck, *Native Tribes and Dialects of Connecticut*, 224.

31. Fawcett, *Medicine Trail*, 32.

32. Melissa Tantaquidgeon Zobel, "The Story Trail of Voices," *ConnecticutHistory.org*, September 4, 2013, accessed November 1, 2017, http://connecticuthistory.org/the-story-trail-of-voices/.

33. See multiple entries in Speck, *Native Tribes and Dialects of Connecticut*, 228–51. Another one of Fielding's diaries was recently located by the Yale Indian Papers Project. This document, housed in the Leffingwell House Museum in Norwich, Connecticut, includes lists of Fielding's relatives and what appear to be the youthful writing attempts of other Mohegans, suggesting that, perhaps, Fielding was teaching her younger relatives.

34. For contemporary Mohegan perspectives on these local traditions, see the chapter "Folks on the Hill" in Fawcett, *Medicine Trail*, 9–19.

35. Ibid., 225.

36. Laura Murray, *To Do Good to My Indian Brethren: The Writings of Joseph Johnson, 1751–1776* (Amherst: University of Massachusetts Press, 1998).

37. Tantaquidgeon, "Frank Speck," 1. See also family stories in Virginia Frances Voight, *Mohegan Chief: The Story of Harold Tantaquidgeon* (New York: Funk and Wagnall's, 1965), 19–20.

38. Emma Baker also served as a tribal political and church leader in various capacities. See Zobel, "The Story Trail of Voices."
39. Speck, *Native Tribes and Dialects of Connecticut*, 224.
40. John Witthoft, "Frank Speck: The Formative Years," in *The Life and Times of Frank G. Speck, 1881–1950*, ed. Roy Blankenship (Philadelphia: Department of Anthropology, University of Pennsylvania, 1991).
41. Frank G. Speck Sr. and Hattie L. Staniford were married on September 1, 1880, in Brooklyn, New York. "New York, Marriage Newspaper Extracts, 1801–1880," Barber Collection (online database), accessed March 23, 2016, https://search .ancestry.com/search/db.aspx?dbid=8936.
42. The 1889, 1890, 1892, 1893, and 1894 New York City Directories all list Frank G. Speck Sr. working as a broker with the Cotton Exchange at 16 Exchange Place, and residing at 328 First Street. New York City Directory, "U.S. City Directories, 1822–1995" (online database), accessed March 23, 2016, https://search.ancestry .com/search/db.aspx?dbid=2469.
43. Virtually all the 1890 federal census records burned in a 1921 warehouse fire, but the state census records survived. Frank G. Speck [Sr.] and family, New York State Census Records, Kings Brooklyn Ward 22 E.D. 16, in *1892 New York State Census* (Albany: New York State Library, 1892), 12.
44. Speck mentioned that Fowler's house was similar to one the Speck family had rented for a vacation at Fish's Eddy. See Speck to Speck, n.d. [after 1897], Frank G. Speck Papers, Series II: Biographical Material, box 20, APS.
45. See Speck to Speck, c. 1898, Frank G. Speck Papers, Subcollection I, Series II: Biographical Material, box 20, APS.
46. This census identifies Frank Jr. as a nineteen-year-old student. Frank G. Speck [Sr.] and family, Hackensack town Ward 4, 5, Bergen, N.J., in *1900 United States Federal Census*, sheet 15B, family 324, NARA microfilm publication T623.
47. Witthoft, "Frank Speck," 2.
48. New York City Department of Records/Municipal Archives, "New York, New York, Death Index, 1862–1948" (online database), accessed March 23, 2016, https:// search.ancestry.com/search/db.aspx?dbid=9131. Frank G. Speck Sr.'s will is archived in *Bergen County Wills*, vol. 33, *1902–1903*, 137–39, available at "New Jersey, Wills and Probate Records, 1739–1991" (online database), accessed March 23, 2016, https://search.ancestry.com/search/db.aspx?dbid=8796.
49. Witthoft, "Frank Speck," 6.
50. Giles is listed as a servant in the Speck household. See Frank G. Speck, Philadelphia Ward 27, Philadelphia, Penn., in *1910 United States Federal Census*, sheet 3A, ED 615, NARA microfilm publication T624.
51. Hattie Speck, 1912 Hackensack, New Jersey. City Directory, "U.S. City Directories, 1822–1995" (online database), accessed March 23, 2016, https://search .ancestry.com/search/db.aspx?dbid=2469.
52. Frank G. Speck, Swarthmore, Delaware, Pennsylvania, in *1930 United States Federal Census*. p. 2B, ED 0135, image 216.0, roll 2033. See also Bureau of the Census, *1940 United States Federal Census* (Washington, D.C.: National Archives and

Records Administration, 1940), p. 9A, ED 23–170, NARA microfilm publication T627_3496.

53. Speck to Prince, May 2, 1938, Frank G. Speck Papers, Series I: Research Material, IV: Southeast 15A3, box 10, APS.

54. Carl A. Weslager, "The Unforgettable Frank Speck," in *The Life and Times of Frank G. Speck, 1881–1950*, ed. Roy Blankenship (Philadelphia: Department of Anthropology, University of Pennsylvania, 1991), 67.

55. Notes from a phone interview with Frank Staniford (Billy) Speck, April 27, 1993, courtesy of Bunny McBride.

56. Notes from a phone interview with Alberta Speck Hartman, April 27, 1993, courtesy of Bunny McBride.

57. Kenneth Heuer, "Introduction," in *The Lost Notebooks of Loren Eiseley*, ed. Kenneth Heuer (Boston, Mass.: Little, Brown, 1987), 16–17.

58. Horace P. Beck, "Frank G. Speck, 1881–1950," *Journal of American Folklore* 64, no. 254 (1951): 415.

59. Loren Eiseley, *All the Strange Hours: The Excavation of a Life* (New York: Charles Scribner's Sons, 1975), 92.

60. Witthoft, "Frank Speck," 2.

61. "Background Note," Frank G. Speck Papers, American Philosophical Society, accessed January 1, 2016, http://amphilsoc.org/collections/view?docId=ead/Mss.Ms .Coll.126-ead.xml.

62. Roy Blankenship, ed., *The Life and Times of Frank G. Speck, 1881–1950* (Philadelphia: Department of Anthropology, University of Pennsylvania, 1991), xii.

63. For a fuller discussion of this concept, see Siobhan Senier, "'Traditionally, Disability Was Not Seen as Such': Writing and Healing in the Work of Mohegan Medicine People," *Journal of Literary & Cultural Disability Studies* 7, no. 2 (2013).

64. See, for example, the experiences of Abenaki Indian doctor Louis Watso, detailed in Margaret Bruchac, "Abenaki Connections to 1704: The Sadoques Family and Deerfield, 2004," in *Captive Histories: Captivity Narratives, French Relations and Native Stories of the 1704 Deerfield Raid*, ed. Evan Haefeli and Kevin Sweeney (Amherst: University of Massachusetts Press, 2006).

65. Zobel, "The Story Trail of Voices." Alonzo (1877–1957), who was also called John, went by several different last names: Cooper, Saunders, and Fielding. Family data from unpublished private Mohegan tribal genealogical records in the Gladys Tantaquidgeon Papers, TIM.

66. Tantaquidgeon, "Frank Speck," 1.

67. Fawcett, *Medicine Trail*, 63.

68. Fawcett, "The Role of Gladys Tantaquidgeon," 138.

69. Tantaquidgeon, "Frank Speck," 1. Gladys suggested that Frank Speck's first visit to Mohegan was in 1902 rather than 1900, but that likely reflects her personal memories of the first time she met him, when she was three years old.

70. Tantaquidgeon, "Frank Speck."

71. Ibid., 2, 4. In the archives of the University of Pennsylvania Museum of Archaeology and Anthropology, in an uncataloged folder of Speck photographs removed

from a photograph album, I discovered a photo of Roscoe Skeesucks showing off the tattoo on his left forearm. No images have survived of Frank's tattoo.

72. Tantaquidgeon, "Frank Speck," 4.

73. Ibid. Additional information is from personal interviews with Gladys Tantaquidgeon, Jayne Fawcett, and Melissa Tantaquidgeon Zobel, 2004–14.

74. Tantaquidgeon, "Frank Speck," 2.

75. Frank Staniford (Billy) Speck, phone interviews with Bunny McBride, October 15, 1992, and April 27, 1993, courtesy of Bunny McBride.

76. Carl A. Weslager, *Delaware's Forgotten Folk: The Story of the Moors and Nanticokes* (Philadelphia: University of Pennsylvania Press, 2006), 88.

77. Tantaquidgeon, "An Affectionate Portrait of Frank Speck," 586.

78. Ibid. See also Fawcett, *Medicine Trail*, 63–67.

79. Mary Ellen Lepionka, "Speck in Riverview," March 26, 2015, unpublished paper in author's possession.

80. Fawcett, "The Role of Gladys Tantaquidgeon," 139.

81. See records in Innu-Montagnais-Naskapi Notebook, Frank G. Speck Papers, Series I: Research Material, A.1, box 4, folder 12, PEM.

82. Expense Accounts and Expedition Reports for Penobscot Fieldwork, 1910–1911, Frank G. Speck Papers, box 10, folders 4–5, PMA.

83. Frank G. Speck, *Penobscot Man: The Life History of a Forest Tribe in Maine* (Philadelphia: University of Pennsylvania Press, 1940), ix.

84. Frank G. Speck, *Ethnology of the Yuchi Indians* (Philadelphia, Penn.: University Museum, 1909).

85. University of Pennsylvania to Frank G. Speck, 1911–1932, Frank G. Speck Papers, Subcollection I, Series II: Biographical Material, box 20, APS. Notices of Speck's PhD and appointments can also be found in the University of Pennsylvania Museum, Board of Managers Minutes, June 1905–June 1910, PMA. See also George B. Gordon, Director's Letterbooks, 1907–13, PMA.

86. See, for example, Mason, "Frank Gouldsmith Speck, 1881–1950"; Hallowell, "Frank Gouldsmith Speck, 1881–1950"; and "Background Note," Frank G. Speck Papers, APS.

87. Alex F. Chamberlain, "Daniel Garrison Brinton," *Journal of American Folklore* 12, no. 46 (1899).

88. Daniel Garrison Brinton, "Anthropology as a Science and as a Branch of University Education in the United States," 1892, and "President's Address to the American Association for the Advancement of Science in 1895," in Regna Darnell, *Daniel Garrison Brinton: The "Fearless Critic" of Philadelphia* (Philadelphia: Department of Anthropology, University of Pennsylvania, 1988), 60.

89. Brinton, "Anthropology as a Science."

90. The entire list of faculty appointments and courses taught from 1886 to 1932 is charted in a 1932 report compiled by Penn archivist Milton Shaham, "Anthropology at the University of Pennsylvania, 1886–1932," in "Anthropology, Department of," University Relations Files, UPF 8.51, box 14, UARC. See also "University

Museum of Archaeology and Anthropology series," Office of the Provost Records, Charles C. Harrison Administration 1854–1943, UPA 6.2H, box 3, UARC.

91. Darnell, *Daniel Garrison Brinton*.

92. Gordon to Harrison, November 5, 1903, Director's Letterbook 1903, PMA.

93. Shaham, "Anthropology at the University of Pennsylvania, 1886–1932."

94. Gordon to Speck, April 6, 1907, Director's Letterbook 1907, PMA.

95. Ames to Gordon, October 20, 1908, Director's Letterbook 1908, PMA.

96. University of Pennsylvania Museum, Board of Managers Minutes, June 1905–June 1910 and October 1910–November 1915, PMA.

97. Gordon to Fisher, April 15, 1910; Director's Letterbook 1910, PMA; and Shaham, "Anthropology at the University of Pennsylvania, 1886–1932."

98. Multiple complaints about Gordon can be found in Edward Sapir Papers, Correspondence, I-A-236M, box 634, folder 1, CMH.

99. For one attempt to resolve the confusion, see the letter from Ruben Reina to Hamilton Cravens, February 29, 1972, "Historical Records Dep't," Department Administrator's files, ADUP. See also Igor Kopytoff, "A Short History of Anthropology at Penn," *Expedition* 48, no. 1 (2012).

100. See, for example, Mason, "Frank Gouldsmith Speck, 1881–1950"; Hallowell, "Frank Gouldsmith Speck, 1881–1950"; and "Background Note," Frank G. Speck Papers, APS.

101. Speck to Sapir, January 25, 1912, Edward Sapir Papers, Correspondence, I-A-236M, box 634, folder 1, CMH.

102. Speck to Sapir, March 28, 1912, and October 2, 1912, Edward Sapir Papers, Correspondence, I-A-236M, box 634, folder 1, CMH. Shotridge and his wife, Florence Kaatxwaantséx, worked in the American section of the Penn Museum from 1912 to 1932.

103. Kopytoff, "A Short History of Anthropology at Penn," 33.

104. Ibid.

105. Ibid.

106. Speck to Sapir, March 2, 1912, and March 18, 1912, Edward Sapir Papers, Correspondence, I-A-236M, box 634, folder 1, CMH.

107. Gordon to Speck, June 12, 1913, Frank G. Speck Papers, Subcollection I, Series II: Biographical Material, box 18, APS; Speck to Gordon, July 1913, and August 17, 1913, Frank G. Speck Papers, box 10, folder 8, PMA.

108. Speck to Sapir, October 1, 1913, Edward Sapir Papers, Correspondence, I-A-236M, box 634, folder 2, CMH.

109. Speck to Gordon, November 5, 1913, and February 4, 1914, Speck to Farabee, May 28, 1917, and Speck to Gordon, January 24, 1923, Frank G. Speck Papers, box 10, folders 4–5, 9–10, PMA.

110. Speck to Ames, March 9, 1915, and Wallis to Speck (n.d. [1915]), Frank G. Speck Papers, Subcollection I, Series II: Biographical Material, box 20, APS.

111. University of Pennsylvania Museum, Board of Managers Minutes, October 1910–November 1915, PMA. For a history of Heye's collection, see Roland Force,

Politics and the Museum of the American Indian: The Heye and the Mighty (Honolulu: Mechas Press, 1999).

112. Blankenship, *The Life and Times of Frank G. Speck*, xii.

113. See Anthropology Department Report, 1927, Frank G. Speck Papers, UPT 50, S741, box 1, folder 5, UARC. See also Mason, "Frank Gouldsmith Speck, 1881–1950."

114. Mason to Eisely, March 7, 1950, in "Anthropology, Department of," University Relations Files, UPF 8.51, box 14, UARC.

115. Shaham, "Anthropology at the University of Pennsylvania, 1886–1932."

116. Weslager, "The Unforgettable Frank Speck," 61.

117. Anthony F. C. Wallace, "The Frank G. Speck Collection," *Proceedings of the American Philosophical Society* 95, no. 3 (1951): 286.

118. Edmund Carpenter, draft notes for an article on Speck, c. 1982 (archived with papers regarding the Museum of the American Indian), William N. Fenton Papers, Series I: Correspondence, box 23, folder 4 APS.

119. Heuer, "Introduction," in *The Lost Notebooks of Loren Eiseley*, 16–17.

120. Speck to Ames, February 11, 1914, Frank G. Speck Papers, Subcollection I, Series II: Biographical Material, box 20, APS.

121. J. Alden Mason, "Frank Gouldsmith Speck, 1881–1950," unpublished manuscript, "Anthropology, Department of," University Relations Files, UPF 8.51, box 14, UARC.

122. Ernest S. Dodge, "Speck on the North Shore," in *The Life and Times of Frank G. Speck, 1881–1950*, ed. Roy Blankenship (Philadelphia: Department of Anthropology, University of Pennsylvania, 1991), 43.

123. Weslager, "The Unforgettable Frank Speck," 62.

124. Speck to Sapir, June 30, 1913, Edward Sapir Papers, Correspondence, I-A-236M, box 634, folder 2, CMH.

125. See, for example, Expense Accounts for 1910–1911, Frank G. Speck Papers, box 10, folders 4–5, PMA.

126. Margaret Bruchac, "The Speck Connection: Recovering Histories of Indigenous Objects," *Beyond the Gallery Walls* (blog), University of Pennsylvania Museum of Archaeology and Anthropology, May 20, 2015, accessed November 1, 2017, http://www.penn.museum/blog/museum/the-speck-connection-recovering-histories-of-indigenous-objects/.

127. Speck to Douglas, October 17, 1941, curatorial correspondence files, Denver Art Museum.

128. This journal was originally mistakenly identified as "Innu-Montagnais-Naskapi Notebook"; it has recently been recataloged as "Account book and ledger," Frank G. Speck Papers, Series III: Personal, B. Accounts, box 8, folder 6, PEM.

129. Edmund Carpenter, draft notes, 1982 (archived with papers regarding the Museum of the American Indian), William N. Fenton Papers, Series I: Correspondence, box 23, folder 4 APS.

130. Bruchac, "The Speck Connection."

131. Fawcett, *Medicine Trail*, 64.

132. "Indian Maiden Here, Descendant of Uncas: Miss Gladys Tantaquidgeon, of the Mohegans, Visiting Dr. Frank Speck, Family Heads Tribe," *Public Ledger* (Philadelphia), undated clipping, Frank G. Speck Papers, Subcollection I, Series I, III. Northeast, D. New England Algonkians, 4. Mohegan-Mohican, box 7, APS.

133. Fawcett, *Medicine Trail*, 61, 72.

134. Tantaquidgeon, Gladys I., College of General Studies, Student Records 1896–1940, UPB 2C.45, box 13, UARC.

135. Copies of Gladys Tantaquidgeon's Penn records are archived in Honorary Degree Files, UARC 5.8, Commencement 1993, Tantaquidgeon, Gladys, box 5, folder 29, UARC.

136. Founded in 1894, the CCT program, a precursor to the College of Liberal and Professional Studies and the School of Education, was designed for public and private schoolteachers who sought not degrees but certificates of proficiency to gain promotions. See Mark Frazier Lloyd, "Women at Penn: Timeline of Pioneers and Achievements," University Archives & Records Center, University of Pennsylvania, July 2001, accessed March 27, 2014, http://www.archives.upenn.edu/histy/features/women/chronbeg.html.

137. Tantaquidgeon, "Frank Speck." Examples of this work can be found in Gladys Tantaquidgeon's publications, as well as her handwritten and typewritten manuscripts, preserved in the uncataloged Gladys Tantaquidgeon Papers, TIM.

138. Eiseley, *All the Strange Hours*, 88.

139. Speck registered Molly Spotted Elk at Swarthmore Preparatory School before admitting her to Penn in 1924, where she audited English and anthropology classes. Like Gladys, she was registered as family and received a tuition waiver. Alumni Records, University of Pennsylvania, UARC.

140. Anonymous, "Education," *Evening News* (Harrisburg, Penn), November 21, 1924.

141. For a history of International House, see Mark Frazier Lloyd, "The Early Years of the International House of Philadelphia and Its Purchase of 3905 Spruce Street 1911–1922," University Archives & Records Center, University of Pennsylvania, August 2000, accessed March 27, 2014, http://www.archives.upenn.edu/histy/features/campuses/3905spruce/3905spruce2.html.

142. For Molly's reminiscences of her time at Penn, see Bunny McBride, *Molly Spotted Elk: A Penobscot in Paris* (Norman: University of Oklahoma Press, 1995), 8–64. For Gladys's reminiscences, see Fawcett, "The Role of Gladys Tantaquidgeon," 140; and Fawcett, *Medicine Trail*, 69–75. Houston Hall, not incidentally, is the same locale where the annual Penn Native American Powwow often takes place today.

143. See note in the University of Pennsylvania Alumni Files and Honorary Degree Files, UARC 5.8, Commencement 1993, Tantaquidgeon, Gladys, box 5, folder 29, UARC.

144. Speck to Ames, February 11, 1914, Frank G. Speck Papers, Subcollection I, Series II: Biographical Material, box 20, APS. See also Records of the Group Committee on Anthropology, "Historical Records Dep't," Department Administrator's files, ADUP. Ida White Cloud, a Carlisle Indian School graduate, worked as a housekeeper in Philadelphia. "Ida White Cloud Student File," 1909, Carlisle Indian

School Digital Resource Center, accessed June 1, 2016, http://carlisleindian .dickinson.edu/student_files/ida-white-cloud-student-file.

145. Notes from a phone interview with Frank Staniford (Billy) Speck, April 27, 1993, courtesy of Bunny McBride.

146. Edmund Carpenter, "Frank Speck: Quiet Listener," in *The Life and Times of Frank G. Speck, 1881–1950*, ed. Roy Blankenship (Philadelphia: Department of Anthropology, University of Pennsylvania, 1991), 80.

147. Ibid.

148. William N. Fenton, "Frank G. Speck's Anthropology," in *The Life and Times of Frank G. Speck, 1881–1950*, ed. Roy Blankenship (Philadelphia: Department of Anthropology, University of Pennsylvania, 1991), 9.

149. Fawcett, *Medicine Trail*, 77. See also "Gladys Tantaquidgeon," Mohegan Tribe, accessed May 15, 2013, http://www.mohegan.nsn.us/Heritage/gt_makiawisug.aspx.

150. Webber's traditional Lenape name, Witapanox'we, is spelled in several different ways in different settings, publications, and archives.

151. See records in "Account book and ledger," Frank G. Speck Papers, Series III: Personal, B. Accounts, box 8, folder 6, PEM.

152. Gladys Tantaquidgeon, "How the Summer Season Was Brought North," *Journal of American Folklore* 54, nos. 213/214 (1941); Gladys Tantaquidgeon, "Notes on the Origin and Uses of Plants of the Lake St. John Montagnais," *Journal of American Folklore* 45, no. 176 (1932).

153. See photographic and film archives in the Frank G. Speck Papers at APS, UPM, and PEM.

154. Speck to Fenton, January 21, 1933, William N. Fenton Papers, Series I: Correspondence, box 33, APS.

155. Frank G. Speck Papers, UPT 50 S741, Class Lecture Notes 1927–1928, box 1, folder 4, UARC.

156. Speck, *Penobscot Man*, ix.

157. Siomonn Pulla, "Frank Speck and the Mapping of Aboriginal Territoriality in Eastern Canada, 1900–1950" (PhD diss., Carleton University, 2006).

158. Malcom Read Lovell, "Penn Professor's Discovery Confounds Indian 'History': Doctor Speck Establishes That the American Redskin Hunts on His Own Family Ground, Is a Protector of Game, and Is No Mere Rover Through the Forests," *Public Ledger* (Philadelphia, Penn.), November 23, 1913.

159. Frank G. Speck, "The Family Hunting Band as the Basis of Algonkian Social Organization," *American Anthropologist*, n.s. 17, no. 2 (1915): 294–95. See also Jocelyn Thorpe, *Temagami's Tangled Wild Rice: Race, Gender, and the Making of Canadian Nature* (Vancouver: University of British Columbia Press, 2012), 51–53.

160. Hallowell, "Ojibwa Ontology, Behavior and World View."

161. The Indian Act was formerly called the "Gradual Enfranchisement Act." See "Chapter 18: An Act to Amend and Consolidate the Laws Respecting Indians," April 12, 1876, Indigenous and Northern Affairs Canada, Government of Canada, accessed August 15, 2017, https://www.aadnc-aandc.gc.ca/eng/1100100010252 /1100100010254.

162. Thorpe, *Temagami's Tangled Wild Rice*, 52.

163. Frank G. Speck, "The Indians and Game Preservation," *Red Man* 6 (1913): 24.

164. See, for example, Harvey A. Feit, "The Construction of Algonquian Hunting Territories: Private Property as Moral Lesson, Policy Advocacy, and Ethnographic Error," in *Colonial Situations: Essay on the Contextualization of Ethnographic Knowledge*, ed. George W. Stocking Jr., History of Anthropology 7 (Madison: University of Wisconsin Press, 1991).

165. Weslager, *Delaware's Forgotten Folk*, 86.

166. Ibid., 91.

167. Ibid., 95.

168. Ibid.

169. Anne Hoffman, "Delaware's Forgotten Folks," *Delaware Public Media*, June 5, 2015.

170. Tantaquidgeon, "Frank Speck," 3.

171. Gladys Tantaquidgeon, "Mohegan Medicinal Practices, Weather-Lore, and Superstitions," in *Native Tribes and Dialects of Connecticut*, ed. Frank G. Speck, Annual Report of the Bureau of American Ethnology 43 (Washington, D.C.: Government Printing Office, 1928).

172. Gladys Tantaquidgeon, "Report on Delaware Ethnobotanical Investigations," in *Fifth Report of the Pennsylvania Historical Commission* (Philadelphia: Commonwealth of Pennsylvania, 1931).

173. Bicknell to Speck, February 11, March 1, and March 11, 1924, Frank G. Speck Papers, Subcollection I, Series I, III. Northeast, New England Algonkians, 4. Mohegan-Mahican, box 7, APS.

174. Ann McMullen, "What's Wrong with This Picture? Context, Coversion, Survival, and the Development of Regional Cultures and Pan-Indianism in Southeastern New England," in *Enduring Traditions: The Native Peoples of New England*, ed. Laurie Weinstein (Westport, Conn.: Bergin and Garvey, 1994).

175. Frank G. Speck, "Indian Girl Saves Legends of Race," *Science News-Letter* 14, no. 386 (1928): 124.

176. Ibid.

177. Ibid.

178. Gladys Tantaquidgeon, notes on Mashpee and Aquinnah folklore, uncataloged Gladys Tantaquidgeon Papers, c. 1930s, TIM. For more details on that project, see Rachel Sayet, "Moshup's Continuance: Sovereignty and the Literature of the Land in the Aquinnah Wampanoag Nation" (master's thesis, Harvard University, 2012).

179. Tantaquidgeon's notes archived among the Frank G. Speck Papers at APS in Subcollection I, Series I, include Tadoussac-Escoumains Field Notes (n.d.), in Mistassini II (4B12), box 3; Botanical notes, c. 1930s, in General (8C1h), box 5; and Plants at Mohegan (n.d.), in Mohegan-Mahican III (10D4b), box 7. There are also several mis-cataloged manuscript drafts for articles that appear to have been authored not by Speck but by Tantaquidgeon, when she was a student and research assistant at Penn.

180. Gladys Tantaquidgeon, "Notes on Mohegan-Pequot Basketry Designs," unpublished manuscript prepared for the Bureau of American Ethnology, Washington, D.C., 1935, from a copy archived in the Gladys Tantaquidgeon Papers at TIM.

181. Speck to Heye, July 15, 1921, and September 9, 1921, Museum of the American Indian/Heye Foundation Records, 1890–1989, Series VI: Collectors, box 74, folder 1, NMAI.

182. Voight, *Mohegan Chief,* 59–61.

183. Speck to Rogers, March 13, 1934, and Rogers to Speck, March 31, 1934, Rogers Indian Papers, uncatalogued correspondence, New London Historical Society.

184. Anonymous, "Running Against Time: Medicine Woman Preserves Mohegan Culture," *Penn Arts & Sciences* (Philadelphia), Summer 2001.

185. Tantaquidgeon to Speck, July 25, 1938, Frank G. Speck Papers, Subcollection I, Series I, Mohegan-Mahican (10D4b), box 7, APS.

186. Gladys Tantaquidgeon, *A Study of Delaware Indian Medicine Practice and Folk Beliefs,* Anthropological Series 3 (Harrisburg: Pennsylvania Historical and Museums Commission, 1942).

187. Donald A. Cadzow, "Foreword," in Tantaquidgeon, *A Study of Delaware Indian Medicine Practice,* v.

188. Anonymous, "Book Relates Indian Medicine Practices," *Daily Notes* (Canonsburg, Penn.), April 11, 1942.

189. "Why Pursue Recognition," Mohegan Tribe, accessed June 10, 2016, https://mohegan.nsn.us/government/recognition/why-persue-recognition.

190. Anonymous, "Running Against Time: Medicine Woman Preserves Mohegan Culture."

191. Fawcett, *Medicine Trail,* 144.

Conclusion

Chapter epigraph: Conversation with Fred McGregor, Kitigan Zibi, Maniwaki, Quebec, May 9, 2017.

1. Browman, *Cultural Negotiations,* 4; Nancy J. Parezo, ed., *Hidden Scholars: Women Anthropologists and the Native American Southwest* (Albuquerque: University of New Mexico Press, 1993), 35n7.

2. See, for example, James Clifford, "Spatial Practices: Fieldwork, Travel, and the Disciplining of Anthropology," in *Anthropological Locations: Boundaries and Grounds of a Field Science,* ed. Akhil Gupta and James Ferguson (Berkeley: University of California Press, 1997).

3. See, for example, Lanita Jacobs-Huey, "The Natives Are Gazing and Talking Back: Reviewing the Problematics of Positionality, Voice, and Accountability Among 'Native' Anthropologists," *American Anthropologist* 104, no. 3 (2002).

4. This is suggested by Miranda J. Brady, "A Dialogic Response to the Problematized Past: The National Museum of the American Indian," in *Contesting Knowledge: Museums and Indigenous Perspectives,* ed. Susan Sleeper-Smith (Lincoln: University of Nebraska Press, 2009).

5. Amy Lonetree, "Museums as Sites of Decolonization: Truth Telling in National and Tribal Museums," in *Contesting Knowledge: Museums and Indigenous Perspectives,* ed.

Susan Sleeper-Smith (Lincoln: University of Nebraska Press, 2009); Lonetree and Cobb, *The National Museum of the American Indian.*

6. Ongoing representational challenges and strategies are discussed in Gerald Mc-Master, "Museums and the Native Voice," *Museums After Modernism: Strategies of Engagement,* ed. Griselda Pollock and Joyce Zemans (London: Blackwell, 2007).

7. Moira McLoughlin, *Museums and the Representation of Native Canadians: Negotiating the Borders of Culture* (New York: Routledge, 1999); Ruth B. Phillips and Mark Salber Phillips, "Double Take: Contesting Time, Place, and Nation in the First Peoples' Hall of the Canadian Museum of Civilization," *American Anthropologist* 104, no. 4 (2006).

8. See the case histories in John H. Merryman, ed., *Imperialism, Art, and Restitution* (Cambridge: Cambridge University Press, 2006).

9. James Clifford, "On Collecting Art and Culture," in *The Predicament of Culture: Twentieth-Century Ethnography, Literature, and Art* (Cambridge, Mass.: Harvard University Press, 1998), 228.

10. See, for example, Erikson, "Decolonizing the Nation's Attic." See also Ann McMullen, "Reinventing George Heye: Nationalizing the Museum of the American Indian and Its Collections," in *Contesting Knowledge: Museums and Indigenous Perspectives,* ed. Susan Sleeper-Smith (Lincoln: University of Nebraska Press, 2009).

11. For a case study of evolving traditions of concealment, see Ruth B. Phillips, "Disappearing Acts: Traditions of Exposure, Traditions of Enclosure, and Iroquois Masks," in *Questions of Tradition,* ed. Mark Salber Phillips and Gordon Schochet (Toronto: University of Toronto Press, 2004).

12. Edmund Carpenter, *Two Essays: Chief and Greed* (North Andover, Mass.: Persimmon Press, 2005). See also Force, *Politics and the Museum of the American Indian,* 44.

13. Leah Gordon, "Trading a Museum's Treasure—A Very Hazardous Business," *New York Times,* March 31, 1974.

14. Fred Ferretti, "Dealer's Papers Sought in Indian Museum Case," *New York Times,* February 26, 1975.

15. Lefkowitz v. The Museum of the American Indian Heye Foundation, no. 41416175 (N.Y. Sup. Ct. 1975), obtained via FOIL request 09506-747. See also Museum of the American Indian/Heye Foundation Records, Series 1, Directors, box 84, folder 13, Smithsonian Institution Archives.

16. On NMAIA, see Smithsonian Institution, National Museum of the American Indian Act, Public Law 101-185 (November 28, 1989), appendix F, accessed November 10, 2017, http://nmai.si.edu/sites/1/files/pdf/about/NMAIAct.pdf. On NAGPRA, see United States Department of the Interior, National Park Service, Native American Graves Protection and Repatriation Act, Public Law 101-601, 25 U.S.C. 3001 et seq. (November 16, 1990).

17. Guidelines regarding repatriation policy are from the National Museum of the American Indian Act, appendix F, accessed September 30, 2017, http://nmai.si.edu /sites/1/files/pdf/about/NMAIAct.pdf.

18. National NAGPRA, "Law, Regulations, and Guidance," accessed November 10, 2017, https://www.nps.gov/nagpra/MANDATES/INDEX.HTM.

19. See, for example, Barbara Isaac, "The Implementation of NAGPRA: The Peabody Museum of Archaeology and Ethnography, Harvard," in *The Dead and Their Possessions: Repatriation in Principle, Policy, and Practice*, ed. Cressida Fforde, Jane Hubert, and Paul Turnbull (New York: Routledge, 2002). See also Lawrence E. Sullivan and Alison Edwards, eds., *Stewards of the Sacred* (Washington, D.C.: American Association of Museums, 2004).

20. Michael F. Brown and Margaret M. Bruchac, "NAGPRA from the Middle Distance: Legal Puzzles and Unintended Consequences," in *Imperialism, Art, and Restitution*, ed. John H. Merryman (Cambridge: Cambridge University Press, 2006).

21. Carpenter to Fenton, April 17, 1991, William N. Fenton Papers, Series I: Correspondence, box 5, APS.

22. Bruchac, "Lost and Found," 137.

23. See Jennifer R. O'Neal, "The Right to Know: Decolonizing Native American Archives," *Journal of Western Archives* 6, no. 1 (2015).

24. Center for Native American and Indigenous Studies (CNAIR), American Philosophical Society, accessed November 19, 2017, https://www.amphilsoc.org/library/CNAIR.

25. CNAIR, "Protocols for the Treatment of Indigenous Materials," accessed November 1, 2017, https://www.amphilsoc.org/sites/default/files/2017-06/attachments/CNAIR%20Protocols.pdf.

26. The classic theoretical discussion of the distinctions among art/artifact and authentic/inauthentic objects can be found in Clifford, "On Collecting Art and Culture."

27. The collection is archived as the Samuel Pennypacker Papers, PMA.

28. See Margaret M. Bruchac, *On the Wampum Trail* (blog), accessed November 10, 2017, http://wampumtrail.wordpress.com/.

29. The first two Kanesatake wampum belts were cataloged as CMH #III-1-929 and #III-1-930; they still reside in the collections of the Canadian Museum of History today. The other two Kanesatake wampum belts were cataloged in 1929 as MAI #16/3826 and MAI #16/3827. One was repatriated to Onondaga in 1999 and eventually returned to Kanesatake.

30. For a fuller discussion of this case, see Margaret M. Bruchac, "Broken Chains of Custody: Possessing, Dispossessing, and Repossessing Lost Wampum" (manuscript submitted for publication and currently under review).

31. Florence Speck to Edmund Carpenter, October 27, 1972, letter archived in uncataloged curatorial files at the New York State Museum Archives, Albany, N.Y.

32. Ibid.

33. Condoled Kanesatake Chief Curtis Nelson, Declaration to the Haudenosaunee Standing Committee on Burial Rules and Regulations, September 8, 2009, copy in author's possession.

34. See Margaret M. Bruchac, "Wampum Research: Notes from the Trail 2014-2015," *Beyond the Gallery Walls* (blog), University of Pennsylvania Museum of Archaeology and Anthropology, June 29, 2015, accessed November 10, 2017, http://www.penn.museum/blog/museum/wampum-research-notes-from-the-trail-june-2015/.

35. He was also attempting to distinguish between Algonkian and Iroquoian wampum belts. See Frank G. Speck, "The Function of Wampum Among the Eastern Algonkian," *American Anthropologist* 6, no. 1 (1919).

36. Barrett Speck to Cotter, October 29, 1992, letter enclosed with "Field trip report on present day status of Eastern Woodland Indians 1967–1968," uncataloged manuscript, University Museum Library, PMA.

37. On historical erasure in New England, see Jean M. O'Brien, "'Vanishing' Indians in Nineteenth-Century New England: Local Historians' Erasure of Still-Present Indian Peoples," in *New Perspectives on Native North America: Cultures, Histories, and Representations*, ed. Sergei A. Kan and Pauline Turner Strong (Lincoln: University of Nebraska Press, 2006).

38. See, for example, Sullivan, "Return of the Sacred Wampum Belts of the Iroquois"; and Hill, "Regenerating Identity."

39. Conversation with Fred McGregor, Kitigan Zibi, Maniwaki, Quebec, May 9, 2017.

40. O'Neal, "The Right to Know."

Archives

Franz Boas Papers. American Philosophical Society, Philadelphia, Penn.

Frederick H. Douglas Papers. Denver Art Museum, Denver, Colo.

William N. Fenton Papers. American Philosophical Society, Philadelphia, Penn.

Mark Raymond Harrington Papers. Braun Research Library Collection (formerly the Southwest Museum of the American Indian), Autry Museum, Los Angeles, Calif.

Julian Hayden Papers. Private collection, Tucson, Ariz. Courtesy of Stephen Hayden.

Joseph Keppler Jr. Papers. Division of Rare and Manuscript Collections, Cornell University Library, Ithaca, N.Y.

Emma Camp Mead Papers. Indian Lake Museum, Indian Lake, N.Y.

Museum of the American Indian/Heye Foundation Papers. Smithsonian National Museum of the American Indian Cultural Resources Center, Suitland, Md.

Arthur C. Parker Papers. New York State Library, Albany, N.Y.

————. Rare Books and Special Collections, River Campus Libraries, University of Rochester, Rochester, N.Y.

————. Rochester Museum and Science Center, Rochester, N.Y.

————. Office of the New York State Archaeologist. New York State Museum, Albany, N.Y.

Frederic Ward Putnam Papers. Harvard University Archives. Peabody Harvard Museum of Archaeology and Ethnography, Cambridge, Mass.

Edward Sapir Papers. Canadian Museum of History, Gatineau, Quebec, Canada.

Frank G. Speck Papers. American Philosophical Society, Philadelphia, Penn.

————. Penn Museum Archives, University of Pennsylvania Museum of Archaeology and Anthropology, Philadelphia, Penn.

————. Phillips Library, Peabody Essex Museum, Salem, Mass.

————. University Archives and Records Center, University of Pennsylvania, Philadelphia, Penn.

Gladys Tantaquidgeon Papers. Private collection, Uncasville, Conn.

Tantaquidgeon Indian Museum. Uncasville, Conn.

Abbreviations for Archives Cited in Notes

APS	American Philosophical Society
ADUP	Anthropology Department, University of Pennsylvania
BRLC	Braun Research Library Collection, Autry Museum
CMH	Canadian Museum of History
CUL	Division of Rare and Manuscript Collections, Cornell University Library
HUA	Harvard University Archives
ILM	Indian Lake Museum
MAI	Museum of the American Indian/Heye Foundation Archives, Smithsonian
NYSL	New York State Library, New York State Museum

NYSM　Office of the New York State Archaeologist, New York State Museum
PEM　Phillips Library, Peabody Essex Museum
PMA　Penn Museum Archives, University of Pennsylvania
RCL　Rare Books and Special Collections, River Campus Libraries, University of Rochester
TIM　Tantaquidgeon Indian Museum
UARC　University Archives and Records Center, University of Pennsylvania

Bibliography

Allen, Chadwick, and Beth H. Piatote, eds. *Society of American Indians and Its Legacies: A Special Combined Issue of SAIL [Studies in American Indian Literature] and AIQ [American Indian Quarterly]*, 25 no. 2 (2013).

Ames, Michael. *Cannibal Tours and Glass Boxes: The Anthropology of Museums.* Vancouver: University of British Columbia Press, 1992.

———. "How to Decorate a House: The Renegotiation of Cultural Representations at the University of British Columbia Museum of Anthropology." *Museum Anthropology* 22, no. 3 (1999): 41–51.

Averkieva, Julia, and Mark A. Sherman. *Kwakiutl String Figures.* Seattle: University of Washington Press; New York: American Museum of Natural History, 1992.

Bahr, Donald, Juan Smith, William Smith Allison, and Julian Hayden. *The Hohokam Chronicles: The Short Swift Time of Gods on Earth.* Berkeley: University of California Press, 1994.

Barbeau, Marius. *Totem Poles: According to Location.* Vol. 2. Ottawa, Ontario: National Museum of Canada, 1950.

———. "Totem Poles: A Recent Native Art of the Northwest Coast of America." *Geographical Review* 20, no. 2 (1930): 258–72.

Barreiro, Jose. "Fenton, William N." In *Encyclopedia of the Haudenosaunee Confederacy*, edited by Bruce Elliott Johansen and Barbara Alice Mann, 80–82. Westport, Conn.: Greenwood, 2000.

Beck, Horace P. "Frank G. Speck, 1881–1950." *Journal of American Folklore* 64, no. 254 (1951): 415–18.

Bell, Lucy Mary Christina. "Kwakwaka'wakw Laws and Perspective Regarding 'Property.'" Master's thesis, University of Victoria, British Columbia, 2005.

Berman, Judith. "George Hunt and the Kwak'wala Texts." *Anthropological Linguistics* 36, no. 4 (1994): 482–514.

———. "Unpublished Materials of Franz Boas and George Hunt: A Record of 45 Years of Collaboration." In *Gateways: Exploring the Legacy of the Jesup North Pacific Expedition, 1897–1902*, edited by Igor Krupnik and William W. Fitzhugh, 181–213. Washington, D.C.: Smithsonian, 2001.

Blanchard, David. "The Seven Nations of Canada: An Alliance and a Treaty." *American Indian Culture and Research Journal* 7, no. 2 (1983): 3–23.

Blankenship, Roy, ed. *The Life and Times of Frank G. Speck, 1881–1950.* Philadelphia: Department of Anthropology, University of Pennsylvania, 1991.

Boas, Franz. "Beiträge zur Erkenntniss der Farbe des Wassers" [Contributions to the understanding of the color of water]. PhD diss., University of Kiel, Germany 1881.

———. *Contributions to the Ethnology of the Kwakiutl.* Columbia University Contributions to Anthropology 3. New York: AMS, 1925.

———. *Ethnology of the Kwakiutl, Based on Data Collected by George Hunt.* Washington, D.C.: Smithsonian Institution, 1921.

———. "The Indians of British Columbia." *Journal of the American Geographical Society* 28, no. 3 (1896): 229–43.

———. *Kwakiutl Ethnography*. Edited by Helen Codere. Chicago: University of Chicago Press, 1966.

———. *The Mind of Primitive Man*. New York: Macmillan, 1911.

———. "On Alternating Sounds." *American Anthropologist* 2, no. 1 (1889): 47–54.

———. "Race Problems in America." *Science* 29, no. 752 (1909): 839–49.

———. *The Religion of the Kwakiutl Indians*. Columbia University Contributions to Anthropology 10. New York: Columbia University Press, 1930.

———. "Sketch of the Kwakiutl Language." *American Anthropologist* 2, no. 4 (1900): 708–21.

———. *The Social Organization and the Secret Societies of the Kwakiutl Indians*. Smithsonian Institution, Report of the U.S. National Museum, 1895. Washington, D.C.: Government Printing Office, 1897.

———. "Some Principles of Museum Administration." *Science* 25, no. 650 (1907): 921–33.

———. "William Jones Obituary." *Southern Workman*, May 1909, 263.

Boas, Franz, and George Hunt. "The Jesup North Pacific Expedition: Kwakiutl Texts." Issued in 3 vols. *Memoirs of the American Museum of Natural History*. New York: G. E. Stechert, 1902–5.

Boas. Norman. *Franz Boas: A Biography*. Mystic, Conn.: Seaport Autographs Press, 2004.

Bostwick, Todd W. Review of *Field Man: Life as a Desert Archaeologist*, by Julian D. Hayden. *Kiva* 77, no. 3 (2012): 15–20.

Bourdieu, Pierre. *Language and Symbolic Power*. Translated by Gino Raymond and Matthew Adamson. Cambridge, Mass.: Harvard University Press, 1991.

Brady, Miranda J. "A Dialogic Response to the Problematized Past: The National Museum of the American Indian." In *Contesting Knowledge: Museums and Indigenous Perspectives*, edited by Susan Sleeper-Smith, 133–55. Lincoln: University of Nebraska Press, 2009.

Briggs, Charles, and Richard Bauman. "'The Foundation of All Future Researches': Franz Boas, George Hunt, Native American Texts, and the Construction of Modernity." *American Quarterly* 51, no. 3 (1999): 479–528.

Brooks, Lisa T. *The Common Pot: The Recovery of Native Space in the Northeast*. Minneapolis: University of Minnesota Press, 2008.

Browman, David L. *Cultural Negotiations: The Role of Women in the Founding of Americanist Archaeology*. Lincoln: University of Nebraska Press, 2013.

Browman, David L., and Stephen Williams, eds. *Anthropology at Harvard: A Biographical History, 1790–1940*. Cambridge, Mass.: Peabody Museum Press, 2013.

Brown, Michael F., and Margaret M. Bruchac. "NAGPRA from the Middle Distance: Legal Puzzles and Unintended Consequences." In *Imperialism, Art, and Restitution*, edited by John H. Merryman, 193–217. Cambridge: Cambridge University Press, 2006.

Bruchac, Margaret M. "Abenaki Connections to 1704: The Sadoques Family and Deerfield, 2004." In *Captive Histories: Captivity Narratives, French Relations and Native Stories of the 1704 Deerfield Raid*, edited by Evan Haefeli and Kevin Sweeney, 262–78. Amherst: University of Massachusetts Press, 2006.

———. "Breaking Ground in the 1930s: Bertha Parker, First Female Native American Archaeologist." Keynote lecture presented at the Sixth Annual Regina Herzfeld Flannery Lecture on the Cultural Heritage of Native Americans at Catholic University, Washington, D.C., April 9, 2014.

———. "Broken Chains of Custody: Possessing, Dispossessing, and Repossessing Lost Wampum." Manuscript submitted for publication and currently under review.

———. "Indian Lake Is the Scene You Should Make: Emma Camp Mead, Indian Doctor/Entrepreneur/Activist/Fashion Plate." Paper presented at the "Native American History: Current and Future Directions" symposium in honor of Neal Salisbury at Smith College, Northampton, Mass., March 5, 2009.

———. "Lost and Found: NAGPRA, Scattered Relics and Restorative Methodologies." *Museum Anthropology* 33, no. 2 (2010): 137–56.

———. "My Sisters Will Not Speak: Boas, Hunt, and the Ethnographic Silencing of First Nations Women." *Curator: The Museum Journal* 57, no. 2 (2014): 153–71.

———. "Resisting Red Power: Scholarly Domination of Haudenosaunee Representation." Paper presented at the Native American and Indigenous Studies Association Conference, Sacramento, Calif., May 19, 2011.

———. "The Speck Connection: Recovering Histories of Indigenous Objects." *Beyond the Gallery Walls* (blog). University of Pennsylvania Museum of Archaeology and Anthropology, May 20, 2015. http://www.penn.museum/blog/museum/the-speck -connection-recovering-histories-of-indigenous-objects/.

———. "Wampum Research: Notes from the Trail 2014–2015." *Beyond the Gallery Walls* (blog). University of Pennsylvania Museum of Archaeology and Anthropology, June 29, 2015. http://www.penn.museum/blog/museum/wampum-research-notes -from-the-trail-june-2015/.

Bruchac, Margaret M., Siobhan Hart, and H. Martin Wobst, eds. *Indigenous Archaeologies: A Reader in Decolonization*. Walnut Creek, Calif.: Left Coast Press, 2010.

Bureau of the Census. *1900 United States Federal Census*. Washington, D.C.: National Archives and Records Administration, 1900.

———. *1910 United States Federal Census*. Washington, D.C.: National Archives and Records Administration, 1910.

———. *1920 United States Federal Census*. Washington, D.C.: National Archives and Records Administration, 1920.

———. *1930 United States Federal Census*. Washington, D.C.: National Archives and Records Administration, 1930.

———. *1940 United States Federal Census*. Washington, D.C.: National Archives and Records Administration, 1940.

Carnicke, Sharon. *Stanislavsky in Focus: An Acting Master for the Twenty-First Century*. Oxford: Routledge Theatre Classics, 2008.

Carola, Chris. "1911 Capitol Fire Commemorated in NY." *Huffington Post*, March 3, 2011.

Carpenter, Edmund. "Frank Speck: Quiet Listener." In *The Life and Times of Frank G. Speck, 1881–1950*, edited by Roy Blankenship, 78–84. Philadelphia: Department of Anthropology, University of Pennsylvania, 1991.

———. *Two Essays: Chief and Greed*. North Andover, Mass.: Persimmon Press, 2005.

Chamberlain, Alex F. "Daniel Garrison Brinton." *Journal of American Folklore* 12, no. 46 (1899): 215–25.

Charland, Thomas M. *Les Abénakis d'Odanak*. Montreal: Editions du Lévrion, 1964.

Clifford, James. "Identity in Mashpee." In *The Predicament of Culture: Twentieth-Century Ethnography, Literature, and Art*, 277–346. Cambridge, Mass.: Harvard University Press, 1988.

———. "On Collecting Art and Culture." In *The Predicament of Culture: Twentieth-Century Ethnography, Literature, and Art*, 215–51. Cambridge, Mass.: Harvard University Press, 1988.

———. "Spatial Practices: Fieldwork, Travel, and the Disciplining of Anthropology." In *Anthropological Locations: Boundaries and Grounds of a Field Science*, edited by Akhil Gupta and James Ferguson, 185–222. Berkeley: University of California Press, 1997.

Cody, Bertha Parker. "A Maidu Myth of the Creation of Indian Women; by Bertha Parker Cody, as Related by Mandy Wilson, Maidu Indian of Chico, California." *Masterkey* 13, no. 2 (1939): 83.

———. "A Maidu Myth of the First Death; by Bertha Parker Cody, as Related by Mandy Wilson of Chico, California." *Masterkey* 13, no. 4 (1939): 144.

———. "Yurok Fish-Dam Dance; as Told by Jane Van Stralen to Bertha Parker Cody." *Masterkey* 16, no. 3 (1942): 81–86.

———. "Yurok Tales: Wohpekumen's Beads, as Told by Jane Van Stralen to Bertha Parker Cody." *Masterkey* 15, no. 6 (1941): 228–31.

Cody, Iron Eyes, and Collin Perry. *Iron Eyes: My Life as a Hollywood Indian*. New York: Everest House, 1982.

Cody, Iron Eyes, and Ye-Was [Bertha Parker Cody]. *Sign Talk in Pictures*. Hollywood, Calif.: H. H. Boelter Lithography, 1958.

Cole, Douglas. *Captured Heritage: The Scramble for Northwest Coast Artifacts*. Vancouver: University of British Columbia Press, 2011.

———. "'The Value of a Person Lies in His Herzensbildung': Franz Boas' Baffin Island Letter-Diary, 1883–1884." In *Observers Observed: Essays on Ethnographic Fieldwork*, edited by George W. Stocking Jr., 13–52. Madison: University of Wisconsin Press, 1983.

Colwell-Chanthaphonh, Chip. *Inheriting the Past: The Making of Arthur C. Parker and Indigenous Archaeology*. Tucson: University of Arizona Press, 2009.

Converse, Harriet Maxwell. "Induction of Women into Iroquois Tribes." *Journal of American Folklore* 6, no. 21 (1893): 147–48.

———. *Myths and Legends of the New York State Iroquois*. Edited and annotated by Arthur Caswell Parker. New York State Museum Bulletin 125, Education Department Bulletin 437. Albany: University of the State of New York, 1908.

[Converse, Harriet Maxwell]. "A Woman Elected a Chief of the Six Nations." *Journal of American Folklore* 5, no. 17 (1892): 146–47.

Coolidge, Sherman. "The Function of the Society of American Indians." *Quarterly Journal of the Society of American Indians* 2, no. 3 (1914): 186–90.

Curland, Richard. "Historically Speaking: Montville Is Home to Largest Boulder." *Bulletin* (Norwich, Conn.), July 1, 2012.

Curtis, Edward. *The North American Indian.* Vol. 10, *The Kwakiutl.* Norwood, Mass.: Plimpton Press, 1915.

Darnell, Regna. *Daniel Garrison Brinton: The "Fearless Critic" of Philadelphia.* Philadelphia: Department of Anthropology, University of Pennsylvania, 1988.

———. *Invisible Genealogies: A History of Americanist Anthropology.* Lincoln: University of Nebraska Press, 2001.

———. "The Pivotal Role of the Northwest Coast in the History of Americanist Anthropology." *British Columbia Studies,* no. 125/126 (Spring/Summer 2000): 33–52.

———. "William N. Fenton (1908–2005)." *Journal of American Folklore* 120, no. 475 (2007): 73–75.

Day, Gordon. "Note on St. Francis Nomenclature." *International Journal of Linguistics* 16, no. 4 (1959): 272–73.

Deloria, Philip J. *Indians in Unexpected Places.* Lawrence: University Press of Kansas, 2004.

———. *Playing Indian.* New Haven, Conn.: Yale University Press, 1998.

Deloria, Vine, Jr. *Custer Died for Your Sins: An Indian Manifesto.* New York: Macmillan, 1969.

Den Ouden, Amy. "Locating the Cannibals: Conquest, North American Ethnohistory, and the Threat of Objectivity." *History and Anthropology* 18, no. 2 (2007): 101–33.

Dirks, Nicholas B. "Franz Boas and the American University: A Personal Account." *Proceedings of the American Philosophical Society* 154, no. 1 (2010): 31–39.

Dennis, Matthew. *Seneca Possessed: Indians, Witchcraft, and Power in the Early Republic.* Philadelphia: University of Pennsylvania Press, 2010.

Dodge, Ernest S. "Speck on the North Shore." In *The Life and Times of Frank G. Speck, 1881–1950,* edited by Roy Blankenship, 38–51. Philadelphia: Department of Anthropology, University of Pennsylvania, 1991.

Eiseley, Loren C. *All the Strange Hours: The Excavation of a Life.* New York: Charles Scribner's Sons, 1975.

Erikson, Patricia Pierce. "Decolonizing the Nation's Attic." In *The National Museum of the American Indian: Critical Conversations,* edited by Amy Lonetree and Amada J. Cobb, 43–83. Lincoln: University of Nebraska Press, 2008.

Everson, Frank. "Renegotiating the Past: Contemporary Tradition and Identity of the Comox First Nation." Master's thesis, University of British Columbia, 2000.

Fawcett, Melissa Jayne. *The Lasting of the Mohegans: The Story of the Wolf People.* Ledyard, Conn.: Pequot Printing, 1995.

———. *Medicine Trail: The Life and Lessons of Gladys Tantaquidgeon.* Tucson: University of Arizona Press, 2000.

———. "The Role of Gladys Tantaquidgeon." In *Papers of the Fifteenth Algonquian Conference,* edited by William Cowan, 135–45. Ottawa, Ont.: Carleton University, 1984.

Feit, Harvey A. "The Construction of Algonquian Hunting Territories: Private Property as Moral Lesson, Policy Advocacy, and Ethnographic Error." In *Colonial Situations: Essays on the Contextualization of Ethnographic Knowledge,* edited by George W. Stocking Jr., 109–34. History of Anthropology 7. Madison: University of Wisconsin Press, 1991.

Fenton, William N. "'Aboriginally Yours': Jesse J. Cornplanter, Hah-Yonh-Wonh-Ish, the Snipe." In *American Indian Intellectuals of the Nineteenth and Early Twentieth Centuries*, edited by Margo Liberty, 199–222. Norman: University of Oklahoma Press, 2002.

———. "Collecting Materials for a Political History of the Six Nations." *Proceedings of the American Philosophical Society* 93, no. 3 (1949): 233–38.

———. *The False Faces of the Iroquois*. Norman: University of Oklahoma Press, 1987.

———. "Frank G. Speck's Anthropology." In *The Life and Times of Frank G. Speck, 1881–1950*, edited by Roy Blankenship, 9–37. Philadelphia: Department of Anthropology, University of Pennsylvania, 1991.

———. *The Great Law and the Longhouse: A Political History of the Iroquois Confederacy*. Norman: University of Oklahoma Press, 1998.

———. "He-Lost-a-Bet (*Howan'eyao*) of the Seneca Hawk Clan." In *Strangers to Relatives: The Adoption and Naming of Anthropologists in Native North America*, edited by Sergei Kan, 81–98. Lincoln: University of Nebraska Press, 2001.

———. "Introduction." In *Parker on the Iroquois*, by Arthur C. Parker, edited by William N. Fenton, 1–47. Syracuse, N.Y.: Syracuse University Press, 1968.

———. *The Little Water Medicine Society of the Seneca*. Norman: University of Oklahoma Press, 2002.

———. "The Lore of the Longhouse: Myth, Ritual and Red Power." In "Anthropology: Retrospect and Prospect: A Special Issue in Honor of Regina Flannery Herzfeld." *Anthropological Quarterly* 48, no. 3 (1975): 131–47.

———. "The New York State Wampum Collection: The Case for the Integrity of Cultural Treasures." *Proceedings of the American Philosophical Society* 115, no. 6 (1971): 437–61.

———. *An Outline of Seneca Ceremonies at Cold Spring Longhouse*. New Haven, Conn.: Yale University Press, 1936.

———. "Return of Eleven Wampum Belts to the Six Nations Iroquois Confederacy on Grand River, Canada." *Ethnohistory* 36, no. 4 (1989): 392–410.

Fixico, Donald L. "Ethics and Responsibilities in Writing American Indian History." In *Natives and Academics: Researching and Writing About American Indians*, edited by Devon A. Mihesuah, 84–99. Lincoln: University of Nebraska Press, 1998.

Force, Roland W. *Politics and the Museum of the American Indian: The Heye and the Mighty*. Honolulu: Mechas Press, 1999.

Ford, Clellan S. *Smoke from Their Fires: The Life of a Kwakiutl Chief*. New Haven, Conn.: Yale University Press, 1941.

Geertz, Clifford. *The Interpretation of Cultures: Selected Essays*. New York: Basic Books, 1973.

Glass, Aaron. "A Cannibal in the Archive: Performance, Materiality, and (In)Visibility in Unpublished Edward Curtis Photographs of the Kwakwaka'wakw Hamat'sa." *Visual Anthropology Review* 25, no. 2 (2009): 128–49.

Gordon, Leah. "Trading a Museum's Treasure—A Very Hazardous Business." *New York Times*, March 31, 1974.

Graybill, Florence Curtis, and Victor Boesen. *Edward Sheriff Curtis: Visions of a Vanishing Race*. Boston, Mass.: Houghton Mifflin, 1986.

Green, Rayna. "The Indian in Popular American Culture." In *Handbook of North American Indians*, vol. 4, *History of Indian-White Relations*, edited by Wilcomb E. Washburn, 587–606. Washington, D.C.: Smithsonian Institution, 1988.

Gupta, Akhil, and James Ferguson, eds. *Anthropological Locations: Boundaries and Grounds of a Field Science*. Berkeley: University of California Press, 1997.

Haber, Alejandro. "This Is Not an Answer to the Question 'Who Is Indigenous?'" *Archaeologies: Journal of the World Archaeological Congress* 3, no. 3 (2007): 213–29.

Hale, Horatio E. *The Iroquois Book of Rites*. Philadelphia, Penn.: D. G. Brinton, 1883.

Hallowell, A. Irving. "Frank Gouldsmith Speck, 1881–1950." *American Anthropologist* 53, no. 1 (1951): 67–87.

———. "Ojibwa Ontology, Behavior and World View." In *Culture in History: Essays in Honor of Paul Radin*, edited by Stanley Diamond, 19–52. New York: Columbia University Press, 1960.

Haraway, Donna. "Teddy Bear Patriarchy: Taxidermy in the Garden of Eden, New York City, 1908–1936." *Social Text* 11 (Winter 1984–85): 20–64.

Harrington, Marie. *On the Trail of Forgotten People: A Personal Account of the Life and Career of Mark Raymond Harrington*. Reno, Nev.: Great Basin Press, 1985.

Harrington, Mark Raymond. "An Abenaki 'Witch-Story.'" *Journal of American Folklore* 14, no. 54 (1901): 160.

———. "A Gypsum Cave Romance." *Masterkey* 5, no. 2 (1931): 49.

———. "The Gypsy Sloth." *Masterkey* 3, no. 8 (1930): 15–16.

———. "The Knife-Maker Understood." *Masterkey* 39, no. 2 (1955): 61.

———. "Man and Beast in Gypsum Cave." *Desert Magazine* 3, no. 6 (1940): 3–5.

———. "In Nevada with Our Expedition." *Masterkey* 2, no. 6 (1929): 22.

———. "Reminiscences of an Archeologist: II." *Masterkey* 37, no. 1 (1963): 22–26.

———. "Reminiscences of an Archeologist: III." *Masterkey* 37, no. 2 (1963): 66–71.

———. "Reminiscences of an Archeologist: IV." *Masterkey* 37, no. 3 (1963): 114–18.

———. "Reminiscences of an Archeologist: VI." *Masterkey* 38, no. 3 (1964): 107–10.

———. "Ruins and Legends of Zuni Land." *Masterkey* 3, no. 1 (1929): 5–16.

———. "Witchcraft Story." *Journal of American Folklore* 15, no. 56 (1902): 62–63.

Hauptman, Laurence M. "Eleanor Roosevelt and the American Indian: The Iroquois as a Case Study." *Hudson Valley Regional Review* 16, no. 1 (1999): 1–15.

———. *The Iroquois and the New Deal*. Syracuse, N.Y.: Syracuse University Press, 1981.

———. "The Iroquois School of Art: Arthur C. Parker and the Seneca Arts Project, 1935–1941." *New York History* 60, no. 3 (1979): 282–312.

Hayden, Julian D. *Field Man: Life as a Desert Archaeologist*. Edited by Bill Broyles and Diane E. Boyer. Tucson: University of Arizona Press, 2011.

Herman, Kali. *Women in Particular*. Phoenix: Oryx Press, 1984.

Hertzberg, Hazel W. "Nationality, Anthropology and Pan-Indianism in the Life of Arthur C. Parker (Seneca)." *Proceedings of the American Philosophical Society* 123, no. 1 (1979): 47–72.

———. *The Search for an American Identity: Modern Pan-Indian Movements*. Syracuse, N.Y.: Syracuse University Press, 1971.

Heuer, Kenneth, ed. *The Lost Notebooks of Loren Eiseley*. Boston, Mass.: Little, Brown, 1987.

Hewitt, J. N. B. "North America." Review of *The Constitution of the Five Nations*, by Arthur C. Parker, *Traditional History of the Confederacy of the Six Nations*, by Duncan Campbell Scott, and *Civil, Religious and Mourning Council and Ceremonies of Adoption of the New York Indians*, by William M. Beauchamp. *American Anthropologist* 19, no. 3 (1917): 429–38.

Hill, Richard W. "Regenerating Identity: Repatriation and the Indian Frame of Mind." In *The Future of the Past: Archaeologists, Native Americans and Repatriation*, edited by Tamara Bray, 127–37. New York: Garland, 2001.

Hinsley, Curtis. *The Smithsonian and the American Indian: Making a Moral Anthropology in Victorian America*. Washington, D.C.: Smithsonian Institution Press, 1994.

Hoffman, Anne. "Delaware's Forgotten Folks." *Delaware Public Media*, June 5, 2015.

Holm, Bill, and George L. Quimby. *Edward S. Curtis in the Land of the War Canoes*. Seattle: University of Washington Press, 1980.

Holmes, W. H. "The World's Fair Congress of Anthropology." *American Anthropologist* 6, no. 4 (1893): 423–34.

Holtz, Jeff. "Mohegans Buy Rock Sacred to Tribe." *New York Times*, July 8, 2007.

Hoxie, Frederick, ed. *Talking Back to Civilization: Indian Voices from the Progressive Era*. Boston, Mass.: Bedford, 1971.

International Directory of Anthropologists. Washington, D.C.: National Research Council, 1938.

Isaac, Barbara. "The Implementation of NAGPRA: The Peabody Museum of Archaeology and Ethnography, Harvard." In *The Dead and Their Possessions: Repatriation in Principle, Policy, and Practice*, edited by Cressida Fforde, Jane Hubert, and Paul Turnbull, 160–70. New York: Routledge, 2002.

Jacknis, Ira. "A New Thing? The NMAI in Historical and Institutional Perspective." *American Indian Quarterly* 30, nos. 3 & 4 (2006): 511–42.

Jacobs-Huey, Lanita. "The Natives Are Gazing and Talking Back: Reviewing the Problematics of Positionality, Voice, and Accountability Among 'Native' Anthropologists." *American Anthropologist* 104, no. 3 (2002): 791–804.

Jemison, G. Peter. "Sovereignty and Treaty Rights: We Remember." *Akwesasne Notes*, n.s. 1, nos. 3–4 (1995): 10–15.

Johansen, Bruce Elliott, and Barbara Alice Mann. *Encyclopedia of the Haudenosaunee (Iroquois Confederacy)*. Westport, Conn.: Greenwood, 2000.

Jones, William. "Some Principles of Algonkin Word Formation." *American Anthropologist*, n.s. 6, no. 3 (1904): 369–407.

Kan, Sergei. *Strangers to Relatives: The Adoption and Naming of Anthropologists in Native North America*. Lincoln: University of Nebraska Press, 2001.

Kappler, Charles J., ed. *Indian Affairs: Laws and Treaties*. Vol. 4, *Laws*. Washington, D.C.: Government Printing Office, 1929.

Kasson, Joy. *Buffalo Bill's Wild West: Celebrity, Memory, and Popular History*. New York: Hill and Wang, 2000.

Kopytoff, Igor. "A Short History of Anthropology at Penn." *Expedition* 48, no. 1 (2012): 29–36.

Krech, Shepard, III, and Barbara Hail, eds. *Collecting Native America, 1870–1960*. Washington, D.C.: Smithsonian Institution Press, 1999.

Kroeber, A. L. "A Mission Record of the California Indians." *University of California Publications in American Archaeology and Ethnology* 8, no. 1 (1908): 1–27.

Lévi-Strauss, Claude. *The Raw and the Cooked: Introduction to a Science of Mythology*. Translated by John and Doreen Weightman. New York: Harper and Row, 1969.

Lloyd, Mark Frazier. "The Early Years of the International House of Philadelphia and Its Purchase of 3905 Spruce Street 1911–1922." University Archives & Records Center, University of Pennsylvania, August 2000. http://www.archives.upenn.edu/histy/features/campuses/3905spruce/3905spruce2.html.

———. "Women at Penn: Timeline of Pioneers and Achievements." University Archives & Records Center, University of Pennsylvania, July 2001. http://www.archives.upenn.edu/histy/features/women/chronbeg.html.

Lonetree, Amy. "Museums as Sites of Decolonization: Truth Telling in National and Tribal Museums." In *Contesting Knowledge: Museums and Indigenous Perspectives*, edited by Susan Sleeper-Smith, 322–38. Lincoln: University of Nebraska Press, 2009.

Lonetree, Amy, and Amada J. Cobb, eds. *The National Museum of the American Indian: Critical Conversations*. Lincoln: University of Nebraska Press, 2008.

Lovell, Malcom Read. "Penn Professor's Discovery Confounds Indian 'History': Doctor Speck Establishes That the American Redskin Hunts on His Own Family Ground, Is a Protector of Game, and Is No Mere Rover Through the Forests." *Public Ledger* (Philadelphia, Penn.), November 23, 1913.

Lowie, Robert H. *Biographical Memoir of Franz Boas 1858–1942*. Washington, D.C.: National Academy of Sciences, 1947.

Lyons, Oren. Review of *The Search for an American Indian Identity: Modern Pan-Indian Movements*, by Hazel W. Hertzberg. *New York History* 53, no. 1 (1972): 107–9.

Mach, Stephanie. "On the Wampum Trail: Balancing Traditional and Museological Care of Wampum." *Beyond the Gallery Walls* (blog). University of Pennsylvania Museum of Archaeology and Anthropology, August 11, 2014. https://www.penn.museum/blog/museum/on-the-wampum-trail-balancing-traditional-and-museological-care-of-wampum/.

MacPherson, Virginia. "Hollywood Tribe on Warpath; Seek More Wampum." *Bend* (OR) *Bulletin*, September 30, 1947.

Maddox, Lucy. *Citizen Indians: Native American Intellectuals, Race, and Reform*. Ithaca, N.Y.: Cornell University Press, 2005.

Mann, Charles C. "The Clovis Point and the Discovery of America's First Culture." *Smithsonian Magazine*, November 2013.

Maroukis, Thomas C. *The Peyote Road: Religious Freedom and the Native American Church*. Norman: University of Oklahoma Press, 2004.

Mason, J. Alden. "Frank Gouldsmith Speck, 1881–1950." *University Museum Bulletin* 15, no. 1 (1950): 2–5.

McBride, Bunny. *Molly Spotted Elk: A Penobscot in Paris*. Norman: University of Oklahoma Press, 1995.

McLoughlin, Moira. *Museums and the Representation of Native Canadians: Negotiating the Borders of Culture*. New York: Routledge, 1999.

McMaster, Gerald. "Museums and the Native Voice." In *Museums After Modernism: Strategies of Engagement*, edited by Griselda Pollock and Joyce Zemans, 70–79. London: Blackwell, 2007.

McMullen, Ann. "Reinventing George Heye: Nationalizing the Museum of the American Indian and Its Collections." In *Contesting Knowledge: Museums and Indigenous Perspectives*, edited by Susan Sleeper-Smith, 65–105. Lincoln: University of Nebraska Press, 2009.

———. "What's Wrong with This Picture? Context, Coversion, Survival, and the Development of Regional Cultures and Pan-Indianism in Southeastern New England." In *Enduring Traditions: The Native Peoples of New England*, edited by Laurie Weinstein, 123–50. Westport, Conn.: Bergin and Garvey, 1994.

Meltzer, David J. *The Great Paleolithic War: How Science Forged an Understanding of America's Ice Age Past*. Chicago: University of Chicago Press, 2015.

Merryman, John H., ed. *Imperialism, Art, and Restitution*. Cambridge: Cambridge University Press, 2006.

Morgan, Lewis Henry. *Ancient Society; or, Researches in the Lines of Human Progress from Savagery Through Barbarism to Civilization*. London: Henry Holt, 1877.

———. *League of the Ho-dé-no-sau-nee or Iroquois*. Rochester, N.Y.: Sage, 1851.

Murray, Laura. *To Do Good to My Indian Brethren: The Writings of Joseph Johnson, 1751–1776*. Amherst: University of Massachusetts Press, 1998.

Nagel, Joane. *American Indian Ethnic Renewal: Red Power and the Resurgence of Identity and Culture*. Oxford: Oxford University Press, 1997.

Nicholas, George. *Being and Becoming Indigenous Archaeologists*. Walnut Creek, Calif.: Left Coast Press, 2010.

Nielsen, Steffen Bohni. "Civilizing Kwakiutl: Contexts and Contests of Kwakiutl Personhood, 1880–1999." PhD diss., University of Aarhus, Denmark, 2001.

O'Brien, Jean M. "'Vanishing' Indians in Nineteenth-Century New England: Local Historians' Erasure of Still-Present Indian Peoples." In *New Perspectives on Native North America: Cultures, Histories, and Representations*, edited by Sergei A. Kan and Pauline Turner Strong, 414–32. Lincoln: University of Nebraska Press, 2006.

O'Neal, Jennifer R. "The Right to Know: Decolonizing Native American Archives." *Journal of Western Archives* 6, no. 1 (2015): 1–17.

Paul, Daniel N. *We Were Not the Savages: A Mi'kmaq Perspective on the Collision Between European and Native American Civilizations*. Black Point, Nova Scotia: Fernwood, 2006.

Parezo, Nancy J., ed. *Hidden Scholars: Women Anthropologists and the Native American Southwest*. Albuquerque: University of New Mexico Press, 1993.

Parker, Arthur C. *The Constitution of the Five Nations*. New York State Museum Bulletin 184. Albany: University of the State of New York, 1916.

———. "The Editor's Viewpoint: A Survey of the Problem— Its Elements and Its End." *Quarterly Journal of the Society of American Indians* 2, no. 4 (1914): 13–22.

———. "Excavations in an Erie Indian Village and Burial Site at Ripley, Chautauqua Co., N.Y." *New York State Museum Bulletin* 117 (December 1907): 459–554.

————. "Fate of the New York State Collections in Archaeology and Ethnology in the Capitol Fire." *American Anthropologist* 13, no. 1 (January–March 1911): 169–71.

————. *The Indian How Book.* New York: George H. Doran, 1931.

————. "Iroquois Uses of Maize and Other Food Plants." *New York State Museum Bulletin* 144 (November 1, 1910): 5–119.

————. "Modern Red Indians." *San Francisco Call*, October 12, 1912.

————. "The New York Indians." *University of the State of New York Bulletin to the Schools* (November 15, 1915).

————. "Secret Medicine Societies of the Seneca." *American Anthropologist*, n.s. 11, no. 2 (1909): 161–85.

————. *Seneca Myths and Folk Tales.* Buffalo, N.Y.: Buffalo Historical Society, 1923.

————. *Skunny Wundy: Seneca Indian Tales.* 1926. Repr., Syracuse, N.Y.: Syracuse University Press, 1994.

————. "Where Questions Are Answered." *Museum Service*, December 1953.

Pearce, Roy Harvey. *Savagism and Civilization: A Study of the Indian and the American Mind.* Baltimore: Johns Hopkins University Press, 1953.

Phillips, Ruth B. "Disappearing Acts: Traditions of Exposure, Traditions of Enclosure, and Iroquois Masks." In *Questions of Tradition*, edited by Mark Salber Phillips and Gordon Schochet, 56–87. Toronto: University of Toronto Press, 2004.

Phillips, Ruth B., and Mark Salber Phillips. "Double Take: Contesting Time, Place, and Nation in the First Peoples' Hall of the Canadian Museum of Civilization." *American Anthropologist* 104, no. 4 (2006): 694–704.

Porter, Joy. "American Indian identity in the life of Arthur Caswell Parker, 1881–1955." PhD diss., University of Nottingham, 1994.

————. *To Be Indian: The Life of Iroquois-Seneca Arthur Caswell Parker.* Norman: University of Oklahoma Press, 2001.

Prince, J. Dyneley. "Last Living Echoes of the Natick." *American Anthropologist*, n.s. 9, no. 3 (1907): 493–98.

Prince, J. Dynely, and Frank G. Speck. "Glossary of the Mohegan-Pequot Language." *American Anthropologist*, n.s. 6, no. 1 (1904): 18–45.

Pulla, Siomonn P. "Frank Speck and the Mapping of Aboriginal Territoriality in Eastern Canada, 1900–1950." PhD diss., Carleton University, 2006.

Raheja, Michelle. *Reservation Reelism: Redfacing, Visual Sovereignty, and Representations of Native Americans in Film.* Lincoln: University of Nebraska Press, 2010.

Raibmon, Paige. "Theatres of Contact: The Kwakwaka'wakw Meet Colonialism in British Columbia and at the World's Fair." *Canadian Historical Review* 81, no. 2 (2000): 157–92.

Reid, Martine J., ed. *Paddling to Where I Stand: Agnes Alfred, Qwiqwasut'inuxw Noblewoman.* Translated by Daisy Sewid-Smith. Vancouver: University of British Columbia Press, 2004.

Rideout, Henry Milner. *William Jones: Indian, Cowboy, American Scholar, and Anthropologist in the Field.* New York: Frederick A. Stokes, 1912.

Robertson, Leslie A., and Kwagu'l Gixsam Clan. *Standing Up with Ga'axsta'las: Jane Constance Cook and the Politics of Memory, Church, and Custom.* Vancouver: University of British Columbia Press, 2012.

Rohner, Ronald P., ed. *The Ethnography of Franz Boas: Letters and Diaries of Franz Boas Written on the Northwest Coast from 1886 to 1931*. Translated by Hedy Parker. Chicago: University of Chicago Press, 1969.

Rowland, Stephen M. "The Career of James E. Thurston and the Extinction of the Professional Field Collector in North American Vertebrate Paleontology." Paper delivered at the Geological Society of America Annual Meeting, Denver, Colo., October 28–31, 2007.

Ryder, Katie. "Hollywood Indian." *Paris Review*, August 1, 2013. http://www.theparis review.org/blog/tag/margaret-tahamont/.

Said, Edward. *Orientalism*. New York: Pantheon, 1978.

Sayet, Melissa Fawcett. "Sociocultural Authority in Mohegan Society." *Artifacts* 16, nos. 3–4 (1988): 11–31.

Sayet, Rachel. "Moshup's Continuance: Sovereignty and the Literature of the Land in the Aquinnah Wampanoag Nation." Master's thesis, Harvard University, 2012.

Scott, James. *Domination and the Arts of Resistance: Hidden Transcripts*. New Haven, Conn.: Yale University Press, 1990.

Senier, Siobhan. "'Traditionally, Disability Was Not Seen as Such': Writing and Healing in the Work of Mohegan Medicine People." *Journal of Literary & Cultural Disability Studies* 7, no. 2 (2013): 213–29.

Shaw, George C. *The Chinook Jargon and How to Use It*. Seattle, Wash.: Rainier Printing Company, 1909.

Simpson, Audra. "On Ethnographic Refusal: Indigeneity, 'Voice,' and Colonial Citizenship." *Junctures* 9 (December 2007): 67–80.

Smith, Harlan Ingersoll. *Archaeology of Lytton, British Columbia*. New York: AMS, 1975. Originally published in *Memoirs of the American Museum of Natural History*, vol. 2, part 3. New York: G. P. Putnam's Sons, 1899.

Smith, Linda Tuhiwai. *Decolonizing Methodologies: Research and Indigenous Peoples*. New York: St. Martin's, 1999.

Smithers, Gregory D. "The Soul of Unity: The Quarterly Journal of the Society of American Indians, 1913–1915." *Society of American Indians and Its Legacies: A Special Combined Issue of SAIL [Studies in American Indian Literature] and AIQ [American Indian Quarterly]* 25, no. 2 (2013): 263–89.

Snyderman, George S. "Witches, Witchcraft, and Alleghany Seneca Medicine." *Proceedings of the American Philosophical Society* 127, no. 4 (1983): 263–77.

Speck, Frank G. *Ethnology of the Yuchi Indians*. Philadelphia, Penn.: University Museum, 1909.

———. "The Family Hunting Band as the Basis of Algonkian Social Organization." *American Anthropologist*, n.s. 17, no. 2 (1915): 289–305.

———. "The Function of Wampum Among the Eastern Algonkian." *American Anthropologist* 6, no. 1 (1919): 3–71.

———. "Game Totems Among the Northeastern Algonkians." *American Anthropologist*, n.s. 19, no. 1 (1917): 9–18.

———. "Indian Girl Saves Legends of Race." *Science News-Letter* 14, no. 386 (1928): 124.

———. "The Indians and Game Preservation." *Red Man* 6 (1913): 21–25.

———. "The Last of the Mohegans." *Papoose* 1, no. 4 (1903): 2–5.

———. "A Modern Mohegan-Pequot Text." *American Anthropologist*, n.s. 6, no. 4 (1904): 469–76.

———. "Mohegan Traditions of 'Muhkeahweesug,' the Little Men." *Papoose* 1, no. 7 (1903): 11–14.

———. *Native Tribes and Dialects of Connecticut: A Mohegan-Pequot Diary*. Bureau of American Ethnology Annual Report 43. Washington, D.C.: U.S. Government Printing Office, 1928.

———. *Penobscot Man: The Life History of a Forest Tribe in Maine*. Philadelphia: University of Pennsylvania Press, 1940.

———. "A Pequot-Mohegan Witchcraft Tale." *Journal of American Folklore* 16, no. 61 (1903): 104–6.

———. "Primitive Religion." In *Religions of the Past and Present: A Series of Lectures Delivered by Members of the Faculty of the University of Pennsylvania*, edited by James A. Montgomery, 9–32. Philadelphia, Penn.: J. B. Lippincott, 1918.

———. "The Remnants of Our Eastern Indian Tribes." *American Inventor* 10 (1903): 266–68.

Speck, Frank G., and J. Dyneley Prince. "The Modern Pequots and Their Language." *American Anthropologist*, n.s. 5, no. 2 (1903): 193–212.

Stocking, George W., Jr. "Afterward: A View from the Center." *Ethnos* 47, nos. 1–2 (1982): 172–286.

———, ed. *Objects and Others: Essays on Museums and Material Culture*. Madison: University of Wisconsin Press, 1985.

Strathern, Marilyn. *Audit Cultures: Anthropological Studies in Accountability, Ethics and the Academy*. New York: Routledge, 2000.

Sturtevant, William C., Donald Colliver, Philip J. C. Dark, and William N. Fenton. "CARM Concerned at Proposed Wampum Return." *Anthropology News* 2, no. 4 (1970): 4.

Sturtevant, William C., Donald Colliver, Philip J. C. Dark, William N. Fenton, and Ernest S. Dodge. "An 'Illusion of Religiosity.'" *Indian Historian* 3, no. 2 (1970): 13–14.

Sullivan, Lawrence E., and Alison Edwards, eds. *Stewards of the Sacred*. Washington, D.C.: American Association of Museums, 2004.

Sullivan, Martin. "Return of the Sacred Wampum Belts of the Iroquois." *History Teacher* 26, no. 1 (1992): 7–14.

Swanton, John R. "Explanation of the Seattle Totem Pole." *Journal of American Folklore* 18, no. 69 (1898): 108–10.

Tantaquidgeon, Gladys. "An Affectionate Portrait of Frank Speck." In *Dawnland Voices: An Anthology of Indigenous Writing from New England*, edited by Siobhan Senier, 581–87. Lincoln: University of Nebraska Press, 2014.

———. *Folk Medicine of the Delaware and Related Algonkian Indians*. Anthropological Series 3. Harrisburg: Pennsylvania Historical and Museum Commission, 1972.

———. "How the Summer Season Was Brought North." *Journal of American Folklore* 54, no. 213/214 (1941): 203–4.

———. "Mohegan Medicinal Practices, Weather-Lore, and Superstitions." In *Native Tribes and Dialects of Connecticut*, edited by Frank G. Speck, 264–76. Annual Report of the Bureau of American Ethnology 43. Washington, D.C.: Government Printing Office, 1928.

———. "Notes on the Origin and Uses of Plants of the Lake St. John Montagnais." *Journal of American Folklore* 45, no. 176 (1932): 265–67.

———. "Report on Delaware Ethnobotanical Investigations." In *Fifth Report of the Pennsylvania Historical Commission*, 112–15. Philadelphia: Commonwealth of Pennsylvania, 1931.

———. *A Study of Delaware Indian Medicine Practice and Folk Beliefs.* Anthropological Series 3. Harrisburg: Pennsylvania Historical and Museum Commission, 1942.

Tehanetorens [Ray Fadden]. *Wampum Belts of the Iroquois.* Summertown, Tenn.: Book Publishing Company, 1999.

Thomas, W. Stephen. "Arthur Caswell Parker: 1881–1955; Anthropologist, Historian and Museum Pioneer." *Rochester History* 17, no. 3 (1955): 1–20.

Thorpe, Jocelyn. *Temagami's Tangled Wild Rice: Race, Gender, and the Making of Canadian Nature.* Vancouver: University of British Columbia Press, 2012.

Thurston, Bertha Parker. "How a Maidu Medicine Man Lost His Power; Related to Bertha Parker Thurston by a Maidu Indian Herbalist." *Masterkey* 9, no. 1 (1935): 28–29.

———. "How He Became a Medicine Man." *Masterkey* 8, no. 3 (1934): 79–81.

———. "A Night in a Maidu Shaman's House." *Masterkey* 7, no. 4 (1933): 111–15.

———. "A Rare Treat at a Maidu Medicine-Man's Feast." *Masterkey* 10, no. 1 (1936): 16–21.

———. "Scorpion Hill." *Masterkey* 7, no. 6 (1933): 171–77.

Tooker, Elisabeth. "Lewis H. Morgan and the Senecas." In *Strangers to Relatives: The Adoption and Naming of Anthropologists in Native North America*, edited by Sergei Kan, 29–56. Lincoln: University of Nebraska Press, 2001.

———. "A Note on the Return of Eleven Wampum Belts to the Six Nations Iroquois Confederacy on Grand River, Canada." *Ethnohistory* 45, no. 2 (1998): 219–36.

Voight, Virginia Frances. *Mohegan Chief: The Story of Harold Tantaquidgeon.* New York: Funk and Wagnall's, 1965.

Wabunaki, Alnoba. "My Race Shall Live Anew." *Quarterly Journal of the Society of American Indians* 2, no. 2 (1914): 90.

———. "With the Passing of Puritanism the Red Man Comes." *Quarterly Journal of the Society of American Indians* 2, no. 2 (1914): 120–25.

Waldman, Amy. "Iron Eyes Cody, 94, an Actor and Tearful Anti-Littering Icon." *New York Times*, January 5, 1999.

Wallace, Anthony F. C. "The Career of William N. Fenton and the Development of Iroquoian Studies." In *Extending the Rafters: Interdisciplinary Approaches to Iroquoian Studies*, edited by Michael K. Foster, Jack Campisi, and Marianne Mithun, 1–12. Albany: State University of New York Press, 1984.

———. "The Dekanawideh Myth Analyzed as the Record of a Revitalization Movement." *Ethnohistory* 5, no. 2 (1958): 118–30.

———. "The Frank G. Speck Collection." *Proceedings of the American Philosophical Society* 95, no. 3 (1951): 286–89.

Warrior, Robert. "The SAI and the End(s) of Intellectual History." *Society of American Indians and Its Legacies: A Special Combined Issue of SAIL [Studies in American Indian Literature] and AIQ [American Indian Quarterly]* 25, no. 2 (2013): 219–35.

Waters, Michael R., and Thomas W. Stafford Jr. "Redefining the Age of Clovis: Implications for the Peopling of the Americas." *Science* 2315, no. 5815 (2007): 1122–26.

Weaver, Sally M. "The Wampum Case." In *The History of Politics on the Six Nations Reserve* (Brantford, Ontario: Records and Council Minutes, Indian Office, 1973), 62–79.

Werner, Wade. "Indians Make Place for Selves in Films, Oust Painted Extras." *Cumberland Evening Times*, September 27, 1927.

Weslager, Carl A. *Delaware's Forgotten Folk: The Story of the Moors and Nanticokes.* Philadelphia: University of Pennsylvania Press, 2006.

———. "The Unforgettable Frank Speck." In *The Life and Times of Frank G. Speck, 1881–1950*, edited by Roy Blankenship, 52–77. Philadelphia: Department of Anthropology, University of Pennsylvania, 1991.

Whiteley, Peter M. "Commemorating Boas." Paper presented at the Colloquium on Collaborative and Engaged Anthropology, American Museum of Natural History, April 1, 2008.

Williams, Paul. "Wampum of the Six Nations Confederacy at the Grand River Territory: 1784–1986." In *Proceedings of the 1986 Shell Bead Conference: Selected Papers*, edited by Charles F. Hayes, 199–204. Rochester, N.Y.: Research Division of the Rochester Museum and Science Center, 1989.

Witthoft, John. "Frank Speck: The Formative Years." In *The Life and Times of Frank G. Speck, 1881–1950*, edited by Roy Blankenship, 1–8. Philadelphia: Department of Anthropology, University of Pennsylvania, 1991.

Woods, Lynn. "A History in Fragments." *Adirondack Life* (November/December 1994): 30–37, 61, 68–71, 78–79.

Yellow Robe, Chauncey. "The Indian and the Wild West Show." *Quarterly Journal of the Society of American Indians* 2, no. 1 (1914): 39–40.

Zobel, Melissa Tantaquidgeon. "The Story Trail of Voices." *ConnecticutHistory.org*, September 4, 2013. http://connecticuthistory.org/the-story-trail-of-voices/.

Index

Abenaki people, 3–5, 64–66, 82, 184

African Americans, 69, 143, 149, 161, 169

Adirondacks, 49–50, 63, 73, 75, 77

Ahhaitty, Glenda, 111, 212n82

Algonkian people: Algonquian language, 5, 14–15, 143–46, 161; as cultural group, 5, 82, 155, 161–62; hunting and fishing traditions, 3, 63, 168–69, 171; ontology of, 3–7, 10–11, 145, 168; oral traditions, 82, 174

Algonquin Indian Council of New England, 5, 141, 170

Algonquin people (also called Anishinaabe or Anishinabeg), 3, 5, 140, 162, 168–69, 189

American Anthropological Association, 113, 133–34, 137

American Museum of Natural History, 9, 11–12, 21, 55, 85

American Philosophical Society, 21, 45, 131, 132, 152, 182

animals. *See* other-than-human beings; hunting traditions

Anislaga, 23–24, *25*, 26, 32–33, 44–45, 47

Annisquam, 150, 154, 187

anthropological studies: as collaborative, ix, 9–10, 90, 117, 141; biases in, 13–14, 16, 23, 157, 189; discursive approach, 183–85, 188–90; gendered relations and, xi–xii, 9, 13, 23–24, 26, 43–44, 62, 113, 164; history of, ix, xi, 9–13, 156–59, 178; Indigenous contributions to, 9–11, 17–19, 178–79; linguistics, 80, 146, 157–58; reflexivity and, xi, 6–8, 12; physical anthropology, 11, 13, 21, 157; salvage anthropology, viii, xii, 6–8, 13, 15–16; social evolution, 9, 12, 26, 61, 68. *See also* ethnographic practice

archaeological theory and practice: as collaborative, 84, 86; excavations, viii, 15, 21, 29–31, 93, 95–96, 123; exhumations, 29–31, 55, 61, 64–65; field instruction, 86–87, 89–91; field surveys, 29,11, 91–92, 104–5; Indigenous archaeology, 89–91, New Archaeology, 95–96

Averkieva, Julia, 44–45

Baker, Emma, 141, 146

Barbeau, Marius, 24, 35, 43–44

basketry, 48–50, 61, 63, 76, 97, 104–6, 145, 147, 171–72, 184

Bear Island, 162, 168–69

Berens, William, 168

Bering Strait, 97, 100, 102

Blankenship, Roy, 152

Boas, Franz: as advocate for Indigenous peoples, 26, 33, 46–47; American Museum of Natural History (AMNH) and, 11–12, 21; career and teaching positions of, 11–12, 21; critiques of, 26, 35, 42, 44–45, 47; Edward Sapir and, 15, 41; Frank Speck and, 140, 156; George Hunt and, 10, 20–21, 24–32, 34–37, 39–41,43, 47; images of, *10*, *22*, *25*; Indigenous material collections and, 26–28, 31, 44; Indigenous perceptions of, 33–34, 46–47; linguistic studies by, 15, 26–27, 41–44; Lucy Homikanis Hunt and, 33–34, 44; Marie Krackowizer and, 20; methodology of, 13, 15, 20–21, 26–28, 41–42; writings and publications, 21, 34, 42, 45, 47

Bonnin, Gertrude Simmons (Zitkala-sa), 67–69

Brinton, Daniel Garrison, 156–57, 160

Brooks, Lisa, 3

Bureau of American Ethnology, 118, 127, 146

Bureau of Indian Affairs, 71, 141, 169–70

California Indian Rights Association, 108

California Institute of Technology, 98–104

Canadian Museum of History (formerly the Canadian Museum of Civilization and the Victoria Museum), 136, 185

Carlisle Indian School, 49, 67–68, 227n144

Carpenter, Edmund, 136–37, 139, 161, 163, 165, 180–81, 185–86

Cayuga people, 5, 62–63, 127, 131, 166. *See also* Haudenosaunee people

Cherokee people, 140, 155, 182

Chicago Field Museum of Natural History, 11, 14, 28

Chicago's World's Fair, 11, 21, 28, 37

About the Author

Photograph by Jason S. Ordaz

Margaret M. Bruchac is an assistant professor of anthropology, associate professor in the Penn Cultural Heritage Center, and coordinator of Native American and Indigenous Studies at the University of Pennsylvania. She is the author of *Dreaming Again: Algonkian Poetry* and a co-editor of *Indigenous Archaeologies: A Reader in Decolonization.*